Study Guide

Financial & Managerial Accounting
2005e

Study Guide

Financial & Managerial Accounting
2005ⓔ

Belverd E. Needles, Jr.
DePaul University

Marian Powers
Northwestern University

Susan V. Crosson
Santa Fe Community College, Florida

CONTRIBUTING EDITOR
Edward H. Julius
California Lutheran University

Houghton Mifflin Company   **Boston**   **New York**

Senior Sponsoring Editor: Bonnie Binkert
Senior Development Editor: Margaret Kearney
Senior Manufacturing Coordinator: Priscilla J. Bailey
Marketing Manager: Todd Berman

Printed in the U.S.A.

ISBN: 0-618-393641

123456789-VHG-08 07 06 05 04

Contents

Appendix

Answers

To the Student

This study guide is designed to help you improve your performance in your first accounting course. It is designed for use with *Financial & Managerial Accounting* 2005© by Needles, Powers, and Crosson.

Reviewing the Chapter

This section provides a concise but thorough summary of the essential points covered by the learning objectives in each corresponding chapter of the text. It also provides a review of key terms and, when appropriate, a summary of journal entries introduced in the text.

Self-Test

The self-test reviews the basic concepts introduced in the text chapter and helps you prepare for examinations based on the chapter's learning objectives.

Testing Your Knowledge

This section provides matching, short-answer, true-false, and multiple-choice questions to test your understanding of the concepts and vocabulary introduced in the text.

Applying Your Knowledge

Developing the ability to work problems is an essential part of learning acounting. In this section, you can exercise your ability to apply principles introduced in the text to "real-life" accounting situations. Many of these sections are followed by crossword puzzles that test your knowledge of key terms.

Answers

The study guide concludes with answers to all the questions, exercises, and puzzles that follow the chapter review. Answers are cross-referenced to the learning objectives in the text chapters.

CHAPTER 1 USES OF ACCOUNTING INFORMATION AND THE FINANCIAL STATEMENTS

REVIEWING THE CHAPTER

Objective 1: Define *accounting,* **identify business goals and activities, and describe the role of accounting in making informed decisions.**

1. **Accounting** is an information system that measures, processes, and communicates financial information about an identifiable economic entity. It provides information that is essential for decision making.

2. A **business** is an economic unit that sells goods and services at prices that will provide an adequate return to its owners. To survive, a business must meet two goals: **profitability,** which means earning enough income to attract and hold investment capital, and **liquidity,** which means keeping sufficient cash on hand to pay debts as they fall due.

3. Businesses pursue their goals by engaging in financing, investing, and operating activities.
   a. **Financing activities** are needed to obtain funding for the business. They include such activities as obtaining capital from owners and creditors, paying a return to owners, and repaying creditors.
   b. **Investing activities** spend the funds raised. They include such activities as buying and selling land, buildings, and equipment.
   c. **Operating activities** are the everyday activities needed to run the business, such as hiring personnel; buying, producing, and selling goods or services; and paying taxes.

4. **Performance measures** indicate the extent to which managers are meeting their business goals

and whether the business activities are well managed. Performance measures thus often serve as the basis for evaluating managers. Examples of performance measures include cash flow (for liquidity), net income or loss (for profitability), and the ratio of expenses to revenue (for operating activities).

5. A distinction is usually made between **management accounting,** which focuses on information for internal users, and **financial accounting,** which involves generating and communicating accounting information in the form of **financial statements** to persons outside the organization.

6. Accounting information is processed by bookkeeping, computers, and management information systems.
   a. A small but important part of accounting, **bookkeeping** is the mechanical and repetitive process of recording financial transactions and keeping financial records.
   b. The **computer** is an electronic tool that rapidly collects, organizes, and communicates vast amounts of information. The computer does not take the place of the accountant, but the accountant must understand how the computer operates because it is an integral part of the accounting information system.
   c. A **management information system (MIS)** is an information network of all major functions (called *subsystems*) of a business. The accounting information system is the financial hub of the management information system.

Objective 2: Identify the many users of accounting information in society.

7. The users of accounting information basically fall into three groups: management, outsiders with a direct financial interest in the business, and outsiders with an indirect financial interest.

   a. **Management** steers a business toward its goals by making the business's important decisions. Specifically, management must ensure that the business is adequately financed; that it invests in productive assets; that it develops, produces, and markets goods or services; that its employees are well managed; and that pertinent information is provided to decision makers.

   b. Present or potential investors and creditors are considered outside users with a direct financial interest in a business. Most businesses publish financial statements that report on their profitability and financial position. Investors use these statements to assess the business's strength or weakness; creditors use them to determine the business's ability to repay debts on time.

   c. Society as a whole, through government officials and public groups, can be viewed as an accounting information user with an indirect financial interest in a business. Such users include tax authorities, regulatory agencies, and other groups, such as labor unions, economic planners, and financial analysts. Among the regulatory agencies is the **Securities and Exchange Commission (SEC),** an agency of the federal government set up by Congress to protect the investing public by regulating the issuing, buying, and selling of stocks in the United States.

8. Managers in government and not-for-profit organizations (hospitals, universities, professional organizations, and charities) also make extensive use of financial information.

Objective 3: Explain the importance of business transactions, money measure, and separate entity to accounting measurement.

9. To make an accounting measurement, the accountant must answer the following basic questions:
   a. What is measured?
   b. When should the measurement be made?
   c. What value should be placed on the item being measured?
   d. How should what is measured be classified?

10. Financial accounting uses money measures to gauge the impact of business transactions on specific business entities.

    a. **Business transactions** are economic events that affect a business's financial position. They can involve an exchange of value (e.g., a purchase, sale, payment, collection, or loan) or a "nonexchange" (e.g., the physical wear and tear on machinery, and losses due to fire or theft).

    b. The **money measure** concept states that business transactions should be measured in terms of money. Financial statements are normally prepared in terms of the monetary unit of the country in which the business resides (i.e., in dollars, euros, etc.). When transactions occur between countries that have different monetary units, the appropriate **exchange rate** must be used to translate amounts from one currency to another.

    c. For accounting purposes, a business is treated as a **separate entity,** distinct from its owner or owners, creditors, and customers—that is, the business owner's personal bank account, resources, debts, and financial records should be kept separate from those of the business.

Objective 4: Describe the corporate form of business organization.

11. The three basic forms of business organization are sole proprietorships, partnerships, and corporations. Accountants recognize each form as an economic unit separate from its owners. A **sole proprietorship** is an unincorporated business owned by one person. A **partnership** is much like a sole proprietorship, except that it is owned by two or more persons. A **corporation,** unlike a sole proprietorship or partnership, is a business unit chartered by the state and legally separate from its owners (the stockholders).

12. The corporation is the dominant form of American business because it enables companies to amass large amounts of capital. The stockholders of a corporation are at risk of loss only to the extent of their investment, and ownership (evidenced by **shares of stock**) can be transferred without affecting operations.

    a. Before a corporation may do business, it must apply for and obtain a charter from the state. The state must approve the **articles of incorporation** included in the application, which describe the basic purpose and structure of the proposed corporation.

b. The stockholders elect a board of directors, which sets corporate policy and appoints managers to oversee the daily operations. Some of the board's specific duties are to declare dividends, authorize contracts, determine executive salaries, and arrange major loans with banks. In addition, the board often appoints an **audit committee,** which, to ensure the board's objectivity in judging management's performance, usually includes directors of other companies. One of the audit committee's functions is to engage independent auditors and review their work.

c. In addition to carrying out the policies set by the board and running the business, a corporation's management is responsible for making at least one comprehensive annual report on the corporation's financial position and the results of operations.

Objective 5: Define *financial position*, state the accounting equation, and show how they are affected by simple transactions.

13. Every business transaction affects a firm's financial position. **Financial position** (a company's economic resources and the claims against those resources) is shown by a balance sheet, so called because the two sides of the balance sheet must always equal each other. In a sense, the balance sheet presents two ways of viewing the same business: the left side shows the assets (resources) of the business, whereas the right side shows who provided the assets. Providers consist of owners (listed under "owners' equity") and creditors (represented by the listing of "liabilities"). Therefore, it is logical that the total dollar amount of assets must equal the total dollar amount of liabilities and owners' equity. This is the **accounting equation**. It is formally stated as

$$\text{Assets} = \text{Liabilities} + \text{Owners' Equity}$$

Another correct form is

$$\text{Assets} - \text{Liabilities} = \text{Owners' Equity}$$

14. **Assets** are the economic resources of a business that are expected to benefit future operations. Examples of assets are cash, accounts receivable, inventory, buildings, equipment, patents, and copyrights.

15. **Liabilities** are a business's present obligations to pay cash, transfer assets, or provide services to other entities in the future. Examples of such debts are money owed to banks, amounts owed to creditors for goods bought on credit, and taxes owed to the government.

16. **Owners' equity** represents the claims by the owners of a business to the assets of the business. It equals the residual interest in assets after deducting the liabilities. Because it is equal to assets minus liabilities, owners' equity is said to equal the **net assets** of the business.

17. The owners' equity of a corporation is called **stockholders' equity**. It consists of contributed capital and retained earnings. **Contributed capital** represents the amount invested by the stockholders, whereas **retained earnings** represent the accumulation of the profits and losses of a company since its inception, less total dividends declared. **Dividends** are distributions of assets to stockholders from past earnings; they appear as a reduction in the statement of retained earnings.

18. Retained earnings are affected not only by dividends, but also by revenues and expenses. **Revenues,** which result from selling goods or services, increase retained earnings. **Expenses,** which represent the costs of doing business, decrease retained earnings. When its revenues exceed its expenses, a company has a **net income**. When its expenses exceed its revenues, a company has a **net loss**.

19. **Accounts** are used to accumulate amounts produced by similar transactions. Examples include Cash, Accounts Payable, and Common Stock.

20. Although every transaction affects the accounting equation in some way, it must always remain in balance. In other words, dollar amounts may change, but assets must always equal liabilities plus owners' equity.

a. The investment of cash by the owners of a corporation will increase both assets and stockholders' equity.

b. The purchase of assets with cash will both increase and decrease assets by the same amount (i.e., total assets will not change).

c. The purchase of assets on credit will increase both assets and liabilities.

d. The payment of a liability will decrease both assets and liabilities.

e. Earning revenue, whether for cash or later payment, will increase both assets and stockholders' equity.

f. The collection of an account receivable will both increase and decrease assets by the same amount (i.e., total assets will not change).

g. Incurring and immediately paying for expenses will decrease both assets and stockholders' equity.

h. Incurring expenses to be paid later will increase liabilities and decrease stockholders' equity.

i. The declaration and payment of a dividend will decrease both assets and stockholders' equity.

Objective 6: Identify the four financial statements.

21. Accountants communicate information through financial statements. The four principal statements are the income statement, statement of retained earnings, balance sheet, and statement of cash flows.

22. Every financial statement has a three-line heading. The first line gives the name of the company. The second line gives the name of the statement. The third line gives the relevant dates (the date of the balance sheet or the period of time covered by the other three statements).

23. The **income statement**, whose components are revenues and expenses, is perhaps the most important financial statement. Its purpose is to measure the business's success or failure in achieving its goal of profitability.

24. The **statement of retained earnings** is a labeled calculation of the changes in retained earnings during an accounting period. Retained earnings at the beginning of the period is the first item on the statement, followed by an addition for net income or a deduction for net loss and a deduction for dividends declared. The ending retained earnings figure that results is transferred to the stockholders' equity section of the balance sheet. Many companies use a **statement of stockholders' equity,** or *shareholders' equity,* in place of the statement of retained earnings. The statement of stockholders' equity is a more comprehensive statement. It incorporates the components of the statement of retained earnings, as well as the changes in all the stockholders' equity accounts over the period.

25. The **balance sheet** shows the financial position of a business as of a certain date. The resources owned by the business are called assets; debts of the business are called liabilities; and the owners' financial interest in the business is called stockholders' equity. The balance sheet is also known as the *statement of financial position.*

26. The **statement of cash flows** focuses on the business's goal of liquidity and contains much infor- mation not found in the other three financial statements. It discloses the cash flows that result from the business's operating, investing, and financing activities during the accounting period. **Cash flows** refer to the business's cash inflows and cash outflows. *Net* cash flows represent the difference between these inflows and outflows. The statement of cash flows indicates the net increase or decrease in cash produced during the period.

Objective 7: State the relationship of generally accepted accounting principles (GAAP) to financial statements and the independent CPA's report, and identify the organizations that influence GAAP.

27. **Generally accepted accounting principles (GAAP)** are the set of conventions, rules, and procedures that constitute acceptable accounting practice at a given time. The set of GAAP changes continually as business conditions change and practices improve.

28. The financial statements of publicly held corpo- rations are audited (examined) by licensed pro- fessionals, called **certified public accountants (CPAs),** to ensure the quality of the statements. CPAs must be independent of their audit clients (without financial or other ties). On completing the **audit,** the CPA reports on whether the audited statements "present fairly, in all material re- spects" and are "in conformity with generally ac- cepted accounting principles."

29. The **Financial Accounting Standards Board (FASB)** is the authoritative body for development of GAAP. This group is separate from the AICPA and issues *Statements of Financial Accounting Standards.*

30. The **American Institute of Certified Public Ac- countants (AICPA)** is the professional associa- tion of CPAs. Its senior technical committees help influence accounting practice.

31. The Securities and Exchange Commission (SEC) is an agency of the federal government. It has the legal power to set and enforce accounting prac- tices for companies whose securities are traded by the general public.

32. The **Governmental Accounting Standards Board (GASB)** was established in 1984 and is responsible for issuing accounting standards for state and local governments.

33. The **International Accounting Standards Board (IASB)** is responsible for developing worldwide accounting standards. To date, it has approved more than 30 international standards.

34. The **Internal Revenue Service (IRS)** enforces and interprets the set of rules governing the assessment and collection of federal income taxes.

Objective 8: Define *ethics* and describe the ethical responsibilities of accountants.

35. **Ethics** is a code of conduct that applies to everyday life. **Professional ethics** is the application of a code of conduct to the practice of a profession. The accounting profession has developed such a code, intended to guide the accountant in carrying out his or her responsibilities to the public. In short, the accountant must act with integrity, objectivity, independence, and due care.

a. **Integrity** means that the accountant is honest, regardless of consequences.

b. **Objectivity** means that the accountant is impartial in performing his or her job.

c. **Independence** is the avoidance of all relationships that impair or appear to impair the objectivity of the accountant, such as owning stock in a company he or she is auditing.

d. **Due care** means carrying out one's responsibilities with competence and diligence.

36. The **Institute of Management Accountants (IMA)** has adopted a code of professional conduct for management accountants. This code emphasizes that management accountants have responsibilities in the areas of competence, confidentiality, integrity, and objectivity.

SELF-TEST

Test your knowledge of the chapter by choosing the best answer for each item below.

1. Which of the following is an important reason for studying accounting?
   a. Accounting information is useful in making economic decisions.
   b. Accounting plays an important role in society.
   c. The study of accounting can lead to a challenging career.
   d. All of the above are important reasons for studying accounting.

2. Which of the following groups uses accounting information for planning a company's profitability and liquidity?
   a. Management
   b. Investors
   c. Creditors
   d. Economic planners

3. Economic events that affect the financial position of a business are called
   a. separate entities.
   b. business transactions.
   c. money measures.
   d. financial actions.

4. For legal purposes, which of the following forms of business organization is (are) treated as a separate economic unit from its owner(s)?
   a. Sole proprietorship
   b. Corporation
   c. Partnership
   d. All of the above

5. If a company has liabilities of $19,000 and owners' equity of $57,000, its assets are
   a. $38,000.
   b. $76,000.
   c. $57,000.
   d. $19,000.

6. The payment of a liability
   a. increases both assets and liabilities.
   b. increases assets and decreases liabilities.
   c. decreases assets and increases liabilities.
   d. decreases both assets and liabilities.

7. Investments by stockholders
   a. increase both total assets and total stockholders' equity.
   b. increase both total assets and total liabilities.
   c. increase total assets and decrease total stockholders' equity.
   d. have no effect on total assets, liabilities, or stockholders' equity.

8. Expenses and dividends appear, respectively, on the
   a. balance sheet and income statement.
   b. income statement and balance sheet.
   c. statement of retained earnings and balance sheet.
   d. income statement and statement of retained earnings.

9. Generally accepted accounting principles
   a. define accounting practice at a point in time.
   b. are similar in nature to the principles of chemistry or physics.
   c. rarely change.
   d. are not affected by changes in the ways businesses operate.

10. Independence is an important characteristic of which of the following in performing audits of financial statements?
    a. Governmental accountants
    b. Certified management accountants
    c. Certified public accountants
    d. Accounting educators

TESTING YOUR KNOWLEDGE

*Matching**

Match each term with its definition by writing the appropriate letter in the blank.

_____ 1. Accounting

_____ 2. Bookkeeping

_____ 3. Computer

_____ 4. Management information system (MIS)

_____ 5. Management accounting

_____ 6. Financial accounting

_____ 7. Accounting equation

_____ 8. Dividend

_____ 9. Certified public accountant (CPA)

_____ 10. Sole proprietorship

_____ 11. Partnership

_____ 12. Corporation

_____ 13. Generally accepted accounting principles (GAAP)

_____ 14. Balance sheet

_____ 15. Income statement

_____ 16. Statement of retained earnings

_____ 17. Statement of cash flows

_____ 18. Separate entity

_____ 19. Money measure

_____ 20. Asset

_____ 21. Liability

_____ 22. Owners' equity

_____ 23. Contributed capital

_____ 24. Statement of stockholders' equity

a. A debt of a business

b. A business owned by stockholders but managed by a board of directors

c. A distribution of earnings to stockholders

d. The concept that all business transactions should be measured in terms of money

e. The statement that shows the financial position of a company on a certain date

f. The repetitive recordkeeping process

g. An economic resource of a business

h. An information system that measures, processes, and communicates economic information

i. A business owned and managed by two or more persons

j. An expert accountant licensed by the state

k. Representation on the balance sheet of stockholders' investments in a corporation

l. The statement that shows a company's profit or loss over a certain period

m. The statement that discloses the operating, investing, and financing activities during a period

n. The branch of accounting concerned with providing external users with financial information needed to make decisions

o. An electronic tool that processes information with great speed

p. The balance sheet section that represents the owners' economic interest in a company

q. The statement that shows the changes in the Retained Earnings account during a period

r. An information network that links a company's functions

s. Assets = Liabilities + Owners' Equity

t. The accounting concept that treats a business as distinct from its owners, creditors, and customers

u. The guidelines that define acceptable accounting practice at a given point in time

v. A business owned and managed by one person

w. The branch of accounting concerned with providing managers with financial information needed to make decisions

x. The financial statement that summarizes changes in the components of stockholders' equity

---

Note to student: The matching quiz might be completed more efficiently by starting with the definition and searching for the corresponding term.

Short Answer

Use the lines provided to answer each item.

1. On the lines that follow, insert the correct heading for the annual income statement of Nolan Corporation on August 31, 20xx.

   _____

   _____

   _____

2. Briefly distinguish between bookkeeping and accounting.

   _____

   _____

   _____

3. Briefly define the terms below, all of which relate to the accountant's Code of Professional Conduct.

   a. Integrity _____

   _____

   b. Objectivity _____

   _____

   c. Independence _____

   _____

   d. Due care _____

   _____

4. What three broad groups use accounting information?

   _____

   _____

   _____

5. What two objectives must be met for a company to survive?

   _____

   _____

6. List the four principal financial statements and briefly state the purpose of each.

   Statement

   a. _____

   _____

   b. _____

   _____

   c. _____

   _____

   d. _____

   _____

   Purpose

   a. _____

   _____

   b. _____

   _____

   c. _____

   _____

   d. _____

   _____

Circle T if the statement is true, F if it is false. Provide explanations for false answers, using the blank lines below.

T F   **1.** Financial position can best be determined by referring to the income statement.

T F   **2.** The IRS is responsible for interpreting and enforcing GAAP.

T F   **3.** One form of the accounting equation is Assets – Liabilities = Owners' Equity.

T F   **4.** Revenues have the effect of increasing owners' equity.

T F   **5.** The existence of Accounts Receivable on the balance sheet indicates that the company has one or more creditors.

T F   **6.** When expenses exceed revenues, a company has suffered a net loss.

T F   **7.** The measurement stage of accounting involves preparation of the financial statements.

T F   **8.** Dividends appear as a deduction on the income statement.

T F   **9.** The current authoritative body dictating accounting practice is the FASB.

T F   **10.** A sole proprietor is personally liable for all debts of the business.

T F   **11.** The statement of cash flows would disclose whether or not land was purchased for cash during the period.

T F   **12.** The statement of retained earnings links a company's income statement to its balance sheet.

T F   **13.** The IASB is responsible for setting guidelines for state and local governments.

T F   **14.** A corporation is managed directly by its stockholders.

T F   **15.** Generally accepted accounting principles are not like laws of math and science; they are guidelines that define correct accounting practice at a given point in time.

T F   **16.** Net assets equal assets plus liabilities.

T F   **17.** The major sections of a balance sheet are assets, liabilities, stockholders' equity, revenues, and expenses.

T F   **18.** A business transaction must always involve an exchange of money.

T F   **19.** A management information system deals not only with accounting, but with other activities of a business as well.

T F   **20.** The income statement is generally considered to be the most important financial statement.

T F   **21.** A business should be understood as an entity that is separate and distinct from its owners, customers, and creditors.

T F   **22.** Economic planners are accounting information users with a direct financial interest.

T F   **23.** The essence of an asset is that it is expected to benefit future operations.

T F   **24.** Cash flow is a measure of profitability.

_____

_____

_____

_____

_____

_____

_____

_____

_____

_____

_____

_____

_____

_____

_____

_____

_____

_____

_____

_____

_____

_____

_____

_____

_____

_____

Multiple Choice

Circle the letter of the best answer.

1. Which of the following accounts would *not* appear on the balance sheet?
   a. Wages Expense
   b. Common Stock
   c. Accounts Receivable
   d. Wages Payable

2. Companies whose stock is publicly traded must file financial statements with the
   a. FASB.
   b. GASB.
   c. SEC.
   d. AICPA.

3. One characteristic of a corporation is
   a. unlimited liability of its owners.
   b. the ease with which ownership is transferred.
   c. ownership by the board of directors.
   d. dissolution upon the death of an owner.

4. Which of the following statements does *not* involve a distinct period of time?
   a. Income statement
   b. Balance sheet
   c. Statement of cash flows
   d. Statement of retained earnings

5. The principal purpose of an audit by a CPA is to
   a. express an opinion on the fairness of a company's financial statements.
   b. detect fraud by a company's employees.
   c. prepare the company's financial statements.
   d. assure investors that the company will be profitable in the future.

6. Collection on an account receivable will
   a. increase total assets and increase total stockholders' equity.
   b. have no effect on total assets, but will increase total stockholders' equity.
   c. decrease both total assets and total liabilities.
   d. have no effect on total assets, liabilities, or stockholders' equity.

7. In a partnership,
   a. profits are always divided equally among partners.
   b. management consists of the board of directors.
   c. no partner is liable for more than a proportion of the company's debts.
   d. dissolution results when any partner leaves the partnership.

8. Which of the following is *not* a major heading on a balance sheet or income statement?
   a. Accounts receivable
   b. Stockholders' equity
   c. Liabilities
   d. Revenues

9. Payment of a liability will
   a. decrease total liabilities and decrease total stockholders' equity.
   b. decrease total assets and increase total stockholders' equity.
   c. decrease total assets and decrease total liabilities.
   d. have no effect on total assets, liabilities, or stockholders' equity.

10. The purchase of an asset for cash will
    a. increase total assets and increase total stockholders' equity.
    b. increase total assets and increase total liabilities.
    c. increase total assets and decrease total liabilities.
    d. have no effect on total assets, liabilities, or stockholders' equity.

11. Which of the following is *not* an activity listed on the statement of cash flows?
    a. Investing activities
    b. Funding activities
    c. Operating activities
    d. Financing activities

APPLYING YOUR KNOWLEDGE

Exercises

1. Atlantic Siding Corporation always publishes annual financial statements. This year, however, it has suffered a very large loss, and it therefore would like to limit access to its financial statements. Why might each of the following insist on seeing Atlantic's financial statements?

   a. Potential investors in Atlantic

   b. The Securities and Exchange Commission

   c. The bank, which is considering a loan request by Atlantic

   d. Present stockholders of Atlantic

   e. Atlantic's management

2. Summit Ridge Corporation had assets of $100,000 and liabilities of $70,000 at the beginning of the year. During the year assets decreased by $15,000 and stockholders' equity increased by $20,000. What is the amount of liabilities at year end?

   $_____

3. Following are the accounts of Farnsworth's TV Repair Corporation as of December 31, 20xx:

Accounts Payable	$ 1,300
Accounts Receivable	1,500
Building	10,000
Cash	?
Common Stock	14,500
Equipment	850
Land	1,000
Retained Earnings	3,000
Truck	4,500

   Using this information, prepare a balance sheet *in good form.* (You must derive the dollar amount for Cash.)

   Farnsworth's TV Repair Corporation
   Balance Sheet
   December 31, 20xx

   Assets

   Liabilities

   Stockholders' Equity

4. Following are the transactions for A-1 Painting, Inc., for the first month of operations.

a. Terri and Keith Ross invested $20,000 cash into the newly formed business in exchange for common stock.
b. Purchased paint supplies and equipment for $650 cash.
c. Purchased a truck on credit for $5,200.
d. Received $525 for painting a house.
e. Paid one-half of the amount due on the truck previously purchased.
f. Billed a customer $150 for painting his garage.
g. Paid $250 for one month's rental of the office.

h. Received full payment from the customer whose garage was painted (transaction **f**).
i. Performed a service for $20. The customer said he would pay next month.
j. The company declared and paid a $200 cash dividend.

In the form below, show the effect of each transaction on the balance sheet accounts by putting the dollar amount, along with a plus or minus sign, under the proper account. Determine the balance in each account at month's end. As an example, transaction **a** already has been recorded.

Transaction	Assets				Liabilities	Stockholders' Equity	
	Cash	Accounts Receivable	Supplies and Equipment	Trucks	Accounts Payable	Common Stock	Retained Earnings
a	+$20,000					+$20,000	
b							
c							
d							
e							
f							
g							
h							
i							
j							
Balance at end of month							

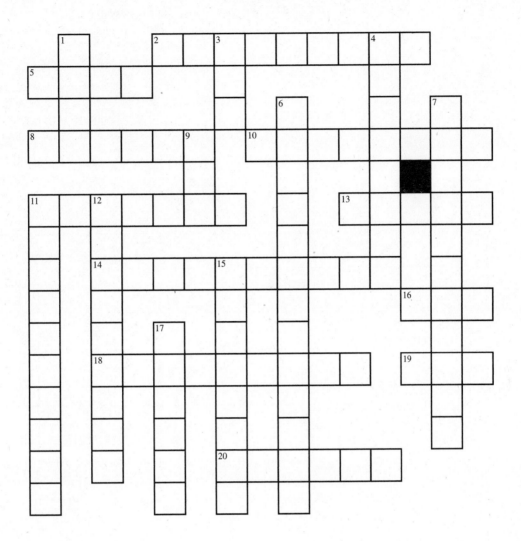

ACROSS

2. Accounting mainly for external use
5. _____ proprietorship
8. Resources of a company
10. One to whom another is indebted
11. _____ sheet
13. Professional organization of accountants (abbr.)
14. The language of business
16. IRS's concern
18. Measure of debt-paying ability
19. Data-generating network
20. Separate _____ concept

DOWN

1. See 3-Down
3. With 1-Down, income statement measure
4. Independent CPA activity
6. Measure of business performance
7. Form of business organization
9. Regulatory agency of publicly held corporations
11. Recorder of business transactions
12. Debt of a company
15. Impartial
17. Ownership in a company

HOW TO READ AN ANNUAL REPORT

REVIEWING THE SUPPLEMENT

1. Most of the more than four million corporations in the United States are small, family-owned businesses. They are called *private* or *closely held* corporations because their stock is not available to the general public. *Public companies,* though fewer in number, have a far greater economic impact than their closely held counterparts. They are often owned by thousands of stockholders.

2. Public companies must register their common stock with the Securities and Exchange Commission (SEC), which regulates the issuance and trading of the stock of public companies. Public companies must also submit to their stockholders an *annual report,* which contains the financial statements and other vital information about the company's financial position and performance. Called the 10-K when filed with the SEC, the annual report is available to the public through a number of sources (including the Internet and such electronic media as *Compact Disclosure*).

3. In addition to the financial statements, an annual report ordinarily contains a list of the corporation's directors and officers, a letter to the stockholders, a multiyear summary of financial highlights, a description of the business, management's discussion of operating results and financial conditions, notes to the financial statements, a report of management's responsibilities, the auditors' report, and supplementary information notes.

4. *Consolidated financial statements* are the combined financial statements of a company and its subsidiaries. The financial statements may present data from consecutive periods side by side for comparison. Such statements are called *comparative financial statements.*

5. The statement of earnings (income statement) should contain information regarding net income and earnings per share. A measure of a company's profitability, earnings per share equals net income divided by the weighted average number of shares of common stock outstanding.

6. The balance sheet usually contains such classifications as current assets, current liabilities, and long-term debt, which are useful in assessing a company's liquidity. In addition, the stockholders' equity section of the balance sheet normally contains information on stock issued and bought back by the corporation, on retained earnings, and on certain unusual items, such as adjustments for foreign currency translations.

7. Whereas the statement of earnings reflects a company's profitability, the consolidated statement of cash flows reflects its liquidity. It provides information about a company's cash receipts, cash payments, and operating, investing, and financing activities during an accounting period.

8. A corporation's annual report usually presents a *statement of stockholders' equity* in place of a statement of retained earnings. This statement explains the changes in each of the components of stockholders' equity.

9. A section called *notes to the financial statements* is an integral part of the financial statements. Its purpose is to help the reader interpret some of the more complex items presented in the statements.

10. A *summary of significant accounting policies* discloses the generally accepted accounting principles used in preparing the statements. It usually appears as the first note to the statements or as a separate section just before the notes.

11. In addition to management's discussion and analysis of operating performance, an annual report usually includes a report of management's responsibilities for the financial statements and the internal control structure.

12. The *independent auditors' report* conveys to third parties that the financial statements were examined in accordance with generally accepted auditing standards (*scope section*) and expresses the auditors' opinion on how fairly the financial statements reflect the company's financial condition (*opinion section*). In addition, the auditors' report clarifies the nature and purpose of the audit and emphasizes management's ultimate responsibility for the financial statements.

13. Corporations are often required to issue *interim financial statements*. These statements present financial information covering less than a year (e.g., quarterly data). Ordinarily, they are reviewed but not audited by the independent CPA.

CHAPTER 2   MEASURING BUSINESS TRANSACTIONS

REVIEWING THE CHAPTER

Objective 1: Explain, in simple terms, the generally accepted ways of solving the measurement issues of recognition, valuation, and classification.

1. Before recording a business transaction, the accountant must determine three things:
   a. When the transaction should be recorded (the **recognition** issue)
   b. What value, or dollar amount, to place on the transaction (the **valuation** issue)
   c. How the components of the transaction should be categorized (the **classification** issue)

2. Normally, a sale is recognized (entered into the accounting records) when the title to merchandise passes from the supplier to the purchaser, regardless of when payment is made or received. This point of sale is referred to as the **recognition point**.
   a. Some business events, such as the hiring of a new employee, are *not* recordable transactions.
   b. Other business events, such as payment to an employee for work performed, *are* recordable transactions.

3. The **cost principle** states that business transactions should be recognized at their original cost (also called *historical cost*). In this case, **cost** (a verifiable measure) refers to a transaction's exchange price at the point of recognition. Generally, any change in value that occurs after the original transaction is not reflected in the accounting records.

Objective 2: Describe the chart of accounts and recognize commonly used accounts.

4. Every business transaction is classified in a filing system consisting of accounts. An account is the basic storage unit for accounting data. Each asset, liability, and component of stockholders' equity, including revenues and expenses, has a separate account.

5. All of a company's accounts are contained in a book or file called the **general ledger** (or simply the *ledger*). In a manual accounting system, each account appears on a separate page. The accounts generally are in the following order: assets, liabilities, stockholders' equity, revenues, and expenses. A list of the accounts with their respective account numbers, called a **chart of accounts,** is presented at the beginning of the ledger for easy reference.

6. Although the accounts that companies use vary, some are common to most businesses. Typical asset accounts are Cash, Notes Receivable, Accounts Receivable, Prepaid Expenses, Land, Buildings, and Equipment. Typical liability accounts are Notes Payable, Accounts Payable, and Mortgage Payable.

7. The stockholders' equity section of a corporation's balance sheet contains a Common Stock account and a Retained Earnings account. The Common Stock account represents the amount of capital invested by stockholders. The Retained Earnings

account represents cumulative profits and losses, less cumulative dividends declared. Dividends are distributions of assets (generally cash) to stockholders and may be declared and paid only when sufficient retained earnings (and cash) exist.

8. A separate account is kept for each type of revenue and expense. The exact revenue and expense accounts used vary according to the type of business and the nature of its operations. Revenues cause an increase in retained earnings, whereas expenses cause a decrease.

Objective 3: Define *double-entry system* and state the rules for double entry.

9. The **double-entry system** of accounting requires that one or more accounts be debited and one or more accounts be credited for each transaction and that total dollar amounts of debits equal total dollar amounts of credits.

10. A **T account** shows an account in its simplest form. It has three parts:
   a. A title that expresses the name of the asset, liability, or stockholders' equity account
   b. A left side, which is called the **debit** side
   c. A right side, which is called the **credit** side

11. To prepare the financial statements at the end of an accounting period, the accountant calculates the **balance** of each account. Using T accounts to determine the account balances involves the following steps:
   a. Foot (add) the debit entries, and do the same with the credit entries.
   b. Write the **footings** (totals) for debits and credits in small numbers beneath the last entry in each column.
   c. Subtract the smaller total from the larger to determine the account balance. A debit balance exists when total debits exceed total credits; a credit balance exists when the opposite is true.

12. To determine which accounts are debited and which are credited in a given transaction, accountants use the following rules:
   a. Increases in assets are debited.
   b. Decreases in assets are credited.
   c. Increases in liabilities and stockholders' equity are credited.
   d. Decreases in liabilities and stockholders' equity are debited.
   e. Revenues, common stock, and retained earnings increase stockholders' equity, and are therefore credited.

   f. Dividends and expenses decrease stockholders' equity, and are therefore debited.

13. Analyzing and processing transactions involves five steps:
   a. Determine the effect (increase or decrease) of the transaction on assets, liabilities, and stockholders' equity accounts. Each transaction should be supported by a **source document,** such as an invoice or a check.
   b. Apply the rules of double entry.
   c. In **journal form,** enter the transaction (record the entry) in the journal.
   d. Post the journal entry to the ledger.
   e. Prepare the trial balance.

Objective 4: Apply the steps for transaction analysis and processing to simple transactions.

14. To record a transaction, one must obtain a description of the transaction, determine the accounts involved in the transaction and the type of each account (e.g., asset or revenue), ascertain the accounts that are increased and decreased by the transaction, and apply the rules described in paragraph 12.

15. For example, if the transaction is described as "purchased office supplies on credit," the transaction analysis would proceed as follows: From the wording, one can determine that the accounts involved are Office Supplies and Accounts Payable. One can also determine that the transaction has increased both accounts. Applying the rules of double entry, an increase in an asset—Office Supplies, in this case—is debited, and an increase in a liability—Accounts Payable—is credited.

Objective 5: Prepare a trial balance and describe its value and limitations.

16. Periodically, the accountant must check the equality of the total of debit and credit balances in the ledger. This is done formally by preparing a **trial balance.** A normal balance for an account is determined by whether it is increased by entries to the debit side or by entries to the credit side. The side on which increases are recorded dictates the account's **normal balance.** For example, asset accounts have a normal debit balance, and liability accounts have a normal credit balance.

17. If the trial balance does not balance, one or more errors have been made in the journal, ledger, or trial balance. The accountant must locate the errors to put the trial balance in balance. It is important to realize that certain errors will not put the trial balance out of balance; in other words, the trial balance cannot detect all errors.

Supplemental Objective 6: Record transactions in the general journal and post transactions from the general journal to the ledger.

18. As transactions occur, they are first recorded chronologically in a book called the **journal.** A separate **journal entry** is made to record each transaction; the process of recording the transactions is called **journalizing.** The **general journal** is the simplest and most flexible type of journal. Each entry in the general journal contains the date of the transaction, the account names, the dollar amounts debited and credited, an explanation of the transaction, and the account numbers if the transaction has been posted to the ledger. A single transaction can have more than one debit or credit; this is called a **compound entry.** A line should be skipped after each journal entry.

19. The general journal records the details of each transaction; the general ledger summarizes these details. Each day's journal entries must be transferred to the appropriate account in **ledger account form.** The process of transferring information from the journal to the general ledger, which updates each account balance, is called **posting.** The dates and amounts are posted to the ledger, and new account balances are calculated. The Post. Ref. columns are used for cross-referencing between the journal and the ledger.

20. Ruled lines appear in financial reports before each subtotal, and a double line customarily is placed below the final amount. Although dollar signs are required in financial statements, they are omitted in journals and ledgers. On paper with ruled columns, commas and decimal points are omitted, and a dash frequently is used to designate zero cents. On unruled paper, however, commas and decimal points are used.

A. (LO 3)   Cash   XX (amount borrowed)
            Notes Payable   XX (amount owed)
                Borrowed cash, issued promissory note in exchange

B. (LO 4)   Cash   XX (amount invested)
            Common Stock   XX (amount invested)
                Owners invested cash into business

C. (LO 4)   Prepaid Rent   XX (amount paid)
            Cash   XX (amount paid)
                Paid rent in advance

D. (LO 4)   Art Equipment   XX (purchase price)
            Cash   XX (amount paid)
                Purchased art equipment for cash

E. (LO 4)   Office Equipment   XX (purchase price)
            Cash   XX (amount paid)
            Accounts Payable   XX (amount to be paid)
                Purchased office equipment, partial payment made

F. (LO 4)   Art Supplies   XX (purchase price)
            Office Supplies   XX (purchase price)
            Accounts Payable   XX (amount to be paid)
                Purchased art and office supplies on credit

G. (LO 4)   Prepaid Insurance   XX (amount paid)
            Cash   XX (amount paid)
                Purchased insurance in advance

H. (LO 4)   Accounts Payable   XX (amount paid)
            Cash   XX (amount paid)
                Made partial payment on a liability

I. (LO 4)   Cash   XX (amount received)
            Advertising Fees Earned   XX (amount earned)
                Received payment for services rendered

J. (LO 4)   Wages Expense   XX (amount incurred)
            Cash   XX (amount paid)
                Recorded and paid wages for the period

K. (LO 4)   Cash   XX (amount received)
            Unearned Art Fees   XX (amount received)
                Received payment for services to be performed

L. (LO 4)   Accounts Receivable   XX (amount to be received)
            Advertising Fees Earned   XX (amount earned)
                Rendered service, payment to be received at later time

M. (LO 4) Utilities Expense   XX (amount incurred)

                  Cash   XX (amount paid)

                      Recorded and paid utility bill

N. (LO 4) Telephone Expense   XX (amount incurred)

                  Accounts Payable   XX (amount to be paid)

                      Recorded telephone bill, payment to be made at later time

O. (LO 4) Dividends   XX (amount declared)

                  Cash   XX (amount paid)

                      Declared and paid a dividend

SELF-TEST

Test your knowledge of the chapter by choosing the best answer for each item below.

1. Deciding whether to record a sale when the order for services is received or when the services are performed is an example of a
   a. recognition issue.
   b. valuation issue.
   c. classification issue.
   d. communication issue.

2. Which of the following statements is *true*?
   a. The chart of accounts usually is presented in alphabetical order.
   b. The general ledger contains all the accounts found in the chart of accounts.
   c. The general journal contains a list of the chart of accounts.
   d. Companies generally use the same chart of accounts.

3. Which of the following is a liability account?
   a. Accounts Receivable
   b. Dividends
   c. Rent Expense
   d. Unearned Art Fees

4. An entry on the left side of an account is called
   a. the balance.
   b. a debit.
   c. a credit.
   d. a footing.

5. Although debits increase assets, they also
   a. decrease assets.
   b. increase stockholders' equity.
   c. increase expenses.
   d. increase liabilities.

6. Payment for a two-year insurance policy is recorded as a debit to
   a. Prepaid Insurance.
   b. Insurance Expense.
   c. Cash.
   d. Accounts Payable.

7. An agreement to spend $100 a month on advertising beginning next month requires
   a. a debit to Advertising Expense.
   b. a debit to Prepaid Advertising.
   c. no entry.
   d. a credit to Cash.

8. Transactions initially are recorded in the
   a. trial balance.
   b. T account.
   c. journal.
   d. ledger.

9. In posting from the general journal to the general ledger, the page number on which the transaction is recorded appears in the
   a. Post. Ref. column of the general ledger.
   b. Item column of the general ledger.
   c. Post. Ref. column of the general journal.
   d. Description column of the general journal.

10. To test that the total of debits and the total of credits are equal, the accountant periodically prepares a
    a. trial balance.
    b. T account.
    c. general journal.
    d. ledger.

TESTING YOUR KNOWLEDGE

Matching*

Match each term with its definition by writing the appropriate letter in the blank.

_____ 1. Original (historical) cost

_____ 2. Account

_____ 3. Debit

_____ 4. Credit

_____ 5. Account balance

_____ 6. Ledger

_____ 7. Posting

_____ 8. Prepaid expenses

_____ 9. Accounts Payable

_____ 10. Common Stock

_____ 11. Retained Earnings

_____ 12. Double-entry system

_____ 13. Trial balance

_____ 14. Journal

_____ 15. Post. Ref.

_____ 16. Footing

_____ 17. Compound entry

_____ 18. Unearned revenue

_____ 19. Dividends

a. Transferring data from the journal to the ledger
b. The amount in an account at a given point in time
c. An entry with more than one debit or credit
d. A distribution of assets to stockholders resulting from profitable operations
e. A procedure for checking the equality of debits and credits in the ledger accounts
f. A record that occupies a page of the ledger
g. The book or file that contains all of a company's accounts
h. Adding a column of numbers
i. A liability that arises when payment for services is received before the services are rendered
j. Cumulative profits and losses, less dividends declared
k. The proper valuation to place on a transaction
l. Amounts owed to others for purchases on credit
m. Amounts paid in advance for goods or services
n. The book of original entry
o. The right side of a ledger account
p. The column in the journal and ledger that provides for cross-referencing between the two
q. The left side of a ledger account
r. The method that requires both a debit and a credit for each transaction
s. The account that represents stockholders' claims arising from their investments in the corporation

Short Answer

Use the lines provided to answer each item.

1. List the five steps that must be executed to analyze and process transactions.

   _____

   _____

   _____

   _____

   _____

2. Indicate which part of the following journal entry applies to each measurement issue listed below:

July 14	Cash	150	
	Accounts Receivable		150
	Collected on account		

   a. Recognition issue _____

   b. Valuation issue _____

   c. Classification issue _____

_____

Note to student: The matching quiz might be completed more efficiently by starting with the definition and searching for the corresponding term.

3. Describe a transaction that would require a debit to one asset and a credit to another asset.

_____

_____

_____

4. Describe a transaction that would require a debit to a liability and a credit to an asset.

_____

_____

_____

5. List the three account types that affect the Retained Earnings account.

_____

_____

_____

6. List the three account types that are credited when increased.

_____

_____

_____

True-False

Circle T if the statement is true, F if it is false. Provide explanations for the false answers, using the blank lines at the end of the section.

T F **1.** A sale should be recorded on the date of payment.

T F **2.** *Historical cost* is another term for *original cost.*

T F **3.** There must be a separate account for each asset, liability, and component of stockholders' equity, including revenues and expenses.

T F **4.** The credit side of an account implies something favorable.

T F **5.** In a given account, total debits must always equal total credits.

T F **6.** Management can determine cash on hand quickly by referring to the journal.

T F **7.** The number and titles of accounts vary among businesses.

T F **8.** Promissory Note is an example of an account title.

T F **9.** Prepaid expenses are classified as assets.

T F **10.** Increases in liabilities are indicated with a credit.

T F **11.** In all journal entries, at least one account must be increased and another decreased.

T F **12.** Journal entries are made after transactions have been entered into the ledger accounts.

T F **13.** In the journal, all liabilities and stockholders' equity accounts must be indented.

T F **14.** A debit is never indented in the journal.

T F **15.** Posting is the process of transferring data from the journal to the ledger.

T F **16.** The Post. Ref. column of a journal or ledger should be empty until posting is done.

T F **17.** In practice, the ledger account form is used, but the T account form is not.

T F **18.** The chart of accounts is a table of contents to the general journal.

T F **19.** Unearned Revenue has a normal debit balance.

T F **20.** Retained Earnings is a cash account that appears in the assets section of the balance sheet.

T F **21.** The Common Stock account represents stockholders' investments but not corporate profits and losses.

T F **22.** Errors caused by transposing digits are divisible by 2.

T F **23.** Dollar signs are omitted from journals and ledgers.

T F **24.** The ordering of a product from a supplier is considered a recordable transaction.

_____   _____
_____   _____
_____   _____
_____   _____
_____   _____
_____   _____
_____   _____
_____   _____
_____   _____
_____   _____
_____   _____

Multiple Choice

Circle the letter of the best answer.

1. Which of the following is *not* an issue when a business transaction is initially recorded?
   a. Classification
   b. Recognition
   c. Summarization
   d. Valuation

2. When a liability is paid, which of the following is *true*?
   a. Total assets and total liabilities remain the same.
   b. Total assets and total stockholders' equity decrease.
   c. Total assets decrease by the same amount that total liabilities increase.
   d. Total assets and total liabilities decrease.

3. Which of the following is *not* true about a proper journal entry?
   a. All credits are indented.
   b. All debits are listed before the first credit.
   c. An explanation is needed for each debit and each credit.
   d. A debit is never indented, even if a liability or stockholders' equity account is involved.

4. What is the last step taken when posting an entry?
   a. The explanation must be transferred.
   b. The account number is placed in the reference column of the ledger.
   c. The journal page number is placed in the reference column of the journal.
   d. The account number is placed in the reference column of the journal.

5. Which of the following errors would the preparation of a trial balance probably disclose (i.e., would cause it to be out of balance)?
   a. Failure to post an entire journal entry.
   b. Failure to record an entire journal entry.
   c. Failure to post part of a journal entry.
   d. Posting the debit of a journal entry as a credit and the credit as a debit.

6. When cash is received in payment of an account receivable, which of the following is *true*?
   a. Total assets increase.
   b. Total assets remain the same.
   c. Total assets decrease.
   d. Total assets and total stockholders' equity increase.

7. Which of the following is increased by debits?
    a. Dividends
    b. Unearned Revenue
    c. Mortgage Payable
    d. Retained Earnings

8. Which of the following accounts is an asset?
    a. Unearned Revenue
    b. Prepaid Rent
    c. Retained Earnings
    d. Fees Earned

9. Which of the following accounts is a liability?
    a. Interest Payable
    b. Interest Expense
    c. Interest Receivable
    d. Interest Income

10. A company that rents an office (i.e., is a lessee, or tenant) would never have an entry for which of the following accounts?
    a. Prepaid Rent
    b. Unearned Rent
    c. Rent Payable
    d. Rent Expense

11. Which of the following accounts has a normal credit balance?
    a. Prepaid Insurance
    b. Dividends
    c. Sales
    d. Advertising Expense

12. Payment of a $50 debt was accidentally debited and posted to Accounts Receivable instead of to Accounts Payable. As a result of the error, the trial balance will
    a. be out of balance by $25.
    b. be out of balance by $50.
    c. be out of balance by $100.
    d. not be out of balance.

APPLYING YOUR KNOWLEDGE

Exercises

1. Following are all the transactions of Natick Printing, Inc., for the month of May. For each transaction, provide *in good form* the journal entries required. Use the journal provided on the next page.

May 2 Natick Printing, Inc., was granted a charter by the state, and investors contributed $28,000 in exchange for 2,800 shares of $10 par value common stock.

3 Rented part of a building for $300 per month. Paid three months' rent in advance.

5 Purchased a small printing press for $10,000 and photographic equipment for $3,000 from Irvine Press, Inc. Paid $2,000 and agreed to pay the remainder as soon as possible.

8 Hired a pressman, agreeing to pay him $200 per week.

9 Received $1,200 from Raymond's Department Store as an advance for brochures to be printed.

11 Purchased paper for $800 from Pacific Paper Company. Issued Pacific a promissory note for the entire amount.

14 Completed a $500 printing job for Sunrise Shoes. Sunrise paid for half, agreeing to pay the remainder next week.

14 Paid the pressman his weekly salary.

15 Paid Irvine Press, Inc., $1,000 of the amount owed for the May 5 transaction.

18 Received the remainder due from Sunrise Shoes for the May 14 transaction.

20 A $700 cash dividend was declared and paid by the corporation.

24 Received an electric bill of $45. Payment will be made in a few days.

30 Paid the electric bill.

2. Following are three balance sheet accounts, selected at random from Patel Company's ledger. For each, determine the account balance.

Accounts Receivable		Accounts Payable	
2,000	1,000	1,200	4,200
750		2,000	

Cash	
15,000	1,000
4,000	1,200
	2,200

a. Accounts Receivable has a (debit or credit) balance of $_____.

b. Accounts Payable has a (debit or credit) balance of $_____.

c. Cash has a (debit or credit) balance of $_____.

General Journal				
Date		**Description**	**Debit**	**Credit**
May	2	Cash	28,000	
		Common Stock		28,000
		Recorded the stockholders' original investment		

3. Two journal entries are presented below. Post both entries to the ledger accounts provided. Only those accounts needed have been provided, and previous postings have been omitted to simplify the exercise.

		General Journal			Page 7
Date		**Description**	**Post. Ref.**	**Debit**	**Credit**
Apr.	3	Cash		1,000	
		Revenue from Services			1,000
		Received payment from Rudley Company for services			
	5	Accounts Payable		300	
		Cash			300
		Paid Garcia Supply Company for supplies purchased on March 31 on credit			

Cash — Account No. 11

						Balance	
Date		**Item**	**Post. Ref.**	**Debit**	**Credit**	**Debit**	**Credit**

Accounts Payable — Account No. 21

						Balance	
Date		**Item**	**Post. Ref.**	**Debit**	**Credit**	**Debit**	**Credit**

Revenue from Services — Account No. 41

						Balance	
Date		**Item**	**Post. Ref.**	**Debit**	**Credit**	**Debit**	**Credit**

CHAPTER 3   MEASURING BUSINESS INCOME

REVIEWING THE CHAPTER

Objective 1: Define *net income* and its two major components, *revenues* and *expenses*.

1. Profitability, or earning a **profit,** is a very important business goal. A major function of accounting is to measure and report a company's success or failure in achieving this goal. This is done by preparing an income statement that shows a company's net income or net loss.

2. **Net income** is the net increase in stockholders' equity that results from a company's operations. Net income occurs when revenues exceed expenses; if expenses exceed revenues, a **net loss** occurs.

3. **Revenues** are increases in stockholders' equity resulting from selling goods, rendering services, or performing other business activities. The revenue for a given period equals the total cash and receivables from goods and services provided to customers during the period.

4. Also described as the *cost of doing business* or as *expired costs,* **expenses** are the costs of goods and services used in the process of earning revenues. Examples of expenses are Telephone Expense, Wages Expense, and Advertising Expense. Expenses decrease stockholders' equity; typically, they also result in an outflow of cash or the incurrence of a liability.

5. Not all increases in stockholders' equity arise from revenues, nor are all decreases in stockholders'

equity produced by expenses. Similarly, not all increases in cash arise from revenues, nor are all decreases in cash produced by expenses.

Objective 2: Explain how the income measurement issues of accounting period, continuity, and matching are resolved.

6. The **accounting period issue** addresses the difficulty of assigning revenues and expenses to a short period of time. In dealing with this problem, accountants make an assumption about **periodicity**—that is, that while measurements of net income for short periods are approximate, they are nonetheless useful estimates of a firm's profitability for the period. To make the comparison of income statements easier, the accounting periods are usually of equal length. Accounting periods of less than a year are called *interim periods*. A **fiscal year** covers any 12-month accounting period. Many firms use a fiscal year that corresponds to a calendar year, the 12-month period ending on December 31. Others choose a fiscal year that corresponds to their yearly business cycles and ends during a slow season. The financial statements should always show the time period covered.

7. The **continuity issue** addresses the difficulty of allocating certain expenses and revenues over several accounting periods when one cannot be certain how long the business will survive. Unless there is evidence to the contrary (such as an imminent bankruptcy), the accountant assumes the business

is a **going concern**—that it will continue to operate indefinitely.

8. The matching issue has to do with the difficulty of assigning revenues and expenses to a period of time. When the **cash basis of accounting** is used, revenues are recorded when cash is received, and expenses are recorded when cash is paid. This method can lead to distortion of net income for the period. According to the **matching rule,** revenues must be recorded in the period(s) in which they are actually earned, and expenses must be recorded in the period(s) in which they are used to produce revenue; the timing of cash payments or receipts is irrelevant.

Objective 3: Define *accrual accounting* **and explain three broad ways of accomplishing it.**

9. **Accrual accounting** consists of all the techniques accountants use to apply the matching rule. Three broad ways of accomplishing accrual accounting are by recognizing revenues when earned (**revenue recognition**), recording expenses when incurred, and adjusting accounts at the end of the period.
   a. Revenue should be recognized when (1) a purchase or sale arrangement exists, (2) goods have been delivered or services rendered, (3) the selling price is fixed or determinable, and (4) collectibility is reasonably assured.
   b. Expenses should be recognized when (1) a purchase or sale arrangement exists, (2) goods have been received or services rendered, (3) the price is fixed or determinable, and (4) the product or service has been used to generate revenue.
   c. Some transactions invariably span the cutoff point for an accounting period. Thus, to ensure that the financial statements for the period are accurate, some accounts will need to be adjusted.

10. Because adjusting entries do not affect cash flow, they never involve the Cash account. They are, however, necessary for the accurate measurement of performance. Good judgment must be exercised when preparing adjusting entries to avoid the abuse and misrepresentation that can occur.

Objective 4: State four principal situations that require adjusting entries and prepare typical adjusting entries.

11. When revenues or expenses apply to more than one accounting period, **adjusting entries** are made at the end of the accounting period. The adjusting entries allocate to the current period the revenues and expenses that apply to the period, deferring the remainder to future periods. A **deferral** is the postponement of the recognition of an expense already paid or of a revenue already received. An **accrual** is the recognition of an expense or revenue that has arisen but that has not yet been recorded.

12. Adjusting entries have several purposes:
   a. To divide recorded costs (such as the cost of machinery or prepaid rent) between two or more accounting periods
   b. To recognize unrecorded expenses (such as wages earned by employees after the last pay period in an accounting period)
   c. To divide recorded revenues (such as commissions collected in advance) between two or more accounting periods
   d. To recognize unrecorded revenues (such as commissions that have been earned but that have not yet been billed to customers)

13. When an expenditure will benefit more than just the current period, the initial debit is usually made to an asset account rather than to an expense account. At the end of the accounting period, the amount that has been used is transferred from the asset account to an expense account.
   a. **Prepaid expenses** (expenses paid in advance, such as Prepaid Rent and Prepaid Insurance) are debited when paid.
   b. An account for supplies, such as Office Supplies, is debited when supplies are purchased. At the end of the accounting period, an inventory of supplies is taken. The difference between supplies available for use during the period and ending inventory is the amount used during the period.
   c. A long-lived asset, such as a building, a truck, or a piece of office equipment, is debited to an asset account when purchased. At the end of each accounting period, an adjusting entry must be made to transfer a part of the original cost of each long-lived asset to an expense account. The amount transferred or allocated is called **depreciation** or *depreciation expense.*
   d. **Accumulated depreciation accounts** are contra-asset accounts used to total the past depreciation expense on specific long-term assets. A **contra account** is so called because on the balance sheet it is subtracted from its associated asset account. Thus, proper balance sheet presentation will show the original cost, the accumulated depreciation as of the balance sheet date, and the undepreciated balance

(called **carrying value** or *book value*). In making the adjusting entry to record depreciation, Depreciation Expense is debited and Accumulated Depreciation is credited.

14. At the end of an accounting period, a company usually has incurred some expenses that have not been recorded in the accounts because it has not yet paid cash for them. An adjusting entry must be made to record these **accrued expenses.** For example, interest on a loan may have accrued during the current period but does not have to be paid until the next period. A debit to Interest Expense and a credit to Interest Payable will record the current period's interest for the income statement. A similar adjusting entry would be made for estimated income taxes and accrued wages. These entries will also record the liabilities for the balance sheet.

15. A company sometimes receives payment for goods or services before delivering them. In such cases, a liability account, such as **Unearned Revenues** or Unearned Fees, appears on the balance sheet. This account is a liability because it represents revenues that must be earned by providing the product or service that is still owed.

16. Often at the end of an accounting period, revenues have been earned but not recorded because no payment has been received. An adjusting entry must be made to record these **accrued** (unrecorded) **revenues.** For example, interest that has been earned might not be received until the next period. A debit must be made to Interest Receivable and a credit to Interest Income to record the current period's interest for the income statement. This entry will also record the asset for the balance sheet.

Objective 5: Prepare financial statements from an adjusted trial balance.

17. After all the adjusting entries have been posted to the ledger accounts and new account balances have been computed, an **adjusted trial balance** should be prepared. Once in balance, the adjusted trial balance is used to prepare the financial statements.

Supplemental Objective 6: Analyze cash flows from accrual-based information.

18. Liquidity, or the ability to pay debts when they fall due, relies on cash flow (not accrual-based) information. Fortunately, cash receipts and payments can be calculated from accrual-based net income and related information. The general rule for determining cash flow received from any revenue or paid for any expense (except depreciation) is to determine the potential cash payments or cash receipts and then deduct the amount not paid or received. For example, cash payments for rent would equal rent expense plus an increase (or minus a decrease) in prepaid rent occurring during the period.

	Cash Flow Formulas (SO 6)		
Type of Account	**Potential Payment or Receipt**	**Not Paid or Received**	**Result**
Prepaid Expense	Ending Balance + Expense for the Period	– Beginning Balance	= Cash Payments for Expenses
Unearned Revenue	Ending Balance + Revenue for the Period	– Beginning Balance	= Cash Receipts from Revenues
Accrued Payable	Beginning Balance + Expense for the Period	– Ending Balance	= Cash Payments for Expenses
Accrued Receivable	Beginning Balance + Revenue for the Period	– Ending Balance	= Cash Receipts from Revenues

Summary of Journal Entries Introduced in Chapter 3

A. (LO 4) Rent Expense   XX (amount expired)
              Prepaid Rent   XX (amount expired)
                  Prepaid rent expired

B. (LO 4) Insurance Expense   XX (amount expired)
              Prepaid Insurance   XX (amount expired)
                  Prepaid insurance expired

C. (LO 4) Art Supplies Expense   XX (amount consumed)
              Art Supplies   XX (amount consumed)
                  Consumed art supplies

D. (LO 4) Office Supplies Expense   XX (amount consumed)
              Office Supplies   XX (amount consumed)
                  Consumed office supplies

E. (LO 4) Depreciation Expense, Art Equipment   XX (amount allocated to period)
              Accumulated Depreciation, Art Equipment   XX (amount allocated to period)
                  Recorded depreciation expense

F. (LO 4) Depreciation Expense, Office Equipment   XX (amount allocated to period)
              Accumulated Depreciation, Office Equipment XX (amount allocated to period)
                  Recorded depreciation expense

G. (LO 4) Wages Expense   XX (amount incurred)
              Wages Payable   XX (amount to be paid)
                  Accrued unrecorded expense

H. (LO 4) Income Taxes Expense   XX (amount estimated)
              Income Taxes Payable   XX (amount estimated to be paid)
                  Accrued estimated income taxes

I. (LO 4) Unearned Art Fees   XX (amount earned)
              Art Fees Earned   XX (amount earned)
                  Performed services paid for in advance

J. (LO 4) Accounts Receivable   XX (amount to be received)
              Advertising Fees Earned   XX (amount earned)
                  Accrued unrecorded revenue

SELF-TEST

Test your knowledge of the chapter by choosing the best answer for each item below.

1. The net increase in stockholders' equity that results from business operations is called
   a. net income.
   b. revenue.
   c. an expense.
   d. an asset.

2. Which of the following accounts is an example of a contra account?
   a. Unearned Art Fees
   b. Depreciation Expense, Buildings
   c. Prepaid Insurance
   d. Accumulated Depreciation, Office Equipment

3. A business can choose a fiscal year that corresponds to
   a. the calendar year.
   b. the yearly business cycle.
   c. any 12-month period.
   d. any of the above.

4. Assigning revenues to the accounting period in which goods are delivered or services are performed and expenses to the accounting period in which they are used to produce revenues is called the
   a. accounting period issue.
   b. continuity assumption.
   c. matching rule.
   d. recognition rule.

5. Accrual accounting involves all of the following *except*
   a. recording all revenues when cash is received.
   b. applying the matching rule.
   c. recognizing expenses when incurred.
   d. adjusting the accounts.

6. Which of the following items is an example of a deferral?
   a. Accruing year-end wages
   b. Recognizing revenues earned but not yet recorded
   c. Recording prepaid rent
   d. Recognizing expenses incurred but not yet recorded

7. Prepaid Insurance shows an ending balance of $2,300. During the period, insurance in the amount of $1,200 expired. The adjusting entry would include a debit to
   a. Prepaid Insurance for $1,200.
   b. Insurance Expense for $1,200.
   c. Prepaid Insurance for $1,100.
   d. Insurance Expense for $1,100.

8. Adjusting entries are used to
   a. make financial statements from one period to the next more comparable.
   b. make net income reflect cash flow.
   c. correct errors that occurred in the recording of earlier transactions.
   d. record initial transactions.

9. On July 31, Wages Payable had a balance of $500; on August 31, the balance was $300. Wages Expense for August was $2,600. How much cash was expended for wages during August?
   a. $2,100
   b. $2,400
   c. $2,600
   d. $2,800

10. Which of the following accounts would probably be contained in an adjusted trial balance but *not* in a trial balance?
    a. Unearned Revenue
    b. Cash
    c. Depreciation Expense
    d. Utilities Expense

TESTING YOUR KNOWLEDGE

Matching*

Match each term with its definition by writing the appropriate letter in the blank.

_____ 1. Net income

_____ 2. Revenues

_____ 3. Expenses

_____ 4. Expired cost

_____ 5. Unexpired cost

_____ 6. Deferral

_____ 7. Accrual

_____ 8. Fiscal year

_____ 9. Going concern assumption

_____ 10. Cash basis of accounting

_____ 11. Accrual accounting

_____ 12. Matching rule

_____ 13. Adjusting entry

_____ 14. Depreciation expense

_____ 15. Accumulated Depreciation

_____ 16. Contra account

_____ 17. Unearned revenue

_____ 18. Adjusted trial balance

a. All the techniques used to apply the matching rule

b. A liability that represents an obligation to deliver goods or render services

c. The portion of an asset that has not yet been charged as an expense

d. A general term for the price of goods sold or services rendered

e. The assumption that a business will continue indefinitely (solution to the continuity issue)

f. Recognition of an expense or revenue that has arisen but has not yet been recorded

g. A method of determining whether accounts are still in balance

h. The requirement that an expense be recognized in the same period as the revenue produced by that expense

i. The amount by which revenues exceed expenses (opposite of net loss)

j. An account that is subtracted from an associated account

k. Any 12-month accounting period

l. An example of a contra account to assets

m. An end-of-period allocation of revenues and expenses relevant to that period

n. The cost of doing business

o. Recording revenues and expenses when payment is received or made

p. The expired cost of a plant asset for a particular accounting period

q. Postponement of the recognition of an expense already paid or of a revenue already received

r. A descriptive term for expense

Note to student: The matching quiz might be completed more efficiently by starting with the definition and searching for the corresponding term.

Short Answer

Use the lines provided to answer each item.

1. Briefly summarize the four situations that require adjusting entries.

_____

_____

_____

_____

2. Briefly explain the matching rule.

_____

_____

_____

3. Define *depreciation*.

_____

_____

_____

4. Distinguish between prepaid expenses and unearned revenues.

_____

_____

_____

5. List the four conditions that must exist before revenue should be recognized.

_____

_____

_____

_____

True-False

Circle T if the statement is true, F if it is false. Provide explanations for the false answers, using the blank lines at the end of the section.

T F 1. Failure to record accrued wages will result in the understatement of total liabilities.

T F 2. Expired costs are listed on the income statement.

T F 3. A calendar year refers to any 12-month period.

T F 4. The cash basis of accounting often violates the matching rule.

T F 5. In accrual accounting, the timing of cash receipts and payments is vital for recording revenues and expenses.

T F 6. Adjusting entries must be made immediately after the financial statements have been prepared.

T F 7. Prepaid insurance represents an unexpired cost.

T F 8. Office Supplies Expense must be debited for the amount of office supplies in ending inventory.

T F 9. Because Accumulated Depreciation appears in the asset section of the balance sheet, it has a debit balance.

T F 10. As a machine is depreciated, its accumulated depreciation increases and its carrying value decreases.

T F 11. On the income statement, Unearned Revenues is a contra account to Earned Revenues.

T F **12.** When an expense has accrued but payment has not yet been made, a debit is needed for the expense and a credit for Prepaid Expenses.

T F **13.** The adjusted trial balance is the same as the trial balance, except that it has been modified by adjusting entries.

T F **14.** If one has made a sale for which the money has not yet been received, one would debit Unearned Revenues and credit Earned Revenues.

T F **15.** The original cost of a long-lived asset should appear on the balance sheet even after depreciation expense has been recorded.

T F **16.** Adjusting entries help make financial statements comparable from one period to the next.

_____

_____

_____

_____

_____

_____

_____

_____

_____

_____

Multiple Choice

Circle the letter of the best answer.

1. Which of the following is an unlikely description for an adjusting entry?
   a. Debit to an expense, credit to an asset
   b. Debit to a liability, credit to a revenue
   c. Debit to an expense, credit to a revenue
   d. Debit to an expense, credit to a liability

2. Depreciation does *not* apply to
   a. trucks.
   b. office supplies.
   c. machinery.
   d. office equipment.

3. An account called Unearned Fees is used when
   a. recorded costs have to be divided among periods.
   b. recorded unearned revenues have to be divided among periods.
   c. unrecorded (accrued) expenses have to be recorded.
   d. unrecorded (accrued) revenues have to be recorded.

4. Depreciation best applies to
   a. recorded costs that must be divided among periods.
   b. recorded revenues that must be divided among periods.
   c. unrecorded expenses that must be recorded.
   d. unrecorded revenues that must be recorded.

5. Which of the following would *not* appear in an adjusted trial balance?
   a. Prepaid Insurance
   b. Unearned Management Fees
   c. Net income
   d. Depreciation Expense

6. An adjusting entry made to record accrued interest on a note receivable due next year would consist of a debit to
   a. Cash and a credit to Interest Income.
   b. Cash and a credit to Interest Receivable.
   c. Interest Expense and a credit to Interest Payable.
   d. Interest Receivable and a credit to Interest Income.

7. The periodicity assumption recognizes that
   a. net income over a short period of time is a useful estimate.
   b. a business is likely to continue indefinitely.
   c. revenues should be recorded in the period earned.
   d. a 12-month accounting period must be used.

8. Prepaid Rent is
   a. an expense.
   b. a contra account.
   c. a liability.
   d. an asset.

9. An adjusting entry would *never* include
   a. Unearned Revenue.
   b. Cash.
   c. Prepaid Advertising.
   d. Wages Expense.

10. Which of the following accounts would probably contain a lower dollar amount on the adjusted trial balance than on the trial balance?
    a. Accounts Receivable
    b. Withdrawals
    c. Office Supplies
    d. Rent Expense

APPLYING YOUR KNOWLEDGE

Exercises

1. On January 1, 20x3, Norton Transit Company began its business by buying a new bus for $24,000. One-eighth of the cost of the bus is depreciated each year. Complete *in good form* the company's partial balance sheet as of December 31, 20x5.

Norton Transit Company
Partial Balance Sheet
December 31, 20x5

Assets

Cash	$5,000
Accounts receivable	3,000
Company vehicles	
Total assets	$_____

2. For each set of facts that follows, provide the dollar amount that would be recorded.

   a. The cost of supplies at the beginning of the period was $510. During the period, supplies that cost $800 were purchased. At the end of the period, supplies that cost $340 remained. Supplies Expense should be recorded for $_____.

   b. The company signed a lease and paid $14,000 on July 1, 20x4, to cover the four-year period beginning July 1, 20x4. How much Rent Expense should it record on December 31, 20x4? $_____

   c. The company was paid $600 in advance for services to be performed. By the end of the period, only one-fourth of the sum had been earned. How much of the $600 will appear as Unearned Revenues on the balance sheet? $_____

3. In the next column is the trial balance of Lehman Company, which operates on a calendar year. The facts that follow are based on this trial balance. For each item, make the adjusting entry in the journal provided on the next page.

Lehman Company
Trial Balance
December 31, 20x6

	Debit	Credit
Cash	$ 77,300	
Notes Receivable	5,000	
Accounts Receivable	9,000	
Prepaid Advertising	8,000	
Prepaid Insurance	1,000	
Supplies	500	
Buildings	90,000	
Accumulated Depreciation, Buildings		$ 6,000
Notes Payable		1,500
Unearned Revenues		2,800
Common Stock		100,000
Dividends	13,000	
Revenues from Services		212,000
Wages Expense	118,500	
	$322,300	$322,300

   a. Cost of supplies on hand, based on a physical count, is $375.

   b. Wages of $2,500 for the five-day workweek ($500 per day) are recorded and paid every Friday. December 31 falls on a Thursday.

   c. During 20x6, services amounting to $600 were rendered for customers who had paid for the services in advance.

   d. Five percent of the cost of buildings is taken as depreciation for 20x6.

   e. One-quarter of the prepaid advertising expired during 20x6.

   f. All the insurance shown on the trial balance was paid for on July 1, 20x6, and covers the two-year period beginning July 1, 20x6.

   g. Work performed for customers that has not been billed or recorded amounts to $2,200.

   h. Accrued interest on a note payable amounts to $52. This interest will be paid when the note matures.

   i. Accrued income tax expense for the year amounts to $21,700. This amount will be paid early next year.

General Journal

Date		Description	Debit	Credit

4. At the beginning and end of the year, Dalton Industries had the following account balances on its balance sheet:

	Jan. 1	Dec. 31
Wages payable	$1,200	$3,700
Unearned revenue	500	900
Prepaid rent	2,400	1,800

The company's income statement for the year showed these figures:

Wages expense	$ 8,700
Revenue from services	35,000
Rent expense	3,600

a. Cash paid for wages during the year =
$_____.

b. Cash received for revenue during the year =
$_____.

c. Cash paid for rent during the year =
$_____.

Crossword Puzzle
for Chapters 2 and 3

ACROSS

1. An account that is subtracted from another
3. See 21-Down
6. Postponement of a revenue or expense
7. Another term for 2-Down (abbr.)
9. Where accounts are kept
13. Source of revenues
16. Test of debit and credit equality (2 words)
18. Left side of ledger
19. Monthly or yearly compensation
22. _____ bookkeeping (hyphenated)
23. Realize (revenues)

DOWN

1. Historical _____
2. Post. _____ column
4. Become an expense
5. Hourly or piecework-rate compensation
8. An income statement item
10. _____ estate (land)
11. Record transactions
12. Rule applied through accrual accounting
14. Right side of ledger
15. Assignment of a dollar amount to a transaction
17. Recognition of unrecorded revenues or expenses
20. A written promise to pay
21. With 3-Across, the term accountants use to refer to profit

CHAPTER 4 ACCOUNTING INFORMATION SYSTEMS

REVIEWING THE CHAPTER

Objective 1: Identify the principles of designing accounting information systems

1. **Accounting information systems** summarize a business's financial data, organize the data into useful form, and (through accountants) communicate the results to management. Management then uses the output to make a variety of business decisions. The means by which an accounting information system accomplishes these objectives is called **data processing.**

2. Most organizations have instituted **enterprise resource planning (ERP) systems,** which are comprehensive information systems that integrate both financial and nonfinancial information about customers, operations, and suppliers in a single database. These computer information systems integrate all functions of a company to provide timely information to decision makers throughout the organization. They are usually set up, monitored, and operated by accountants.

3. The design of an accounting information system should adhere to the following general principles of systems design:
   a. The **cost-benefit principle** states that the benefits derived from an accounting information system must match or exceed the system's cost.
   b. The **control principle** states that the accounting information system must contain the safeguards necessary to protect assets and to ensure that the data are reliable.

   c. The **compatibility principle** states that the accounting information system must be in harmony with the organization and its employees.
   d. The **flexibility principle** states that the accounting information system must be able to accommodate changes in the volume of transactions as well as organizational changes.

Objective 2: State all the steps in the accounting cycle.

4. The steps in the **accounting cycle** are as follows:
   a. *Analyze* business transactions from the source documents.
   b. *Record* the transactions in the journal.
   c. *Post* the entries to the ledger and prepare a trial balance.
   d. *Adjust* the accounts at the end of the period and prepare an adjusted trial balance.
   e. *Close* the revenue, expense, and Dividends accounts to conclude the current accounting period and prepare for the beginning of the new accounting period, and prepare a post-closing trial balance.
   f. *Prepare* financial statements from the adjusted trial balance.

Objective 3: Describe the use and structure of spreadsheet software and general ledger systems in computerized accounting systems.

5. In most small companies and even in large, multinational corporations, the microcomputer is a

critical element in the processing of information. It has become even more critical as companies have expanded their use of the Internet to transact business directly with vendors, suppliers, and clients.

6. Accountants commonly use spreadsheet software and general ledger systems.

   a. Spreadsheet software, such as Microsoft® Excel and Lotus®, assists in data analysis. A **spreadsheet** is a computerized grid of rows and columns into which the user places data or formulas related to such accounting tasks as financial planning and cost estimation.

   b. **General ledger systems** are integrated computer programs that are useful for double-entry transactions. They are usually organized so that each module performs a major accounting function. Accountants use these systems to account for such functions as sales, accounts receivable, purchases, accounts payable, and payroll.

   c. Most general ledger software uses the Windows® operating system, which has a **graphical user interface (GUI)** that employs symbols, called **icons,** to represent operations. General Ledger Software, Peachtree Complete Accounting™ for Windows, and Quickbooks® are among the most commonly used general ledger systems.

   d. **Source documents** (invoices, etc.) should support each transaction entered into the accounting system. Posting can be accomplished on a batch basis (at the end of a day, week, or month) or on a real-time (immediate) basis.

Objective 4: Explain how accountants and businesses use the Internet.

7. The **Internet** is the world's largest computer network, enabling individuals and organizations around the world to communicate with one another. Access to the Internet is generally gained via a modem connected to a phone line or a cable.

8. Accountants and businesses use the Internet in a variety of ways, including those described below.

   a. Most companies publish electronic versions of their annual reports on their web sites. The financial information of large companies is also available on Edgar, the SEC's online warehouse of financial information.

   b. **Extensible Business Reporting Language (XBRL)** is a computer language that allows users to access financial information on the Web and to summarize it, perform computations, and format it in any manner they wish.

   c. Businesses, individuals, and the government conduct business over the Internet in a practice called **electronic commerce (ecommerce).**

   d. **Electronic Data Interchange (EDI)** is ecommerce facilitated through private networks.

   e. Many manufacturers use the Internet to track the supplies and materials they need on a daily or hourly basis. This system, called **supply-chain management,** may also include a link to customers.

   f. **Event-to-knowledge (E2K) management** uses the Internet to convey information to internal and external users as quickly as possible after a transaction has occurred.

   g. Even when transactions are conducted electronically, source documents are still needed to back up the transactions. Ways of eliminating the need for such documentation are gradually being developed.

Objective 5: Explain the purposes of closing entries and prepare required closing entries.

9. Balance sheet accounts are called **permanent** (or *real*) **accounts** because their balances can extend past the end of an accounting period. They are *not* set back to zero.

10. Revenue and expense accounts are called **temporary** (or *nominal*) **accounts** because of their transient nature. Their purpose is to record revenues and expenses during a particular accounting period. At the end of that period, their totals are transferred to Retained Earnings (via the Income Summary account), leaving zero balances to begin the next accounting period.

11. **Closing entries** serve two purposes. First, they set the stage for the new accounting period by clearing revenue and expense accounts of their balances. (So that the Retained Earnings account can be updated, the Dividends account also is closed.) Second, they summarize the period's revenues and expenses by transferring the balance of revenue and expense accounts to the **Income Summary** account. The Income Summary account exists only during the closing process and does not appear in the financial statements. Closing entries must be made at the end of each period for which financial statements are prepared (such as at the end of each quarter).

12. There are four closing entries:

    a. Temporary credit balances are closed. This is accomplished with a compound entry that debits each revenue account for the amount required to give it a zero balance and credits Income Summary for the revenue total.

  b. Temporary debit balances are closed. This is accomplished with a compound entry that credits each expense for the amount required to give it a zero balance and debits Income Summary for the expense total.

  c. The Income Summary account is closed. After the revenue and expense accounts have been closed, the Income Summary account will have either a debit balance or a credit balance. If a credit balance exists, then Income Summary must be debited for the amount required to give it a zero balance, and Retained Earnings is credited for the same amount. The reverse is done when Income Summary has a debit balance.

  d. The Dividends account is closed. This is accomplished by crediting Dividends for the amount required to give it a zero balance, and debiting Retained Earnings for the same amount. Note that the Income Summary account is not involved in this closing entry.

13. The closing process prepares the books for the next accounting period. After closing, the revenue, expense, and Dividends accounts (temporary accounts) have zero balances. The updated Retained Earnings account reflects dividend declarations and net income or net loss for the period just ended. The balance sheet accounts (permanent accounts) show the correct balances, which are carried forward to the next period.

Objective 6: Prepare the post-closing trial balance.

14. After the closing entries are posted to the ledger, a **post-closing trial balance** must be prepared to verify again the equality of the debits and credits in the ledger. Only balance sheet accounts appear in the post-closing trial balance because all income statement accounts, as well as the Dividends account, have zero balances at this point.

Supplemental Objective 7: Prepare reversing entries as appropriate.

15. At the end of each accounting period, the accountant makes adjusting entries to bring revenues and expenses into conformity with the matching rule. The accrual type of adjusting entry is followed in the next period by the receipt or payment of cash. Thus, it would become necessary in the next period to make a special entry dividing amounts between the two periods. To avoid this inconvenience, the accountant can make

reversing entries (dated the beginning of the new period). Reversing entries, though not required, allow the bookkeeper to simply make the routine bookkeeping entry when cash finally changes hands. Not all adjusting entries may be reversed. In the system we use, only adjustments for accruals are reversed. Deferrals should not be reversed because such reversals would not simplify the bookkeeping process in future accounting periods.

Supplemental Objective 8: Prepare and use a work sheet.

16. Accountants use **working papers** to help organize their work and to provide evidence in support of the financial statements. The **work sheet** is one such working paper. The work sheet decreases the chance of overlooking an adjustment, acts as a check on the arithmetical accuracy of the accounts, and helps in preparing the financial statements. The work sheet is never published and is rarely seen by management. It is a useful tool for the accountant.

17. The five steps in the preparation of the work sheet are as follows:
  a. Enter and total the account balances in the Trial Balance columns.
  b. Enter and total the adjustments in the Adjustments columns. (A letter identifies the debit and credit for each adjustment and can act as a key to a brief explanation at the bottom of the work sheet.)
  c. Enter and total (by means of **crossfooting,** or adding and subtracting horizontally) the adjusted account balances in the Adjusted Trial Balance columns.
  d. Extend (transfer) the account balances from the Adjusted Trial Balance columns to the Income Statement columns or the Balance Sheet columns (depending on which type of account is involved).
  e. Total the Income Statement columns and the Balance Sheet columns. Enter the net income or net loss in both pairs of columns (one will be a debit and the other a credit) as a balancing figure, and recompute the column totals.

18. Once the work sheet is completed, the accountant can use it to (a) record the adjusting entries, (b) record the closing entries, thus preparing the records for the new period, and (c) prepare the financial statements.
  a. Formal adjusting entries must be recorded in the journal and posted to the ledger so that the

account balances on the books will agree with those on the financial statements. This is easily accomplished by referring to the Adjustments columns (and footnoted explanations) of the work sheet.

b. Formal closing entries are entered into the journal and posted to the ledger, as explained in Learning Objective 5. This is accomplished by referring to the work sheet's Income Statement columns (for the revenue and expense accounts) and its Balance Sheet columns (for the Dividends account).

c. The income statement may be prepared from the information found in the work sheet's Income Statement columns. Calculations of the change in retained earnings for the period are shown on the statement of retained earnings. Information for this calculation may be found in the Balance Sheet columns of the work sheet (beginning retained earnings, net income, and dividends). The balance sheet may be prepared from information found in the work sheet's Balance Sheet columns and in the statement of retained earnings.

Summary of Journal Entries Introduced in Chapter 4

A. (LO 5)   Advertising Fees Earned   XX (current credit balance)
            Art Fees Earned   XX (current credit balance)
                Income Summary   XX (sum of revenue amounts)
                    Closed the revenue accounts

B. (LO 5)   Income Summary   XX (sum of expense amounts)
                Wages Expense   XX (current debit balance)
                Utilities Expense   XX (current debit balance)
                Telephone Expense   XX (current debit balance)
                Rent Expense   XX (current debit balance)
                Insurance Expense   XX (current debit balance)
                Art Supplies Expense   XX (current debit balance)
                Office Supplies Expense   XX (current debit balance)
                Depreciation Expense, Art Equipment   XX (current debit balance)
                Depreciation Expense, Office Equipment   XX (current debit balance)
                Income Taxes Expense   XX (current debit balance)
                    Closed the expense accounts

C. (LO 5)   Income Summary   XX (current credit balance)
                Retained Earnings   XX (net income amount)
                    Closed the Income Summary account
                    (profit situation)

D. (LO 5)   Retained Earnings   XX (dividends for period)
                Dividends   XX (dividends for period)
                    Closed the Dividends account

E. (SO 7)   Wages Expense   XX (amount accrued)
                Wages Payable   XX (amount to be paid)
                    Accrued unrecorded wages

F. (SO 7)   Wages Payable   XX (amount previously accrued)
            Wages Expense   XX (amount incurred this period)
                Cash   XX (amount paid)
                    Payment of wages (Entry E was *not* reversed.)

G. (SO 7)   Wages Payable   XX (amount to be paid)
                Wages Expense   XX (amount accrued)
                    Reversed adjusting entry for E above (Assume
                    Wages Expense had been closed at end of period.)

H. (SO 7)   Wages Expense   XX (amount paid)
                Cash   XX (amount paid)
                    Payment of wages (Entry E *was* reversed.)

I. (SO 7)   Income Taxes Payable   XX (amount in adjusting entry)
                Income Taxes Expense   XX (amount in adjusting entry)
                    Reversed adjusting entry for estimated income taxes

J. (SO 7)   Advertising Fees Earned   XX (amount accrued)
                Accounts Receivable   XX (amount accrued)
                    Reversed adjusting entry for accrued fees earned

SELF-TEST

Test your knowledge of the chapter by choosing the best answer for each item below.

1. Which of the following sequences of actions describes the sequence of the accounting cycle?
   a. Post, record, analyze, prepare, close, adjust
   b. Analyze, record, post, adjust, close, prepare
   c. Prepare, record, post, adjust, analyze, close
   d. Enter, record, close, prepare, adjust, analyze

2. One important purpose of closing entries is to
   a. adjust the accounts in the ledger.
   b. set balance sheet accounts to zero to begin the next accounting period.
   c. set income statement accounts to zero to begin the next accounting period.
   d. summarize assets and liabilities.

3. After all the closing entries have been posted, the balance of the Income Summary account should be
   a. a debit if a net income has been earned.
   b. a debit if a net loss has been incurred.
   c. a credit if a net loss has been incurred.
   d. zero.

4. After the closing entries have been posted, all of the following accounts should have a zero balance *except*
   a. Service Revenue Earned.
   b. Depreciation Expense.
   c. Unearned Service Revenue.
   d. Wages Expense.

5. The post-closing trial balance
   a. lists income statement accounts only.
   b. lists balance sheet accounts only.
   c. lists both income statement and balance sheet accounts.
   d. is prepared before closing entries are posted to the ledger.

6. For which of the following adjustments would a reversing entry facilitate bookkeeping procedures?
   a. An adjustment for depreciation expense
   b. An adjustment to allocate prepaid insurance to the current period
   c. An adjustment made as a result of an inventory of supplies
   d. An adjustment for wages earned by but not yet paid to employees

7. The work sheet is a type of
   a. ledger.
   b. journal.
   c. working paper.
   d. financial statement.

8. A decision to go ahead with a costly computer system because of potential sales loss and customer discontent under the current system is probably a result of applying the
   a. cost-benefit principle.
   b. control principle.
   c. compatibility principle.
   d. flexibility principle.

9. Using the Internet to get information to users as quickly as possible is called
   a. enterprise resource planning.
   b. event-to-knowledge management.
   c. graphical user interface.
   d. Electronic Data Interchange.

10. All of the following are source documents *except*
    a. time cards.
    b. vendor invoices.
    c. checks.
    d. financial statements.

TESTING YOUR KNOWLEDGE

*Matching**

Match each term with its definition by writing the appropriate letter in the blank.

_____ 1. Post-closing trial balance

_____ 2. Working papers

_____ 3. Work sheet

_____ 4. Crossfooting

_____ 5. Reversing entry

_____ 6. Closing entries

_____ 7. Income Summary

_____ 8. Temporary (nominal) accounts

_____ 9. Permanent (real) accounts

_____ 10. Spreadsheet

_____ 11. Icon

_____ 12. Data processing

_____ 13. Internet

_____ 14. Accounting cycle

_____ 15. Electronic commerce (ecommerce)

_____ 16. Supply-chain management

a. Use of the Internet to track supplies and materials daily

b. Accounts whose balances extend beyond the end of an accounting period

c. Gathering, organizing, and communicating information

d. A symbol representing a common computer operation

e. The world's largest computer network

f. The means of transferring net income or net loss to the Retained Earnings account

g. A working paper that facilitates the preparation of financial statements

h. A final proof that the accounts are in balance

i. The opposite of an adjusting entry, journalized to facilitate routine bookkeeping

j. An account used only during the closing process

k. The sequence of steps followed in the accounting system

l. Software employing a grid of rows and columns

m. Adding or subtracting from left to right

n. Business conducted over the Internet

o. Documents that help accountants organize their work

p. Accounts that begin each period with zero balances

Note to student: The matching quiz might be completed more efficiently by starting with the definition and searching for the corresponding term.

Use the lines provided to answer each item.

1. What four accounts or kinds of accounts are closed out each accounting period?

   _____

   _____

   _____

   _____

2. List the five column headings of a work sheet in their proper order.

   _____

   _____

   _____

   _____

   _____

3. In general, what accounts appear in the post-closing trial balance? What accounts do *not* appear?

   _____

   _____

4. Briefly explain the purpose of reversing entries.

   _____

   _____

   _____

5. The six steps in the accounting cycle are presented below in the wrong order. Place the numbers 1 through 6 in the spaces provided to indicate the correct order.

   _____ The entries are posted to the ledger.

   _____ The temporary accounts are closed.

   _____ The transactions are analyzed from the source documents.

   _____ The accounts are adjusted.

   _____ The transactions are recorded in the journal.

   _____ Financial statements are prepared from the adjusted trial balance.

6. List the four general principles of systems design, and briefly describe the significance of each.

   a. _____

   _____

   b. _____

   _____

   c. _____

   _____

   d. _____

   _____

Circle T if the statement is true, F if it is false. Provide explanations for the false answers, using the blank lines below.

T F **1.** The work sheet is prepared before formal adjusting entries are made in the journal.

T F **2.** Preparing a work sheet reduces the possibility of overlooking an adjustment.

T F **3.** In the Balance Sheet columns of a work sheet, total debits differ from total credits by the amount of the net income or loss.

T F **4.** The statement of retained earnings is prepared after the income statement but before the balance sheet.

T F **5.** The Income Summary account appears in the statement of retained earnings.

T F **6.** Closing entries convert real and nominal accounts to zero balances.

T F **7.** When revenue accounts are closed, the Income Summary account is credited.

T F **8.** The Dividends account is closed to the Income Summary account.

T F **9.** When the Income Summary account is closed, it always requires a debit.

T F **10.** Reversing entries are never required.

T F **11.** The work sheet is published as a supplement to the balance sheet and income statement.

T F **12.** A key letter is needed in the Adjusted Trial Balance columns of a work sheet to show whether the entry is extended to the Balance Sheet columns or the Income Statement columns.

T F **13.** If total debits exceed total credits (before balancing) in the Income Statement columns of a work sheet, it means that a net loss has occurred.

T F **14.** The post-closing trial balance includes the Dividends account.

T F **15.** Reversing entries update the accounts at the end of the accounting period.

T F **16.** Retained Earnings is an example of a permanent (real) account.

T F **17.** The icons of a graphical user interface (GUI) make software easier to use.

T F **18.** Extensible Business Reporting Language facilitates the use of financial information on the Internet.

T F **19.** Edgar is an example of a general ledger system.

_____

_____

_____

_____

_____

_____

_____

_____

_____

Circle the letter of the best answer.

1. Which of the following accounts would appear in a post-closing trial balance?
   a. Interest Income
   b. Income Summary
   c. Retained Earnings
   d. Dividends

2. Which of the following statements is true?
   a. Closing entries are prepared before formal adjusting entries.
   b. The work sheet is prepared after the post-closing trial balance.
   c. Formal adjusting entries are prepared before the work sheet.
   d. Closing entries are prepared after the adjusted trial balance.

3. Reversing entries
   a. are dated as of the end of the period.
   b. are the opposite of adjusting entries.
   c. may be made for depreciation previously recorded.
   d. are the opposite of closing entries.

4. If total debits exceed total credits (before balancing) in the Balance Sheet columns of a work sheet,
   a. a net income has occurred.
   b. a net loss has occurred.
   c. a mistake has definitely been made.
   d. no conclusions can be drawn until the closing entries have been made.

5. Which of the following accounts would *not* be involved in closing entries?
   a. Unearned Commissions
   b. Retained Earnings
   c. Telephone Expense
   d. Dividends

6. When a net loss has occurred,
   a. all expense accounts are closed with debits.
   b. the Income Summary account is closed with a credit.
   c. the Dividends account is closed with a debit.
   d. all revenue accounts are closed with credits.

7. Which of the following is *not* an objective of closing entries?
   a. To transfer net income or loss to Retained Earnings
   b. To produce zero balances in all nominal accounts
   c. To update the revenue and expense accounts
   d. To be able to measure net income for the following period

8. A corporation began the accounting period with $50,000 in retained earnings and ended it with $75,000 in retained earnings. During the period it declared $30,000 in dividends. What was the corporation's net income or loss for the period?
   a. $55,000 net income
   b. $30,000 net loss
   c. $5,000 net loss
   d. $5,000 net income

9. Which of the following is an example of a temporary account?
   a. Prepaid Rent
   b. Unearned Revenues
   c. Wages Expense
   d. Accumulated Depreciation, Building

10. An accounting information system that can accommodate changes in a business adheres to the
    a. control principle.
    b. compatibility principle.
    c. flexibility principle.
    d. cost-benefit principle.

APPLYING YOUR KNOWLEDGE

Exercises

1. Following are the accounts of an adjusted trial balance for the month of July. In the journal provided below, make the necessary closing entries. All accounts have normal balances.

Accounts Payable	$ 1,000
Accounts Receivable	2,000
Cash	13,500
Common Stock	10,000
Dividends	2,500
Rent Expense	500
Retained Earnings	3,000
Revenue from Services	4,700
Telephone Expense	50
Utilities Expense	150

General Journal				
Date		Description	Debit	Credit

2. Using the information from Exercise 1, complete the following statement of retained earnings.

Frank's Fix-It Services, Inc.
Statement of Retained Earnings
For the Month Ended July 31, 20xx

---

3. The items below provide the information needed to make adjustments for Mike's Maintenance, Inc., as of December 31, 20xx. Complete the entire work sheet on the next page using this information. Remember to use key letters for each adjustment.

a. On December 31, there is $200 of unexpired rent on the storage garage.

b. Depreciation taken on the lawn equipment during the period amounts to $1,500.

c. An inventory of lawn supplies shows $100 remaining on December 31.

d. Accrued wages on December 31 amount to $280.

e. Grass-cutting fees earned but as yet uncollected amount to $50.

f. Of the $300 landscaping fees paid for in advance, $120 had been earned by December 31.

g. Accrued income tax expense for the year amounts to $1,570. This amount will be paid early next year.

Mike's Maintenance, Inc.
Work Sheet
For the Year Ended December 31, 20xx

Account Name	Trial Balance		Adjustments		Adjusted Trial Balance		Income Statement		Balance Sheet	
	Debit	Credit	Debit	Credit	Debit	Credit	Debit	Credit	Debit	Credit
Cash	2,560									
Accounts Receivable	880									
Prepaid Rent	750									
Lawn Supplies	250									
Lawn Equipment	10,000									
Accum. Deprec., Lawn Equipment		2,000								
Accounts Payable		630								
Unearned Landscaping Fees		300								
Common Stock		5,000								
Retained Earnings		1,000								
Dividends	6,050									
Grass-Cutting Fees Earned		15,000								
Wages Expense	3,300									
Gasoline Expense	140									
	23,930	23,930								
Rent Expense										
Depreciation Expense, Lawn Equipment										
Lawn Supplies Expense										
Wages Payable										
Landscaping Fees Earned										
Income Taxes Expense										
Income Taxes Payable										
Net Income										

4. On December 1, Krantz Company borrowed $20,000 from a bank on a note for 90 days at 12 percent (annual) interest. Interest is not included in the face amount. Make the following entries in the journal provided below:

a. December 1 entry to record the note
b. December 31 entry to record accrued interest
c. December 31 entry to close interest account
d. January 1 reversing entry
e. March 1 entry to record payment of the note plus interest

	General Journal			
Date		**Description**	**Debit**	**Credit**

CHAPTER 5 FINANCIAL REPORTING AND ANALYSIS

REVIEWING THE CHAPTER

Objective 1: State the objectives of financial reporting.

1. Financial reporting should fulfill three objectives. It should (a) furnish information that is useful in making investment and credit decisions; (b) provide information that is useful in assessing cash flow prospects; and (c) provide information about business resources, claims to those resources, and changes in them. General-purpose external financial statements are the main way of presenting financial information to interested parties. They consist of the balance sheet, income statement, statement of retained earnings, and statement of cash flows.

Objective 2: State the qualitative characteristics of accounting information and describe their interrelationships.

2. Accounting attempts to provide decision makers with information that displays certain **qualitative characteristics,** or standards:
   a. **Understandability** is the qualitative characteristic of information that communicates an intended message.
   b. Another very important standard is **usefulness.** To be useful, information must be relevant and reliable. **Relevance** means that the information is capable of influencing a decision. Relevant information provides feedback, helps in making predictions, and is timely. **Reliability** means that the information accurately reflects

what it is meant to reflect, that it is credible, verifiable, and neutral.

Objective 3: Define and describe the conventions of *comparability* and *consistency, materiality, conservatism, full disclosure,* and *cost-benefit*.

3. To help users interpret financial information, accountants depend on five **conventions,** or rules of thumb: comparability and consistency, materiality, conservatism, full disclosure, and cost-benefit.
   a. **Comparability** means that the information allows the decision maker to compare the same company over two or more accounting periods or different companies over the same accounting period. **Consistency** means that a particular accounting procedure, once adopted, should not be changed unless management decides it is no longer appropriate or unless reporting requirements change. The nature of the change, its justification, and its dollar effect on income should be disclosed in the notes to the financial statements.
   b. The **materiality** convention states that strict accounting practice need not be applied to items of insignificant dollar value. Whether a dollar amount is material is a matter of professional judgment, which should be exercised in a fair and accurate manner.
   c. The **conservatism** convention states that an accountant who has a choice of acceptable accounting procedures should choose the one that is least likely to overstate assets and

income. Applying the lower-of-cost-or-market rule to inventory valuation is an example of conservatism.

   d. The **full disclosure** convention states that financial statements and their notes should contain all information relevant to the user's understanding of the statements. Disclosures of such matters as accounting changes, commitments and contingencies, and the accounting methods used are essential for a full understanding of the financial statements.

   e. The **cost-benefit** convention states that the benefits to be gained from providing accounting information should be greater than the cost of providing it.

Objective 4: Explain management's responsibility for ethical financial reporting and define *fraudulent financial reporting.*

4. Users of financial statements depend on a company's management and accountants to act ethically and with good judgment in preparing the statements. This responsibility is often addressed in the management report that appears in a company's annual report.

5. The intentional preparation of misleading financial statements is called **fraudulent financial reporting.** It can be the result of the distortion of records, falsification of transactions, or misapplication of accounting principles. Persons guilty of fraudulent financial reporting are subject to criminal penalties and fines.

Objective 5: Identify and describe the basic components of a classified balance sheet.

6. **Classified financial statements** are general-purpose external financial statements that divide assets, liabilities, stockholders' equity, revenues, and expenses into subcategories, thus making the statements more useful to readers.

7. On a classified balance sheet, assets are usually divided into four categories: (a) current assets; (b) investments; (c) property, plant, and equipment; and (d) intangible assets. These categories are listed in order of liquidity (the ease with which an asset can be turned into cash). For simplicity, some companies group investments, intangible assets, and miscellaneous assets into a category called **other assets**.

   a. **Current assets** are cash and other assets (including short-term investments, accounts and notes receivable, prepaid expenses, supplies, and inventory) that are expected to be turned into cash or used up within a company's normal operating cycle or within one year, whichever is longer. (From here on, we will call this time period the current period.) A company's normal operating cycle is the average time between the purchase of inventory and the collection of cash from the sale of that inventory.

   b. Examples of **investments** include stocks and bonds held for long-term investment, land held for future use, plant or equipment that is not used in the business, special funds, and large permanent investments made to control another company.

   c. **Property, plant, and equipment** (also called *operating assets, fixed assets, tangible assets, long-lived assets,* or *plant assets*) include things like land, buildings, delivery equipment, machinery, office equipment, and natural resources. Most of the assets in this category are subject to depreciation.

   d. **Intangible assets** have no physical substance. Their value stems from the rights or privileges they extend to their owners. Examples are patents, copyrights, goodwill, franchises, and trademarks.

8. Liabilities on a classified balance sheet are divided into current and long-term liabilities.

   a. **Current liabilities** are obligations for which payment (or performance) is due in the current period. They are paid from current assets or by incurring new short-term liabilities. Examples of current liabilities include notes payable, accounts payable, taxes payable, and unearned revenues.

   b. **Long-term liabilities** are debts that are due after the current period or that will be paid from noncurrent assets. Examples are mortgages payable, long-term notes payable, bonds payable, employee pension obligations, and long-term leases.

9. The owners' equity section of a classified balance sheet is usually called owner's equity, partners' equity, or stockholders' equity. The exact name depends on whether the business is a sole proprietorship, a partnership, or a corporation. Other descriptive terms for owners' equity are *proprietorship, capital,* and the somewhat misleading term *net worth.*

   a. The stockholders' equity section consists of contributed capital and retained earnings. Contributed capital is generally shown on the balance sheet as the par value of the issued stock and as the paid-in, or contributed, capital in excess of par value.

b. In a sole proprietorship or partnership, the owner's or partners' equity section shows the name of the owner or owners. Each is followed by the word *capital* and the dollar amount of investment as of the balance sheet date.

10. Using software to present balance sheet figures in graphic form makes it easier to understand the numerical relationships and patterns among the various accounts. The visual presentation enables the reader to easily grasp the relative magnitude of the numbers and to plainly see their relationship to the whole.

Objective 6: Prepare multistep and single-step classified income statements.

11. An income statement may be presented in either multistep or single-step form. The **multistep income statement** is the more detailed of the two, containing several subtractions and subtotals. A merchandiser's or manufacturer's multistep income statement has separate sections for cost of goods sold, operating expenses, and other (nonoperating) revenues and expenses.

12. On the multistep income statements of **merchandising companies** (which buy and sell finished products) and **manufacturing companies** (which make and sell products), net income is computed as follows:

  Net sales
  − Cost of goods sold
  = Gross margin
  − Operating expenses
  = Income from operations
  ± Other revenues and expenses
  = Income before income taxes
  − Income taxes
  = Net income

The multistep income statement of a service company is prepared in the same manner, except that it does not contain cost of goods sold or gross margin.

a. **Net sales** consist of gross proceeds from the sale of merchandise (**gross sales**) less sales returns and allowances and sales discounts.

b. **Cost of goods sold** (also called *cost of sales*) is the amount a merchandising company paid for the goods that it sold during an accounting period. If, for example, a merchandiser sells for $100 a radio that cost the firm $70, then revenue from the sale is $100, cost of goods sold is $70, and **gross margin** (also called *gross profit*) is $30. The gross margin helps pay for **operating expenses** (all expenses other than cost of goods sold and income taxes). What is left after subtracting operating expenses represents **income from operations** (also called *operating income*).

c. Operating expenses consist of selling expenses and general and administrative expenses. Selling expenses are directly related to the sales effort. They include advertising expenses, salespeople's salaries, sales office expenses, and **freight out expense**. General and administrative expenses are not directly related to the manufacturing or sales effort. Examples are general office expenses and executive salaries.

d. **Other revenues and expenses** are nonoperating items, such as interest income and interest expense. They are added to or deducted from income from operations to arrive at **income before income taxes.** A corporate income statement should disclose **income taxes** (also called *provision for income taxes*) separately from the other expenses. (The income statement of a sole proprietorship or a partnership does not contain a provision for income taxes because these forms of business are not taxable units.)

e. **Net income,** often described as the *bottom line,* is what remains of the gross margin after operating expenses have been deducted, other revenues and expenses have been added or deducted, and income taxes have been deducted.

f. **Earnings per share,** also called *net income per share,* equals net income divided by the average number of shares of common stock outstanding. It usually appears below net income in the income statement and is a measure of the company's profitability.

13. Managers are continually trying to improve net income and profitability, and a multistep income statement provides them with much useful information. A graphic presentation of the income statement can facilitate analysis of the data.

14. In the **single-step income statement**, the revenues section lists all revenues, including other revenues, and the costs and expenses section lists all expenses (except for income taxes), including

cost of goods sold and other expenses. A condensed version of the single-step form (omitting earnings per share data) is as follows:

Revenues	X
- Costs and expenses	X
= Income before income taxes	X
- Income taxes	X
= Net income	X

Objective 7: Evaluate liquidity and profitability using classified financial statements.

15. Classified financial statements help the reader evaluate liquidity and profitability.

16. **Liquidity** refers to a company's ability to pay its bills when they are due and to meet unexpected needs for cash. Two measures of liquidity are working capital and the current ratio.
    a. **Working capital** equals current assets minus current liabilities. It is the amount of current assets that would remain if all current debts were paid.
    b. The **current ratio** equals current assets divided by current liabilities. A current ratio of 1:1, for example, shows that current assets are just enough to pay current liabilities. A 2:1 current ratio is considered more satisfactory.

17. **Profitability** refers to a company's ability to earn a satisfactory income. To draw conclusions about profitability, one must compare profitability measures with past performance and industry averages. Five common measures of profitability are profit margin, asset turnover, return on assets, debt to equity ratio, and return on equity.
    a. The **profit margin** equals net income divided by net sales. A 12.5 percent profit margin, for example, means that 12½ cents has been earned on each dollar of sales.
    b. **Asset turnover** equals net sales divided by average total assets. This measure shows how efficiently a company is using its assets to produce sales.
    c. **Return on assets** equals net income divided by average total assets. This measure shows how efficiently a company is using its assets to produce income.
    d. The **debt to equity ratio** measures the proportion of a business financed by creditors relative to the proportion financed by owners. It equals total liabilities divided by stockholders' equity. A debt to equity ratio of 1.0, for instance, indicates equal financing by creditors and owners.
    e. **Return on equity** shows what percentage was earned on the owners' investment. It equals net income divided by average stockholders' equity.

SELF-TEST

Test your knowledge of the chapter by choosing the best answer for each item below.

1. Goodwill is categorized as
   a. a current asset.
   b. revenue.
   c. an intangible asset.
   d. property, plant, and equipment.

2. Accounting information is said to be useful if it is
   a. timely and biased.
   b. relevant and reliable.
   c. relevant and certain.
   d. accurate and faithful.

3. To ignore an amount because it is small in relation to the financial statements as a whole is an application of
   a. materiality.
   b. conservatism.
   c. full disclosure.
   d. comparability.

4. Accounting is concerned with providing information to decision makers. The overall framework of rules within which accountants work to provide this information is best described as
   a. business transactions.
   b. data processing.
   c. generally accepted accounting principles.
   d. income tax laws.

5. A note receivable due in two years normally would be classified as
   a. a current asset.
   b. an investment.
   c. property, plant, and equipment.
   d. an intangible asset.

6. The current portion of long-term debt is normally classified as
   a. current assets.
   b. current liabilities.
   c. long-term liabilities.
   d. stockholders' equity.

7. A disadvantage of the single-step income statement is that
   a. gross margin is not disclosed separately.
   b. other revenues and expenses are separated from operating items.
   c. interest expense is not disclosed.
   d. the cost of goods sold cannot be determined.

8. Net income is a component in determining each of the following ratios *except*
   a. profit margin.
   b. return on assets.
   c. debt to equity ratio.
   d. return on equity.

9. Asset turnover is expressed
   a. in dollars.
   b. as a percentage.
   c. in times.
   d. in days.

10. Which of the following terms does *not* mean the same as the others listed?
    a. Net worth
    b. Owners' equity
    c. Proprietorship
    d. Working capital

TESTING YOUR KNOWLEDGE

*Matching**

Match each term with its definition by writing the appropriate letter in the blank.

_____ **1.** Qualitative characteristics

_____ **2.** Relevance

_____ **3.** Reliability

_____ **4.** Fraudulent financial reporting

_____ **5.** Classified financial statements

_____ **6.** Liquidity

_____ **7.** Current assets

_____ **8.** Property, plant, and equipment

_____ **9.** Intangible assets

_____ **10.** Current liabilities

_____ **11.** Long-term liabilities

_____ **12.** Other revenues and expenses

_____ **13.** Earnings per share

_____ **14.** Merchandising company

_____ **15.** Cost of goods sold

_____ **16.** Gross margin

_____ **17.** Operating expenses

a. A buyer and seller of goods in finished form

b. Long-lived tangible assets

c. The intentional preparation of misleading financial statements

d. All expenses except for cost of goods sold and income taxes

e. Guidelines for evaluating the quality of accounting reports

f. Short-term obligations

g. Financial reports broken down into subcategories

h. What a merchandising company paid for the goods it sold during an accounting period

i. Net income divided by the average number of shares of common stock outstanding

j. The income statement section that contains non-operating items

k. The subcategory of assets that are expected to be turned into cash or used up within one year or the normal operating cycle, whichever is longer

l. The standard that accounting information should be related to the user's needs

m. Long-term assets that lack physical substance and that grant rights or privileges to their owner

n. Net sales minus cost of goods sold

o. Obligations due after the current period

p. The standard that accounting information should accurately reflect what it is meant to represent

q. The ability to pay bills when due and to meet unexpected needs for cash

---

Note to student: The matching quiz might be completed more efficiently by starting with the definition and searching for the corresponding term.

Short Answer

Use the lines provided to answer each item.

1. List the three forms of business organization and each one's name for the owners' equity section of the balance sheet.

Business Organization

_____
_____
_____

Name for Owners' Equity Section

_____
_____
_____

2. What does each of the following ratios show about a company's profitability?

Profit margin

_____
_____
_____

Asset turnover

_____
_____
_____

Return on assets

_____
_____
_____

Return on equity

_____
_____
_____

Debt to equity ratio

_____
_____
_____

3. Define each of the following liquidity ratios:

Working capital

_____
_____

Current ratio

_____
_____

4. Explain the basic point of each of the following conventions:

Consistency and comparability

_____
_____
_____

Materiality

_____
_____

Cost-benefit

_____
_____

Conservatism

_____
_____

Full disclosure

_____
_____

True-False

Circle T if the statement is true, F if it is false. Provide explanations for the false answers, using the blank lines below.

T F 1. Receivables are not current assets if collection requires more than one year.

T F 2. Freight out expense is a type of operating expense.

T F 3. Gross margin minus operating expenses equals income from operations.

T F 4. Operating expenses consist of selling expenses and cost of goods sold.

T F 5. Accounting information is relevant if it could make a difference to the outcome of a decision.

T F 6. The net income figure is needed to compute the profit margin, the return on assets, and the return on equity.

T F 7. The investments section of a balance sheet includes both short- and long-term investments in stock.

T F 8. One meaning of the term *profitability* is the ease with which an asset can be converted to cash.

T F 9. A company's normal operating cycle cannot be less than one year.

T F 10. Net worth refers to the current value of a company's assets.

T F 11. Other revenues and expenses is a separate category in a multistep income statement.

T F 12. Multistep and single-step income statements for the same company in the same accounting period will produce different net income figures.

T F 13. Working capital equals current assets divided by current liabilities.

T F 14. The debt to equity ratio shows the proportion of a company financed by the owners.

T F 15. The qualitative characteristic of relevance means that independent parties can confirm or duplicate accounting information.

T F 16. Earnings per share is an important measure of liquidity.

T F 17. The customary dividing line between a material amount and an immaterial one is $500.

Circle the letter of the best answer.

1. The basis for classifying assets as current or noncurrent is the period of time that a business normally needs to turn cash invested in
   a. noncurrent assets back into current assets.
   b. receivables back into cash, or one year, whichever is shorter.
   c. inventories back into cash, or one year, whichever is longer.
   d. inventories back into cash, or one year, whichever is shorter.

2. Which of the following will *not* be found anywhere in a single-step income statement?
   a. Cost of goods sold
   b. Other expenses
   c. Gross margin
   d. Operating expenses

3. The current ratio would probably be of *most* interest to
   a. stockholders.
   b. creditors.
   c. management.
   d. customers.

4. Which of the following would *not* appear in the stockholders' equity section of a corporation's balance sheet?
   a. Retained earnings
   b. Common stock
   c. Paid-in capital in excess of par value
   d. Dale Richards, Capital

5. Net income divided by net sales equals
   a. profit margin.
   b. return on assets.
   c. working capital.

d. income from operations.

6. Operating expenses consist of
   a. other expenses and cost of goods sold.
   b. selling expenses and cost of goods sold.
   c. selling expenses and general and administrative expenses.
   d. selling expenses, general and administrative expenses, and other expenses.

7. According to FASB *Statement of Financial Accounting Concepts No. 1, w*hich of the following is *not* an objective of financial reporting?
   a. To provide information about the timing of cash flows
   b. To provide information to investors and creditors
   c. To provide information about business resources
   d. To provide information to management

8. If a company has a profit margin of 4.0 percent and an asset turnover of 3.0 times, its return on assets is approximately
   a. 1.3 percent.
   b. 3.0 percent.
   c. 4.0 percent.
   d. 12.0 percent.

9. The multistep income statement of a service company would *not* contain which of the following components?
   a. Income taxes
   b. Gross margin
   c. Other revenues and expenses
   d. Operating expenses

APPLYING YOUR KNOWLEDGE

Exercises

1. Gledhill Company uses the following headings on its classified balance sheet:

   a. Current Assets
   b. Investments
   c. Property, Plant, and Equipment
   d. Intangible Assets
   e. Current Liabilities
   f. Long-Term Liabilities
   g. Stockholders' Equity

   Indicate by the letters preceding these headings where each of the following items should be placed. Write an *X* next to items that do not belong on the balance sheet.

   _____ 1. Franchises
   _____ 2. Short-term advances from customers
   _____ 3. Accumulated depreciation
   _____ 4. Common stock
   _____ 5. Prepaid rent
   _____ 6. Delivery truck
   _____ 7. Office supplies
   _____ 8. Fund for the purchase of land
   _____ 9. Notes payable due in ten years
   _____ 10. Bonds payable currently due (payable out of current assets)
   _____ 11. Goodwill
   _____ 12. Short-term investments
   _____ 13. Provision for income taxes
   _____ 14. Inventory
   _____ 15. Accounts payable

2. The following information relates to A-1 Appliance, Inc., for 20xx:

Current Assets	$ 60,000
Average Total Assets	200,000
Current Liabilities	20,000
Long-Term Liabilities	30,000
Average Stockholders' Equity	150,000
Net Sales	250,000
Net Income	25,000

   Using this information, compute the following measures of liquidity and profitability:

   a. Working capital = $ _____
   b. Current ratio = _____
   c. Profit margin = _____%
   d. Return on assets = _____%
   e. Return on equity = _____%
   f. Asset turnover = _____ times

3. The following data relate to Lassen Corporation for 20xx:

Cost of Goods Sold	$150,000
Interest Income	2,000
Income Taxes	5,000
Net Sales	200,000
Common Stock Outstanding	3,500 shares
Operating Expenses	30,000

   a. In the space provided on the next page, complete a condensed multistep income statement in good form. Include earnings per share information in the proper place.

Newcastle Company Income Statement (Multistep) For the Year Ended December 31, 20xx		

b. In the space provided below, complete a condensed single-step income statement in good form. Include earnings per share information in the proper place.

Lassen Corporation Income Statement (Single-step) For the Year Ended December 31, 20xx		

Crossword Puzzle
for Chapters 4 and 5

ACROSS

1. Strong proponent of 10-Across
3. Relevance and reliability
6. Ownership stake in company assets
8. Short-term
9. Inventory-related expense (4 words)
10. _____ disclosure
11. _____ turnover
12. _____ out expense
13. _____ revenues and expenses
14. Provision _____ income taxes
18. Cost-_____ convention
19. Cleared, as temporary accounts
22. Another term for 13-Across
23. _____ worth

DOWN

2. Financial statement form
4. Profits (verb)
5. Income statement form (hyphenated)
6. Normal operating _____
7. Hourly pay
8. Add or subtract horizontally
12. Issuer of financial-reporting objectives
15. Balance of a cleared account
16. Asset category
17. Property, _____, and equipment
20. _____ to equity ratio
21. A natural resource

CHAPTER 6 MERCHANDISING OPERATIONS AND INTERNAL CONTROL

REVIEWING THE CHAPTER

Objective 1: Identify the management issues related to merchandising businesses.

1. A **merchandising business** earns income by buying and selling goods. This type of firm, whether wholesale or retail, uses the same basic accounting methods as a service company. However, accounting for a merchandising concern is more complicated because, unlike a service firm, a merchandiser must account for the inventory of goods it holds for resale.

2. Careful **cash flow management**—planning receipts and payment of cash to ensure liquidity—is important in any type of business. It is particularly important in a merchandising business because to ensure that it has **merchandise inventory** on hand to sell to customers, a merchandiser must be able to pay its suppliers when their bills fall due.
   a. A merchandiser engages in a series of transactions known as the **operating cycle.** The transactions involved in the operating cycle are the purchase of merchandise inventory for cash or on credit, payment for purchases made on credit, sale of the inventory for cash or on credit, and collection of cash from credit sales.
   b. Cash flow can be improved by reducing the **financing period** (also called the *cash gap*), which is the length of time a business will be without cash from merchandise inventory transactions. Technically, it is the amount of time from the purchase of inventory to the collection of cash from its sale minus the time the business takes to pay for the inventory.

3. **Profitability management** is also important for the merchandiser. It involves purchasing goods at favorable prices, selling those goods at a price that will cover costs and help earn a profit, and controlling operating expenses. One effective way of controlling expenses is to use operating budgets. An **operating budget** is a detailed listing of selling expenses and general and administrative expenses and their projected amounts. Periodically, management should compare these budgeted amounts with actual expenditures, analyze items that are significantly over or under budget, and adjust operations accordingly.

4. A merchandising company must choose a system or a combination of systems to account for its inventory. The two basic systems are the perpetual inventory system and the periodic inventory system.
   a. Under the **perpetual inventory system** continuous records are kept of the quantity and, usually, the cost of individual items as they are bought and sold. The detailed data available from the perpetual inventory system enable managers to quickly determine product availability, avoid running out of stock, and control the costs of carrying inventory.
   b. Merchandisers use the **periodic inventory system** when it is unnecessary or impractical to keep track of the quantity of inventory or the cost of each item (e.g., when a retailer sells a high volume of low-value items). With this system, no detailed records of inventory are kept during the accounting period; the merchandiser

waits until the end of the period to take a physical count of the inventory.

c. The periodic inventory system is simpler and less costly to maintain than the perpetual inventory system. However, its lack of detailed records may lead to inefficiencies, lost sales, and higher operating costs.

5. A merchandising business typically handles a great deal of cash and inventory—assets that are very susceptible to theft and embezzlement. Thus, a good system of internal control must be established to protect the company's assets.

a. A **physical inventory**—an actual count of the merchandise on hand—is a means of maintaining control over merchandise inventory. Such a count is conducted under both the perpetual and periodic inventory systems. It usually takes place on the last day of the fiscal year. To simplify the process, many retailers end their fiscal year during a slow season, when inventories are relatively low.

b. Merchandise inventory appears as an asset on the balance sheet and includes all salable goods owned by the company, no matter where the goods are located. Goods in transit to which a company has acquired title are included in ending inventory; goods that the company has formally sold are not included even if they are still in transit.

c. Inventory losses from theft and spoilage are included in the cost of goods sold. It is easier to track such losses under the perpetual inventory system than under the periodic inventory system.

Objective 2: Define and distinguish the terms of sale for merchandising transactions.

6. As a matter of convenience, manufacturers and wholesalers frequently quote prices of merchandise based on a discount from the list or catalogue price (called a **trade discount**). Neither the list price nor the trade discount is entered into the accounting records.

7. When goods are sold on credit, terms vary as to when payment must be made. For instance, n/30 means that full payment is due within 30 days of the invoice date, and n/10 eom means that full payment is due 10 days after the end of the month.

8. When a merchandising firm gives a customer a discount for early payment, it records a **sales discount.** Terms of 2/10, n/30, for example, mean that a 2 percent discount will be given if payment

is made within 10 days of the invoice date. Otherwise, the full amount is due within 30 days.

9. The terms of sale designate whether the buyer or seller of the goods bears the freight charges. A buyer in Chicago, for instance, must pay the freight in from Boston if the terms specify FOB (free on board) Boston or **FOB shipping point.** However, the seller in Boston pays if the terms are FOB Chicago or **FOB destination.** FOB terms also pertain to when the title of the merchandise passes from the seller to the buyer.

10. Companies that allow customers to make purchases on credit cards (such as MasterCard or Visa) must follow special accounting procedures. In reimbursing a merchant for a sale, credit card companies take a discount as payment for establishing the customer's credit and collecting money from the customer. When the merchant communicates its credit card sales to its bank (resulting in a cash deposit to its account), it debits Cash and Credit Card Discount Expense and credits Sales.

Objective 3: Prepare an income statement and record merchandising transactions under the perpetual inventory system.

11. The net income of a merchandising firm is computed as follows:

Net sales
– Cost of goods sold
= Gross margin
– Operating expenses
= Income before income taxes
– Income taxes
= Net income

12. Under the perpetual inventory system, the Cost of Goods Sold and Merchandise Inventory accounts are updated whenever a purchase, sale, or other inventory transaction takes place. Transactions are recorded under the perpetual inventory system as follows:

a. For the purchase of merchandise on credit, Merchandise Inventory is debited, and Accounts Payable is credited.

b. Transportation costs for goods received are recorded with a debit to **Freight In** (also called *transportation in*) and a credit to Accounts Payable or Cash.

c. A return of goods to the supplier for credit is recorded with a debit to Accounts Payable and a credit to Merchandise Inventory.

d. Payment on account is recorded with a debit to Accounts Payable and a credit to Cash.

e. When goods are sold on credit, Accounts Receivable is debited, and Sales is credited. However, an additional entry must be made, debiting Cost of Goods Sold and crediting Merchandise Inventory.

f. Delivery costs for goods sold are recorded with a debit to **Freight Out Expense** (also called *Delivery Expense*) and a credit to Accounts Payable or Cash.

g. When a credit customer returns goods for a refund, **Sales Returns and Allowances** is debited and Accounts Receivable is credited. (The purpose in accumulating returns and allowances in a Sales Returns and Allowances account rather than in the Sales account is to make data on customer dissatisfaction readily available to managers.) A second entry is needed to reinstate Merchandise Inventory (a debit) and to reduce Cost of Goods Sold (a credit).

h. The receipt of payment on account is recorded with a debit to Cash and a credit to Accounts Receivable.

Objective 4: Prepare an income statement and record merchandising transactions under the periodic inventory system.

13. Under the periodic inventory system, the Merchandise Inventory and Cost of Goods Sold accounts are *not* updated as purchases, sales, and other inventory transactions occur. Cost of goods sold is therefore computed on the income statement as follows:

Beginning inventory

+ Net cost of purchases (see paragraph 14)

= **Goods available for sale**

– Ending inventory

= Cost of goods sold

14. Net cost of purchases is calculated as follows:

Purchases

– Purchases returns and allowances

– Purchases discounts

= **Net purchases**

+ Freight in

= Net cost of purchases

15. Transactions are recorded under the periodic inventory system as follows:

a. All purchases of merchandise are debited to the **Purchases** account and credited to Accounts Payable. The purpose of the Purchases account is to accumulate the cost of merchandise purchased for resale during the period.

b. Transportation costs for goods purchased are recorded with a debit to Freight In and a credit to Accounts Payable or Cash.

c. The return of goods to the supplier for credit is recorded with a debit to Accounts Payable and a credit to **Purchases Returns and Allowances.** The latter appears as a contra account to purchases on the income statement.

d. Payment on account is recorded with a debit to Accounts Payable and credit to Cash.

e. When a cash sale is made, Cash is debited and Sales is credited for the amount of the sale. When a credit sale is made, Accounts Receivable is debited and Sales is credited.

f. Delivery costs for goods sold are recorded with a debit to Freight Out Expense and a credit to Accounts Payable or Cash.

g. When a credit customer returns goods for a refund, Sales Returns and Allowances is debited and Accounts Receivable is credited. The former functions as a contra account to sales on the income statement.

h. The receipt of payment on account is recorded with a simple debit to Cash and credit to Accounts Receivable.

Objective 5: Define *internal control* and its basic components, give examples of control activities, and describe the limitations of internal control.

16. Internal control encompasses all the policies and procedures management uses to ensure the reliability of financial reporting, compliance with laws and regulations, and the effectiveness and efficiency of operations. To achieve these objectives, management must establish five components of internal control: the control environment, risk assessment, information and communication, control activities, and monitoring.

a. The **control environment** reflects management's integrity and ethics, philosophy and operating style, method of assigning authority and responsibility, as well as the company's organizational structure and personnel policies and practices.

b. **Risk assessment** entails identifying areas in which risk of asset loss or inaccuracy of accounting records is especially high.

c. **Information and communication** relates to the accounting system that management sets up and to the communication of individual responsibilities within that system.

    d. Control activities are the procedures and policies that management establishes to ensure that the objectives of internal control are met. (See paragraph 17.)

    e. Monitoring consists of management's regular assessment of the quality of internal control.

17. Examples of control activities are (a) requiring authorization for all transactions, (b) recording all transactions, (c) using well-designed documents, (d) instituting physical controls, as over the accounting records, (e) making periodic independent checks of records and assets, (f) separating duties, and (g) employing sound personnel procedures. **Bonding** an employee (a good example of a sound personnel procedure) means insuring the company against theft by that person.

18. A system of internal control relies on the people who carry out the control procedures. In addition to human error, collusion and changing conditions can limit the effectiveness of a system of internal control.

Objective 6: Apply internal control activities to common merchandising transactions.

19. Proper controls over merchandising transactions not only help prevent losses from theft or fraud; they also help ensure accuracy in the accounting records. In addition, they can foster balanced inventory levels, help a company keep enough cash on hand to make timely payments for purchases discounts, and enable a company to avoid credit losses.

20. Some common procedures for maintaining control over cash are (a) separating the authorization, recordkeeping, and custodianship of cash; (b) limiting access to cash; (c) specifying the persons responsible for handling cash; (d) maximizing the use of banking facilities and minimizing cash on hand; (e) bonding employees who have access to cash; (f) physically protecting cash on hand by using cash registers, safes, and similar equipment; (g) performing unannounced audits of the cash on hand; (h) recording cash receipts promptly; (i) depositing cash receipts promptly; (j) paying by check; and (k) having someone who does not deal with cash reconcile the Cash account.

21. Cash received by mail should be handled by two or more employees. Cash received from sales over the counter should be controlled through the use of cash registers and prenumbered sales tickets. At the end of each day, total cash receipts should be reconciled and recorded in the cash receipts journal. All these tasks should be performed in accordance with the separation of duties.

22. All cash payments for purchases should be made by check and only with authorization. The system of authorization and the documents used differ among companies. The most common documents are described below.

    a. When a department needs to acquire materials, it fills out a **purchase requisition** form requesting that the company purchase them.

    b. The department responsible for the company's purchasing activities completes a **purchase order** and sends it to the vendor.

    c. After shipping the goods, the vendor sends an **invoice**, or bill, to the company.

    d. When the goods arrive, the receiving department completes a **receiving report** and forwards it to the accounting department; it contains information about the quantity and condition of the goods received.

    e. A **check authorization**, issued by the accounting department, is a document attached to the purchase order, invoice, and receiving report; it indicates that the information on those three documents is in agreement and that payment is approved.

    f. When payment is approved, the company's treasurer issues a **check** to the vendor for the amount of the invoice less any appropriate discount. A remittance advice, which shows what the check is paying, should be attached to the check.

Supplemental Objective 7: Apply sales and purchases discounts to merchandising transactions.

23. Sales discounts for early payment are customary in some industries. These discounts are recorded only when payment is received within the discount period. Cash and Sales Discounts are debited; Accounts Receivable is credited. Sales Discounts is a contra account to sales on the income statement.

24. **Purchases discounts** are discounts taken for early payment of merchandise purchased for resale. They are to the buyer what sales discounts are to the seller. A purchase is initially recorded at the gross purchase price. If the company makes payment within the discount period, it debits Accounts Payable, credits Purchases Discounts, and credits Cash. Purchases Discounts is a contra account to Purchases on the Income Statement.

Summary of Journal Entries Introduced in Chapter 6

A. (LO 2)   Cash   XX (amount net of fee)
    Credit Card Discount Expense   XX (fee charged)
      Sales   XX (gross amount sold)
        Made sales on credit cards

Perpetual Inventory System

B. (LO 3)   Merchandise Inventory   XX (purchase price)
    Accounts Payable   XX (amount due)
      Purchased merchandise on credit

C. (LO 3)   Freight In   XX (price charged)
    Accounts Payable   XX (amount due)
      Received bill for transportation charges

D. (LO 3)   Accounts Payable   XX (amount returned)
    Merchandise Inventory   XX (amount returned)
      Returned merchandise to supplier for credit

E. (LO 3)   Accounts Payable   XX (amount paid)
    Cash   XX (amount paid)
      Made payment on account to supplier

F. (LO 3)   Accounts Receivable   XX (amount to be received)
    Sales   XX (sales price)
      Sold merchandise on credit

    Cost of Goods Sold   XX (inventory cost)
    Merchandise Inventory   XX (inventory cost)
      Transferred cost of merchandise inventory
      to Cost of Goods Sold account

G. (LO 3)   Freight Out Expense   XX (amount incurred)
    Cash   XX (amount paid)
      Paid delivery costs for goods shipped
      to customer

H. (LO 3)   Sales Returns and Allowances   XX (price of goods returned)
    Accounts Receivable   XX (amount credited to account)
      Accepted returned merchandise for credit

    Merchandise Inventory   XX (inventory cost)
    Cost of Goods Sold   XX (inventory cost)
      Transferred cost of merchandise returned to
      Merchandise Inventory account

I. (LO 3)   Cash   XX (amount received)
    Accounts Receivable   XX (amount settled)
      Received payment on account from customer

J. (LO 4) Purchases   XX (purchase price)
                Accounts Payable   XX (amount due)
                    Purchased merchandise on credit

K. (LO 4) Freight In   XX (price charged)
                Accounts Payable   XX (amount due)
                    Received bill for transportation charges

L. (LO 4) Accounts Payable   XX (amount returned)
                Purchases Returns and Allowances   XX (amount returned)
                    Returned merchandise to supplier for credit

M. (LO 4) Accounts Payable   XX (amount paid)
                Cash   XX (amount paid)
                    Made payment on account to supplier

N. (LO 4) Accounts Receivable   XX (amount to be received)
                Sales   XX (sales price)
                    Sold merchandise on credit

O. (LO 4) Freight Out Expense   XX (amount incurred)
                Cash   XX (amount paid)
                    Paid delivery costs for goods shipped to customer

P. (LO 4) Sales Returns and Allowances   XX (price of goods returned)
                Accounts Receivable   XX (amount credited to account)
                    Accepted return of merchandise, account credited

Q. (LO 4) Cash   XX (amount received)
                Accounts Receivable   XX (amount settled)
                    Received payment on account from customer

---

R. (SO 7) Accounts Receivable   XX (amount due)
                Sales   XX (sales price)
                    Sold merchandise on credit

S. (SO 7) Cash   XX (net amount received)
                Sales Discounts   XX (discount taken)
                    Accounts Receivable   XX (gross amount settled)
                        Received payment from customer within
                        discount period

T. (SO 7) Cash   XX (amount received)
                Accounts Receivable   XX (gross amount settled)
                    Received payment on account after
                    discount period

U. (SO 7) Accounts Payable   XX (gross amount settled)
                Purchases Discounts   XX (discount taken)
                Cash   XX (net amount paid)
                    Paid supplier within discount period

V. (SO 7) Accounts Payable   XX (gross amount settled)
                Cash   XX (amount paid)
                    Paid supplier after discount period

SELF-TEST

Test your knowledge of the chapter by choosing the best answer for each item below.

1. Management determines that, on average, customers are taking five more days to pay for sales made on credit. To which of the following management concerns does this payment pattern directly relate?
   a. Cash flow management
   b. Profitability management
   c. Choice of inventory system
   d. Control of merchandise operations

2. A pretax income always results when
   a. cost of goods sold exceeds operating expenses.
   b. revenues exceed the cost of goods sold.
   c. revenues exceed operating expenses.
   d. the gross margin exceeds operating expenses.

3. Which of the following appears as an operating expense on the income statement of a merchandising concern?
   a. Freight In
   b. Freight Out Expense
   c. Sales Returns and Allowances
   d. Purchases Returns and Allowances

4. If a firm's beginning merchandise inventory is $400, its ending merchandise inventory is $700, and its cost of goods sold is $3,400, the net cost of purchases
   a. is $3,700.
   b. is $3,400.
   c. is $3,100.
   d. cannot be determined.

5. A sale is made on June 1 for $200, terms 2/10, n/30, on which a sales return of $50 is granted on June 7. The dollar amount received for payment in full on June 9 is
   a. $200.
   b. $150.
   c. $147.
   d. $196.

6. Under a periodic inventory system, a purchase of merchandise for $750 that includes freight of $50 under terms of n/30, FOB shipping point, would result in a
   a. debit to Freight In of $50.
   b. debit to Purchases of $750.
   c. credit to Accounts Payable of $700.
   d. credit to Freight Payable of $50.

7. A firm that maintains perpetual inventory records sells on account for $2,000 goods that cost the firm $1,400. The entries to record this transaction should include a
   a. debit to Merchandise Inventory for $1,400.
   b. debit to Sales for $2,000.
   c. credit to Accounts Receivable for $2,000.
   d. debit to Cost of Goods Sold for $1,400.

8. Which of the following is *not* a component of internal control?
   a. Monitoring
   b. Risk assessment
   c. Reporting
   d. Control activities

9. The separation of duties in terms of cash transactions means that different persons should be responsible for authorization, custody, and
   a. approval.
   b. recordkeeping.
   c. control.
   d. protection.

10. Which of the following documents must be presented and in agreement before a check authorization is prepared?
    a. Purchase requisition and purchase order
    b. Purchase order and receiving report
    c. Purchase requisition, purchase order, and invoice
    d. Purchase order, invoice, and receiving report

TESTING YOUR KNOWLEDGE

*Matching**

Match each term with its definition by writing the appropriate letter in the blank.

_____ 1. Trade discount

_____ 2. Invoice

_____ 3. Receiving report

_____ 4. Check authorization

_____ 5. Sales Returns and Allowances

_____ 6. Sales Discounts

_____ 7. Freight out expense

_____ 8. Purchases

_____ 9. Goods available for sale

_____ 10. Perpetual inventory system

_____ 11. Periodic inventory system

_____ 12. Freight in

_____ 13. FOB (free on board)

_____ 14. Purchases Returns and Allowances

_____ 15. Purchases Discounts

_____ 16. Internal control

_____ 17. Purchase requisition

_____ 18. Purchase order

a. Transportation cost for goods purchased
b. A document that authorizes payment
c. Delivery charge for goods sold
d. A system that maintains continuous records of the quantity and, usually, the cost of goods as they are bought and sold
e. A vendor's bill
f. The point after which the buyer must bear the transportation cost
g. Under the periodic inventory system, the account used to accumulate the cost of goods bought during the period
h. A deduction off a list or catalogue price
i. Beginning inventory plus net cost of purchases
j. A document that asks the purchasing department to order certain items
k. The account used by sellers when a buyer pays for goods within the discount period
l. The account used by sellers when a buyer returns goods
m. A system that does *not* maintain continuous records of merchandise inventory
n. The account used by buyers when they pay for goods within the discount period
o. An order for goods that is sent to a vendor
p. Under the periodic inventory system, the account used by buyers when they return goods
q. A description of goods received by a company
r. A system designed to ensure the reliability of financial reporting, compliance with laws and regulations, and the effectiveness and efficiency of operations

---

Note to student: The matching quiz might be completed more efficiently by starting with the definition and searching for the corresponding term.

Short Answer

Use the lines provided to answer each item.

1. List seven control activities that help make a system of internal control effective.

   _____

   _____

   _____

   _____

   _____

   _____

   _____

2. List any six procedures that may be employed to control and safeguard cash.

   _____

   _____

   _____

   _____

   _____

   _____

3. What three documents should be in agreement before an invoice is paid?

   _____

   _____

   _____

4. Assuming a company uses the periodic inventory system, list the items that would appear in a condensed cost of goods sold section of its income statement. Use mathematical signs to indicate their relationship.

   _____

   _____

   _____

   _____

5. Using mathematical signs, list the sequence of items involved in computing net cost of purchases in a periodic inventory system.

   _____

   _____

   _____

   _____

   _____

   _____

True-False

Circle T if the statement is true, F if it is false. Provide explanations for the false answers, using the blank lines at the end of the section.

T F 1. Ending merchandise inventory is needed to calculate goods available for sale.

T F 2. Terms of n/10 eom mean that payment must be made ten days before the end of the month.

T F 3. An operating budget is a detailed listing of selling, general, and administrative expenses and their projected amounts.

T F 4. Inventory losses are normally included in the cost of goods sold.

T F 5. FOB destination means that the seller bears the transportation cost.

T F 6. Sales Discounts is a contra account to Net Sales.

T F 7. Under the periodic inventory system, ending inventory is a necessary component of both the balance sheet and the income statement.

T F 8. Cost of goods available for sale minus cost of goods sold equals ending inventory.

T F 9. The perpetual inventory system requires more detailed recordkeeping than the periodic system.

T F 10. The beginning inventory of an accounting period is the same as the ending inventory of the previous period.

T F 11. Sales Returns and Allowances normally has a credit balance.

T F 12. Under the periodic inventory system, a cash purchase of office supplies for use in daily operations requires a debit to Purchases and a credit to Cash.

T F 13. A Purchases Returns and Allowances account is not used in the perpetual inventory system.

T F 14. Merchants treat Credit Card Discount Expense as a contra account to Sales.

T F 15. Under the periodic inventory system, the cost of goods sold must be recorded and the inventory account must be decreased as soon as a sale is made.

T F 16. An example of a trade discount is 2/10, n/30.

T F 17. When goods are shipped FOB shipping point, title passes when the buyer receives the goods.

T F 18. A good system of internal control will guarantee that the accounting records are accurate.

T F 19. *Collusion* refers to a secret agreement between two or more persons to defraud a company.

T F 20. Mail should be opened in the accounting department so that transactions can be recorded immediately.

T F 21. A company orders goods by sending the supplier a purchase requisition.

T F 22. Rotating employees in job assignments is poor internal control because employees are continually forced to learn new job skills.

T F 23. One of the five components of internal control is "information and communication."

Multiple Choice

Circle the letter of the best answer.

1. Dew buys $600 of merchandise from Allen, with terms of 2/10, n/30. Dew immediately returns $100 of goods and pays for the remainder eight days after the purchase. Dew's entry on the date of payment would include a
   a. debit to Accounts Payable for $600.
   b. debit to Sales Discounts for $12.
   c. credit to Purchases Returns and Allowances for $100.
   d. credit to Purchases Discounts for $10.

2. Which of the following accounts normally has a credit balance?
   a. Sales Discounts
   b. Merchandise Inventory
   c. Purchases Returns and Allowances
   d. Freight In

3. Under a periodic inventory system, which of the following accounts is irrelevant in computing cost of goods sold ?
   a. Freight In
   b. Freight Out Expense
   c. Merchandise Inventory, beginning
   d. Merchandise Inventory, ending

4. When a company is buying goods, which of the following documents is prepared first?
   a. Purchase order
   b. Receiving report
   c. Check authorization
   d. Purchase requisition

5. Which of the following is an example of poor internal control?
   a. Having the receiving department compare goods received with the related purchase order
   b. Forcing employees to take earned vacations
   c. Requiring someone other than the petty cash custodian to enter petty cash transactions in the accounting records
   d. Bonding employees

6. Which of the following accounts is *not* used in conjunction with a perpetual inventory system?
   a. Cost of Goods Sold
   b. Freight In
   c. Purchases
   d. Merchandise Inventory

7. Which of the following transactions is *not* part of the operating cycle?
   a. Sale of inventory
   b. Cash payment for operating expenses
   c. Purchase of inventory
   d. Cash collection from inventory sales

8. A company has credit card sales for the day of $1,000. If the credit card company charges 5 percent, the company's journal entry to record sales and the receipt of cash when it deposits the credit card invoices at its bank would include a
   a. credit to Sales for $950.
   b. credit to Credit Card Discount Expense for $50.
   c. debit to Sales for $1,000.
   d. debit to Cash for $950.

9. On average, it takes Ledbetter Corporation 45 days to sell its inventory and 60 days to collect payment from customers. Ledbetter normally pays for inventory purchases within 30 days. Its financing period is
   a. 75 days.
   b. 135 days.
   c. 15 days.
   d. 105 days.

APPLYING YOUR KNOWLEDGE

Exercises

1. Morris Merchandising Company uses the periodic inventory system. Listed below are its transactions during the month of May. Record each transaction in the journal provided on the opposite page.

May   1   Purchased merchandise for $500 on credit, terms 2/10, n/60.

       3   Sold merchandise for $500 on credit, terms 2/10, 1/20, n/30.

       4   Paid $42 for freight charges relating to a merchandise purchase in April.

       5   Purchased office supplies for $100, on credit.

       6   Returned $20 of the May 5 office supplies, for credit.

       7   Returned $50 of merchandise purchased on May 1, for credit.

       9   Sold merchandise for $225, on credit, terms 2/10, 1/15; n/30.

     10   Paid for the merchandise purchased on May 1, less the return and a discount.

     14   The customer of May 9 returned $25 of merchandise, for credit.

     22   The customer of May 9 paid for the merchandise, less the return and a discount.

     26   The customer of May 3 paid for the merchandise purchased on that date.

2. The following data are from the records of the Gaviota Merchandising Company:

Advertising Expense	$ 5,000
Dividends	12,000
Freight In	2,000
Freight Out Expense	4,000
Income Taxes Expense	4,780
Income Taxes Payable	4,780
Interest Income	150
Merchandise Inventory (Jan. 1)	10,000
Merchandise Inventory (Dec. 31)	8,000
Purchases	50,000
Purchases Discounts	500
Purchases Returns and Allowances	500
Rent Expense	3,000
Retained Earnings	15,000
Sales	100,000
Sales Discounts	300
Sales Returns and Allowances	200
Wages Expense	7,000

Using this information, complete the form below, showing only the computation of gross margin.

Gaviota Merchandising Company Partial Income Statement For the Year Ended December 31, 20xx			

	General Journal		
Date	Description	Debit	Credit

CHAPTER 7 SHORT-TERM FINANCIAL ASSETS

REVIEWING THE CHAPTER

Objective 1: Identify and explain the management issues related to short-term financial assets.

1. A company must use its assets to maximize income while maintaining liquidity. **Short-term financial assets** are assets that arise from cash transactions, the investment of cash, and the extension of credit. Examples are cash and cash equivalents, short-term investments, accounts receivable, and notes receivable.

2. A common measure of the adequacy of short-term financial assets is the **quick ratio,** which equals short-term financial assets divided by current liabilities. A quick ratio of 1.0 is generally considered the minimum benchmark, but industry characteristics and company trends should also be carefully examined.

3. Three key management issues in maintaining adequate liquidity are managing cash needs during seasonal cycles, setting credit policies, and financing receivables.

   a. During the course of a year, most businesses experience periods of both strong and weak sales and variations in cash flow. To remain liquid throughout these seasonal cycles, a business must carefully plan for cash inflows, cash outflows, borrowing, and investing.

   b. Companies that sell on credit do so to be competitive and to increase sales. To minimize the risk of incurring bad debts, they establish policies and procedures for checking the financial backgrounds of potential credit customers. The effectiveness of a company's credit policies is commonly measured by the **receivable turnover** (net sales divided by average net accounts receivable) and the **average days' sales uncollected** (365 divided by the receivable turnover).

   c. Companies sometimes cannot afford to wait until their receivables are collected. They can use the receivables to obtain cash by borrowing funds and pledging the accounts receivable as collateral. They can also raise funds by selling or transferring their receivables to a **factor** (e.g., a bank or finance company) through a process called **factoring.** Receivables can be factored with recourse or without recourse. With recourse means that the seller of the receivable has a **contingent liability** (potential obligation) to "make good" on the debt if the debtor fails to pay the receivable. When receivables are factored without recourse (as with major credit cards), the factor bears any losses from uncollectible accounts; because the risk involved is greater, the factoring fee is also greater. **Securitization** is the process of grouping receivables into batches and selling them (with or without recourse) at a discount to companies and investors. **Discounting** is a method of selling notes receivable in which the holder of a note receives cash upon endorsing the note and turning it over to a bank. However, the bank has recourse against the note's endorser, who is contingently liable for payment if the note's maker fails to pay the bank at the maturity date.

Objective 2: Explain *cash, cash equivalents,* **and the importance of electronic funds transfer.**

4. **Cash** consists of currency and coins on hand, checks and money orders from customers, and deposits in checking and savings accounts. Cash may also include a **compensating balance,** the minimum amount a bank requires a company to keep in its bank account as part of a credit-granting arrangement.

5. **Cash equivalents** consist of investments, such as certificates of deposit and U.S. Treasury notes, that have a term of less than 90 days. Cash and cash equivalents often are combined on the balance sheet.

6. Many companies use an imprest system to maintain control over the petty cash they keep on hand for cash registers, for paying for small purchases, and for making cash advances. The checking accounts that banks offer improve control by minimizing the amount of currency a company needs to keep on hand and by providing permanent records of payments. Today, instead of writing checks to pay for purchases or to repay loans, companies often use **electronic funds transfer (EFT)**—that is, the transfer of funds between banks through electronic communication. Automated teller machines (ATMs), banking by telephone, and *debit cards* have also become commonplace. When a purchase is made with a debit card, the purchase amount is deducted directly from the customer's bank account.

Objective 3: Identify types of short-term investments and explain the financial reporting implications.

7. Companies frequently have excess cash on hand for short periods of time. To put this cash to good use, many companies purchase **short-term investments,** or **marketable securities.** Short-term investments are categorized as held-to-maturity securities, trading securities, or available-for-sale securities.

8. **Held-to-maturity securities** are debt securities, such as U.S. Treasury bills, that are expected to be held until their maturity date and whose cash value is not needed until then. When these securities are purchased, Short-Term Investments is debited, and Cash is credited. At year end, accrued interest is recognized with a debit to Short-Term Investments and a credit to Interest Income; the investment is valued on the balance sheet at its amortized cost. At maturity, Cash is debited for the maturity amount, and Short-Term Investments and Interest Income are credited.

9. **Trading securities** consist of both debt and equity securities that will be held for just a short time. These securities are often bought and sold to generate profits on short-term increases in their prices. They are valued on the balance sheet at their fair value (normally, market value). An increase or decrease in the total trading portfolio during an accounting period is reflected in that period's income statement.
   a. When trading securities are purchased, Short-Term Investments is debited, and Cash is credited.
   b. At the end of the accounting period, the cost and market (fair) value of the securities are compared, and an adjustment is made. If their value has declined, Unrealized Loss on Investments (an income statement account) is debited, and Allowance to Adjust Short-Term Investments to Market (a contra-asset account) is credited. If their value has increased, Allowance to Adjust Short-Term Investments to Market is debited, and Unrealized Gain on Investments is credited. In either case, the investments are reported on the balance sheet at market value.
   c. When a trading security is sold, Cash is debited for the proceeds, Short-Term Investments is credited for the original cost, and Realized Gain (or Realized Loss) on Investments is credited (or debited) for the difference.

10. **Available-for-sale securities** are debt and equity securities that do not qualify as either held-to-maturity or trading securities. They are recorded in the same way as trading securities, except that unrealized gains and losses are reported in the stockholders' equity section of the balance sheet (as accumulated other comprehensive income) rather than on the income statement.

11. Dividend and interest income for all three categories of investments appears in the other income and expenses section of the income statement.

Objective 4: Define *accounts receivable* **and apply the allowance method of accounting for uncollectible accounts.**

12. **Accounts receivable** are short-term financial assets that represent payment due from credit customers. This type of credit is often called **trade credit. Installment accounts receivable** are receivables that will be collected in a series of payments; they usually are classified on the balance

sheet as current assets. When loans or credit sales are made to a company's employees, officers, or owners, they are shown separately on the balance sheet with a title like "receivables from employees" rather than "assets receivable." Accounts Receivable should appear on the balance sheet as the sum of all accounts with debit balances. Customers' accounts sometimes show credit balances because of overpayment; the sum of the credit balances should appear on the balance sheet as a current liability.

13. A company will always have some customers who cannot or will not pay. **Uncollectible accounts** (also called *bad debts*) are an expense of selling on credit. A company can afford such an expense because extending credit allows it to sell more and thereby increase its earnings.

14. Some companies recognize the loss from an uncollectible account at the time it is determined to be uncollectible. Because of government regulations, all companies use this method, called the **direct charge-off method,** for tax purposes, but companies that follow GAAP do not use it on their financial statements because it does not conform to the matching rule.

15. The matching rule requires that uncollectible accounts expense be recognized in the same accounting period as the corresponding sale. Of course, at the time of a credit sale, a company does not know which customers are not going to pay or how much money will be lost. An estimate must therefore be made at the end of the accounting period. At that time, an adjusting entry is made, debiting Uncollectible Accounts Expense and crediting Allowance for Uncollectible Accounts for the estimated amount. This method of accounting for uncollectible accounts is called the **allowance method.** Uncollectible Accounts Expense appears on the income statement as an operating expense and is closed out, as are other expenses. **Allowance for Uncollectible Accounts** (also called *Allowance for Doubtful Accounts and Allowance for Bad Debts*) is a contra account to Accounts Receivable; it reduces Accounts Receivable to the amount estimated to be collectible.

16. Two common methods of estimating uncollectible accounts are the percentage of net sales method and the accounts receivable aging method.
   a. With the **percentage of net sales method,** the estimated percentage of uncollectible accounts is multiplied by net sales for the period

to determine the amount of the adjusting entry for uncollectible accounts.
   b. With the **accounts receivable aging method,** accounts receivable are placed in a "not yet due" category or in one of several "past due" categories; this procedure is called the **aging of accounts receivable**. The amounts in each category are totaled, and each total is then multiplied by an estimated percentage for bad debts. The sum of these figures represents estimated bad debts in ending Accounts Receivable. As with the percentage of net sales method, the debit is to Uncollectible Accounts Expense, and the credit is to Allowance for Uncollectible Accounts. However, the entry is for the amount that will bring Allowance for Uncollectible Accounts to the figure arrived at in the aging calculation.
   c. The percentage of net sales method can be described as an income statement approach to estimating uncollectible accounts because net sales (an income statement component) is the basis for the calculation. The accounts receivable aging method is more of a balance sheet approach because it uses accounts receivable (a balance sheet component) as its computational basis.

17. When it becomes clear that a specific account receivable will not be collected, it is written off by a debit to Allowance for Uncollectible Accounts (not to Uncollectible Accounts Expense, which was already charged when the allowance was set up). When this happens, Accounts Receivable and Allowance for Uncollectible Accounts decrease by a similar amount, and the estimated net figure for receivables stays the same.

18. When a customer whose account has been written off pays in part or in full, two entries must be made. First, the customer's receivable is reinstated by a debit to Accounts Receivable and a credit to Allowance for Uncollectible Accounts for the amount now thought to be collectible. Second, for each collection, Cash is debited, and Accounts Receivable is credited .

Objective 5: Define *promissory note,* and compute and record promissory notes receivable.

19. A **promissory note** is an unconditional written promise to pay a definite sum, or principal, on demand or at a future date. The person who signs the note and thereby promises to pay is called the *maker* of the note. The person to whom money is owed is called the *payee.* The payee records all

promissory notes due in less than one year as short-term **notes receivable;** the maker records them as short-term **notes payable.**

20. The **maturity date** (the date on which the note must be paid) and **duration of note** (the length of time between its issuance and the maturity date) must be stated on the promissory note or be determinable from the facts stated on the note.

21. **Interest** is the cost of borrowing money or the reward for lending money, depending on whether one is the borrower or the lender. The amount of interest is based on the principal (the amount of money borrowed or lent), the interest rate (the annual charge for borrowing money, which is expressed as a percentage), and the loan's length of time. It is computed as follows:

    $$\text{Interest} = \text{Principal} \times \text{Rate of Interest} \times \text{Time (length of loan)}$$

22. The **maturity value** of an interest-bearing note is the face value of the note (the principal) plus interest at the maturity date. A note can also be non-interest-bearing. In that case, maturity value is equal to the principal, but the principal includes implied interest.

23. Journal entries for promissory notes are required in the four situations described below.
    a. When a promissory note is received—for example, in settlement of an existing account receivable—Notes Receivable is debited, and Accounts Receivable is credited. Other situations could require the credit to be made to a revenue account instead.
    b. When collection is made on a note, Cash is debited for the maturity value, Notes Receivable is credited for the face value, and Interest Income is credited for the difference.
    c. A **dishonored note** is one that is not paid at the maturity date. When a note is dishonored, the payee debits Accounts Receivable for the maturity value and credits Notes Receivable and Interest Income.

    d. End-of-period adjustments must be made for notes that apply to both the current and future periods. In this way, interest can be divided correctly among the periods.

Supplemental Objective 6: Prepare a bank reconciliation.

24. The end-of-month balance in a bank statement rarely agrees with the balance of a company's Cash account on that date. Certain transactions shown in the company's books may not yet appear in the bank statement, and certain bank transactions may not yet appear in the company's books. Thus, the accountant must prepare a **bank reconciliation** to account for the difference between the balance in the bank statement and the balance in the company's Cash account. Each figure is adjusted by additions and deductions, resulting in two adjusted cash balance figures, which must agree. For example:
    a. Outstanding checks are deducted from the balance per the bank.
    b. Deposits in transit are added to the balance per the bank.
    c. The bank's service charges appear on the bank statement and are deducted from the balance per the books.
    d. A customer's nonsufficient (NSF) check is deducted from the balance per the books.
    e. Miscellaneous charges are deducted and miscellaneous credits are added to the balance per the books.
    f. Interest earned on a checking account is added to the balance per the books.
    Errors by either the bank or the company must, of course, be identified and corrected immediately.

25. After the bank reconciliation has been prepared, adjusting entries must be made so that the accounting records reflect the information supplied by the bank statement. Each adjustment includes either a debit or a credit to Cash. Adjustments are recorded only for the items that affected the book balance.

A. (LO 3) Short-Term Investments   XX (purchase price)
            Cash   XX (amount paid)
                Purchase of U.S. Treasury bills

B. (LO 3) Short-Term Investments   XX (accrued interest)
            Interest Income   XX (accrued amount)
                Accrual of interest on U.S. Treasury bills

C. (LO 3) Cash   XX (maturity amount)
            Short-Term Investments   XX (debit balance)
            Interest Income   XX (interest this period)
                Receipt of cash at maturity of U.S. Treasury bills
                and recognition of related income

D. (LO 3) Short-Term Investments   XX (purchase price)
            Cash   XX (amount paid)
                Investment in stocks for trading

E. (LO 3) Unrealized Loss on Investments   XX (market decline)
            Allowance to Adjust Short-Term Investments to Market   XX (market decline)
                Recognition of unrealized loss on trading portfolio

F. (LO 3) Cash   XX (proceeds on sale)
            Short-Term Investments   XX (purchase price)
            Realized Gain on Investments   XX (the difference)
                Sale of stock at a gain

G. (LO 3) Allowance to Adjust Short-Term Investments to Market   XX (market increase)
            Unrealized Gain on Investments   XX (market increase)
                Recognition of unrealized gain on trading portfolio

H. (LO 4) Uncollectible Accounts Expense   XX (amount estimated)
            Allowance for Uncollectible Accounts   XX (amount estimated)
                To record the estimated uncollectible accounts
                expense for the year

I. (LO 4) Allowance for Uncollectible Accounts   XX (defaulted amount)
            Accounts Receivable   XX (defaulted amount)
                To write off receivable of a specific customer as
                uncollectible

J. (LO 4) Accounts Receivable   XX (amount reinstated)
            Allowance for Uncollectible Accounts   XX (amount reinstated)
                To reinstate the portion of a specific customer's
                account now considered collectible

K. (LO 4) Cash   XX (amount received)
            Accounts Receivable   XX (amount received)
                Collection from customer in J

L. (LO 5) Notes Receivable   XX (establishing amount)
     Accounts Receivable   XX (eliminating amount)
      Received note in payment of account

M. (LO 5) Cash   XX (maturity amount)
     Notes Receivable   XX (face amount)
     Interest Income   XX (amount earned)
      Collected note

N. (LO 5) Accounts Receivable   XX (maturity amount)
     Notes Receivable   XX (face amount)
     Interest Income   XX (amount earned)
      To record dishonored note

O. (LO 5) Interest Receivable   XX (amount accrued)
     Interest Income   XX (amount earned)
      To accrue interest earned on a note receivable

P. (LO 5) Cash   XX (maturity amount)
     Notes Receivable   XX (face amount)
     Interest Receivable   XX (interest previously accrued)
     Interest Income   XX (interest this period)
      Receipt of note receivable plus interest (see O above)

Q. (SO 6) After a bank reconciliation is prepared, journal entries must be made to record items on the bank statement that the company has not yet recorded (service charges, NSF checks, etc.). The sample entries presented in the text are not duplicated here. Note, however, that all entries contain either a debit or a credit to Cash.

Test your knowledge of the chapter by choosing the best answer for each item below.

1. Because Tamara Company's sales are concentrated in the summer, its managers must carefully plan for borrowing needs and short-term investments. This is an example of management's responsibility to
   a. finance receivables.
   b. manage cash needs during seasonal cycles.
   c. set reasonable credit policies.
   d. finance purchases of long-term assets.

2. At year end, RJN Company has $3,400 on hand in currency and coins, deposits in checking accounts of $32,000, U.S. Treasury bills due in 60 days worth $58,000, and U.S. Treasury bonds due in 180 days worth $88,000. On its balance sheet, cash and cash equivalents will be shown as
   a. $3,400.
   b. $35,400.
   c. $93,400.
   d. $181,400.

3. A company purchases a $100,000 U.S. Treasury bill due in 180 days for $97,000. When it receives cash for this transaction in the amount of $100,000, the journal entry should contain a
   a. credit to Interest Income for $3,000.
   b. debit to Gain on Investment for $3,000.
   c. credit to Investment Loss for $3,000.
   d. credit to Gain on Investment for $3,000.

4. The matching rule
   a. necessitates the recording of an estimated amount for bad debts.
   b. is violated when the allowance method is used.
   c. results in the recording of an exact amount for losses from bad debts.
   d. requires that losses from bad debts be recorded whenever a customer defaults.

5. Which of the following methods of recording uncollectible accounts expense would best be described as an income statement method?
   a. Accounts receivable aging method
   b. Direct charge-off method
   c. Percentage of net sales method
   d. Both a and b

6. Using the percentage of net sales method, uncollectible accounts expense for the year is estimated to be $54,000. If the balance of Allowance for Uncollectible Accounts is a $16,000 credit before adjustment, what is the balance after adjustment?
   a. $16,000
   b. $38,000
   c. $54,000
   d. $70,000

7. Using the accounts receivable aging method, estimated uncollectible accounts are $74,000. If the balance of Allowance for Uncollectible Accounts is an $18,000 credit before adjustment, what is the balance after adjustment?
   a. $18,000
   b. $56,000
   c. $74,000
   d. $92,000

8. Each of the following is a characteristic of a promissory note *except*
   a. a payee who has an unconditional right to receive a definite amount on a definite date.
   b. an amount to be paid that can be determined on the date the note is signed.
   c. a due date that can be determined on the date the note is signed.
   d. a maker who agrees to pay a definite sum subject to conditions to be determined at a later date.

9. The maturity value of a $6,000, 90-day note at 10 percent is
   a. $600.
   b. $5,850.
   c. $6,600.
   d. $6,150.

10. In a bank reconciliation, which of the following items would be added to the balance on the bank statement?
   a. Outstanding checks
   b. Deposits in transit
   c. A service charge
   d. Interest on the average balance

TESTING YOUR KNOWLEDGE

Matching*

Match each term with its definition by writing the appropriate letter in the blank.

_____ **1.** Trade credit

_____ **2.** Factoring

_____ **3.** Uncollectible accounts expense

_____ **4.** Allowance for uncollectible accounts

_____ **5.** Installment accounts receivable

_____ **6.** Promissory note

_____ **7.** Maker

_____ **8.** Payee

_____ **9.** Bank reconciliation

_____ **10.** Maturity value

_____ **11.** Interest rate

_____ **12.** Interest

_____ **13.** Principal

_____ **14.** Contingent liability

_____ **15.** Dishonored note

_____ **16.** Discounting

_____ **17.** Compensating balance

_____ **18.** Cash equivalents

_____ **19.** Cash

_____ **20.** Securitization

a. Short-term investments of less than 90 days

b. Coins, currency, checks, money orders, and bank deposits

c. The charge for borrowing money, expressed as a percentage

d. A note that is not paid at the maturity date

e. A written promise to pay

f. Estimated bad debts as shown on the income statement

g. Selling or transferring accounts receivable

h. A potential obligation

i. An accounting for the difference between book balance and bank balance at a particular date

j. Allowing customers to pay for merchandise over a period of time

k. The grouping of receivables into batches for selling at a discount

l. The creditor named in a promissory note

m. Estimated bad debts as represented on the balance sheet

n. Selling a note before its maturity date

o. The charge for borrowing money, expressed in dollars

p. Receivables that will be collected in a series of payments

q. A minimum amount that a bank requires a company to keep in its account

r. The debtor named in a promissory note

s. The amount of money borrowed or lent

t. A note's principal plus interest

**Note to student:* The matching quiz might be completed more efficiently by starting with the definition and searching for the corresponding term.

Short Answer

Use the lines provided to answer each item.

1. List three methods used to compute uncollectible accounts expense.

_____

_____

_____

2. Explain the concept of contingent liability as it relates to discounted notes receivable.

_____

_____

_____

_____

3. Under what circumstance would there be a debit balance in Allowance for Uncollectible Accounts?

_____

_____

_____

4. List the three categories of short-term investments.

_____

_____

_____

5. List four examples of short-term financial assets.

_____

_____

_____

_____

6. List three items that would be deducted from the book balance in a bank reconciliation.

_____

_____

_____

True-False

Circle T if the statement is true, F if it is false. Provide explanations for the false answers, using the blank lines at the end of the section.

T F **1.** Under the direct charge-off method, Allowance for Uncollectible Accounts does not exist.

T F **2.** The percentage of net sales method violates the matching rule.

T F **3.** Under the accounts receivable aging method, the balance in Allowance for Uncollectible Accounts is ignored in making the adjusting entry.

T F **4.** Allowance for Uncollectible Accounts is a contra account to Accounts Receivable.

T F **5.** Loans to a company's officers should not be included in Accounts Receivable on the balance sheet.

T F **6.** When a customer overpays, his or her account on the company's books has a credit balance.

T F **7.** Interest of 5 percent on $700 for 90 days would be computed as follows:

$700 \times .05 \times 90$.

T F **8.** *Trade credit* refers to sales that wholesalers and retailers make on credit.

T F **9.** When a note is discounted at a bank, the maker must make good on the note if the payee defaults.

T F **10.** A note dated December 14 and due February 14 has a duration of 60 days.

T F   **11.** The figure for receivable turnover is a component in the calculation of average days' sales uncollected.

T F   **12.** Under the allowance method, the entry to write off a specific account as uncollectible decreases total assets.

T F   **13.** The maturity value of an interest-bearing note equals principal plus interest.

T F   **14.** Under the allowance method, a specific account is written off with a debit to Uncollectible Accounts Expense and a credit to Accounts Receivable.

T F   **15.** The payee of a dishonored note should record interest earned on the note.

T F   **16.** A credit memorandum on a bank statement indicates an addition to the bank balance.

T F   **17.** Accounts receivable are an example of a cash equivalent.

T F   **18.** The use of a major credit card (e.g., MasterCard) is an example of factoring with recourse.

T F   **19.** The quick ratio equals current assets divided by current liabilities.

T F   **20.** *Imprest system* refers to the mechanics of a petty cash fund.

T F   **21.** Held-to-maturity securities do not include equity securities.

T F   **22.** Trading securities appear on the balance sheet at original cost.

T F   **23.** Securitization involves selling batched receivables at a discount.

Multiple Choice

Circle the letter of the best answer.

1. Which of the following does *not* equal the others?
   a. $600 for 60 days at 6 percent
   b. $1,200 for 120 days at 3 percent
   c. $300 for 120 days at 6 percent
   d. $600 for 30 days at 12 percent

2. At the balance sheet date, a company estimates that $1,500 of net sales for the year will not be collected. A debit balance of $600 exists in Allowance for Uncollectible Accounts. Under the percentage of net sales method, Uncollectible Accounts Expense would be debited and Allowance for Uncollectible Accounts would be credited for
   a. $600.
   b. $1,100.
   c. $1,500.
   d. $2,100.

3. A contingent liability exists when
   a. a note is discounted.
   b. a note is dishonored.
   c. interest accrues on a note.
   d. a note reaches maturity.

4. Based on the accounts receivable aging method, a company estimates that $850 of end-of-period accounts receivable will not be collected. A credit balance of $300 exists in Allowance for Uncollectible Accounts. Uncollectible Accounts Expense should be recorded for
   a. $300.
   b. $550.
   c. $850.
   d. $1,150.

5. Under the accounts receivable aging method, a specific customer's account is written off by debiting
   a. Uncollectible Accounts Expense and crediting Allowance for Uncollectible Accounts.
   b. Accounts Receivable and crediting Allowance for Uncollectible Accounts.
   c. Allowance for Uncollectible Accounts and crediting Accounts Receivable.
   d. Uncollectible Accounts Expense and crediting Accounts Receivable.

6. Which of the following *cannot* be determined from the information on a note?
   a. Discount rate
   b. Interest rate
   c. Interest
   d. Maturity date

7. Which of the following methods of handling bad debts often violates the matching rule?
   a. Percentage of net sales method
   b. Direct charge-off method
   c. Accounts receivable aging method
   d. Both **a** and **c**

8. Which of the following is *not* considered a short-term financial asset?
   a. Notes receivable
   b. Short-term investments
   c. Inventory
   d. Cash

9. Unrealized gains and losses on available-for-sale securities are reported on
   a. the income statement.
   b. the balance sheet as a contra-asset account.
   c. the balance sheet in the stockholders' equity section.
   d. no financial statement.

10. After a bank reconciliation has been completed, journal entries must be made to adjust for all of the following *except*
   a. bank service charges.
   b. deposits in transit.
   c. a note collected by the bank.
   d. an error made by the bank.

APPLYING YOUR KNOWLEDGE

Exercises

1. For the following set of facts, make the necessary entries for Doherty's Department Store in the journal provided on the next page.

Dec. 31 Interest of $75 has accrued on notes receivable.

31 Net sales for the year were $600,000. It is estimated that 4 percent will not be collected. Make the entry for uncollectible accounts.

Jan. 3 Anna Kohn purchased $10,000 worth of goods on credit in November. She now issues Doherty's a $10,000, 30-day, 6 percent note, thus extending her credit period.

8 Tom O'Brien goes bankrupt and notifies Doherty's that he cannot pay for the $1,000 worth of goods that he purchased last year on account.

25 Tom O'Brien notifies Doherty's that he will be able to pay $600 of the $1,000 that he owes.

28 A check for $200 is received from Tom O'Brien.

2. Calculate interest on the following amounts:

a. $7,200 at 4% for 20 days = _____

b. $52,000 at 7% for 3 months = _____

c. $4,317 at 6% for 60 days = _____

d. $18,000 at 8% for 1 day = _____

3. On November 17, 20x1, Valdez Corporation purchased 2,000 shares of Welu Corporation's stock for $30 per share. The purchase was made for trading purposes. At December 31, 20x1, the stock had a market value of $28 per share. On January 12, 20x2, Valdez sold all 2,000 shares for $66,000. In the journal provided below, prepare the entries for November 17, December 31, and January 12.

		General Journal		
Date		**Description**	**Debit**	**Credit**

General Journal				
Date		Description	Debit	Credit

Crossword Puzzle
for Chapters 6 and 7

ACROSS

 4. Banking transaction
 5. Purchase _____
 6. Conspiracy for fraudulent purposes
 8. Cost of _____ (2 words)
 9. Receiving _____
 13. System of regulatory procedures (2 words)
 17. Temporary, as investments (hyphenated)
 19. Written promises to pay
 20. Uncollectible accounts (2 words)

DOWN

 1. Invoice
 2. Available-_____ securities (2 words, hyphenated)
 3. Method of accounting for 20-Across
 4. Method of selling notes receivable
 6. _____ equivalent
 7. The "OB" of FOB (2 words)
 10. _____ charge-off method
 11. The "T" of EFT
 12. Buyer of accounts receivable
 14. Account like Allowance of Uncollectible Accounts
 15. Unrealized _____ on Investments
 16. Engages in interest-earning activities
 18. Banking convenience, for short

CHAPTER 8 INVENTORIES

REVIEWING THE CHAPTER

Objective 1: Identify and explain the management issues associated with accounting for inventories.

1. **Merchandise inventory** consists of all the goods that a merchandising company owns and holds for sale in the regular course of business. The inventory of a manufacturer, on the other hand, consists of raw materials, work in process, and finished goods. The costs of work in process and finished goods inventories include the costs of raw material, labor, and overhead (indirect manufacturing costs) incurred in producing the finished product. Inventory appears in the current assets section of the balance sheet.

2. The objective of accounting for inventory is the proper determination of income through the matching of costs and revenues, not the determination of the most realistic inventory value. Thus, in accounting for inventory, the following two questions must be answered:
   a. How much of the asset has been used up (expired) during the current period and should be transferred to expense?
   b. How much of the asset is unused (unexpired) and should remain on the balance sheet as an asset?

3. A company has a number of choices with regard to inventory systems and methods. Because these systems and methods usually produce different amounts of reported net income, the choices that a company makes affect external evaluations of the company, as well as such internal evaluations

as performance reviews. In addition, because income is affected, the valuation of inventory can have a considerable effect on the amount of income taxes paid, which will in turn affect cash flows.

4. It is important for a merchandiser to maintain a sufficient level of inventory to satisfy customer demand. However, the higher the level maintained, the more costly it is for the business. Management can evaluate the level of inventory by calculating and analyzing the inventory turnover and average days' inventory on hand.
   a. **Inventory turnover** indicates the number of times a company's average inventory is sold during an accounting period. It equals cost of goods sold divided by average inventory.
   b. **Average days' inventory on hand** indicates the average number of days required to sell the inventory on hand. It equals 365 divided by the inventory turnover.

5. To reduce their levels of inventory, many companies use supply-chain management in conjunction with a just-in-time operating environment With **supply-chain management**, a company manages its inventory and purchasing through business-to-business transactions conducted over the Internet. In a **just-in-time operating environment,** companies work closely with suppliers to coordinate and schedule shipments so that the goods arrive just in time to be used or sold. As a result, the costs of carrying inventory are greatly reduced.

Objective 2: Define *inventory cost* **and relate it to goods flow and cost flow.**

6. **Inventory cost** includes the invoice price of the inventory less purchases discounts; freight in, including insurance in transit; and applicable taxes and tariffs.

7. Goods in transit should be included in inventory only if the company has title to the goods. When goods are sent FOB (free on board) shipping point, title passes to the buyer when the goods reach the common carrier. When goods are sent FOB destination, title passes when the goods reach the buyer.

8. Goods that have been sold but are awaiting delivery to the buyer should not be included in the seller's inventory count. When goods are held on **consignment,** the consignee (who earns a commission on making the sale) has possession of the goods, but the consignor retains title until the consignee sells the goods. The consignor therefore includes them in its physical inventory.

9. When identical items of merchandise are purchased at different prices during the year, it is usually impractical to monitor the actual **goods flow** and record the corresponding costs. Instead, the accountant makes an assumption about the **cost flow** using one of the following costing methods: specific identification, average-cost, first-in, first-out (FIFO), or last-in, first-out (LIFO).

Objective 3: Calculate the pricing of inventory, using the cost basis under the periodic inventory system.

10. If the units of ending inventory can be identified as having come from specific purchases, the **specific identification method** can be used. In this case, the flow of costs reflects the actual flow of goods. However, the specific identification method is not practical in most cases.

11. Under the **average-cost method,** inventory is priced at the average cost of the goods available for sale during the period. Average cost is computed by dividing the total cost of goods available for sale by the total units available for sale. The average cost per unit is then multiplied by the number of units in ending inventory to arrive at the cost of ending inventory.

12. Under the **first-in, first-out (FIFO) method,** the costs of the first items purchased are assigned to the first items sold. Thus, ending inventory cost is determined from the prices of the most recent purchases. During periods of rising prices, FIFO

yields a higher income before income taxes than any of the other three costing methods.

13. Under the **last-in, first-out (LIFO) method,** the costs of the last items purchased are assigned to the first items sold. Thus, the ending inventory cost is determined from the prices of the earliest purchases. During periods of rising prices, LIFO yields a lower income before income taxes than any of the other three methods. However, it matches current merchandise costs with current sales prices.

Objective 4: Apply the perpetual inventory system to the pricing of inventories at cost.

14. The pricing of inventories differs under the periodic and perpetual inventory systems. When the periodic system is used, only the ending inventory is counted and priced, and the cost of goods sold is calculated by subtracting ending inventory from the cost of goods available for sale. When the perpetual system is used, a company has more control over its inventory because a continuous record is kept of the balance of each inventory item; as goods are sold, costs are transferred from the Inventory account to the Cost of Goods Sold account.

15. The specific identification and FIFO methods produce the same figures for inventory and cost of goods sold under the periodic and perpetual inventory systems. The results differ for the average-cost method because under the perpetual system, an average is calculated after each purchase rather than at the end of the accounting period. The results for the LIFO method also differ because under the perpetual system, the cost components of inventory change constantly as goods are bought and sold.

Objective 5: State the effects of inventory methods and misstatements of inventory on income determination, income taxes, and cash flows.

16. During periods of rising prices, FIFO produces a higher net income figure than LIFO. During periods of falling prices, the reverse is true. The average-cost method produces a net income figure somewhere between the figures produced by FIFO and LIFO. Because the specific identification method depends on the particular items sold, no generalization can be made about the effect of changing prices. LIFO is best suited for the income statement because it matches revenues and cost of goods sold. FIFO, however, provides a more up-to-date ending inventory figure for the balance sheet.

17. Several rules govern the valuation of inventory for federal income tax purposes. For example, even though a business has a wide choice of methods, once it has chosen a method, it must apply that method consistently. In addition, several regulations apply to LIFO, such as the requirement that if LIFO is used for tax purposes, it must also be used in the accounting records.

18. A **LIFO liquidation** occurs when sales have reduced inventories below the levels established in earlier years. When prices have been rising steadily, a LIFO liquidation produces unusually high profits.

19. Beginning inventory plus purchases equals the cost of goods available for sale. The cost of goods sold is determined indirectly by deducting ending inventory from the cost of goods available for sale. If the value of ending inventory is understated or overstated, a corresponding error—dollar for dollar—will be made in income before income taxes. It is important to match the cost of goods sold with sales so that income before income taxes is reasonably accurate.

20. Because the ending inventory of one period becomes the beginning inventory of the next period, a misstatement in inventory will affect both periods. Although over a two-year period, the errors in income before income taxes will counterbalance each other, the misstatements are a violation of the matching rule. Moreover, management, investors, and creditors make many annual decisions on an annual basis, and in doing so, they rely on the accuracy of the net income figure.

21. The inventory method that a company uses will affect not only its reported profitability, but also its reported liquidity and cash flows. LIFO, for example, will usually produce a lower figure for income before income taxes than will FIFO. However, the reduced tax liability under LIFO will have a positive effect on cash flows. Measures of liquidity, such as the current ratio, inventory turnover, and average days' inventory on hand, will also be affected by the inventory method used.

Objective 6: Apply the lower-of-cost-or-market (LCM) rule to inventory valuation.

22. The **market** value (current replacement cost) of inventory can fall below its historical cost as a result of physical deterioration, obsolescence, or a decline in price level. When that happens, the inventory valuation should be based on the **lower-of-cost-or-market (LCM) rule.** The two basic methods of valuing inventory at the lower of cost or market are the **item-by-item method** and the **major category method.** Both methods are accepted by GAAP and the IRS for federal income tax purposes.

Supplemental Objective 7: Estimate the cost of ending inventory using the retail inventory method and gross profit method.

23. The **retail method** of inventory estimation can be used when the difference between the cost and sale prices of goods is a constant percentage over a period of time. It can be used regardless of whether a business makes a physical count of goods. To apply the retail method, goods available for sale are figured both at cost and at retail. Next, a cost-to-retail ratio is computed. Sales for the period are then subtracted from goods available for sale at retail to produce ending inventory at retail. Finally, ending inventory at retail is multiplied by the cost-to-retail ratio to produce an estimate of the cost of ending inventory.

24. The **gross profit method** of inventory estimation (also called the *gross margin method*) assumes that a business's gross margin ratio remains relatively stable from year to year. This method is used when a business does not keep records of the retail prices of beginning inventory and purchases and when inventory records are lost or destroyed. To apply the gross profit method, the cost of goods available for sale is determined by adding purchases to beginning inventory. The cost of goods sold is then estimated by deducting the estimated gross margin from sales. Finally, the estimated cost of goods sold is subtracted from the cost of goods available for sale to arrive at the estimated cost of ending inventory.

SELF-TEST

Test your knowledge of the chapter by choosing the best answer for each item below.

1. An overstatement of ending inventory in one period results in
   a. an overstatement of the ending inventory in the next period.
   b. an understatement of income before income taxes in the next period.
   c. an overstatement of income before income taxes in the next period.
   d. no effect on income before income taxes in the next period.

2. Which of the following costs would *not* be included in the cost of inventory?
   a. Goods held on consignment
   b. Taxes and tariffs applicable to the goods
   c. Freight in
   d. Invoice price

3. Sept. 1 Inventory 10 @ $4.00
   8 Purchased 40 @ $4.40
   17 Purchased 20 @ $4.20
   25 Purchased 30 @ $4.80   Sold 70

   Based on this information and assuming that the periodic inventory system is used, cost of goods sold under the average-cost method would be
   a. $133.20.
   b. $444.00.
   c. $310.80.
   d. $304.50.

4. Assuming the same facts as in **3,** cost of goods sold under the first-in, first-out (FIFO) method would be
   a. $144.00.
   b. $300.00.
   c. $388.50.
   d. $444.00.

5. Assuming the same facts as in **3,** ending inventory under the last-in, first-out (LIFO) method would be
   a. $316.
   b. $444.
   c. $300.
   d. $128.

6. Inventory turnover equals cost of goods sold divided by
   a. number of days in a year.
   b. cost of goods available for sale.
   c. number of months in a year.
   d. average inventory.

7. In a period of rising prices, which of the following inventory costing methods generally results in the lowest figure for income before income taxes?
   a. Average-cost method
   b. FIFO method
   c. LIFO method
   d. Cannot tell without more information

8. When applying the lower-of-cost-or-market rule to inventory, *market* generally means
   a. original cost less physical deterioration.
   b. resale value.
   c. original cost.
   d. current replacement cost.

9. Which of the following companies would be most likely to use the retail inventory method?
   a. A farm supply company
   b. A TV repair company
   c. A dealer in heavy machinery
   d. A men's clothing shop

10. A retail company has goods available for sale of $1,000,000 at retail and $600,000 at cost, and ending inventory of $100,000 at retail. What is the estimated cost of goods sold?
    a. $60,000
    b. $100,000
    c. $900,000
    d. $540,000

*Matching**

Match each term with its definition by writing the appropriate letter in the blank.

_____ 1. LIFO liquidation

_____ 2. Merchandise inventory

_____ 3. Specific identification method

_____ 4. FIFO method

_____ 5. LIFO method

_____ 6. Average-cost method

_____ 7. Lower of cost or market

_____ 8. Retail method

_____ 9. Gross profit method

_____ 10. Periodic inventory system

_____ 11. Perpetual inventory system

_____ 12. Market

_____ 13. Consignment

_____ 14. Cost flow

_____ 15. Goods flow

_____ 16. Supply-chain management

a. The association of costs with their assumed flow

b. The current replacement cost of inventory

c. The inventory estimation method used when inventory records are lost or destroyed

d. The inventory method in which the assumed flow of costs matches the actual flow of goods

e. The inventory system that maintains continuous records

f. The actual physical movement of inventory

g. The inventory method that yields the highest net income figure during periods of rising prices

h. Goods that a merchandiser holds for sale in the regular course of business

i. A method of managing inventory and purchasing by conducting business-to-business transactions over the Internet

j. The inventory method that best follows the matching rule

k. An arrangement whereby one company sells goods for another company, for a commission

l. The inventory system that does not maintain continuous records

m. An occurrence that produces unusually high profits under steadily rising prices

n. The inventory method that utilizes an average-cost-per-unit figure

o. A rule that governs how inventory should be valued when its replacement cost falls below its historical cost

p. The inventory estimation method that uses a cost-to-retail ratio

---

Note to student: The matching quiz might be completed more efficiently by starting with the definition and searching for the corresponding term.

Short Answer

Use the lines provided to answer each item.

1. List the four basic methods used to determine the cost of merchandise inventory.

   _____

   _____

   _____

   _____

2. List the two basic methods of valuing inventory at the lower of cost or market.

   _____

   _____

3. List two methods of estimating ending inventory.

   _____

   _____

4. Briefly distinguish between the periodic and perpetual inventory systems in terms of recordkeeping and inventory taking.

   _____

   _____

   _____

   _____

   _____

5. List the three types of inventory involved in the manufacture of goods.

   _____

   _____

   _____

True-False

Circle T if the statement is true, F if it is false. Provide explanations for the false answers, using the blank lines at the end of the section.

T F **1.** The inventory turnover figure is needed to calculate average days' inventory on hand.

T F **2.** When beginning inventory is understated, the cost of goods sold for the period is also understated.

T F **3.** When ending inventory is overstated, income before income taxes for the period is also overstated.

T F **4.** An error in 20x1's ending inventory will cause income before income taxes to be misstated in both 20x1 and 20x2.

T F **5.** Goods in transit belong in a buyer's inventory only if the buyer has paid for them.

T F **6.** If prices never changed, all methods of inventory valuation would result in identical figures for income before income taxes.

T F **7.** Under FIFO, goods are sold in exactly the same order as they are purchased.

T F **8.** Of the four inventory costing methods, LIFO yields the lowest net income figure during periods of falling prices.

T F **9.** Under the retail method, inventory must be figured both at cost and at retail.

T F **10.** Under the gross profit method, the cost of goods sold is estimated by multiplying the gross margin percentage by sales.

T F **11.** In periods of rising prices, the average-cost method results in a lower income before income taxes than LIFO does.

T F **12.** If FIFO is used for tax purposes, it must be used for reporting purposes as well.

T F **13.** When goods are held on consignment, the consignee retains possession of the goods as well as title to them until they are sold.

T F **14.** The inventory costing method that produces the highest profitability will not necessarily generate the highest cash flow.

T F **15.** In a just-in-time operating environment, a significant amount of money is tied up in inventories.

_____ _____

_____ _____

_____ _____

_____ _____

_____ _____

_____ _____

_____ _____

_____ _____

_____ _____

_____ _____

Multiple Choice

Circle the letter of the best answer.

1. Which of the following is least likely to be included in the cost of inventory?
   a. Freight in
   b. The cost of storing goods
   c. The purchase cost of goods
   d. The excise tax on goods purchased

2. In periods of rising prices, which inventory method yields the highest income before income taxes?
   a. FIFO
   b. LIFO
   c. Specific identification
   d. Average-cost

3. If an item of merchandise in a warehouse is overlooked and not included in inventory, it results in
   a. overstated income before income taxes.
   b. overstated total assets.
   c. understated stockholders' equity.
   d. understated cost of goods sold.

4. Which inventory method is best suited for costing low-volume, high-priced goods?
   a. FIFO
   b. LIFO
   c. Specific identification
   d. Average-cost

5. Which of the following does the retail method of estimating inventory *not* use or compute?
   a. Ending inventory at retail
   b. Freight in at retail
   c. Beginning inventory at cost
   d. Sales during the period

6. The cost of merchandise inventory becomes an expense in the period in which the merchandiser
   a. sells the inventory.
   b. obtains title to the inventory.
   c. pays for the inventory.
   d. receives payment for the inventory that it has sold.

7. Goods in transit should be included in the inventory of
   a. neither the buyer nor the seller.
   b. the buyer when the goods have been shipped FOB destination.
   c. the seller when the goods have been shipped FOB shipping point.
   d. the company that has title to the goods.

8. Insurance companies often verify the extent of inventory lost or destroyed by applying the
   a. specific identification method.
   b. retail method.
   c. item-by-item method.
   d. gross profit method.

9. For a manufacturer, the cost of work in process and finished goods inventories includes all of the following *except*
   a. indirect materials costs.
   b. office wages.
   c. indirect labor costs.
   d. factory rent.

Inventories

APPLYING YOUR KNOWLEDGE

Exercises

1. Rutland Company uses the periodic inventory system. The company had a beginning inventory of 100 units that cost $20 each. It then made the following purchases:

Feb. 20 Purchased 200 units at $22 each
May   8 Purchased 150 units at $20 each
Oct. 17 Purchased 250 units at $24 each

Calculate the cost that would be assigned to an ending inventory of 310 units and the cost of goods sold under the LIFO, FIFO and average-costing methods.

		Cost of Ending Inventory	Cost of Goods Sold
a.	LIFO	$ _____	$ _____
b.	FIFO	$ _____	$ _____
c.	Average-cost	$ _____	$ _____

2. The records of Pinnacle Company show the following data for the month of May:

Sales	$156,000
Beginning inventory, at cost	70,000
Beginning inventory, at retail	125,000
Net purchases, at cost	48,000
Net purchases, at retail	75,000
Freight in	2,000

Use the retail method to compute the estimated cost of ending inventory.

3. At the beginning of the accounting period, the cost of merchandise inventory was $150,000. During the period, net sales were $300,000, and net purchases totaled $120,000; the historical gross margin has been 20 percent. Compute the estimated cost of ending inventory using the gross profit method.

4. Martino Enterprises uses the perpetual inventory system and the LIFO costing method. On May 1, its inventory consisted of 100 units that cost $10 each. Successive purchases and sales for May were as follows:

May 4 Purchased 60 units at $12 each
       8 Sold 50 units
      17 Purchased 70 units at $11 each
      31 Sold 100 units

Calculate ending inventory and cost of goods sold.

5. Assume the same facts as in Exercise **4,** except that Martino uses the average-cost method. Calculate ending inventory and cost of goods sold (round dollar amounts to the nearest cent).

CHAPTER 9 CURRENT LIABILITIES

REVIEWING THE CHAPTER

Objective 1: Identify the management issues related to recognition, valuation, classification, and disclosure of current liabilities.

1. Liabilities, one of the three major parts of the balance sheet, are legal obligations for the future payment of assets or the future performance of services. The primary reason for incurring current liabilities is to meet needs for cash during the operating cycle.

2. If a company's cash flows are inadequate to meet its current liabilities, the company could be forced into bankruptcy; thus, careful management of cash flows related to current liabilities is critical. Another issue in managing cash flows and current liabilities is the length of time creditors allow for payment. Common measures of this time are payables turnover and average days' payable. **Payables turnover** (measured in number of "times") shows the relative size of a company's accounts payable. The formula for calculating it is as follows:

$$\frac{\text{Cost of Goods Sold} \pm \text{Change in Merchandise Inventory}}{\text{Average Accounts Payable}}$$

Average days' payable shows the average length of time a company takes to pay its accounts payable. It is computed as follows:

$$\frac{365 \text{ days}}{\text{Payables Turnover}}$$

3. A liability should be recorded at the time it is incurred. However, for accrued and estimated liabilities, it is necessary to make adjusting entries at the end of an accounting period. Contracts representing future obligations are not recorded as liabilities until they become current obligations.

4. Liabilities are valued at the actual or estimated amount of money necessary to satisfy the obligation or at the fair market value of the goods or services that must be delivered.

5. **Current liabilities** are obligations expected to be satisfied within one year or the normal operating cycle, whichever is longer. They are normally paid out of current assets or with cash generated from operations. **Long-term liabilities** are obligations due beyond one year or the normal operating cycle.

6. Supplemental disclosure of some liabilities may be required in the notes to the financial statements—for example, when a company has special credit arrangements that can influence potential investors' decisions.

Objective 2: Identify, compute, and record definitely determinable and estimated current liabilities.

7. Current liabilities consist of definitely determinable liabilities and estimated liabilities.

8. **Definitely determinable liabilities** are obligations that can be measured exactly. They include accounts payable, bank loans and commercial

paper, notes payable, accrued liabilities, dividends payable, sales and excise taxes payable, current portions of long-term debt, payroll liabilities, and unearned revenues.

a. Accounts payable, sometimes called *trade accounts payable,* are obligations currently due to suppliers of goods and services.

b. To finance current operations by borrowing funds, companies often obtain a **line of credit** with a bank. Companies with excellent credit ratings can also borrow short-term funds by issuing **commercial paper** (unsecured loans sold to the public).

c. Short-term notes payable are current obligations evidenced by promissory notes. Interest may be stated on the face of the note or included in the face amount. In the latter case, the actual amount borrowed is less than the face amount.

d. Accrued liabilities are actual or estimated liabilities that exist at the balance sheet date but are unrecorded at that date. An end-of-period adjustment is needed to record both the interest expense and the accrued liability.

e. Dividends payable represent a corporation's obligation to distribute earnings to stockholders. This obligation arises only when the board of directors declares a dividend.

f. Most states and many cities levy a sales tax on retail transactions. The federal government also charges an excise tax on some products. The merchant must collect payment for these taxes at the time of the sale; the related journal entry records both the receipt of cash and the tax liabilities.

g. If a portion of long-term debt is due within the next year and is to be paid from current assets, that amount should be classified as a current liability; the remaining debt should be classified as a long-term liability.

h. Payroll liabilities are a business's employee-related obligations. Payroll accounting applies only to an organization's employees, who are under its direct supervision and control; it does not apply to independent contractors, such as lawyers and CPAs. A business is not only responsible for paying its employees **wages** or **salaries**; it is also obligated for such items as social security (FICA) taxes, Medicare, and unemployment taxes. In addition, it must withhold income taxes from its employees' gross earnings and remit them to the appropriate government agencies. Some companies also contribute to medical insurance for employees and to pension funds.

i. **Unearned revenues** represent obligations to deliver goods or services in return for advance payment. When delivery takes place, Unearned Revenue is debited, and a revenue account is credited.

9. **Estimated liabilities** are definite obligations, but the amount of the obligations must be estimated at the balance sheet date because the exact figure will not be known until a future date. Examples of estimated liabilities are corporate income taxes, property taxes, product warranties, and vacation pay.

a. A corporation's income tax depends on its net income, a figure that often is not determined until well after the balance sheet date.

b. Property taxes are levied on real and personal property. Very often, a company's accounting period ends before property taxes have been assessed, and the company must therefore estimate the taxes.

c. When a company sells a product with a warranty, a liability exists for the length of the warranty. Many warranties will remain in effect in subsequent accounting periods. However, the warranty expense and liability must be recorded in the period of the sale no matter when the company makes good on the warranty. Therefore, at the end of each accounting period, the company should make an estimate of future warranty expense that will apply to the present period's sales.

d. In a company in which employees earn vacation pay for working a certain length of time, the company must estimate the vacation pay that applies to each payroll period. The debit is to Vacation Pay Expense, and the credit is to Estimated Liability for Vacation Pay. The liability decreases (is debited) when an employee receives vacation pay.

Objective 3: Distinguish *contingent liabilities* from *commitments.*

10. Businesses are required to disclose contingent liabilities and commitments in the notes to their financial statements. A **contingent liability** is a potential liability that may or may not become an actual liability. The uncertainty about its outcome is settled when a future event does or does not occur. Contingent liabilities arise from things like pending lawsuits, tax disputes, and failure to fol-

low government regulations. Two conditions must be met before a contingency is entered in the accounting records: the liability must be probable, and it can be reasonably estimated. A **commitment** is a legal obligation that does not qualify for recognition as a liability. Leases and purchase agreements are the most common examples of commitments.

Supplemental Objective 4: Compute and record the liabilities associated with payroll accounting.

11. Computations for payroll liabilities must be made for each employee's compensation, for withholdings from each employee's total pay, and for the employer's portion of payroll taxes.

12. An employee's take-home pay equals gross earnings less total withholdings. Pay is withheld for social security and Medicare taxes and for federal income taxes. The amount withheld for federal income taxes depends on the amount the employee earns and the number of exemptions claimed on the employee's W-4 form (Employee's Withholding Exemption Certificate). The amount that the employer withholds and remits to the government should be close to the employee's actual federal income tax liability. The procedures for withholding state and local income taxes are generally similar to those for federal income taxes. Pay may also be withheld from an employee's earnings for pension plans, insurance premiums, union dues, and savings plans.

13. The **payroll register,** which is prepared each pay period, is a detailed list of a company's total payroll for the period. It includes each employee's name, hours, earnings, deductions, net pay, and payroll classification. The journal entry to record the payroll is based on the column totals of the payroll register.

14. Employers must keep an **employee earnings record** for each employee showing all payroll data: earnings, amounts withheld (listed by category), and payment. Each year, the company must inform the employee of his or her total earnings and tax deductions on a W-2 form (Wage and Tax Statement). The employee uses this form to complete his or her individual tax return. The employer must send a copy of each W-2 to the IRS.

15. Both the employee and the employer pay social security and Medicare taxes. Employers alone pay federal unemployment insurance taxes (FUTA) and state unemployment insurance taxes. The employer treats all these taxes as operating expenses. The entry to record them shows a debit to Payroll Taxes Expense and a credit to each of the four tax liabilities.

16. Many companies use a special payroll bank account against which payroll checks are drawn. In addition to issuing paychecks each pay period, companies must pay the social security and Medicare taxes (both employees' and employers' shares) and the federal income taxes at least quarterly. The FUTA tax is paid yearly if the amount is less than $100; if it exceeds $100 at the end of any quarter, a payment is necessary. Payment dates for unemployment insurance vary among the states.

Interest Stated Separately

A. (LO 2) Cash   XX (amount received)
      Notes Payable   XX (face amount)
        Issued promissory note with interest stated
        separately

B. (LO 2) Notes Payable   XX (face amount)
      Interest Expense   XX (amount incurred)
        Cash   XX (maturity amount)
        Payment of note with interest stated separately

C. (LO 2) Interest Expense   XX (amount accrued)
      Interest Payable   XX (amount accrued)
        To record interest expense on note with interest
        stated separately

Interest in Face Amount

D. (LO 2) Cash   XX (face amount minus interest)
      Discount on Notes Payable   XX (interest in face amount)
        Notes Payable   XX (face amount)
        Issued promissory note with interest included in
        face amount

E. (LO 2) Notes Payable   XX (face amount)
        Cash   XX (face amount)
        Payment of note with interest included in face
        amount (see also entry F)

F. (LO 2) Interest Expense   XX (amount accrued)
        Discount on Notes Payable   XX (amount accrued)
        To record interest expense on note with interest
        in face amount

G. (LO 2) Cash   XX (amount collected)
        Sales   XX (price charged)
        Sales Tax Payable   XX (amount to remit)
        Excise Tax Payable   XX (amount to remit)
        Sale of merchandise and collection of sales and
        excise taxes

H. (LO 2) Wages Expense   XX (gross amount)
        Employees' Federal Income Taxes Payable   XX (amount withheld)
        Employees' State Income Taxes Payable   XX (amount withheld)
        Social Security Tax Payable   XX (employees' share)
        Medicare Tax Payable   XX (employees' share)
        Medical Insurance Premiums Payable   XX (employees' share)
        Pension Contributions Payable   XX (employees' share)
        Wages Payable   XX (take-home pay)
        To record payroll

I. (LO 2) Payroll Taxes and Benefits Expense   XX (total employer payroll taxes)
    Social Security Tax Payable   XX (employer's share)
    Medicare Tax Payable   XX (employer's share)
    Medical Insurance Premiums Payable   XX (employer's share)
    Pension Contributions Payable   XX (employer's share)
    Federal Unemployment Tax Payable   XX (amount incurred)
    State Unemployment Tax Payable   XX (amount incurred)
        To record payroll taxes and other costs

J. (LO 2) Cash   XX (amount prepaid)
    Unearned Subscriptions   XX (amount to earn)
        Receipt of annual subscriptions in advance

K. (LO 2) Unearned Subscriptions   XX (amount earned)
    Subscription Revenues   XX (amount earned)
        Delivery of monthly magazine issues

L. (LO 2) Income Taxes Expense   XX (amount estimated)
    Estimated Income Taxes Payable   XX (amount estimated)
        To record estimated federal income taxes

M. (LO 2) Product Warranty Expense   XX (estimated amount)
    Estimated Product Warranty Liability   XX (estimated amount)
        To record estimated product warranty expense

N. (LO 2) Cash   XX (fee charged)
    Estimated Product Warranty Liability   XX (cost of part)
    Service Revenue   XX (fee charged)
    Merchandise Inventory   XX (cost of part)
        Replacement of part under warranty

O. (LO 2) Vacation Pay Expense   XX (amount incurred)
    Estimated Liability for Vacation Pay   XX (amount owed or accrued)
        Estimated vacation pay expense

P. (LO 2) Estimated Liability for Vacation Pay   XX (amount taken)
    Cash (or Wages Payable)   XX (amount paid or payable)
        Wages of employees on vacation

SELF-TEST

Test your knowledge of the chapter by choosing the best answer for each item below.

1. Failure to record a liability will probably
   a. have no effect on net income.
   b. result in overstated net income.
   c. result in overstated total assets.
   d. result in overstated total liabilities and owner's equity.

2. Which of the following is most likely to be a definitely determinable liability?
   a. Property taxes payable
   b. Product warranty liability
   c. Income taxes payable
   d. Interest payable

3. Which of the following is a payroll tax borne by both employee and employer?
   a. Excise tax
   b. Income tax
   c. FUTA tax
   d. Medicare tax

4. The amount received by a borrower on a one-year, $3,000, 10 percent note with interest included in the face value is
   a. $3,000.
   b. $2,700.
   c. $3,300.
   d. $2,990.

5. Which of the following is most likely to be an estimated liability?
   a. Deferred revenues
   b. Vacation pay liability
   c. Current portion of long-term debt
   d. Payroll liabilities

6. If product J cost $100 and had a 2 percent failure rate, the estimated warranty expense in a month in which 1,000 units were sold would be
   a. $2,000.
   b. $100.
   c. $20.
   d. $20,000.

7. Seventy percent of a company's employees typically qualify to receive two weeks' paid vacation per year. The amount of estimated vacation pay liability for a week in which the total payroll is $3,000 is
   a. $2,100.
   b. $42.
   c. $84.
   d. $120.

8. A contingent liability should be recorded in the accounting records if it is
   a. not probable but can be reasonably estimated.
   b. not probable but cannot be estimated.
   c. probable and can be reasonably estimated.
   d. probable but cannot be reasonably estimated.

9. An employee has gross earnings of $500 and withholdings of $31 for social security tax, $7 for Medicare tax, and $60 for income taxes. The employer pays $31 for social security tax, $7 for Medicare tax, and $20 for FUTA. The total cost of the employee to the employer is
   a. $402.
   b. $500.
   c. $558.
   d. $596.

10. Payroll Taxes Expense includes all of the following *except*
   a. federal unemployment tax payable.
   b. social security tax payable.
   c. federal income tax payable.
   d. state unemployment tax payable.

TESTING YOUR KNOWLEDGE

Matching*

Match each term with its definition by writing the appropriate letter in the blank.

_____ 1. Current liabilities

_____ 2. Long-term liabilities

_____ 3. Definitely determinable liabilities

_____ 4. Estimated liabilities

_____ 5. Unearned (deferred) revenues

_____ 6. Vacation pay

_____ 7. Withholdings

_____ 8. Commercial paper

_____ 9. W-2 form

_____ 10. W-4 form

_____ 11. Take-home pay

_____ 12. Employee earnings record

_____ 13. Payroll register

_____ 14. Payroll taxes expense

_____ 15. Contingent liabilities

_____ 16. Wages

_____ 17. Salaries

_____ 18. Line of credit

_____ 19. Commitment

a. A detailed listing of a company's total payroll for one pay period

b. Obligations that are expected to be satisfied within one year or the normal operating cycle, whichever is longer

c. An arrangement with a bank that allows a company to borrow funds when needed

d. Compensation of employees at an hourly rate

e. Obligations that exist but cannot be measured exactly on the balance sheet date

f. Gross earnings less total withholdings

g. Obligations that can be measured exactly

h. Deductions from employees' earnings that employers remit to the appropriate agencies

i. A yearly statement on which tax exemptions are claimed

j. Payment for time off that an employee has earned

k. A statement of an employee's total annual earnings and withholdings that employers are required to give to each employee

l. Unsecured loans sold to the public

m. Social security, Medicare, and unemployment taxes levied on the employer

n. A record containing all payroll data for one employee

o. Obligations to deliver goods or services in return for advance payment

p. Employment compensation at a monthly or yearly rate

q. Potential liabilities that may or may not become actual liabilities

r. Obligations that are not expected to be satisfied in the current period

s. A legal obligation that does not qualify for recognition as a contingent liability

---

*Note to student: The matching quiz might be completed more efficiently by starting with the definition and searching for the corresponding term.

Short Answer

Use the lines provided to answer each item.

1. Current liabilities fall into two main categories. What are these categories?

   _____

   _____

2. Provide three examples of contingent liabilities.

   _____

   _____

   _____

3. Provide three examples of estimated liabilities.

   _____

   _____

   _____

4. Provide three examples of definitely determinable liabilities.

   _____

   _____

   _____

5. List three taxes for which deductions must be made from an employee's earnings and one for which a deduction is often, but not always, made.

   _____

   _____

   _____

6. List the four components of payroll taxes expense.

   _____

   _____

   _____

   _____

True-False

Circle T if the statement is true, F if it is false. Provide explanations for the false answers, using the blank lines at the end of the section.

T F 1. Deferred revenues appear on the income statement.

T F 2. A contract to purchase goods in the future does not require that a current liability be recorded.

T F 3. The failure to record an accrued liability results in an overstatement of net income.

T F 4. The current portion of a long-term debt is a current liability if it is to be satisfied with cash.

T F 5. Sales tax payable is an example of an estimated liability.

T F 6. Warranties fall into the category of definitely determinable liabilities.

T F 7. The amount withheld for federal income taxes depends in part on the number of exemptions claimed on the W-4 form.

T F 8. The journal entry to record the payroll is based on the column totals of the payroll register.

T F 9. FUTA is a tax borne by both the employer and the employee.

T F 10. Every contingent liability must eventually become an actual liability or no liability at all.

T F 11. The Discount on Notes Payable account is associated with notes whose interest is stated separately on the face of the note.

T F **12.** Liabilities basically are obligations that result from past transactions.

T F **13.** A CPA is an example of an independent contractor.

T F **14.** If a refrigerator is sold with a warranty in year 1 and repairs are made in year 2, Product Warranty Expense should be recorded in year 2.

T F **15.** When the payroll is recorded, the Wages and Salaries Payable account is credited for total take-home pay.

T F **16.** Social security and Medicare taxes are borne by the employee, not the employer.

T F **17.** Typically, unemployment taxes are a component of Payroll Taxes and Benefits Expense.

T F 18. A decrease in the payables turnover will produce an increase in the average days' payable.

_____

_____

_____

_____

_____

_____

_____

_____

_____

_____

_____

Circle the letter of the best answer.

1. Which of the following is *not* a definitely determinable liability?
   a. Dividends payable
   b. Deferred revenues
   c. Property taxes payable
   d. Excise taxes payable

2. Estimated liabilities always apply to all of the following *except*
   a. warranties.
   b. vacation pay.
   c. a corporation's income tax.
   d. pending lawsuits.

3. Which of the following is *not* deducted from an employee's earnings?
   a. FUTA tax
   b. Union dues
   c. Social security tax
   d. Charitable contributions

4. The amount of federal income tax withheld on behalf of an employee is recorded as a
   a. payroll expense.
   b. contra account.
   c. current asset.
   d. current liability.

5. When an employee receives vacation pay, the company should debit
   a. Vacation Pay Expense and credit Cash.
   b. Vacation Pay Receivable and credit Cash.
   c. Estimated Liability for Vacation Pay and credit Cash.
   d. Vacation Pay Expense and credit Estimated Liability for Vacation Pay.

6. Balboa Engraving, Inc., purchased some equipment by executing a $10,000 non-interest-bearing note (i.e., interest is included in the face amount) due in three years. Balboa should record the equipment at
   a. $10,000 minus the discounted interest on the note.
   b. $10,000 plus the discounted interest on the note.
   c. the amount of the discounted interest on the note.
   d. $10,000.

7. When accounting for a note whose interest is included in its face amount, the Discount on Notes Payable account eventually is converted into
   a. Interest Receivable.
   b. Interest Expense.
   c. Interest Payable.
   d. Interest Income.

APPLYING YOUR KNOWLEDGE

Exercises

1. During 20x5, Hall's Appliance Store sold 300 washing machines, each with a one-year guarantee. It estimated that 5 percent of the washing machines eventually would require some type of repair, at an average cost of $35. Prepare the adjusting entry that Hall's would make concerning the warranty, as well as the entry that it would make on April 9, 20x6, for a repair that cost $48.

General Journal				
Date		**Description**	**Debit**	**Credit**

2. Pat Bauer, an office worker who is paid $6.50 per hour, worked 40 hours during the week that ended May 7. Social security taxes are 6.20 percent, Medicare taxes are 1.45 percent, union dues are $5, state taxes withheld are $8, and federal income taxes withheld are $52. Bauer's employer must pay (on the basis of gross earnings) social security taxes of 6.20 percent, Medicare taxes of 1.45 percent, federal unemployment taxes of 0.8 percent, and state unemployment taxes of 5.4 percent. In the journal provided below, record an entry that summarizes Pat Bauer's earnings for the week and an entry that records the employer's payroll taxes. Round off amounts to the nearest cent.

General Journal				
Date		**Description**	**Debit**	**Credit**

3. Tillit Corporation has current assets of $100,000 and current liabilities of $40,000, of which accounts payable are $30,000. Last year, its accounts payable were $20,000. Its cost of goods sold is $290,000, and its merchandise decreased by $15,000. Using these data, compute the following short-term liquidity measures:

a. Working capital

b. Payables turnover

c. Average days' payable

Crossword Puzzle
for Chapters 8 and 9

ACROSS

3. See 4-Down
5. Employee earnings _____
6. Cost of goods available for _____
8. Compensation at an hourly rate
10. Merchandise
11. _____ paper
12. _____ credit (2 words)
13. _____ (take-home) pay
14. Merchandise movement (2 words)
18. Product liability
19. Ownership of goods
21. A payroll tax, for short

DOWN

1. Inventory estimation technique (2 words)
2. _____ payable
4. With 3-Across, liability arising from payment received in advance
7. Type of current liability
9. Just-_____ operating environment (2 words, hyphenated)
11. Major _____ method (of applying LCM)
12. The "L" of LIFO
15. The "L" of LCM
16. Average _____ inventory on hand
17. _____ transactions (from which liabilities result)
20. Goods _____ transit

CHAPTER 10 LONG-TERM ASSETS

REVIEWING THE CHAPTER

Objective 1: Identify the types of long-term assets and explain the management issues related to accounting for them.

1. **Long-term assets** (sometimes called *fixed assets*) are assets that (a) have a useful life of more than one year, (b) are acquired for use in the operation of a business, and (c) are not intended for resale to customers. Assets that are not being used in the normal course of business, such as land held for speculative purposes, should be classified as long-term investments rather than as long-term assets.

2. Property, plant, and equipment is the balance sheet classification for **tangible assets,** which are long-term assets that have physical substance, and for **natural resources,** which are long-term assets in the form of valuable substances, such as standing timber, oil and gas fields, and mineral deposits. **Intangible assets** is the balance sheet classification for long-term assets without physical substance whose value is based on rights or advantages accruing to the owners; examples are patents, copyrights, trademarks, franchises, leasehold improvements, and goodwill. The allocation of costs to different accounting periods is called **depreciation** in the case of plant and equipment (plant assets), **depletion** in the case of natural resources, and **amortization** in the case of intangible assets. Because land has an unlimited useful life, its cost is never converted into an expense.

3. Long-term assets are generally reported at **carrying value** (also called *book value*), which is the unexpired part of a plant asset's cost. Carrying value is calculated by deducting accumulated depreciation from original cost. If **asset impairment** (loss of revenue-generating potential) occurs, the long-term asset's carrying value is reduced to reflect its current fair value (measured by the present value of future cash flows). A loss for the amount of the write-down would also be recorded.

4. Capital budgeting is the process of evaluating a decision to acquire a long-term asset. One common capital budgeting technique compares the amount and timing of cash inflows and outflows over the life of the asset under consideration. If the net present value of those cash flows is positive, the asset should probably be purchased. Information about long-term asset acquisitions may be found in the investing activities section of the statement of cash flows.

5. Long-term assets not purchased for cash must be financed. Common financing techniques include issuing stock, bonds, and long-term notes.

6. The major problem in accounting for long-term assets is to figure out how much of the asset has benefited the current period and how much should be carried forward as an asset that will benefit future periods. To resolve these issues, one must determine (a) the cost of the asset; (b) the method of matching the cost with revenues; (c) the treatment of subsequent expenditures, such as repairs and additions; and (d) the treatment of the asset at the time of disposal.

Objective 2: Distinguish between capital and revenue expenditures, and account for the cost of property, plant, and equipment.

7. Before recording an **expenditure** (a payment or the incurrence of liability) for a long-term asset, one must determine whether it was a capital expenditure or a revenue expenditure. A **capital expenditure** is an expenditure for the purchase or expansion of long-term assets. Capital expenditures are recorded in the asset accounts because they will benefit several future accounting periods. A **revenue expenditure** is an expenditure for repairs, maintenance, and anything else necessary to enable the asset to fulfill its originally estimated useful life. A revenue expenditure is charged as an expense in the period in which it is incurred because it benefits only the current accounting period.

8. Treating a capital expenditure as a revenue expenditure, or vice versa, can result in a mismatching of revenues and expenses. Great care must therefore be taken to draw the appropriate distinction.

9. The acquisition cost of a long-term asset includes the purchase price, freight charges, insurance while in transit, installation, and other costs involved in acquiring the asset and getting it ready for use. These costs are allocated to the useful life of the asset rather than charged as expenses in the current period. Also included in the acquisition cost is interest incurred during the construction of a plant asset. However, interest incurred in the purchase of an asset is expensed when incurred. Small expenditures for such items as office supplies are also often expensed immediately because the amounts involved are immaterial.
   a. When land is purchased, the Land account should be debited not only for the price paid for the land, but also for such expenses as real estate commissions, lawyers' fees, back taxes paid by the buyer; the cost (less salvage value) of razing buildings on the land; draining, clearing, and grading costs; assessments for local improvements; and (usually) the cost of landscaping. Land is not subject to depreciation because of its unlimited useful life.
   b. Unlike land, land improvements, such as fences, driveways, and parking lots, have a limited life and are therefore subject to depreciation. They are recorded in a Land Improvements account rather than in the Land account.
   c. When a business constructs a building for its own use, it debits the Buildings account for such costs as materials, labor, overhead, architects' fees, insurance during construction, interest on construction loans, legal fees, and building permits. Because they have a limited useful life, buildings are considered depreciable assets.
   d. The cost of equipment includes the invoice price less cash discounts, freight charges (including insurance), excise taxes and tariffs, buying expenses, installation costs, and test runs. Like land improvements and buildings, equipment is subject to depreciation.
   e. When long-term assets are purchased for a lump sum, the cost should be divided among the assets acquired in proportion to their appraised values.

Objective 3: Define *depreciation* and compute depreciation under the straight-line, production, and declining-balance methods.

10. *Depreciation,* as the term is used in accounting, refers to the allocation of the cost (less the residual value) of a tangible asset to the periods benefited by the asset. It does not refer to the asset's physical deterioration or to a decrease in its market value. Thus, depreciation is not a process of valuation but of allocating the cost of the asset over the asset's estimated useful life. All tangible assets except land have limited useful lives, generally because of **physical deterioration** (resulting from use and exposure to the elements) and **obsolescence** (the process of becoming out of date).

11. Depreciation is computed after the asset's cost, residual value, depreciable cost, and estimated useful life have been determined. **Residual value** (often called *salvage value* or *disposal value*) is the estimated value of the asset at the estimated disposal date. **Depreciable cost** is the asset's cost less its residual value. **Estimated useful life** can be measured in time or in units and requires the accountant's careful consideration.

12. The most common depreciation methods are the straight-line, production, and declining-balance methods. The last is described as an accelerated method.
   a. Under the **straight-line method,** the depreciable cost is spread evenly over the life of the asset. Depreciation for each year is computed as follows:

$$\frac{\text{Cost} - \text{Residual Value}}{\text{Estimated Useful Life (Years)}}$$

b. Under the **production method,** depreciation is based not on time, but on use of the asset in units. Under this method, depreciation for each year is computed as follows:

$$\frac{\text{Cost} - \text{Residual Value}}{\substack{\text{Estimated Units of} \\ \text{Useful Life}}} \times \substack{\text{Actual Units} \\ \text{of Output}}$$

c. The declining-balance method is called an **accelerated method** because depreciation is greatest in the first year and decreases each year thereafter. This method is consistent with the matching rule because the highest depreciation is charged in the most productive years, when the asset is new, and because of the smoothing effect that results when annual depreciation and repair expense are combined (i.e., over the years, depreciation charges decrease, while repair costs increase). With the **declining-balance method,** depreciation is computed by multiplying the remaining carrying value (the unexpired part of the cost) of the asset by a fixed percentage. The **double-declining-balance method** is a form of the declining-balance method; it uses a fixed percentage that is twice the straight-line percentage. Under the double-declining-balance method, depreciation for each year is computed as follows:

$$2 \times \frac{100\%}{\text{Useful Life in Years}} \times \substack{\text{Remaining} \\ \text{Carrying} \\ \text{Value}}$$

Under the declining-balance or double-declining-balance method, as under the other methods, an asset should not be depreciated below its residual value.

Objective 4: Account for the disposal of depreciable assets.

13. When an asset is still in use after it has been fully depreciated, no more depreciation should be recorded, but the asset should not be written off until its disposal. Disposal occurs when the asset is discarded, sold, or traded in for another asset.

14. When a business disposes of an asset, depreciation should be recorded for the partial period up to the date of the disposal. This brings the asset's Accumulated Depreciation account up to that date. For example, when a machine is discarded (thrown out), Accumulated Depreciation, Machinery is debited and Machinery is credited for the present balance in the Accumulated Depreciation ac-

count. If the machine has not been fully depreciated, then to balance the entry, Loss on Disposal of Machinery must be debited for the carrying value.

15. When a machine is sold for cash, both the Cash and the Accumulated Depreciation, Machinery accounts are debited, and the Machinery account is credited. If the cash received is less than the carrying value of the machine, then Loss on Sale of Machinery is debited. If the cash received is greater than the carrying value, Gain on Sale of Machinery is credited to balance the entry.

16. When an asset is traded in (exchanged) for a similar one, the gain or loss is computed as follows:

$$\begin{array}{l} \quad \text{Trade-In Allowance} \\ - \quad \underline{\text{Carrying Value of Asset Traded In}} \\ = \quad \text{Gain (Loss) on Trade-In} \end{array}$$

a. For financial reporting purposes, both gains and losses on the exchange of dissimilar assets should be recognized. When similar assets are exchanged, only losses should be recognized.

b. For income tax purposes, both gains and losses on the exchange of similar assets should be recognized, but neither should be recognized on the exchange of dissimilar assets.

c. When a gain or loss is recognized, the asset acquired should be debited for its list price—cash paid plus trade-in allowance—using a realistic trade-in value. The old asset is removed from the books, as described in paragraph 15.

d. When a gain or loss is not recognized, the asset acquired should be debited for the carrying value of the asset traded in plus cash paid (this results in the nonrecognition of the gain or loss).

Objective 5: Identify the issues related to accounting for natural resources and compute depletion.

17. *Depletion* refers both to the exhaustion of a natural resource and to the allocation of its cost to accounting periods, which is based on the amount of the resource extracted in each period. Depletion for each period is computed as follows:

$$\frac{\text{Cost} - \text{Residual Value}}{\substack{\text{Estimated Units} \\ \text{Available}}} \times \substack{\text{Units Extracted} \\ \text{and Sold} \\ \text{During Period}}$$

Units extracted but not sold within an accounting period are recorded as inventory, to be charged as an expense in the period in which they are sold.

18. Assets acquired in conjunction with a natural resource that have no useful purpose after the natural resource is depleted (e.g., drills and pumps) should be depreciated on the same basis as the depletion.

19. Two methods are used to account for the exploration and development of oil and gas resources. Under the **successful efforts method,** the cost of a dry well is written off immediately as a loss. The **full-costing method,** on the other hand, capitalizes and depletes the costs of both productive and dry wells. Both methods are in accordance with GAAP.

Objective 6: Identify the issues related to accounting for intangible assets, including research and development costs and goodwill.

20. Intangible assets acquired from others should initially be recorded as assets. Those with determinable useful lives (such as patents, copyrights, and leaseholds) should be written off over their useful lives through periodic amortization. This is normally accomplished by a direct reduction of the asset account and an increase in amortization expense. Any substantial and permanent decline (impairment) in value must also be recognized. However, a business must expense the costs of *developing* its intangible assets.
   a. **Goodwill** is the excess of the cost of a group of assets (usually a business) over the fair market value of the individual assets.
   b. A **trademark** or **brand name** is a registered symbol or name that gives the owner the exclusive right to use it to identify a product or service.
   c. A **copyright** is an exclusive right granted by the federal government to reproduce and sell literary, musical, and other artistic materials and computer programs for a period of the author's life plus 70 years.
   d. A **patent** is an exclusive right granted by the federal government for a period of 20 years (14 years for a design) to make a particular product or use a specific process.
   e. A **license** or **franchise** is the right to an exclusive territory or market, or the right to use a formula, technique, process, or design.
   f. A **leasehold** is a right to occupy land or buildings under a long-term rental contract.
   g. **Leasehold improvements** are improvements to leased property that become the property of the lessor when the lease expires.
   h. **Technology** is capitalized software developed for sale or lease or for use within the firm.
   i. A **noncompete covenant** is a contract that limits the rights of others to compete in a specific industry or line of business for a specified time.
   j. Customer lists are lists of customers or of subscribers.

21. *Research and development (R&D)* refers to developing new products, testing existing ones, and doing pure research. The costs associated with these activities should be charged as expenses in the period in which they are incurred.

22. The costs of developing computer software should be treated as R&D costs until the product is deemed technologically feasible (i.e., when a detailed working program has been designed). At that point, the costs should be recorded as assets and amortized over the estimated economic life of the product using the straight-line method.

23. The costs of leasehold improvements are amortized over the remaining term of the lease or the useful life of the improvement, whichever is shorter.

24. *Goodwill,* as the term is used in accounting, refers to a company's ability to earn more than is normal within its industry. Goodwill equals the excess of the purchase cost over the fair market value of the net assets if the assets were purchased separately. It should be recorded only when an entire company is purchased; it is reported as a separate line item on the balance sheet. Once recorded, it is subject to annual impairment reviews. When its fair value goes below its carrying value, an impairment loss is reported on the income statement, and goodwill is reduced on the balance sheet.

Supplemental Objective 7: Apply depreciation methods to problems of partial years, revised rates, groups of similar items, special types of capital expenditures, and cost recovery.

25. When an asset is purchased after the beginning of the year or discarded before the end of the year, depreciation should be recorded for only part of the year. The accountant figures the year's depreciation and multiplies this figure by the fraction of the year that the asset was in use.

26. Often, the estimated useful life or residual value of an asset is found to be significantly over- or under-

stated after some depreciation has been taken. In that case, the accountant must produce a revised figure for the asset's remaining useful life or remaining depreciable cost. Future depreciation is then calculated by spreading the remaining depreciable cost over the remaining useful life, leaving previous depreciation unchanged.

27. When a company has a number of plant assets that are similar in nature, such as trucks or pieces of office equipment, it may use a method known as **group depreciation** rather than individual depreciation. Under group depreciation, the original costs of all similar assets are lumped together in one summary account. Depreciation is then figured for the group of assets as a whole.

28. Businesses make capital expenditures not only for plant assets, natural resources, and intangible assets, but also for **additions** (such as a building wing) and **betterments** (such as the installation of an air-conditioning system). **Ordinary repairs** are expenditures necessary to maintain an asset in good operating condition so that it can attain its originally intended useful life. They are charged as expenses in the period in which they are incurred. **Extraordinary repairs** are expenditures that either increase an asset's residual value or lengthen its useful life. They are recorded by debiting Accumulated Depreciation (thereby increasing the asset's carrying value) and crediting Cash or Accounts Payable.

29. The Tax Reform Act of 1986 changed the ways in which businesses depreciate assets for income tax purposes. Since 2003, it has permitted companies to expense the first $25,000 of equipment costs immediately rather than recording them as assets (before 2003, the figure was $17,500). The act also inaugurated the **Modified Accelerated Cost Recovery System (MACRS),** which ignores estimated useful life and residual value and allows rapid write-offs of expenditures recorded as assets. Under MACRS, each depreciable asset is placed in a category for tax purposes and is depreciated according to percentages and over a prescribed number of years. For example, most property other than real estate is depreciated by a 200 percent declining balance with a half-year convention. Recovery of the cost of property placed in service after December 31, 1986, is calculated according to MACRS for tax purposes. MACRS depreciation enables companies to reduce current taxes, but it normally is not acceptable for financial reporting because the shortened recovery periods violate the matching rule.

A. (LO 3) Depreciation Expense, Asset Name   XX (amount allocated)
        Accumulated Depreciation, Asset Name   XX (amount allocated)
           To record depreciation for the period (review of
           entry introduced in Chapter 3)

B. (LO 4) Depreciation Expense, Machinery   XX (amount allocated)
        Accumulated Depreciation, Machinery   XX (amount allocated)
           To record depreciation up to date of disposal

C. (LO 4) Accumulated Depreciation, Machinery   XX (existing balance)
        Loss on Disposal of Machinery   XX (carrying value)
          Machinery   XX (purchase price)
           Discarded machine no longer used in the business

D. (LO 4) Cash   XX (proceeds on sale)
        Accumulated Depreciation, Machinery   XX (existing balance)
          Machinery   XX (purchase price)
           Sale of machine for carrying value; no gain or loss

E. (LO 4) Cash   XX (proceeds on sale)
        Accumulated Depreciation, Machinery   XX (existing balance)
        Loss on Sale of Machinery   XX (CV minus cash)
          Machinery   XX (purchase price)
           Sale of machine at less than carrying value (CV);
           loss recorded

F. (LO 4) Cash   XX (proceeds on sale)
        Accumulated Depreciation, Machinery   XX (existing balance)
          Gain on Sale of Machinery   XX (cash minus CV)
          Machinery   XX (purchase price)
           Sale of machine at more than carrying value (CV);
           gain recorded

G. (LO 4) The journal entries to record exchanges of plant assets
        are all very similar (see entry H). The amounts, however,
        depend on a variety of factors, among them the similarity
        or dissimilarity of assets exchanged and the purpose of the
        entry (financial accounting or income tax). In addition,
        gains and losses sometimes are recognized, sometimes not.
        Please see the textbook for a thorough explanation.

H. (LO 4) Machinery (new)   XX (see textbook)
        Accumulated Depreciation, Machinery   XX (existing balance)
          Machinery (old)   XX (purchase price)
          Cash   XX (payment required)
           Exchange of machines—cost of old machine and its
           accumulated depreciation removed from the records,
           and new machine recorded at list price. (Note: If gain
           or loss must be recognized, it would be credited or
           debited, respectively.)

I.   (LO 5)   Depletion Expense, Coal Deposits   XX (amount allocated)
                   Accumulated Depletion, Coal Deposits   XX (amount allocated)
                       To record depletion of coal mine

J.   (SO 7)   Capital expenditures typically are debited to an asset
                   account (such as Buildings or Equipment), and revenue
                   expenditures typically are debited to an expense account
                   (such as Repair Expense). An exception to these rules is
                   for extraordinary repairs, as shown below.

K.   (SO 7)   Accumulated Depreciation, Machinery   XX (amount of repair)
                       Cash   XX (amount of repair)
                           Extraordinary repair to machinery

SELF-TEST

Test your knowledge of the chapter by choosing the best answer for each item below.

1. Which of the following does *not* characterize all long-term assets?
   a. Used in the operation of a business
   b. Possess physical substance
   c. Have a useful life of more than one year
   d. Are not for resale

2. Which of the following would *not* be included in the cost of land?
   a. The cost of paving the land for parking
   b. An assessment from the local government for installing a sewer
   c. The cost of razing a building on the land
   d. A commission to the real estate agent involved in the purchase of the land

3. Which of the following most appropriately describes depreciation?
   a. Allocation of the cost of a plant asset
   b. Decline in the value of a plant asset
   c. Gradual obsolescence of a plant asset
   d. Physical deterioration of a plant asset

4. Assuming an asset has a useful life of six years, which of the following methods would result in the greatest depreciation in the first year?
   a. Cannot tell from data given
   b. Double-declining-balance
   c. Production
   d. Straight-line

5. The sale of equipment costing $16,000, with accumulated depreciation of $13,400 and a sale price of $4,000, would result in a
   a. gain of $4,000.
   b. gain of $1,400.
   c. loss of $1,400.
   d. loss of $12,000.

6. A truck that cost $16,800 and on which $12,600 of accumulated depreciation has been recorded was disposed of on January 2, the first business day of the year. The truck was traded for a similar truck having a price of $19,600; a $2,000 trade-in was allowed, and the balance was paid in cash. According to generally accepted accounting principles, the amount of the gain or loss recognized on this transaction would be
   a. a $2,200 gain.
   b. a $2,200 loss.
   c. a $2,000 gain.
   d. no gain or loss recognized.

7. Which of the following is *not* classified as a natural resource?
   a. Timberland
   b. Gas reserve
   c. Goodwill
   d. Oil well

8. Which of the following intangible assets grants its owner the exclusive right to publish and sell sheet music?
   a. Copyright
   b. Noncompete covenant
   c. Patent
   d. Trademark

9. According to generally accepted accounting principles, the proper accounting treatment of the cost of most research and development is to
   a. amortize the cost over a period not to exceed 40 years.
   b. amortize the cost over five years.
   c. carry the cost as an asset indefinitely.
   d. write the cost off immediately as an expense.

10. Reliable Insurance Company has many items of office equipment in its home office. Rather than compute depreciation on each item individually, the company may combine like items in one account and use
    a. statistical depreciation.
    b. combined depreciation.
    c. group depreciation.
    d. direct charge off.

TESTING YOUR KNOWLEDGE

*Matching**

Match each term with its definition by writing the appropriate letter in the blank.

_____ 1. Long-term assets

_____ 2. Depreciation

_____ 3. Obsolescence

_____ 4. Franchise

_____ 5. Residual value (salvage or disposal value)

_____ 6. Accelerated method

_____ 7. Straight-line method

_____ 8. Production method

_____ 9. Full-costing method

_____ 10. Double-declining-balance method

_____ 11. Group depreciation

_____ 12. Natural resources

_____ 13. Depletion

_____ 14. Amortization

_____ 15. Modified Accelerated Cost Recovery System (MACRS)

_____ 16. Capital expenditure

_____ 17. Revenue expenditure

_____ 18. Patent

_____ 19. Copyright

_____ 20. Leasehold

_____ 21. Trademark

_____ 22. Successful efforts method

a. The exclusive right to make a particular product or use a specific process for 20 years

b. Using one depreciation rate for several similar items

c. The allocation of an intangible asset's cost to the periods benefited by the asset

d. The right to occupy property under a long-term rental contract

e. Assets to be used in the business for more than one year

f. The allocation of the cost of a tangible asset to the periods benefited by the asset

g. An expenditure for services needed to maintain and operate plant assets (an expense)

h. The depreciation method under which cost allocation is based on units, not time

i. The exclusive right to publish literary, musical, and other artistic materials and computer programs for the author's life plus 70 years

j. The accelerated depreciation method based on twice the straight-line rate

k. A depreciation method used for tax purposes only

l. The estimated value of an asset on the disposal date

m. An expenditure for the purchase or expansion of long-term assets (an asset)

n. One reason for an asset's limited useful life

o. Assets in the form of valuable substances that can be extracted and sold

p. An identifying symbol or name for a product or service that can be used only by its owner

q. The method of accounting for oil and gas that immediately writes off the cost of dry wells

r. The depreciation method that charges equal depreciation each year

s. The exclusive right to sell a product within a certain territory

t. The practice of charging the highest depreciation in the first year and decreasing depreciation each year thereafter

u. The allocation of a natural resource's cost to the periods over which the resource is consumed

v. The method of accounting for oil and gas that capitalizes the cost of dry wells

---

Note to student: The matching quiz might be completed more efficiently by starting with the definition and searching for the corresponding term.

Short Answer

Use the lines provided to answer each item.

1. Distinguish between an addition and a betterment.

_____

_____

_____

_____

2. When a plant asset is sold for cash, under what unique circumstance would no gain or loss be recorded?

_____

_____

3. List four pieces of information necessary to compute the depletion expense of an oil well for a given year.

_____

_____

_____

_____

4. Distinguish between ordinary and extraordinary repairs.

_____

_____

_____

_____

5. For each asset category listed below, provide the accounting term for the allocation of its cost to the periods benefited.

Category	Term for Cost Allocation
Intangible assets	_____
Plant and equipment	_____
Natural resources	_____

6. Plant assets have limited useful lives for two reasons. What are they?

_____

_____

True-False

Circle T if the statement is true, F if it is false. Provide explanations for the false answers, using the blank lines at the end of the section.

T F **1.** Land is not subject to depreciation.

T F **2.** The loss recorded on a discarded asset is equal to the carrying value of the asset at the time it is discarded.

T F **3.** Land held for speculative reasons is not classified as property, plant, and equipment.

T F **4.** Depreciation is a process of valuation, not allocation.

T F **5.** Depreciation for a machine can be calculated by having an appraiser determine the extent of the machine's deterioration.

T F **6.** When land is purchased for use as a plant site, its cost should include the cost of clearing and draining the land.

T F **7.** Each type of depreciable asset should have its own accumulated depreciation account.

T F **8.** Estimated useful life in years is irrelevant when applying the production method of depreciation.

T F **9.** If depreciation expense under the straight-line method is $1,000 in the first year, it will be $2,000 in the second year.

T F **10.** When the estimated useful life of an asset is revised after some depreciation has been taken, the accountant should not go back to previous years to make corrections.

T F **11.** For financial accounting purposes, both gains and losses on the exchange of dissimilar assets are recognized in the accounting records.

T F **12.** In an asset's last year of depreciation, accelerated depreciation generally results in less net income than does straight-line depreciation.

T F **13.** Depreciable cost equals cost minus accumulated depreciation.

T F **14.** Estimated useful life and residual value are ignored when applying MACRS depreciation.

T F **15.** A copyright is a name or symbol that can be used only by its owner.

T F **16.** If ordinary maintenance is mistakenly capitalized instead of being charged as an expense, net income for the period will be overstated.

T F **17.** A betterment is an example of a revenue expenditure.

T F **18.** Recording an extraordinary repair leaves the carrying value of the asset unchanged.

T F **19.** When a machine is sold for less than its carrying value, one of the debits is to Loss on Sale of Machinery and one of the credits is to Accumulated Depreciation, Machinery.

T F **20.** *Capital expenditure* is another term for *expense.*

T F **21.** For income tax purposes, neither gains nor losses are recognized on the exchange of similar plant assets.

T F **22.** When a plant asset is sold, depreciation expense need not be recorded for the partial period up to the date of the sale.

T F **23.** In determining the number of years over which to amortize copyrights and patents, useful life is more important than the period legally covered by these assets.

T F **24.** As accumulated depreciation increases, carrying value decreases.

T F **25.** Goodwill should be recorded only when an entire company has been purchased.

T F **26.** Research and development costs should be capitalized when they can be associated with a specific new product.

T F **27.** The full-costing method capitalizes the cost of both successful and dry wells.

T F **28.** A long-term asset's carrying value should be reduced when its value is impaired.

Multiple Choice

Circle the letter of the best answer.

1. A building and land are purchased for a lump-sum payment of $66,000. How much should be allocated to land if the land is appraised at $20,000 and the building is appraised at $60,000?
   a. $22,000
   b. $20,000
   c. $16,500
   d. $13,750

2. The expired cost of a plant asset is called its
   a. accumulated depreciation.
   b. carrying value.
   c. depreciable cost.
   d. residual value.

3. When applied to an asset in its first year of use, which depreciation method results in the greatest depreciation charge?
   a. Declining-balance
   b. Production
   c. Straight-line
   d. Impossible to determine without more data

4. When a machine was purchased, its estimated useful life was 20 years. However, after it had been depreciated for 5 years, the company decided that it originally had overestimated the machine's useful life by 3 years. What should be done?
   a. Go back and adjust depreciation for the first 5 years.
   b. Depreciate the remainder of the depreciable cost over the next 15 years.
   c. Depreciate the remainder of the depreciable cost over the next 12 years.
   d. Both a and b should be done.

5. According to GAAP, goodwill should
   a. be expensed when acquired.
   b. be amortized over its useful life.
   c. be written down when an impairment occurs.
   d. never be expensed, amortized, or written down.

6. The costs of land improvements
   a. should be included in the cost of the land.
   b. are subject to depreciation.
   c. should be deducted from the cost of the land.
   d. should be charged as expenses in the year they are incurred.

7. A machine that cost $9,000 has a carrying value of $2,000 and is sold for $1,700. Which of the following is true about the entry made to record the sale?
   a. Accumulated Depreciation is debited for $2,000.
   b. Machinery is credited for $2,000.
   c. Loss on Sale of Machinery is credited for $300.
   d. Accumulated Depreciation is debited for $7,000.

8. Which of the following items is *not* a revenue expenditure?
   a. Ordinary maintenance of a machine
   b. Replacing an old roof with a new one
   c. The installation of new light bulbs
   d. Repair of a tire on a company truck

9. Charging a depreciable item as an expense instead of capitalizing it results in
   a. overstated total assets.
   b. understated net income in the next period.
   c. overstated depreciation expense in the next period.
   d. understated net income in the current period.

10. Overestimating the number of barrels that can be pumped from an oil well over its lifetime results in
    a. understated net income each year.
    b. understated depletion cost per unit each year.
    c. overstated depletion expense each year.
    d. understated total assets each year.

11. The cost of developing computer software should be
    a. expensed up to the point that the product is technologically feasible.
    b. capitalized in its entirety and amortized over 14 years.
    c. expensed after the product is deemed to be technologically feasible.
    d. expensed in its entirety when incurred.

12. Which of the following normally is charged as an expense in the period of expenditure?
    a. Goodwill
    b. Leaseholds
    c. Leasehold improvements
    d. Research and development costs

APPLYING YOUR KNOWLEDGE

Exercises

1. A machine that cost $26,000 had an estimated useful life of five years and a residual value of $2,000 when purchased on January 2, 20x4. Fill in the amount of depreciation expense for 20x5, as well as the accumulated depreciation and carrying value of the machine as of December 31, 20x5, under both of the methods listed below.

	Depreciation Expense for 20x5	Accumulated Depreciation as of 12/31/x5	Carrying Value as of 12/31/x5
a. Straight-line	$ _____	$ _____	$ _____
b. Double-declining-balance	$ _____	$ _____	$ _____

2. A machine that was to produce a certain type of toy was purchased for $35,000 on April 30, 20x6. The machine was expected to produce 100,000 toys during the ten years that the company expected to keep the machine. The company estimated that it then could sell the machine for $5,000. Using the production method, calculate the depreciation expense in 20x6, when the machine produced 7,500 toys.

3. Classify each of the following as a capital expenditure or a revenue expenditure by placing a *C* or an *R* next to each item.

_____ **a.** Replacement of a roof

_____ **b.** Replacement of the battery in a company vehicle

_____ **c.** Painting of a firm's executive offices

_____ **d.** Installation of aluminum siding

_____ **e.** Replacement of the motor in a machine

_____ **f.** Repair of an air-conditioning unit

_____ **g.** Installation of a piece of machinery

_____ **h.** Addition of a building wing

_____ **i.** Tune-up of a company vehicle

4. Reiner Manufacturing is investigating the purchase of a piece of equipment that would cost $22,000. It is estimated that the equipment would be used for six years, have a residual value of $3,000, and generate positive net cash flows of $4,000 in each of its six years of use. Using Tables 3 and 4 in the text's appendix on future and present value tables, calculate the equipment's net present value, and state whether Reiner should make the purchase. Assume an interest rate of 8 percent.

5. On January 2, 20xx, Brooks Enterprises traded in a machine that cost $25,000 and had a carrying value of $8,000 for a new machine with a retail price of $23,000; Brooks paid $15,500 in cash. The machines are similar in nature. Prepare the journal entry that Brooks would make to conform to GAAP and the entry it would make to conform to income tax regulations. Use the journal provided at the top of the next page.

General Journal

Date		Description	Debit	Credit

6. In 20xx, Porter Coal Company purchased a coal mine for $800,000. It is estimated that 2 million tons of coal can be extracted from the mine. In the journal provided below, prepare Porter's adjusting entry for December 31, 20xx, to reflect the extraction and sale of 100,000 tons during the year.

General Journal

Date		Description	Debit	Credit

CHAPTER 11 LONG-TERM LIABILITIES

REVIEWING THE CHAPTER

Objective 1: Identify the management issues related to issuing long-term debt.

1. To foster growth, companies often invest in long-term assets and in research and development and other activities that will benefit the business in the long run. To finance these investments, they must obtain long-term funding. They commonly do so by issuing stock and long-term debt in the form of bonds, notes, mortgages, and leases. Long-term debt consists of liabilities to be settled beyond one year or the normal operating cycle, whichever is longer. The management issues related to issuing long-term debt are whether to issue it, how much of it to carry, what types of it to incur, and how to handle debt repayment.

2. In considering whether to issue long-term debt, management must weigh the advantages of this method of obtaining funds against the advantages of relying solely on stockholders' equity.

   a. One advantage of issuing long-term debt is that bondholders and other creditors do not have voting rights, and common stockholders therefore retain their level of control. Another advantage is that interest on debt is tax-deductible, which lowers the company's tax burden. A third advantage of issuing long-term debt is that it may give the company **financial leverage**—that is, if earnings on the funds obtained exceed the interest incurred, then stockholders' earnings will increase (this is also called *trading on equity*).

   b. One disadvantage of issuing long-term debt is that the more of it a company issues, the more periodic interest it must pay. Failure to pay either periodic interest or the principal at maturity can force a company into bankruptcy. Another disadvantage is that financial leverage can work against a company if the earnings from its investments do not exceed its interest payments.

3. The use of debt financing varies widely across industries. A common measure of how much risk a company undertakes in issuing debt is the **interest coverage ratio.** It is expressed in "times" and is calculated as follows:

$$\frac{\text{Income Before Taxes} + \text{Interest Expense}}{\text{Interest Expense}}$$

The higher the interest coverage ratio, the lower the company's risk will be of defaulting on interest payments.

Objective 2: Identify and contrast the major characteristics of bonds.

4. A **bond** is a security representing money borrowed from the investing public. The holders of bonds are creditors of the issuing organizations. They are entitled to periodic interest and to the principal of the debt on some specified date. Their claims to a corporation's assets, like the claims of all creditors, have priority over stockholders' claims.

5. When a corporation issues bonds, it enters into a contract, called a **bond indenture,** with the bondholders. It may also give each bondholder a **bond certificate** as evidence of the corporation's debt. A **bond issue** is the total value of bonds issued at one time. Bonds are usually issued with a face value that is some multiple of $1,000. Bond prices are expressed as a percentage of face value; for example, when bonds with a face value of $100,000 are issued at 97, the corporation receives $97,000. A corporation can issue several types of bonds, each having different features.

   a. **Unsecured bonds** (also called *debenture bonds*) are issued on the general credit of the corporation. **Secured bonds** give the bondholders a pledge of certain of the corporation's assets as a guarantee of repayment.

   b. When all the bonds in an issue mature on the same date, they are called **term bonds.** When the bonds in an issue mature on different dates, they are called **serial bonds.**

   c. **Registered bonds** are those for which the corporation maintains a record of bondholders and pays them interest by check on the interest payment date. **Coupon bonds** have detachable coupons stating the amount of interest due and the payment date, which the bondholders remove and present at a bank for collection of the interest due.

Objective 3: Record the issuance of bonds at face value and at a discount or premium.

6. Bonds payable (along with any unamortized discounts or premiums) usually appear in the long-term liabilities section of the balance sheet. However, bonds that will mature within one year and that will be retired by using current assets are classified as current liabilities. Important provisions of the bond indenture are disclosed in the notes to the financial statements.

7. Regardless of the price at which bonds are issued, bondholders are entitled to interest. The formula for calculating interest for a period is as follows:

   Interest = Principal × Rate × Time

8. The **face interest rate** is the rate paid to bondholders based on the face value, or principal, of the bonds. The **market interest rate** (also called the *effective interest rate*) is the rate paid in the market on bonds of similar risk. When the face interest rate equals the market interest rate on the issue date, the corporation will probably receive face value for the bonds.

9. When the face interest rate is less than the market interest rate for similar bonds on the issue date, the bonds will probably sell at a **discount** (less than face value). Unamortized Bond Discount appears on the balance sheet as a contra-liability to Bonds Payable. The difference between the two amounts is the carrying value, or present value, of the bonds. The carrying value increases as the discount is amortized and equals the face value of the bonds at maturity.

10. When the face interest rate is greater than the market interest rate for similar bonds on the issue date, the bonds usually sell at a **premium** (greater than face value). Unamortized Bond Premium is added to Bonds Payable on the balance sheet to produce the carrying value.

11. The costs involved in issuing bonds benefit the entire life of a bond issue. The usual way of treating these costs is to establish a separate account for them and to spread them out over the life of the bonds, often through the amortization of a discount or premium.

Objective 4: Use present values to determine the value of bonds.

12. Theoretically, the value of a bond is equal to the sum of the present values of (a) the periodic interest payments and (b) the single payment of the principal at maturity. The discount rate used is based on the current market rate of interest.

Objective 5: Amortize bond discounts and bond premiums using the straight-line and effective interest methods.

13. When a company issues bonds at a discount or premium, the interest payments it makes do *not* equal the actual total interest cost. Instead, total interest cost equals the interest payments over the life of the bond plus the original discount amount or minus the original premium amount.

14. A discount on bonds payable is considered an interest charge that must be amortized (spread out) over the life of the bond. Amortization is usually recorded on the interest payment dates, using either the straight-line method or the effective interest method.

   a. The **straight-line method** allocates a bond discount equally over each interest period in the life of the bond. The amount to be amortized each period is calculated by dividing the bond discount by the total number of interest payments.

b. The **effective interest method** is more difficult to apply than the straight-line method, but it must be used when the results of the two methods differ significantly. To apply the effective interest method to the amortization of a discount, it is first necessary to determine the market interest rate for similar securities on the issue date. This rate (halved for semi-annual interest) is multiplied by the carrying value of the bonds for each interest period to obtain the bond interest expense to be recorded. The actual interest paid is then subtracted from the recorded bond interest expense to obtain the discount amortization for the period. Because the unamortized discount is now less, the carrying value is greater. The new carrying value is applied to the next period, and the same procedure is repeated.

c. A **zero coupon bond** is a promise to pay a fixed amount at maturity, with no periodic interest payments. Investors' earnings consist of the large discount given when the bond is issued, which the issuing organization then amortizes over the life of the bond.

15. Amortization of a premium acts as an offset against interest paid in determining the interest expense to be recorded.

a. Under the straight-line method, the premium to be amortized in each period equals the bond premium divided by the number of interest payments during the life of the bond.

b. The effective interest method is applied to the amortization of bond premiums in almost exactly the same way as it is applied to the amortization of bond discounts. The only difference is that the amortization for the period is computed by subtracting the bond interest expense recorded from the actual interest paid (rather than by subtracting actual interest paid from the bond interest expense recorded).

Objective 6: Record bonds issued between interest dates and year-end adjustments.

16. When an organization issues bonds between interest payment dates, it collects from investors the interest that has accrued since the last interest payment date. At the end of the first interest period, it reimburses the investors for this amount and pays them the rest of the interest earned during the period.

17. When an accounting period ends between interest payment dates, the accrued interest and the proportionate discount or premium amortization must be recorded.

Supplemental Objective 7: Account for the retirement of bonds and the conversion of bonds into stock.

18. **Callable bonds** give the issuer the right to buy back and retire the bonds at a specified **call price** before the maturity date. The retirement of a bond issue before its maturity date is called **early extinguishment of debt.** A company may decide to retire its callable bonds for a number of reasons—for example, because it wants to restructure its debt to equity ratio or, if the market interest rate drops, because it wants to issue new debt at a lower interest rate. Whenever bonds are called, an entry is needed to eliminate Bonds Payable and any unamortized premium or discount and to record the payment of cash at the call price. In addition, a gain or loss on the retirement of the bonds must be recorded.

19. **Convertible bonds** give the bondholder the option of converting them to the common stock or other securities of the issuing corporation. Because of this feature, the interest rate the corporation pays is usually lower than the rate it pays on other types of bonds. When a bondholder converts his or her bonds into common stock, the company records the common stock at the carrying value of the bonds. The entry eliminates Bonds Payable and any unamortized discount or premium and records common stock and paid-in capital in excess of par value. No gain or loss is recorded.

Supplemental Objective 8: Explain the basic features of mortgages payable, long-term leases, and pensions and other postretirement benefits as long-term liabilities.

20. A **mortgage** is a long-term debt secured by real property. It is usually paid in equal monthly installments. When a payment is made, both Mortgage Payable and Mortgage Interest Expense are debited, and Cash is credited. Each month, the interest portion of the payment decreases, while the principal portion of the payment increases.

21. A lease is a contract that allows a business or individual to use an asset for a specific length of time in return for periodic payments. The parties involved in a lease are the lessor, who owns the lease asset, and the lessee, who pays rent to the lessor for use of the leased asset. A **capital lease**

is a long-term lease in which the risks of ownership lie with the lessee and whose terms resemble those of a purchase on installment. It is, in fact, so much like a purchase that the lessee should record it as an asset (to be depreciated) and a related liability. An **operating lease** is a short-term lease in which the risks of ownership remain with the lessor; each monthly lease payment should be charged to Rent Expense.

22. A **pension plan** is a contract under which a company agrees to pay benefits to its employees after they retire. Benefits to retirees are usually paid out of a **pension fund.** Pension plans are classified as *defined contribution plans* or *defined benefit plans.* **Other postretirement benefits,** such as health care, should be estimated and accrued while the employee is still working (in accordance with the matching rule).

A. (LO 3)   Cash   XX (amount received)
           Bonds Payable   XX (face value)
              Sold bonds at face value

B. (LO 3)   Bond Interest Expense   XX (amount incurred)
           Cash (or Interest Payable)   XX (amount paid or due)
              Paid (or accrued) interest to bondholders

C. (LO 3)   Cash   XX (amount received)
           Unamortized Bond Discount   XX (amount of discount)
           Bonds Payable   XX (face value)
              Sold bonds at a discount

D. (LO 3)   Cash   XX (amount received)
           Unamortized Bond Premium   XX (amount of premium)
           Bonds Payable   XX (face value)
              Sold bonds at a premium

E. (LO 5)   Bond Interest Expense   XX (amount incurred)
           Unamortized Bond Discount   XX (amount amortized)
           Cash (or Interest Payable)   XX (amount paid or due)
              Paid (or accrued) interest to bondholders and
              amortized the discount

F. (LO 5)   Bond Interest Expense   XX (amount incurred)
           Unamortized Bond Premium   XX (amount amortized)
           Cash (or Interest Payable)   XX (amount paid or due)
              Paid (or accrued) interest to bondholders and
              amortized the premium

G. (LO 6)   Cash   XX (amount received)
           Bond Interest Expense   XX (accrued amount)
           Bonds Payable   XX (face value)
               Sold bonds at face value plus accrued interest
              (see entry H)

H. (LO 6)   Bond Interest Expense   XX (six months' amount)
           Cash (or Interest Payable)   XX (amount paid or due)
              Paid (or accrued) semiannual interest on bonds issued
              in entry G

I. (LO 6)   The year-end accrual for bond interest expense is identical
           to entry E for discounts and entry F for premiums, except that
           in both cases Interest Payable is credited instead of Cash.

J. (LO 6)   Bond Interest Expense   XX (amount incurred)
           Interest Payable   XX (amount accrued)
           Unamortized Bond Premium   XX (amount amortized)
           Cash   XX (amount paid)
              Paid semiannual interest including interest
              previously accrued, and amortized the
              premium for the period since the end of
              the fiscal year

K. (SO 7) Bonds Payable .... XX (face value)
          Unamortized Bond Premium .... XX (current credit balance)
          Loss on Retirement of Bonds .... XX (see explanation)
             Cash .... XX (amount paid)
               Retired bonds at a loss (the loss equals the excess of
               the call price over the carrying value)

L. (SO 7) Bonds Payable .... XX (face value)
          Unamortized Bond Premium .... XX (current credit balance)
             Cash .... XX (amount paid)
             Gain on Retirement of Bonds .... XX (see explanation)
               Retired bonds at a gain (the gain equals
               the excess of the carrying value over the
               call price)

M. (SO 7) Bonds Payable .... XX (face value)
          Unamortized Bond Premium .... XX (current credit balance)
             Common Stock .... XX (par value)
             Paid-in Capital in Excess of Par Value, Common ... XX (excess of par)
               Converted bonds payable into common stock
               (Note: No gain or loss is recorded; also, when
               appropriate, an unamortized bond discount would
               be credited in the entry.)

N. (SO 8) Mortgage Payable .... XX (principal)
          Mortgage Interest Expense .... XX (interest)
             Cash .... XX (monthly payment)
               Made monthly mortgage payment

O. (SO 8) Capital Lease Equipment .... XX (present value)
             Capital Lease Obligations .... XX (present value)
               To record capital lease

P. (SO 8) Depreciation Expense, Capital Lease Equipment ... XX (amount allocated)
             Accumulated Depreciation, Capital Lease Equipment ... XX (amount allocated)
               To record depreciation expense on capital lease

Q. (SO 8) Interest Expense .... XX (amount incurred)
          Capital Lease Obligations .... XX (amount reduced)
             Cash .... XX (amount paid)
               Made payment on capital lease

                                                       Chapter 11

SELF-TEST

Test your knowledge of the chapter by choosing the best answer for each item below.

1. It is advantageous for a company to use financial leverage when
   a. its investments in assets earn more than the interest it pays to finance the investments.
   b. it wants to promote its serial bonds.
   c. its debt to equity ratio is very high.
   d. it needs to conserve cash.

2. A bond indenture is
   a. a bond on which interest is past due.
   b. a bond secured by corporate assets.
   c. an agreement between the issuing corporation and the bondholders.
   d. an unsecured bond.

3. If the market interest rate is lower than the face interest rate on the date on which bonds are issued, the bonds will
   a. sell at a discount.
   b. sell at a premium.
   c. sell at face value.
   d. not sell until the face interest rate is adjusted.

4. The current value of a bond can be determined by calculating the present value of the
   a. face value of the bond.
   b. interest payments.
   c. interest payments plus any discount or minus any premium.
   d. interest payments and of the single payment of principal at maturity.

5. When the straight-line method is used to amortize a bond discount, the interest expense for an interest period is calculated by
   a. deducting the amount of discount amortized for the period from the amount of cash paid for interest during the period.
   b. adding the amount of discount amortized for the period to the amount of cash paid for interest during the period.
   c. multiplying the face value of the bonds by the face interest rate.
   d. multiplying the carrying value of the bonds by the market interest rate.

6. The total interest cost on a 9 percent, ten-year, $1,000 bond that is issued at 95 is
   a. $50.
   b. $140.
   c. $900.
   d. $950.

7. Foley Corporation issued a ten-year, 10 percent bond payable in 20x5 at a premium. During 20x6, the corporation's accountant failed to amortize any of the bond premium. The omission of the premium amortization
   a. does not affect the net income reported for 20x6.
   b. causes the net income for 20x6 to be overstated.
   c. causes the net income for 20x6 to be understated.
   d. causes retained earnings at the end of 20x6 to be overstated.

8. Simms Corporation has authorized a bond issue with interest payment dates of January 1 and July 1. If the bonds are sold at the face amount on March 1, the cash Simms receives is equal to the face amount of the bonds
   a. plus the interest accrued from March 1 to July 1.
   b. plus the interest accrued from January 1 to March 1.
   c. minus the interest accrued from March 1 to July 1.
   d. minus the interest accrued from January 1 to March 1.

9. Bonds that allow the holders to exchange them for other securities of the issuing corporation are called
   a. secured bonds.
   b. callable bonds.
   c. debenture bonds.
   d. convertible bonds.

10. Which of the following is most likely a capital lease?
    a. A five-year lease on a new building
    b. A two-year lease on a truck with an option to renew for one more year
    c. A five-year lease on a computer with an option to buy it for a small amount at the end of the lease
    d. A monthly lease on a building that can be canceled with ninety days' notice

TESTING YOUR KNOWLEDGE

Matching*

Match each term with its definition by writing the appropriate letter in the blank.

_____ **1.** Bonds

_____ **2.** Bond indenture

_____ **3.** Secured bonds

_____ **4.** Debentures

_____ **5.** Term bonds

_____ **6.** Serial bonds

_____ **7.** Registered bonds

_____ **8.** Coupon bonds

_____ **9.** Callable bonds

_____ **10.** Bond discount

_____ **11.** Bond premium

_____ **12.** Effective interest method

_____ **13.** Capital lease

_____ **14.** Operating lease

_____ **15.** Convertible bonds

_____ **16.** Pension plan

_____ **17.** Pension fund

_____ **18.** Bond certificate

_____ **19.** Early extinguishment of debt

_____ **20.** Zero coupon bonds

_____ **21.** Financial leverage (trading on the equity)

a. Unsecured bonds

b. A lease that amounts to a purchase

c. Bonds that the issuing corporation can retire before their maturity date

d. A method of borrowing that can increase stockholders' earnings

e. The amount by which the face value of a bond exceeds its issue price

f. Bonds with detachable forms that are redeemed for interest

g. A short-term lease that is recorded with debits to Rent Expense

h. Proof of a company's debt to a bondholder

i. Long-term debt instruments

j. Bonds whose owners receive interest by check directly from the company

k. The retirement of a bond issue before its maturity date

l. The amortization method based on carrying value

m. The amount by which the issue price of a bond exceeds its face value

n. A contract under which a company agrees to pay benefits to its employees after they retire

o. Bonds that mature on the same date

p. The source of benefits paid to retirees

q. Bonds backed by certain corporate assets

r. Bonds that may be exchanged for common stock

s. Bonds that mature in installments

t. Bonds that pay no periodic interest but that are issued at a large discount

u. A contract between bondholders and the issuing corporation

---

*Note to student: The matching quiz might be completed more efficiently by starting with the definition and searching for the corresponding term.

Short Answer

Use the lines provided to answer each item.

1. Distinguish between *debenture* and *indenture* as these terms apply to bonds.

   _____

   _____

   _____

2. Under what circumstances would a bond issue be likely to sell at a premium?

   _____

   _____

   _____

   _____

3. What is the formula for computing interest for a time period?

   _____

   _____

4. When valuing a bond, what two components are added together to determine the present value of the bond?

   _____

   _____

   _____

5. Describe three advantages of issuing long-term debt rather than common stock.

   _____

   _____

   _____

   _____

   _____

   _____

   _____

True-False

Circle T if the statement is true, F if it is false. Provide explanations for the false answers, using the blank lines at the end of the section.

T F **1.** Bondholders are owners of a corporation.

T F **2.** Financial leverage is also known as trading on equity.

T F **3.** Bond interest can be paid only when declared by the board of directors.

T F **4.** Bonds with a lower interest rate than the market rate for similar bonds will probably sell at a discount.

T F **5.** When a bond premium is amortized, the bond interest expense recorded is greater than the cash paid.

T F **6.** When the effective interest method is used to amortize a bond discount, the amount amortized increases each year.

T F **7.** When bonds are issued between interest dates, Bond Interest Expense is debited for interest accrued since the last interest date.

T F **8.** As a bond premium is amortized, the carrying value of bonds payable decreases.

T F **9.** When bonds are issued at a discount, the total interest cost to the issuing corporation equals the interest payments minus the bond discount.

T F **10.** When bonds are retired, all of the premium or discount associated with the bonds must be canceled.

T F **11.** When the effective interest method is used to amortize a premium on bonds payable, the premium amortized decreases each year.

T F **12.** When bonds are issued at a premium, the total interest cost to the issuing corporation equals the interest payments minus the bond premium.

T F **13.** For operating leases, assets should be recorded at the present value of future lease payments.

T F **14.** Pension expense is usually difficult to measure because it is based on estimates of many factors, such as employees' life expectancy and employee turnover.

T F **15.** When bonds are converted into stock, a gain or loss should be recorded.

T F **16.** Bond issue costs should be amortized over the life of the bonds.

T F **17.** Postretirement health care benefits should be expensed while the employee is still working.

T F **18.** A disadvantage of issuing long-term debt is the increased risk of default.

T F **19.** A low interest coverage ratio indicates a low risk of default on interest payments.

Multiple Choice

Circle the letter of the best answer.

1. Assume that $900,000 of 5 percent bonds are issued at face value two months before the next semiannual interest payment date. Which of the following statements correctly describes the related journal entry?
   a. Cash is debited for $900,000.
   b. Cash is debited for $907,500.
   c. Bond Interest Expense is credited for $7,500.
   d. Bond Interest Expense is credited for $15,000.

2. As a mortgage is paid off, the
   a. principal portion of a fixed payment increases.
   b. interest portion of a fixed payment increases.
   c. principal and interest portions do not change.
   d. monthly payments increase.

3. Unamortized Bond Premium is presented on the balance sheet as
   a. a long-term asset.
   b. a stockholders' equity account.
   c. a deduction from Bonds Payable.
   d. an addition to Bonds Payable.

4. When the interest dates on a bond issue are May 1 and November 1, the adjusting entry to record bond interest expense on December 31 might include a
   a. debit to Interest Payable.
   b. credit to Cash.
   c. credit to Unamortized Bond Discount.
   d. credit to Bond Interest Expense.

5. Under the effective interest method, as a discount is amortized each period, the
   a. amount amortized decreases.
   b. interest expense recorded increases.
   c. interest paid to bondholders increases.
   d. bonds' carrying value decreases.

6. Which of the following would most likely be considered an operating lease?
   a. A 6-year lease on equipment with an option to renew for another 6 years
   b. A 5-year lease on machinery, which the lessor can cancel at the end of the lease
   c. A 40-year lease on a building, which covers the building's useful life
   d. A 7-year lease on a company vehicle with an option to buy the vehicle for $1 at the end of the lease

7. A $200,000 bond issue with a carrying value of $195,000 is called at 102 and retired. Which of the following statements about the journal entry for this transaction is true?
   a. A gain of $5,000 is recorded.
   b. A loss of $4,000 is recorded.
   c. A loss of $9,000 is recorded.
   d. No gain or loss is recorded.

8. A company has $600,000 in bonds payable with an unamortized premium of $12,000. If one-third of the bonds are converted to common stock, the carrying value of the bonds payable will decrease by
   a. $196,000.
   b. $200,000.
   c. $204,000.
   d. $208,000.

APPLYING YOUR KNOWLEDGE

Exercises

1. A corporation issues $600,000 of 7 percent, 10-year bonds at 98½ on one of its semiannual interest dates. Assuming straight-line amortization, answer each of the following questions:

   a. What is the amount of the bond discount? $_____

   b. How much interest is paid on the next interest date? $_____

   c. How much bond interest expense is recorded on the next interest date? $_____

   d. After three years, what is the carrying value of the bonds? $_____

2. A corporation issues $500,000 of 7 percent, 20-year bonds at 110. Interest is paid semiannually, and the effective interest method is used for amor-tization. Assume that the market rate for similar investments is 6 percent and that the bonds are issued on an interest date.

   a. What amount was received for the bonds? $_____

   b. How much interest is paid each interest period? $_____

   c. How much bond interest expense is recorded on the first interest date? $_____

   d. How much of the premium is amortized on the first interest date? $_____

   e. What is the carrying value of the bonds after the first interest date? $_____

3. A corporation issued $600,000 of 8 percent, 10-year bonds at 106. Calculate the total interest cost.

Crossword Puzzle
for Chapters 10 and 11

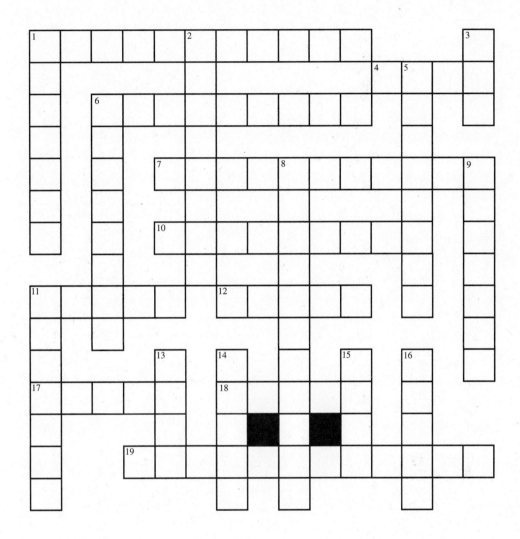

ACROSS

1. Arrangement for retirement income (2 words)
4. Estimated useful _____
6. Registered symbol or brand name
7. Type of note settled in a series of payments
10. Exclusive right to a market
11. Buys back bonds before maturity
12. Residual _____
17. Sale of bonds or stock
18. Use another's property for a fee
19. Bonds, e.g. (3 words, first 2 hyphenated)

DOWN

1. Bond _____ (opposite of bond discount)
2. Category of repairs
3. _____ present value
5. _____ coverage ratio
6. Possessing physical substance
8. Type of depreciation method
9. Exchange (2 words)
11. _____ expenditure
13. _____ coupon bonds
14. Long-term asset account (abbr.)
15. Bonds with one maturity date
16. Older term for long-term assets

CHAPTER 12 CONTRIBUTED CAPITAL

REVIEWING THE CHAPTER

Objective 1: Identify and explain the management issues related to contributed capital.

1. A **corporation** is a legal entity, separate from its owners, that is authorized by the state to conduct business. The management of contributed capital is critical to the financing of a corporation. It includes the issues of forming a corporation, managing under the corporate form of business, using equity financing, determining dividend policies, evaluating performance using return on equity, and using stock options as compensation.

2. Before a corporation can do business, it must apply for and receive a charter from the state. The application contains the **articles of incorporation,** which describe the basic purpose and structure of the proposed corporation and which, if approved, become part of the corporate charter.

   a. A corporation raises beginning capital by issuing shares of stock. Each **share of stock** represents a unit of ownership in the corporation.

   b. The owners of a corporation's common stock elect a board of directors. The board sets corporate policies, appoints the corporation's officers, and has the sole authority to declare **dividends,** which are distributions of resources, generally in the form of cash, to the stockholders. The board also authorizes contracts, decides on executive salaries, and arranges major loans with banks. In addition, it often appoints an **audit committee,** which, to ensure the board's objectivity in judging management's performance, usually includes directors of other companies. One of the audit committee's functions is to engage independent auditors and review their work.

   c. A corporation's officers are responsible for carrying out the policies set by the board, running the business, and making at least one comprehensive annual report on the corporation's financial position and the results of operations.

3. Because of the ease with which a corporation can raise large amounts of capital, it is the dominant form of business in the United States. The corporation has several advantages over the sole proprietorship and partnership. In addition to its ability to raise capital, it is a separate legal entity, offers its owners limited liability, lacks the mutual agency that characterizes a partnership, has a continuous life, and allows for centralized authority and responsibility, as well as for professional management. It is also easy to transfer ownership in a corporation. However, a corporation has several disadvantages when compared with a sole proprietorship or partnership. It is subject to greater government regulation and to **double taxation** (i.e., the corporation's income is subject to income taxes, and its stockholders are taxed on any dividends), and the owners' limited liability can limit the amount a small corporation can borrow. Moreover, separation of ownership and control may allow management to make harmful decisions.

4. Ownership in a corporation is evidenced by a document called a **stock certificate,** which shows the

number of shares the stockholder owns. A stockholder sells stock by endorsing the stock certificate and sending it to the corporation's secretary. The secretary—or in many instances, an independent registrar or transfer agent—is responsible not only for transferring the stock, but also for maintaining stockholders' records, preparing a list of stockholders for stockholders' meetings, and paying dividends. The maximum number of shares a corporation is allowed to issue is called **authorized stock** and is specified in the corporate charter. **Par value** (also specified in the corporate charter) is the legal capital of a share of stock. **Legal capital** equals the number of shares issued times the par value; it is the minimum amount that can be reported as contributed capital.

a. Corporations often hire an **underwriter,** an intermediary between the corporation and the investing public, to help in their **initial public offering (IPO)** of capital stock. A corporation in this instance is said to be "going public." The underwriter guarantees the sale of the stock and charges a fee for this service.

b. The costs of forming a corporation are called **start-up and organization costs.** Incurred before a corporation starts operations, they include state incorporation fees, attorneys' fees, accountants' fees, and the cost of printing stock certificates. Such costs are expensed when incurred.

5. Although a board of directors has the sole authority to declare dividends, senior managers, who usually serve on the board, influence dividend policies. Among the factors that affect the decision to pay dividends are the extent of profitable operations, the dividend policy that prevails among other companies in the same industry, the expected volatility of earnings, and the actual amount of cash available for dividend payments. Investors evaluate the amount of the dividends they receive by looking at the **dividends yield,** which is calculated as follows:

$$\frac{\text{Dividends per Share}}{\text{Market Price per Share}}$$

Expressed as a percentage, the dividends yield measures the return, in terms of dividends, per share of stock. The **price/earnings (P/E) ratio,** on the other hand, measures investors' confidence in a company's future. The P/E ratio is calculated as follows:

$$\frac{\text{Market Price per Share}}{\text{Earnings per Share}}$$

A P/E ratio of 15 times, for example, means that investors are confident enough in a company to pay $15 per share for every dollar of earnings accruing to one share.

6. Management's decisions about a variety of matters matters, including the issuance of stock, affect **return on equity.** Return on equity is therefore commonly used as a measure of management's performance. Expressed as a percentage, it is calculated as follows:

$$\frac{\text{Net Income}}{\text{Average Stockholders' Equity}}$$

7. A **stock option plan** allows a corporation's employees to purchase a certain quantity of the corporation's stock at a certain price at a certain time. Usually, stock options are offered only to management personnel. On the date on which the options are granted, their fair value must be estimated, and the amount in excess of the option price must either be recorded as compensation expense over the grant period or reported in the notes to the financial statements. Most companies choose the latter approach, which requires that they also disclose how the failure to record compensation expense on the income statement affects income and earnings per share.

Objective 2: Identify the components of stockholders' equity.

8. On a corporation's balance sheet, the owners' claims to the business are called *stockholders' equity.* The stockholders' equity section is divided into two parts: contributed capital (the stockholders' investments in the corporation) and retained earnings (earnings that have remained in the business). If a corporation issues only one type of stock, it is called **common stock.** A second type of stock, called **preferred stock,** can also be issued. Because common stockholders' claims to corporate assets rank behind the claims of creditors and preferred stockholders in the case of liquidation, common stock is considered a corporation's **residual equity. Issued stock** consists of shares that a corporation has sold or otherwise transferred to stockholders. **Outstanding stock** consists of issued stock that is still in circulation. Treasury stock consists of shares bought back and held by the issuing corporation.

Objective 3: Account for cash dividends.

9. A corporation's board of directors decides on the timing of dividend payments. The **date of declaration** is the date on which the board formally

declares a dividend, specifying that the owners of the stock on the **date of record** will receive their dividends on the **date of payment.** After the date of record, the stock is said to be **ex-dividend** (without dividend rights). The liability for payment of cash dividends arises on the date of declaration. The declaration is recorded with a debit to Cash Dividends Declared and a credit to Cash Dividends Payable. No journal entry is made on the date of record. On the date of payment, Cash Dividends Payable is debited, and Cash is credited. The Cash Dividends Declared account is closed to Retained Earnings at the end of the accounting period. A **liquidating dividend** is a dividend that exceeds retained earnings. It represents a return of contributed capital to the stockholders and is usually issued when a corporation is going out of business or reducing its operations.

Objective 4: Identify the characteristics of preferred stock, including the effect on distribution of dividends.

10. Each share of preferred stock entitles its owner to a dividend each year. Although holders of preferred stock usually lack the voting rights that common stockholders enjoy, they have preference over common stockholders in terms of the receipt of dividends; that is, when a board of directors declares dividends, holders of preferred stock must receive a certain amount of dividends before common stockholders receive anything. The amount they receive is a specific dollar amount or a percentage of the par value of the preferred shares. If a board of directors fails to declare an annual dividend to preferred stockholders, the consequences vary according to the terms under which the shares were issued. If the stock is **cumulative preferred stock**, the unpaid amount is carried over to the next year. Unpaid back dividends are called **dividends in arrears.** They become a liability only when the board declares a dividend, and they should then be disclosed in the financial statements or in a note to the financial statements. If the stock is **noncumulative preferred stock,** the corporation is under no obligation to make up the missed dividends.

11. In addition to having preference over common stockholders in terms of receipt of dividends, holders of preferred stock have preference in terms of assets when a corporation is liquidated. In this case, preferred stockholders must receive the par value of their shares or a larger stated liquidation per share before common stockholders receive any share of the corporation's assets.

12. An owner of **convertible preferred stock** has the option of exchanging each share of preferred stock for a specified number of shares of common stock.

13. Most preferred stock is **callable preferred stock,** which means that the corporation has the right to buy the stock back at a specified price, which is usually higher than the par value of the stock. If the stock is nonconvertible, the holder must surrender it to the corporation when asked to do so. If it is convertible preferred stock, the holder has the option of converting it to common stock.

Objective 5: Account for the issuance of stock for cash and other assets.

14. Capital stock may or may not have a par value, depending on the specifications in the corporate charter. When par value stock is issued, the Capital Stock account is credited for the legal capital (par value), and any excess is recorded as Paid-in Capital in Excess of Par Value. The entire amount is labeled total contributed capital in the stockholders' equity section of the balance sheet. On the rare occasions that stock is issued at a discount (less than par value), Discount on Capital Stock is debited.

15. **No-par stock** is stock for which a par value has not been established. It can be issued with or without a **stated value.** The stated value can be any value assigned by the board of directors unless state law specifies a minimum amount. The total stated value is recorded in the Capital Stock account. Any amount received in excess of the stated value is part of the corporation's contributed capital; it is recorded as Paid-in Capital in Excess of Stated Value. When a corporation issues no-par stock without a stated value, the entire amount received is credited to Capital Stock. Unless state law specifies a different amount, that amount is designated as legal capital, which can be withdrawn only if the corporation is being liquidated.

16. Stock is sometimes issued in exchange for noncash assets or for services received. This kind of transaction should be recorded at the fair market value of the stock. If the stock's fair market value cannot be determined, the fair market value of the assets or services received should be used.

Objective 6: Account for treasury stock.

17. **Treasury stock** is stock that the issuing corporation has reacquired (i.e., the stock is issued but is no longer outstanding). Companies may purchase their own stock for several reasons: to distribute it

to employees through stock option plans, to maintain a favorable market for the stock, to increase earnings per share, to use in purchasing other companies, or to prevent a hostile takeover by another company. Treasury stock can be held indefinitely, reissued, or retired. It has no rights until it is reissued. It appears as the last item in the stockholders' equity section of the balance sheet as a deduction from the total of contributed capital and retained earnings.

18. When treasury stock is reacquired, its account is debited for the purchase cost, and Cash is credited. The par value, stated value, or original issue price of the stock is ignored.

19. Treasury stock may be reissued at the purchase cost, above that cost, or below it. When cash received from a reissue exceeds the purchase cost, the difference is credited to Paid-in Capital, Treasury Stock. When cash received is less than the purchase cost, the difference is debited to Paid-in Capital, Treasury Stock. If Paid-In Capital, Treasury Stock does not exist or if the balance in that account is insufficient to cover the difference, Retained Earnings should be debited. In no case should a gain or loss on the reissuance of treasury stock be recorded.

20. When treasury stock is retired, all the contributed capital associated with the retired shares must be removed from the accounts. If less was paid to reacquire the stock than was contributed originally, the difference is credited to Paid-in Capital, Retirement of Stock. If more was paid, the difference is debited to Retained Earnings.

A. (LO 3)   Cash Dividends Declared   XX (amount declared)
            Cash Dividends Payable   XX (amount to be paid)
                Declared cash dividend to common stockholders

B. (LO 3)   Cash Dividends Payable   XX (amount paid)
            Cash   XX (amount paid)
                Paid cash dividends declared in Entry A

C. (LO 5)   Cash   XX (amount invested)
            Common Stock   XX (legal capital amount)
                Issued par value common stock for par value

D. (LO 5)   Cash   XX (amount invested)
            Common Stock   XX (legal capital amount)
            Paid-in Capital in Excess of Par Value, Common   XX (excess of par value)
                Issued par value common stock for amount in excess
                of par value

E. (LO 5)   Cash   XX (amount invested)
            Common Stock   XX (legal capital amount)
                Issued no-par common stock (no stated value
                established)

F. (LO 5)   Cash   XX (amount invested)
             Common Stock   XX (legal capital amount)
            Paid-in Capital in Excess of Stated Value, Common   XX (excess of stated value)
                Issued no-par common stock with stated value for
                amount in excess of stated value

G. (LO 5)   Start-up and Organization Expense   XX (fair market value of services)
            Common Stock   XX (par value)
            Paid-in Capital in Excess of Par Value, Common   XX (excess of par value)
                Issued par value common stock for incorporation
                services

H. (LO 5)   Land   XX (fair market value of stock)
            Common Stock   XX (par value)
            Paid-in Capital in Excess of Par Value, Common   XX (excess of par value)
                Issued par value common stock with a market value
                in excess of par value for a piece of land

I. (LO 6)   Treasury Stock, Common   XX (cost)
            Cash   XX (amount paid)
                 Acquired shares of the company's common stock

J. (LO 6)   Cash   XX (amount received)
            Treasury Stock, Common   XX (cost)
                Reissued shares of treasury stock at cost

K. (LO 6) Cash   XX (amount received)
               Treasury Stock, Common   XX (cost)
               Paid-in Capital, Treasury Stock   XX ("gain")
                   Sold shares of treasury stock at amount above cost

L. (LO 6) Cash   XX (amount received)
               Paid-in Capital, Treasury Stock   XX ("loss")
               Retained Earnings (only if needed)   XX ("loss")
                   Treasury Stock, Common   XX (cost)
                   Sold shares of treasury stock at amount below cost

M. (LO 6) Common Stock   XX (par value)
               Paid-in Capital in Excess of Par Value, Common XX (excess of par value)
               Retained Earnings (only if needed)   XX (premium paid)
                   Treasury Stock, Common   XX (cost)
                   Retired treasury stock; cost exceeded original
                   investment amount

N. (LO 6) If the treasury stock in Entry M were retired for an
               amount less than the original investment, then instead of
               Retained Earnings being debited for the excess paid,
               Paid-in Capital, Retirement of Stock would be credited
               for the difference.

SELF-TEST

Test your knowledge of the chapter by choosing the best answer for each item below.

1. One disadvantage of the corporate form of business is
   a. government regulation.
   b. centralized authority and responsibility.
   c. the corporation's status as a separate legal entity.
   d. continuous existence.

2. The start-up and organization costs of a corporation should
   a. be recorded and maintained as an intangible asset for the life of the corporation.
   b. be recorded as an intangible asset and amortized over a reasonable length of time.
   c. be written off as an expense when incurred.
   d. not be incurred before the state grants the corporation its charter.

3. All of the following normally are found in the stockholders' equity section of a corporate balance sheet *except*
   a. paid-in capital in excess of par value.
   b. retained earnings.
   c. cash dividends payable.
   d. common stock.

4. The board of directors of the Green Corporation declared a cash dividend on January 18, 20x8, to be paid on February 18, 20x8, to shareholders holding stock on February 2, 20x8. February 2, 20x8, is the
   a. date of declaration.
   b. date of record.
   c. payment date.
   d. ex-dividend date.

5. The journal entry to record the declaration of a cash dividend
   a. reduces assets.
   b. increases liabilities.
   c. increases total stockholders' equity.
   d. does not affect total stockholders' equity.

6. Dividends in arrears are dividends on
   a. noncumulative preferred stock that have not been declared for a specific period.
   b. cumulative preferred stock that have been declared but not paid.
   c. cumulative preferred stock that have not been declared for a specific period.
   d. common stock that can never be declared.

7. The par value of common stock represents the
   a. amount entered in a corporation's Common Stock account when the shares are issued.
   b. exact amount a corporation receives when it issues the stock.
   c. liquidation value of the stock.
   d. stock's market value.

8. The Paid-in Capital in Excess of Stated Value account is used when
   a. the par value of capital stock is greater than the stated value.
   b. capital stock is sold at an amount greater than stated value.
   c. the market value of the stock rises above its stated value.
   d. the number of shares issued exceeds the stock's stated value.

9. Which of the following is properly deducted from stockholders' equity?
   a. Treasury stock
   b. Retained earnings
   c. Dividends in arrears
   d. Paid-in capital in excess of par value

10. A plan under which employees are allowed to purchase shares of stock in a company at a specified price is called a stock
    a. option plan.
    b. subscription plan.
    c. dividend plan.
    d. compensation plan.

TESTING YOUR KNOWLEDGE

Matching*

Match each term with its definition by writing the appropriate letter in the blank.

_____ 1. Corporation

_____ 2. Start-up and organization costs

_____ 3. Issued stock

_____ 4. Authorized stock

_____ 5. Outstanding stock

_____ 6. Common stock

_____ 7. Preferred stock

_____ 8. Dividends in arrears

_____ 9. Par value

_____ 10. No-par stock

_____ 11. Stated value

_____ 12. Treasury stock

_____ 13. Ex-dividend

_____ 14. Liquidating dividend

_____ 15. Convertible preferred stock

_____ 16. Callable preferred stock

_____ 17. Cumulative preferred stock

_____ 18. Stock option plan

_____ 19. Stock certificate

_____ 20. Residual equity

a. Unpaid back dividends

b. The common stock of a corporation

c. Without dividend rights

d. The amount of legal capital of a share of no-par stock

e. Stock currently held by stockholders

f. The dominant form of business in the United States

g. The type of stock whose holders have prior claim to dividends over common stockholders

h. Stock that the issuing corporation has reacquired

i. Stock whose unpaid dividends carry over to future years

j. Proof of ownership in a corporation

k. Expenditures necessary to form a corporation

l. The maximum amount of stock that a corporation may issue

m. The name of the stock when only one type of stock is issued

n. Stock that may or may not have a stated value

o. The legal value of a share of stock

p. Stock that has been sold to stockholders and may or may not have been bought back by the corporation

q. Stock that may be bought back at the option of the issuing corporation

r. An agreement whereby a corporation allows certain employees to purchase its stock at a fixed price

s. The return of contributed capital to a corporation's stockholders

t. Preferred stock that the holder may exchange for common stock

---

Note to student: The matching quiz might be completed more efficiently by starting with the definition and searching for the corresponding term.

Short Answer

Use the lines provided to answer each item.

1. List eight advantages of the corporate form of business.

   _____

   _____

   _____

   _____

   _____

   _____

   _____

   _____

2. List four disadvantages of the corporate form of business.

   _____

   _____

   _____

   _____

3. Name the two major parts of the stockholders' equity section of a balance sheet.

   _____

   _____

4. Under what two circumstances are preferred shareholders given preference over common shareholders?

   _____

   _____

5. Under what circumstance would a corporation have more shares of stock issued than outstanding?

   _____

   _____

   _____

6. What is the difference between treasury stock and unissued stock?

   _____

   _____

   _____

Circle T if the statement is true, F if it is false. Provide explanations for the false answers, using the blank lines below.

T F **1.** Corporate earnings are taxed twice: once as corporate income and once as stockholders' income from dividend payments.

T F **2.** The concept of legal capital was designed to protect a corporation's stockholders.

T F **3.** Creditors cannot attach the personal assets of a corporation's stockholders.

T F **4.** Start-up and organization costs should be charged as expenses in the year the corporation is formed.

T F **5.** Contributed capital consists of capital stock plus paid-in capital in excess of par (stated) value.

T F **6.** A transfer agent keeps records of stock transactions.

T F **7.** Preferred stock cannot be both convertible and cumulative.

T F **8.** Dividends in arrears do not exist when preferred stock is noncumulative.

T F **9.** The worth of a share of stock can be measured by its par value.

T F **10.** The purchase of treasury stock reduces total assets and total stockholders' equity.

T F **11.** Preferred stockholders are guaranteed annual dividends; common stockholders are not.

T F **12.** Preferred stock is considered the residual equity of a corporation.

T F **13.** The amount of compensation in connection with a stock option plan is measured on the date the option is exercised.

T F **14.** On the date a dividend is paid, total assets and total stockholders' equity decrease.

T F **15.** Dividends in arrears should always appear as a liability on the balance sheet.

T F **16.** Treasury Stock is listed on the balance sheet as an asset.

T F **17.** When corporations initially sell their stock to the public, they often engage the services of an underwriter.

T F **18.** When treasury stock is sold at more than its cost, Gain on Sale of Treasury Stock is credited.

T F **19.** The higher the market price per share of stock, the lower the dividends yield is.

T F **20.** A corporation's purchase of treasury stock will decrease its return on equity.

T F **21.** The higher the price/earnings ratio, the higher investors' confidence in a firm's future is.

Multiple Choice

Circle the letter of the best answer.

1. When treasury stock is reissued below cost, all of the following may be true *except*
   a. Retained Earnings is debited.
   b. Treasury Stock is credited.
   c. Paid-in Capital, Treasury Stock is debited.
   d. Loss on Reissue of Treasury Stock is debited.

2. The purchase of treasury stock does *not* affect
   a. the amount of stock outstanding.
   b. the amount of stock issued.
   c. total assets.
   d. total stockholders' equity.

3. Which of the following statements is true?
   a. Outstanding shares plus issued shares equal authorized shares.
   b. Unissued shares plus outstanding shares equal authorized shares.
   c. Authorized shares minus unissued shares equal issued shares.
   d. Unissued shares minus issued shares equal outstanding shares.

4. Rosen Corporation has outstanding 20,000 shares of $10 par value common stock and 1,000 shares of $100 par value, 7 percent noncumulative preferred stock. Last year, the company paid no dividends; this year, it paid $40,000 in dividends. What portion of this $40,000 should common stockholders receive?
   a. $0
   b. $2,800
   c. $26,000
   d. $33,000

5. Which of the following is *not* a characteristic of corporations?
   a. Separation of ownership and management
   b. Ease of transfer of ownership
   c. Double taxation
   d. Unlimited liability of stockholders

6. On which of the following dates is a journal entry made?
   a. Date of record
   b. Date of payment
   c. Date of declaration
   d. Both b and c

7. Stock is said to be "ex-dividend" after
   a. it has been sold to another party.
   b. the date of record
   c. the date of payment.
   d. the date of declaration.

8. When callable preferred stock is called and surrendered to a corporation, the stockholder is *not* entitled to
   a. a call premium.
   b. the par value of the stock.
   c. any dividends in arrears.
   d. the market value of the stock.

APPLYING YOUR KNOWLEDGE

Exercises

1. In the journal provided below, prepare entries for
   the following transactions:

   Jan. 1 Paid $8,000 in legal and incorporation fees to
   form EHJ Corporation.

   Feb. 9 Issued 5,000 shares of $100 par value common stock at $115 per share.

   Apr. 12 Exchanged 2,000 shares of 4 percent, no-par preferred stock, which had a stated value of $100 per share, for a building with a market value of $240,000. The market value of the stock cannot be determined.

   June 23 Declared a $4 per share dividend on the preferred stock, to be paid on July 8. The date of record is July 1.

   July 8 Paid the dividend declared on June 23.

		General Journal		
Date		**Description**	**Debit**	**Credit**

2. Davis Corporation began operations on August 10, 20x5, by issuing 50,000 shares of $10 par value common stock at $50 per share. As of January 1, 20x6, its capital structure was the same. During January 20x6, Davis Corporation engaged in the transactions described below. Prepare the proper entry for each transaction in the journal that follows. In all cases, assume sufficient cash and retained earnings.

Jan. 12 Purchased 5,000 shares of stock from its stockholders at $60 per share.

20 Reissued 2,000 shares of treasury stock at $65 per share.

27 Reissued another 2,000 shares of treasury stock at $58 per share.

31 Retired the remaining 1,000 treasury shares.

3. Grainger Corporation paid no dividends in its first two years of operations. In its third year, it paid $51,000 in dividends. In all three years, it has had outstanding 5,000 shares of $10 par value common stock and 1,000 shares of 6 percent, $100 par value cumulative preferred stock. How much of the $51,000 in dividends goes to

a. preferred stockholders? $ _____

b. common stockholders? $ _____

4. Assume the same facts as in Exercise **3** except that Grainger's preferred stock is *noncumulative*. How much of the $51,000 in dividends goes to

a. preferred stockholders? $ _____

b. common stockholders? $ _____

General Journal				
Date		**Description**	**Debit**	**Credit**

CHAPTER 13 THE CORPORATE INCOME STATEMENT AND THE STATEMENT OF STOCKHOLDERS' EQUITY

REVIEWING THE CHAPTER

Objective 1: Prepare a corporate income statement and identify the issues related to evaluating the quality of earnings.

1. Corporate financial statements should report **comprehensive income**—that is, the change in a company's equity from sources other than stockholders during an accounting period. Comprehensive income includes net income, changes in unrealized investment gains and losses, and other items affecting equity. Although sometimes reported in a separate statement or in the income statement, comprehensive income is most often reported in the statement of stockholders' equity.

2. The most commonly used predictors of a company's performance are expected changes in earnings per share and expected return on equity. Net income is a key component of both measures.

3. Net income or loss for a period includes all revenues, expenses, gains, and losses, with the exception of prior period adjustments. A corporate income statement may therefore contain many line items and subtotals. On the income statement of a corporation that has both continuing and discontinued operations, the operating income section is called **income from continuing operations.** This section, which includes revenues, costs and expenses, gains and losses on the sale of assets, write-downs of assets, and restructurings, is followed by a section on income taxes. Appearing below that are nonoperating items, such as discontinued operations, extraordinary gains and

losses, and the cumulative effect of a change in accounting principle. Earnings per share data appear at the bottom of the statement.

4. Because net income is so important in measuring a company's prospects, it is equally important to evaluate the quality of the net income figure, or the **quality of earnings.** The quality of earnings refers to the substance of earnings and their sustainability into future accounting periods. It is affected by the accounting methods and estimates that management chooses and by the gains and losses, write-downs and restructurings, and nature of the nonoperating items reported on the income statement. Management also has choices about the content and positioning of these income-statement categories.

5. The different estimates and methods that management can choose for dealing with such matters as uncollectible accounts, inventory, and depreciation produce different net income figures. In general, an accounting method or estimate that produces a lower, or more conservative, figure produces a more reliable quality of earnings. Management's choices about how nonoperating and nonrecurring items (discontinued operations, extraordinary gains and losses, and the effects of accounting changes) are reported on the income statement also affect the "bottom line." Financial analysts should therefore look beyond the net income figure to the notes to the financial statements, where generally accepted accounting principles require full disclosure of the significant

accounting methods used in preparing the statements and any changes in those methods.

6. Although gains or losses on the sale of assets appear in the operating section of the income statement, they usually represent one-time events. They are not sustainable, ongoing operations, and management often has some choice as to their timing. Analysts should therefore ignore them when considering operating income.

7. A **write-down** (also known as a *write-off*) is recorded when the value of an asset drops below its carrying value. (Write-downs are reflected on both the balance sheet and the income statement.) A **restructuring** is the estimated cost of altering a company's operations, often involving plant closures and layoffs. Write-downs and restructurings are frequently an indication of bad management decisions in the past. Both reduce current operating income; however, because they shift future costs to the current period, they make it more likely that future earnings will show improvement. They are therefore often taken when a company is having a bad year anyway or when there is a change in management.

8. Generally speaking, gains and losses, asset write-downs, restructurings, and nonoperating items have no effect on cash flows; the cash expenditures for these items were made in previous periods. However, sustainable earnings generally *do* have a relationship to future cash flows.

9. The quality of earnings is especially relevant when considering return on assets and return on equity, two measures often used to measure management's performance and to help in determining its compensation. The numerator in these ratios—net income—should, as noted earlier, not always be taken at face value. The denominators—assets or stockholders' equity—likewise can be "manipulated"; for example, a write-down or restructuring of assets, in addition to a reduction in net income, reduces assets and stockholders' equity, which tends to improve future ratios.

Objective 2: Show the relationships among income taxes expense, deferred income taxes, and net of taxes.

10. A corporation's taxable income is determined by subtracting allowable business deductions from includable gross income. Tax rates currently range from a 15 percent to a 39 percent marginal rate.

11. Income taxes expense is the expense recognized in the accounting records on an accrual basis that applies to income from continuing operations. It may or may not equal the amount of taxes actually paid and recorded as income taxes payable in the current period. The difference arises because generally accepted accounting principles govern how income taxes are computed for financial reporting purposes, whereas the Internal Revenue Code dictates methods of computing income taxes owed to the federal government.

12. When income computed for financial reporting purposes differs from taxable income, the **income tax allocation** method should be used. Under this method, the difference between the income taxes expense and income taxes payable is debited or credited to an account called **Deferred Income Taxes.** This account is evaluated yearly to determine whether changes in income tax laws and regulations have made adjustments necessary.

13. Deferred income taxes are the result of temporary differences in the treatment of certain items (such as depreciation) for tax and financial reporting purposes. They are classified as current or noncurrent, depending on the classification of the asset or liability that created the difference.

14. To avoid distorting net operating income on the income statement, certain items must be reported **net of taxes**—that is, after considering applicable tax effects. These items are discontinued operations, extraordinary gains and losses, and accounting changes.

Objective 3: Describe the disclosure on the income statement of discontinued operations, extraordinary items, and accounting changes.

15. **Segments** are distinct parts of a company, such as a separate major line of business or class of customer. Any gain or loss on the **discontinued operations** of a segment must be disclosed on the income statement separately from continuing operations and net of taxes.

16. **Extraordinary items** are events that are both unusual in nature and infrequent. Gains and losses arise from such extraordinary events as natural disasters, theft, the passage of a new law, and a foreign government's takeover of property. Extraordinary gains and losses that are material in amount should be disclosed separately on the income statement (net of taxes) after discontinued operations.

17. A company may change from one accounting method to another (e.g., from FIFO to LIFO) only if it can justify the new procedure as better accounting practice, and it must then disclose the change in the financial statements. The **cumulative effect of an accounting change** refers to the effect that the new method would have had on net income in previous periods. It should appear on the income statement (net of taxes) immediately after extraordinary items.

Objective 4: Compute earnings per share.

18. Readers of financial statements use earnings per share of common stock to judge a company's performance and to compare it with the performance of other companies. Appearing on the income statement just below net income, the earnings per share section always shows (a) income from continuing operations, (b) income before extraordinary items and the cumulative effect of accounting changes, (c) the cumulative effect of accounting changes, and (d) net income.

19. A company that has issued no securities that are convertible to common stock has a **simple capital structure.** In this case, the income statement presents only **basic earnings per share**, which is calculated as follows:

$$\frac{\text{Net Income} - \text{Nonconvertible Preferred Dividends}}{\text{Weighted-Average Common Shares Outstanding}}$$

20. A company that has issued securities that can be converted to common stock has a **complex capital structure. Potentially dilutive securities,** such as stock options and convertible preferred stocks or bonds, are so called because they have the potential to decrease earnings per share. When a company has a complex capital structure, its income statement must present both basic and **diluted earnings per share.** Diluted earnings per share shows the maximum potential effect of dilution on the ownership position of common stockholders.

Objective 5: Prepare a statement of stockholders' equity.

21. The **statement of stockholders' equity** (also called the *statement of changes in stockholders' equity*) is often used in place of the statement of retained earnings. It is a labeled computation of the changes in stockholders' equity accounts during an accounting period. It contains all the components of the statement of retained earnings, a summary of the period's stock transactions, and accumulated other comprehensive income, such as adjustments for foreign currency translations.

22. **Retained earnings** are the profits a corporation has earned since its beginning, minus any losses, dividends declared, or transfers to contributed capital. Ordinarily, Retained Earnings has a credit balance. When a debit balance exists, the corporation is said to have a **deficit.** Retained earnings are not the same as cash or any other asset; they are simply an intangible representation of earnings "plowed back into the business."

23. When retained earnings are unrestricted, a company may use the assets for dividend payments and other purposes. A **restriction on retained earnings** means that a certain amount of the assets generated by earnings must remain in the business to be used for purposes other than dividend payments; in other words, it restricts the amount of retained earnings available for dividends. Contractual agreements or state laws may require a company to restrict all or a part its retained earnings, or a board of directors may decide to keep assets in the business for future needs. Restrictions on retained earnings are most commonly disclosed in the notes to the financial statements.

Objective 6: Account for stock dividends and stock splits.

24. A **stock dividend** is a proportional distribution of shares among stockholders. A board of directors may declare a stock dividend to (a) give evidence of the company's success without paying a cash dividend, (b) reduce the stock's market price by increasing the number of shares outstanding, (c) make a nontaxable distribution to stockholders, or (d) increase the company's permanent capital. A stock dividend results in the transfer of a part of retained earnings to contributed capital. For a small stock dividend (less than 20 to 25 percent of outstanding common stock), the market value of the shares distributed is transferred from retained earnings; for a large stock dividend (greater than 20 to 25 percent), the par or stated value is transferred. A stock dividend does not change total stockholders' equity or any individual's proportionate equity in the company.

25. A **stock split** is an increase in the number of shares of stock outstanding, with a corresponding

decrease in the par or stated value of the stock. For example, a 3-for-1 split on 40,000 shares of $30 par value would result in the distribution of 80,000 additional shares (i.e., someone who owned one share would now own three shares). The par value would be reduced to $10. A stock split does not change the number of shares authorized or the balances in stockholders' equity. Its main purpose is to improve a stock's marketability by pushing its market price down. In our example, if the stock was selling for $180 per share, a 3-for-1 split would probably cause its market price to fall to about $60 per share. Although a stock split does not have to be recorded, it is appropriate to document it with a memorandum entry in the general journal.

Objective 7: Calculate book value per share.

26. The **book value** of a company's stock represents the company's total assets less its liabilities. It is simply the stockholders' equity or, to put it another way, the company's net assets. If a company has common stock only, the **book value per share** is computed by dividing total stockholders' equity by the number of outstanding and distributable shares. If the company also has preferred stock, the call or par value of the preferred stock, plus any dividends in arrears, is deducted from stockholders' equity in computing the book value per share of common stock.

Summary of Journal Entries Introduced in Chapter 15

A. (LO 2)   Income Taxes Expense .... XX (amount per GAAP)
               Income Taxes Payable .... XX (currently payable)
               Deferred Income Taxes .... XX (eventually payable)
                  To record estimated current and deferred income taxes

B. (LO 6)   Stock Dividends Declared .... XX (amount transferred)
               Common Stock Distributable .... XX (par value amount)
               Paid-in Capital in Excess of Par Value, Common .... XX (excess of par)
                  Declared a stock dividend on common stock

C. (LO 6)   Common Stock Distributable .... XX (par value amount)
               Common Stock .... XX (par value amount)
                  Distributed a stock dividend

SELF-TEST

Test your knowledge of the chapter by choosing the best answer for each item below.

1. The balance of the Retained Earnings account represents
   a. an excess of revenues over expenses for the most current operating period.
   b. the profits of a company since its inception, less any losses, dividends to stockholders, or transfers to contributed capital.
   c. cash set aside for specific future uses.
   d. cash available for daily operations.

2. A corporation should account for the declaration of a 3 percent stock dividend by
   a. transferring from retained earnings to contributed capital an amount equal to the market value of the dividend shares.
   b. transferring from retained earnings to contributed capital an amount equal to the legal capital represented by the dividend shares.
   c. making only a memorandum entry in the general journal.
   d. transferring from retained earnings to contributed capital whatever amount the board of directors deems appropriate.

3. Which of the following increases the number of shares of common stock outstanding?
   a. A stock split
   b. A restriction on retained earnings
   c. Treasury stock
   d. A cash dividend

4. When retained earnings are restricted, total retained earnings
   a. increase.
   b. decrease.
   c. may increase or decrease.
   d. are unaffected.

5. The purpose of a statement of stockholders' equity is to
   a. summarize the changes in the components of stockholders' equity over the accounting period.
   b. disclose the computation of book value per share of stock.
   c. budget for the transactions expected to occur during the forthcoming period.
   d. replace the statement of retained earnings.

6. All of the following elements of a corporation's common stock can be determined from the accounting records *except*
   a. par value.
   b. stated value.
   c. book value.
   d. market value.

7. Which of the following items appears on the corporate income statement before income from continuing operations?
   a. Income from operations of a discontinued segment
   b. Income taxes expense
   c. The cumulative effect of a change in accounting principle
   d. An extraordinary gain

8. When there is a difference in the timing of revenues and expenses for financial reporting and income tax purposes, it is usually necessary to
   a. prepare an adjusting entry.
   b. adjust figures on the corporate tax return.
   c. use the income tax allocation method.
   d. do nothing because the difference is a result of two different sets of rules.

9. A loss due to discontinued operations should be reported on the income statement
   a. before both extraordinary items and the cumulative effect of an accounting change.
   b. before the cumulative effect of an accounting change and after extraordinary items.
   c. after both extraordinary items and the cumulative effect of an accounting change.
   d. after the cumulative effect of an accounting change and before extraordinary items.

10. Which of the following would be involved in the computation of earnings per common share for a company with a simple capital structure?
    a. Common shares authorized
    b. Dividends declared on nonconvertible preferred stock
    c. The shares of nonconvertible preferred stock outstanding
    d. Treasury shares

TESTING YOUR KNOWLEDGE

*Matching**

Match each term with its definition by writing the appropriate letter in the blank.

_____ 1. Retained earnings

_____ 2. Deficit

_____ 3. Statement of stockholders' equity

_____ 4. Income tax allocation

_____ 5. Simple capital structure

_____ 6. Complex capital structure

_____ 7. Discontinued operations

_____ 8. Comprehensive income

_____ 9. Stock dividend

_____ 10. Stock split

_____ 11. Restricted retained earnings

_____ 12. Segments

_____ 13. Potentially dilutive securities

_____ 14. Extraordinary item

_____ 15. Earnings per share

_____ 16. Accounting change

_____ 17. Book value per share

_____ 18. Restructuring

a. An event resulting in an unusual and infrequent gain or loss

b. The make-up of a corporation that has issued convertible securities

c. A negative figure for retained earnings

d. Distinct parts of a business

e. A summary of the changes in stockholders' equity accounts during an accounting period

f. The net assets represented by one share of a corporation's stock

g. The change in a company's equity during a period from sources other than owners, including net income, changes in unrealized investment gains and losses, and other items affecting equity

h. Use of a different but more appropriate accounting method

i. A proportional distribution of shares among stockholders

j. The profits that a corporation has earned since its inception, minus any losses, dividends declared, or transfers to contributed capital

k. A measure of the net income earned by each share of common stock

l. The estimated cost of plant closings and layoffs

m. The makeup of a corporation that has not issued convertible securities

n. The income statement section immediately before extraordinary gains or losses

o. The method used to reconcile accounting income and taxable income

p. A portion of retained earnings that cannot be used for dividend payments

q. Options and convertible preferred stocks that can lower earnings per share

r. A corporate stock maneuver that results in a change in par or stated value

---

Note to student: The matching quiz might be completed more efficiently by starting with the definition and searching for the corresponding term.

Short Answer

Use the lines provided to answer each item.

1. List three ways in which the Retained Earnings account can be reduced.

   _____

   _____

   _____

2. What are the two major distinctions between a stock dividend and a stock split?

   _____

   _____

   _____

3. What two conditions must be met for an item to qualify as extraordinary?

   _____

   _____

4. Number the following items to indicate the order of their appearance on an income statement:

   _____ Cumulative effect of accounting change

   _____ Revenues

   _____ Extraordinary gains and losses

   _____ Net income

   _____ Discontinued operations

   _____ Income from continuing operations

5. What are the three ways in which corporations report comprehensive income?

   _____

   _____

   _____

True-False

Circle T if the statement is true, F if it is false. Provide explanations for the false answers, using the blank lines at the end of the section.

T F 1. If an extraordinary gain of $20,000 has occurred, it should be reported net of taxes at more than $20,000.

T F 2. A restriction on retained earnings represents cash set aside for a special purpose.

T F 3. The book value of a share of common stock decreases when dividends are declared.

T F 4. After a stock dividend is distributed, each stockholder owns a greater percentage of the corporation.

T F 5. The market value of a stock on the date a small stock dividend is declared has no bearing on the journal entry.

T F 6. The main purpose of a stock split is to reduce the stock's par value.

T F 7. A gain on the sale of a plant asset qualifies as an extraordinary item.

T F 8. Extraordinary items should appear on the statement of stockholders' equity.

T F 9. The effect of a change from the straight-line method of depreciation to an accelerated method should be reported on the income statement immediately after extraordinary items.

T F 10. Common Stock Distributable is a current liability on the balance sheet.

T F **11.** The income statement of a corporation with a complex capital structure should present both basic and diluted earnings per share.

T F **12.** If taxable income always equaled accounting income, there would be no need for income tax allocation.

T F **13.** The quality of earnings is affected by the existence of an extraordinary item on the income statement.

T F **14.** Potentially dilutive securities are included in the calculation of basic earnings per share.

T F **15.** Stock Dividends Declared is closed to Retained Earnings at the end of an accounting period.

T F **16.** Write-downs often are an indication that management has made bad decisions in the past.

_____

_____

_____

_____

_____

_____

_____

_____

_____

_____

_____

_____

_____

_____

_____

_____

_____

_____

_____

_____

_____

_____

_____

_____

Circle the letter of the best answer.

1. Which of the following has no effect on retained earnings?
   a. Stock split
   b. Stock dividend
   c. Cash dividend
   d. Net loss

2. A company with 10,000 shares of common stock outstanding has distributed a 10 percent stock dividend and then split its stock 4 for 1. How many shares are now outstanding?
   a. 2,750
   b. 41,000
   c. 44,000
   d. 55,000

3. When retained earnings are restricted, which of the following statements is true?
   a. Total retained earnings increase.
   b. The company is no longer limited in the amount of dividends it can pay.
   c. Total retained earnings are reduced.
   d. Total stockholders' equity remains the same.

4. On the date that a stock dividend is distributed,
   a. Common Stock Distributable is credited.
   b. Cash is credited.
   c. Retained Earnings remains the same.
   d. no entry is made.

5. The effect of an accounting change should appear on
   a. the income statement.
   b. the balance sheet.
   c. the statement of stockholders' equity.
   d. no financial statement.

6. Chen Corporation had 60,000 shares of common stock outstanding from January 1 to October 1; from October 1 to December 31, it had 40,000 shares outstanding. What is the weighted-average number of shares used to calculate earnings per share?
   a. 45,000 shares
   b. 50,000 shares
   c. 55,000 shares
   d. 100,000 shares

7. If retained earnings were $70,000 on January 1, 20xx, and $100,000 on December 31, 20xx, and if cash dividends of $15,000 were declared and paid during the year, net income for the year must have been
   a. $30,000.
   b. $45,000.
   c. $55,000.
   d. $85,000.

8. Which of the following would *not* appear on a statement of stockholders' equity?
   a. Conversion of preferred stock into common stock
   b. Dividends declared
   c. Discontinued operations
   d. Accumulated other comprehensive income

9. A corporation has issued only one type of stock and wants to compute book value per share. It needs all of the following information *except*
   a. retained earnings.
   b. the current year's dividends.
   c. total contributed capital.
   d. total shares outstanding and distributable.

10. Retained earnings
    a. are the same as cash.
    b. are the amount invested by stockholders in a corporation.
    c. equal cumulative profits, less any losses, dividends declared, or transfers to contributed capital.
    d. are not affected by revenues and expenses.

11. The quality of a company's earnings may be affected by the
    a. countries in which the company operates.
    b. choice of independent auditors.
    c. industry in which the company operates.
    d. accounting methods used by the company.

APPLYING YOUR KNOWLEDGE

Exercises

1. In the journal provided below, prepare the proper entry for each of the following:

Sept. 1 Mettler Corporation begins operations by issuing 10,000 shares of $100 par value common stock at $120 per share.

Mar. 7 A 5 percent stock dividend is declared. The market price of the stock is $130 per share on March 7.

   30 This is the date of record for the stock dividend declared on March 7.

Apr. 13 The stock dividend is distributed.

General Journal				
Date		**Description**	**Debit**	**Credit**

2. A company has $100,000 in operating income before taxes. It had an extraordinary loss of $30,000 when lightning struck one of its warehouses. The company must pay a 40 percent tax on all items. Complete the partial income statement below in good form.

Operating income before taxes	$100,000

3. Hiller Corporation had taxable income of $40,000, $40,000, and $80,000 in 20x3, 20x4, and 20x5, respectively. Its income for accounting purposes was $60,000, $30,000, and $70,000 in 20x3, 20x4, and 20x5, respectively. The difference between taxable income and accounting income was due to $30,000 in expenses that were deductible in full for tax purposes in 20x3 but were expensed one-third per year for accounting purposes. Make the correct journal entry to record income taxes expense in each of the three years. Assume a 40 percent tax rate.

	General Journal		
Date	**Description**	**Debit**	**Credit**

4. Simms Corporation's balance sheet as of December 31, 20xx, includes the following information about stockholders' equity:

Contributed capital		
Preferred stock, $50 par value, $50 call price, 7% cumulative, 4,000 shares authorized, issued, and outstanding	$200,000	
Paid-in capital in excess of par value, preferred	40,000	
Common stock, no-par, 30,000 shares authorized, issued, and outstanding	360,000	
Total contributed capital	$600,000	
Retained earnings	80,000	
Total stockholders' equity	$680,000	

Dividends in arrears total $28,000.

Compute the book value per share of both the preferred stock and the common stock.

5. Throughout 20xx, Tatum Corporation had 10,000 shares of common stock and 30,000 shares of nonconvertible preferred stock outstanding. Tatum's net income for the year was $50,000, dividends on preferred stock totaled $20,000, and dividends on common stock totaled $5,000. Calculate basic earnings per share.

CHAPTER 14 THE STATEMENT OF CASH FLOWS

REVIEWING THE CHAPTER

Objective 1: State the principal purposes and uses of the statement of cash flows, and identify its components.

1. The **statement of cash flows** focuses on a company's liquidity and contains much information not found in the income statement, balance sheet, or statement of stockholders' equity. It explains the changes in cash and cash equivalents from one accounting period to the next by showing the cash inflows and outflows from a company's operating, investing, and financing activities during an accounting period. For the statement of cash flows, **cash** is defined as including both cash and cash equivalents. **Cash equivalents** are short-term, highly liquid investments, such as money market accounts, commercial paper (short-term notes), and U.S. Treasury bills. Marketable securities are not considered cash equivalents.

2. The principal purpose of the statement of cash flows is to provide information about a company's cash receipts and cash payments during an accounting period. A secondary purpose is to provide information about a company's operating, investing, and financing activities.

3. Management uses the statement of cash flows to assess the company's debt-paying ability, to determine dividend policy, and to plan for investing and financing needs. Investors and creditors use the statement to assess such things as the company's ability to manage cash flows, to generate positive future cash flows, to pay its liabilities, to

pay dividends and interest, and to anticipate its need for additional financing.

4. The statement of cash flows classifies cash receipts (inflows) and cash payments (outflows) as stemming from operating, investing, and financing activities. The statement may be accompanied by a schedule of significant noncash transactions.
   a. **Operating activities** include receiving cash from the sale of goods and services, receiving interest and dividends on loans and investments, receiving cash from the sale of trading securities, and making cash payments for wages, goods and services, interest, taxes, and purchases of trading securities.
   b. **Investing activities** include purchasing and selling long-term assets and marketable securities (other than trading securities or cash equivalents) and making and collecting on loans to other entities.
   c. **Financing activities** include issuing and buying back stock, as well as borrowing and repaying loans on a short- or long-term basis (i.e., issuing bonds and notes). Dividend payments are also included in this category, but payments of accounts payable and accrued liabilities are not (they are classified as operating activities).
   d. Settling a debt by issuing stock and purchasing land by taking out a mortgage are significant financing and investing activities, but they do not involve cash inflows and outflows and are therefore not reflected on the statement of cash

flows. However, because they will affect future cash flows, they should be disclosed in a separate schedule of **noncash investing and financing transactions** that accompanies the statement of cash flows. These transactions involve only long-term assets, long-term liabilities, and stockholders' equity.

5. The sections on operating, investing, and financing activities are the three main divisions of a statement of cash flows. A reconciliation of the beginning and ending balances of cash appears near the bottom of the statement.

Objective 2: Analyze the statement of cash flows.

6. Two areas that analysts focus on when evaluating a firm's statement of cash flows are cash-generating efficiency and free cash flow. Because cash flows can vary from year to year, it is best to look at trends in these areas over several years.

7. **Cash-generating efficiency** is a company's ability to generate cash from its current or continuing operations. It can be expressed in terms of three ratios: cash flow yield, cash flows to sales, and cash flows to assets.

   a. **Cash flow yield** equals net cash flows from operating activities divided by net income (or by income from continuing operations). A cash flow yield of 2.0 times, for example, means that operating activities have generated twice as much cash flow as net income.

   b. **Cash flows to sales** equals net cash flows from operating activities divided by net sales. A ratio of 5.7 percent, for example, means that operating cash flows of 5.7 cents have been generated for every dollar of net sales.

   c. **Cash flows to assets** equals net cash flows from operating activities divided by average total assets. A ratio of 4.8 percent, for example, means that operating cash flows of 4.8 cents have been generated for every dollar of average total assets.

8. **Free cash flow** is the cash that remains from operating activities after deducting the funds a company must commit to continue operating at its planned level. It equals net cash flows from operating activities minus dividends minus net capital expenditures (purchases minus sales of plant assets). A *positive* free cash flow means that the company has met its cash commitments and has cash remaining to reduce debt or expand further. A *negative* free cash flow means that the company will have to sell investments, borrow money, or issue stock to continue at its planned level.

Objective 3: Use the indirect method to determine cash flows from operating activities.

9. To determine cash flows from operating activities, the figures on the income statement must be converted from an accrual basis to a cash basis using either the **direct method** or the **indirect method**. The direct and indirect methods produce the same net figure, and both conform to GAAP, but the indirect method is far more widely used.

10. Under the indirect method, the net cash flows from operating activities are determined by adding to or deducting from net income items that do not affect cash flows from operations. Items that are added include depreciation expense, amortization expense, depletion expense, losses, decreases in certain current assets (accounts receivable, inventory, and prepaid expenses), and increases in certain current liabilities (accounts payable, accrued liabilities, and income taxes payable). Items that are deducted include gains, increases in certain current assets (see above), and decreases in certain current liabilities (see above).

Objective 4: Determine cash flows from investing activities.

11. To determine cash flows from investing activities, each account involving cash receipts and cash payments from investing activities is examined. The objective is to explain the change in each account balance from one year to the next.

12. Investing activities center on long-term assets shown on the balance sheet, but they also include transactions affecting short-term investments from the current assets section of the balance sheet and investment gains and losses from the income statement.

Objective 5: Determine cash flows from financing activities.

13. The procedure for determining cash flows from financing activities is similar to the procedure for determining cash flows from investing activities. The difference is that the accounts to be analyzed involve short-term borrowings, long-term liabilities, and stockholders' equity. Cash dividends from the statement of stockholders' equity are also considered.

14. Exhibit 4 in the text shows a statement of cash flows that was prepared using the indirect method. As already noted, the essence of the indirect approach is the conversion of net income to net cash flows from operating activities.

SELF-TEST

Test your knowledge of the chapter by choosing the best answer for each item below.

1. Cash equivalents include
   a. three-month Treasury bills.
   b. marketable securities.
   c. accounts receivable.
   d. long-term investments.

2. The primary purpose of the statement of cash flows is to provide information about
   a. the results of a company's operations in an accounting period.
   b. a company's financial position at the end of an accounting period.
   c. a company's operating, investing, and financing activities during an accounting period.
   d. a company's cash receipts and cash payments during an accounting period.

3. Which of the following is supplemental to the statement of cash flows?
   a. Operating activities
   b. Investing activities
   c. Significant noncash transactions
   d. Financing activities

4. Which of the following would be classified as an operating activity on the statement of cash flows?
   a. Paying a cash dividend
   b. Issuing long-term notes for plant assets
   c. Paying interest on a long-term note
   d. Purchasing a patent with cash

5. Which of the following would be classified as an investing activity on the statement of cash flows?
   a. Paying a cash dividend
   b. Issuing long-term notes for plant assets
   c. Paying interest on a long-term note
   d. Purchasing a patent with cash

6. Which of the following would be classified as a financing activity on the statement of cash flows?
   a. Paying a cash dividend
   b. Purchasing a trading security with cash
   c. Paying interest on a long-term note
   d. Purchasing a patent with cash

7. On the statement of cash flows, the net amount of the major components of cash flow will equal the increase or decrease in
   a. cash and accounts receivable.
   b. working capital.
   c. cash and cash equivalents.
   d. short-term investments.

8. Cash flow yield is expressed in terms of
   a. dollars.
   b. times.
   c. a percentage.
   d. days.

9. In a statement of cash flows, all of the following would be classified as operating activities *except*
   a. paying wages.
   b. purchasing inventory with cash.
   c. selling trading securities.
   d. purchasing treasury stock with cash.

10. The calculation of free cash flow includes a subtraction for
    a. the sale of plant assets.
    b. interest.
    c. dividends.
    d. net cash flows from operating activities.

TESTING YOUR KNOWLEDGE

Matching*

Match each term with its definition by writing the appropriate letter in the blank.

_____ 1. Statement of cash flows

_____ 2. Cash equivalents

_____ 3. Operating activities

_____ 4. Investing activities

_____ 5. Financing activities

_____ 6. Noncash investing and financing transactions

_____ 7. Direct method

_____ 8. Indirect method

_____ 9. Cash-generating efficiency

_____ 10. Free cash flow

a. The items in a separate schedule that may accompany the statement of cash flows

b. Net cash flows from operating activities minus dividends minus net capital expenditures

c. The procedure for determining cash flows from operations that starts with the net income figure

d. A company's ability to produce cash flows from its current or continuing operations

e. The section in a statement of cash flows that deals mainly with stockholders' equity accounts and borrowing

f. A financial report that explains the change in a company's cash during an accounting period

g. The section in a statement of cash flows that deals mainly with long-term assets and marketable securities other than trading securities or cash equivalents

h. The procedure for determining cash flows from operations that adjusts each income statement item from an accrual basis to a cash basis

i. The section in a statement of cash flows that most closely relates to net income (loss)

j. Short-term, highly liquid investments

Short Answer

Use the lines provided to answer each item.

1. Give two examples of noncash investing and financing transactions.

   _____

   _____

2. When the statement of cash flows is prepared under the indirect method, why are depreciation, amortization, and depletion expenses added back to net income to determine cash flows from operating activities?

   _____

   _____

   _____

3. List three examples of cash equivalents.

   _____

   _____

   _____

Note to student: The matching quiz might be completed more efficiently by starting with the definition and searching for the corresponding term.

True-False

Circle T if the statement is true, F if it is false. Provide explanations for the false answers, using the blank lines below.

T F **1.** Much of the information presented in the statement of cash flows cannot be found in the other major financial statements.

T F **2.** Payment on an account payable is considered a financing activity.

T F **3.** Proceeds from the sale of available-for-sale securities, whether the securities are short-term or long-term, are considered cash inflows from investing activities.

T F **4.** Under the indirect method, a decrease in prepaid expenses is added to net income in determining net cash flows from operating activities.

T F **5.** The schedule of noncash investing and financing transactions may include line items for depreciation, depletion, and amortization recorded during the period.

T F **6.** A net positive figure for cash flows from investing activities implies that the business is generally expanding.

T F **7.** The issuance of common stock for cash is disclosed in the financing activities section of the statement of cash flows.

T F **8.** Under the indirect method, a loss on the sale of buildings is deducted from net income in the operating activities section of the statement of cash flows.

T F **9.** Cash obtained by borrowing, whether the debt is short-term or long-term, is considered a financing activity.

T F **10.** The purchase of land in exchange for common stock represents both an investing and a financing activity.

T F **11.** Free cash flow does not include a deduction for dividends because a dividend payment is never required.

T F **12.** Both the direct method and the indirect method convert the figures on the income statement from an accrual basis to a cash basis.

T F **13.** The purchase of treasury stock is disclosed in the investing activities section of the statement of cash flows.

Multiple Choice

Circle the letter of the best answer.

1. On a statement of cash flows that employs the indirect method, interest and dividends received would be
   a. included as components of net income in the operating activities section.
   b. deducted from net income in the operating activities section.
   c. included in the investing activities section.
   d. included in the financing activities section.
   e. included in the schedule of noncash investing and financing transactions.

2. On a statement of cash flows that employs the indirect method, a gain on the sale of investments would be
   a. added to net income in the operating activities section.
   b. deducted from net income in the operating activities section.
   c. included in the investing activities section.
   d. included in the financing activities section.
   e. included in the schedule of noncash investing and financing transactions.

3. On a statement of cash flows that employs the indirect method, an increase in accounts payable would be
   a. added to net income in the operating activities section.
   b. deducted from net income in the operating activities section.
   c. included in the investing activities section.
   d. included in the financing activities section.
   e. included in the schedule of noncash investing and financing transactions.

4. On a statement of cash flows that employs the indirect method, the purchase of a building by incurring a mortgage payable would be
   a. added to net income in the operating activities section.
   b. deducted from net income in the operating activities section.
   c. included in the investing activities section.
   d. included in the financing activities section.
   e. included in the schedule of noncash investing and financing transactions.

5. On a statement of cash flows that employs the indirect method, dividends paid would be
   a. added to net income in the operating activities section.
   b. deducted from net income in the operating activities section.
   c. included in the investing activities section.
   d. included in the financing activities section.
   e. included in the schedule of noncash investing and financing transactions.

6. On a statement of cash flows that employs the indirect method, an increase in inventory would be
   a. added to net income in the operating activities section.
   b. deducted from net income in the operating activities section.
   c. included in the investing activities section.
   d. included in the financing activities section.
   e. included in the schedule of noncash investing and financing transactions.

7. All of the following represent cash flows from operating activities *except* cash
   a. payments for income taxes.
   b. receipts from sales.
   c. receipts from the issuance of stock.
   d. payments for purchases.

8. The calculations of cash flow yield, cash flows to sales, and cash flows to assets are all based on
   a. net cash flows from financing activities.
   b. net increase or decrease in cash.
   c. net cash flows from operating activities.
   d. net cash flows from investing activities.

APPLYING YOUR KNOWLEDGE

Exercises

1. For 20x7, Cerritos Corporation had average total assets of $800,000, net sales of $900,000, net income of $60,000, net cash flows from operating activities of $120,000, dividend payments of $30,000, purchases of plant assets of $75,000, and sales of plant assets of $40,000. Using this information, compute the following cash flow measures.

   a. Cash flow yield = _____ times

   b. Cash flows to sales = _____%

   c. Cash flows to assets = _____%

   d. Free cash flow = $_____

2. Harding Corporation's comparative balance sheets as of December 31, 20x5, and 20x4, and its income statement for the year ended December 31, 20x5, are as follows:

Harding Corporation
Comparative Balance Sheets
December 31, 20x5 and 20x4

	20x5	20x4
Assets		
Sales	$108,000	$103,000
Accounts receivable (net)	96,000	72,000
Merchandise inventory	61,000	75,000
Equipment	77,000	70,000
Accumulated depreciation, equipment	(28,000)	(19,000)
Total assets	$314,000	$301,000
Liabilities and Stockholders' Equity		
Accounts payable	$ 50,000	$ 46,000
Income taxes payable	2,500	1,800
Notes payable (long-term)	30,000	25,000
Bonds payable	45,000	60,000
Common stock, $10 par value	95,000	80,000
Paid-in capital in excess of par value, Common	35,000	35,000
Retained earnings	56,500	53,200
Total liabilities and stockholders' equity	$314,000	$301,000

Harding Corporation
Income Statement
For the Year Ended December 31, 20x5

Net sales		$842,000
Cost of goods sold		333,000
Gross margin		$509,000
Operating expenses (including depreciation expense of $14,000)		412,000
Income from operations		$97,000
Loss on sale of equipment	($4,000)	
Interest expense	(9,000)	(13,000)
Income before income taxes		$ 84,000
Income taxes		29,000
Net income		$ 55,000

During 20x5, Harding sold for $11,000 equipment that cost $20,000 and that had accumulated depreciation of $5,000. It also purchased equipment for $27,000, paid a $10,000 note and borrowed $15,000 on a new note, converted bonds with a face value of $15,000 into 1,500 shares of common stock, and paid $51,700 in cash dividends. Using the indirect method, complete the statement of cash flows that appears on the next page.

Harding Corporation	
Statement of Cash Flows	
For the Year Ended December 31, 20x5	

Cash flows from operating activities

Cash flows from investing activities

Cash flows from financing activities

Net increase (decrease) in cash
Cash at beginning of year
Cash at end of year

Schedule of Noncash Investing and Financing Transactions

Crossword Puzzle
for Chapters 12, 13, and 14

ACROSS

5. _____ (all-inclusive) income
7. Dividends in _____
8. Commercial _____
9. Corporate stock maneuver
12. Unusual and infrequent (event)
15. Distinct part of a business's operations
19. Canceled, as treasury stock
20. Distribution of resources to stockholders

DOWN

1. First-time public stock issue, for short
2. Stock units
3. Reader of financial statements
4. Negative retained earnings
5. Type of capital structure
6. A legal-capital designation (hyphenated)
7. Term for maximum number of shares that can be issued
10. _____/earnings ratio
11. Type of stock
13. _____ on equity
14. The "_____" line
15. Stock value for 6-Down
16. _____ sale of investments (2 words)
17. Cash outflow classified under operating activities
18. Item "added back" under the indirect method

CHAPTER 15 THE CHANGING BUSINESS ENVIRONMENT: A MANAGER'S PERSPECTIVE

REVIEWING THE CHAPTER

Objective 1: Distinguish management accounting from financial accounting and explain the role of management accounting in the management cycle.

1. **Management accounting** is the process of identifying, measuring, accumulating, analyzing, preparing, interpreting, and communicating information that management uses to plan, evaluate, and control an organization and to ensure that its resources are used and accounted for appropriately. The information that management accounting provides should be timely and accurate and support management decisions about pricing, planning, operations, and many other matters. The need for management accounting information exists regardless of the type of organization or its size.

2. Although both management accounting and financial accounting provide information essential to decision making, they differ in a number of ways. The primary users of management accounting information are people inside the organization—managers, as well as employees, who depend on the information to make informed decisions, to perform their jobs effectively, and to achieve their organization's goals. Financial accounting, on the other hand, uses the actual results of management decisions to prepare financial reports primarily for use by parties outside the organization—owners or stockholders, lenders, customers and governmental agencies. Whereas the format of management accounting reports is flexible, driven by the users' needs, financial accounting reports must conform to GAAP. The nature of the information in the reports also differs (historical or future-oriented in management accounting reports; historical and verifiable in financial accounting reports), as do the units of measure used and the frequency of the reports.

3. The management cycle involves four stages: planning, executing, reviewing, and reporting. Management accounting can provide an ongoing stream of relevant information that supports management decisions in each stage of this cycle.
   a. In the planning stage, managers use management accounting information to establish **strategic objectives** and **operating objectives** that support their company's **mission** and to formulate a comprehensive **business plan** for achieving those objectives. The business plan is usually expressed in financial terms in the form of budgets.
   b. In the executing stage, managers implement the business plan in ways that make optimal use of available resources. The information that management accounting provides about such matters as deliveries and sales is extremely useful in managing the **supply chain**—the path that leads from the supplier of the materials from which a product is made to the final consumer.
   c. In the reviewing stage, managers compare actual performance with planned performance and take steps to correct any problems.

d. The reports prepared in the final stage of the management cycle reflect the results of the efforts undertaken in the previous three stages. Any report, whether prepared for internal or external use, should present accurate information that is clear and useful to the reader. The key to preparing such a report is to apply the four *w*'s: who, what, why, and when.

Objective 2: Describe the value chain and its usefulness in analyzing a business.

4. The **value chain** conceives of each step in the manufacture of a product or the delivery of a service as a link in a chain that adds value to the product or service. These value-adding steps—research and development, design, supply, production, marketing, distribution, and customer service—are called **primary processes.** The value chain also includes **support services**—human resources, legal services, information services, and management accounting. Support services facilitate the primary processes but do not add value to the final product. Value chain analysis enables a company to focus on its **core competency.** It frequently results in the **outsourcing** of parts of the value chain that are not among a company's core competencies.

Objective 3: Identify the management tools used for continuous improvement and describe how they work to meet the demands of global competition and how management accounting supports them.

5. Several management tools have been developed to help firms compete in an expanding global market. They include the just-in-time (JIT) operating philosophy, total quality management (TQM), activity-based management (ABM), and the theory of constraints (TOC). All these methods are based on the concept of **continuous improvement**—that is, that management should never be satisfied with the status quo but should continue to seek better methods, better products or services, better processes, and better resources.

a. The **just-in-time (JIT) operating philosophy** requires that all resources—materials, personnel, and facilities—be acquired and used only as needed. Its objectives are to improve productivity and eliminate waste. Management accounting responds to a JIT environment by providing an information system that is sensitive to changes in production processes.

b. **Total quality management (TQM)** requires that all parts of a business work together to build quality into the firm's products or services. The **costs of quality** include both the costs of achieving quality and the costs of poor quality. Managers share accounting information about the magnitude and classification of costs of quality with their employees to stimulate improvement.

c. **Activity-based management (ABM)** identifies all major operating activities, determines the resources consumed by each of those activities and the cause of the resource usage, and categorizes the activities as value-adding or non-value-adding. **Value-adding activities** add value to a product or service, as perceived by the customer. **Nonvalue-adding activities** add cost to a product or service but do not increase its market value. ABM seeks to eliminate or reduce the cost of non-value adding activities. In assigning costs, ABM relies on **activity-based costing (ABC),** a management accounting practice that identifies all of an organization's major operating activities (both production and nonproduction), traces costs to those activities, and then assigns costs to the products or services that use the resources supplied by those activities.

d. According to the **theory of constraints (TOC),** limiting factors, or bottlenecks, occur during the production of any product or service, but by using management accounting information to identify such constraints, managers can focus attention and resources on them and achieve significant improvements. TOC thus helps managers set priorities on how they spend their time and other resources.

Objective 4: Explain the balanced scorecard and its relationship to performance measures.

6. Performance measures are quantitative tools that gauge an organization's performance in relation to a specific goal or an expected outcome. Performance measures may be either financial or nonfinancial.

a. Financial performance measures use monetary data to assess the performance of an organization or its segments. Examples of these measures include return on investment, net income as a percentage of sales, and the costs of poor quality as a percentage of sales.

b. Nonfinancial performance measures include the number of times an activity occurs or the time taken to perform a task. Examples are number of customer complaints, the time it takes to fill an order, number of orders shipped the same day, and the hours of inspection. Such performance measures are useful in reducing or eliminating waste and inefficiencies in operating activities.

7. Managers use performance measures in each stage of the management cycle. In the planning stage, they establish performance measures that will support the organization's mission and the objectives of its business plan. In the executing stage, performance measures guide and motivate the performance of employees and assist in assigning costs. In the reviewing stage, managers use the information that performance measures have provided to analyze significant differences between actual and planned performance and to improvise ways of improving performance. In the reporting stage, they use the results of performance measurement in preparing performance evaluations and in developing new budgets.

8. The **balanced scorecard** helps an organization measure and evaluate itself from a variety of viewpoints. It links the perspectives of an organization's four stakeholder groups—financial (owners, investors, and creditors), learning and growth (employees), internal business processes, and customers—with the organization's mission, objectives, resources, and performance measures. The balanced scorecard uses both financial and nonfinancial performance measures to assess whether the objectives of the four perspectives are being met.

9. To ensure its success, a company must compare its performance with that of similar companies in the same industry. **Benchmarking** is a technique for determining a company's competitive advantage by comparing its performance with that of its closest competitors. **Benchmarks** are measures of the best practices in an industry.

Objective 5: Prepare an analysis of nonfinancial data.

10. Using management tools like TQM and ABM and comprehensive frameworks like the balanced scorecard requires analysis of both financial and nonfinancial data. In analyzing nonfinancial data, it is important to compare performance measures with the objectives that are to achieved.

Objective 6: Identify the standards of ethical conduct for management accountants.

11. Conflicts between external parties (e.g., owners, creditors, governmental agencies, and the local community) can create ethical dilemmas for management and for management accountants, who have a responsibility to help management balance the interests of external parties. Throughout their careers, management accountants have an obligation to the public, their profession, the organizations they serve, and themselves to maintain the highest standards of ethical conduct. To provide guidance, the Institute of Management Accountants has issued standards of ethical conduct for practitioners of management accounting and financial management. These standards emphasize practitioners' responsibility in the areas of competence, confidentiality, integrity, and objectivity.

SELF-TEST

Test your knowledge of the chapter by choosing the best answer for each item below.

1. Management accounting information is needed in
   a. manufacturing companies only.
   b. large companies only.
   c. not-for-profit organizations only.
   d. all types and sizes of organizations.

2. When applied to a company's financial, production, and distribution data, management accounting procedures will
   a. guarantee the generation of a profit.
   b. satisfy requirements of the Internal Revenue Service.
   c. satisfy management's information needs.
   d. represent the union's basic collective bargaining agreement.

3. Which of the following statements is *false?*
   a. The primary users of financial accounting reports are parties outside the organization.
   b. Management accountants are not restricted to using historical data and can employ any unit of measure useful in a particular situation.
   c. The only restrictive guideline on financial accounting is that the accounting practice or technique used must produce accurate and useful information.
   d. Financial accounting typically records and reports on the assets, liabilities, equities, and net income of a company as a whole.

4. Which of the following is *not* a stage in the management cycle?
   a. Planning
   b. Executing
   c. Preparing financial statements
   d. Reviewing

5. Which of the following management philosophies evolved to help firms compete in a global market?
   a. Just-in-time operating philosophy
   b. Total quality management
   c. Activity-based management
   d. All of the above

6. Performance measures may be either financial or nonfinancial. Which of the following is *not* a financial performance measure?
   a. Number of customer complaints
   b. Return on equity
   c. Sales for the month
   d. Total costs of production

7. The standards of ethical conduct issued by the Institute of Management Accountants state that the management accountant has a responsibility in all of the following areas *except*
   a. compliance with IRS regulations.
   b. confidentiality.
   c. competence.
   d. objectivity.

TESTING YOUR KNOWLEDGE

Matching*

Match each term with its definition by writing the appropriate letter in the blank.

_____ **1.** Theory of constraints (TOC)

_____ **2.** Value-adding activity

_____ **3.** Activity-based management (ABM)

_____ **4.** Total quality management (TQM)

_____ **5.** Continuous improvement

_____ **6.** Management accounting

_____ **7.** Balanced scorecard

_____ **8.** Nonvalue-adding activity

_____ **9.** Just-in-time (JIT) operating philosophy

_____ **10.** Activity-based costing (ABC)

a. A framework that uses both financial and nonfinancial performance measures to assess whether the objectives of a company's stakeholder groups are being met

b. Something that increases both product cost and desirability

c. A management tool that identifies and analyzes all major operating activities and seeks to eliminate those that do not add value to a product or service

d. A management approach that creates an environment in which materials, personnel, and facilities are acquired and used only as needed

e. The concept that management should never be satisfied with the status quo but should constantly seek better ways of doing things

f. A management tool that enables managers to identify limitations on production and to set priorities on their time and resources

g. A management approach that focuses on coordinating employees' efforts to achieve product or service excellence

h. A management accounting practice that traces costs to major operating activities and assigns the costs to the products that use the resources supplied by the activities

i. The field involved with providing useful information to managers for decision-making purposes

j. Something that increases product cost but does not enhance product desirability

Short Answer

Use the lines provided to answer each item.

1. What are the four traditional stages of the management cycle?

_____

_____

_____

_____

2. Briefly explain what is meant by a just-in-time operating philosophy.

_____

_____

_____

_____

Note to student: The matching quiz might be completed more efficiently by starting with the definition and searching for the corresponding term.

3. List the four areas emphasized by the standards of ethical conduct for management accountants.

_____

_____

_____

_____

4. Briefly explain the "four *w*'s" of preparing a management report.

_____

_____

_____

True-False

Circle T if the statement is true, F if it is false. Provide explanations for the false answers, using the blank lines at the end of the section.

T F **1.** The function of the management accountant is to make important decisions for the company.

T F **2.** Management accounting exists primarily for the benefit of people inside the company.

T F **3.** A management accountant for a not-for-profit or government organization relies more on financial accounting principles than on management accounting rules.

T F **4.** The business entity as a whole is the focal point of analysis in financial accounting.

T F **5.** The data that support management accounting reports often are subjective.

T F **6.** Financial accounting reports may be prepared whenever management requests them.

T F **7.** Avoiding conflicts of interest relates most closely to the ethical standard of confidentiality.

T F **8.** Enhancing one's professional skills relates most closely to the ethical standard of objectivity.

T F **9.** The just-in-time operating philosophy emphasizes the elimination of waste.

T F **10.** Performance measures may be either financial or nonfinancial.

T F **11.** Nonvalue-adding activities are prime targets for elimination.

T F **12.** Management accountants frequently use nonfinancial units in their analyses.

T F **13.** Planning is the second stage in the management cycle.

T F **14.** Activity-based management identifies activities as being value-adding or nonvalue-adding.

T F **15.** Activities that add value to a product, as perceived by the manufacturer, are known as value-adding activities.

_____

_____

_____

_____

_____

_____

_____

_____

_____

_____

_____

_____

_____

_____

_____

_____

_____

_____

Multiple Choice

Circle the letter of the best answer.

1. Developing skills on an ongoing basis relates most closely to which of the following standards of ethical conduct?
   a. Integrity
   b. Objectivity
   c. Confidentiality
   d. Competence

2. Refusing a gift that might influence one's actions relates most closely to which of the following standards of ethical conduct?
   a. Integrity
   b. Objectivity
   c. Confidentiality
   d. Competence

3. Management accounting and financial accounting do *not* differ with respect to
   a. the primary users of the accounting reports.
   b. the timeliness of the information presented in the reports.
   c. restrictive guidelines.
   d. the units of measurement used in analyses.

4. Which of the following adhere(s) to the concept of continuous improvement?
   a. Just-in-time operating philosophy
   b. Total quality management
   c. Activity-based management
   d. All of the above

5. The content of management accounting reports normally is dictated by
   a. the double-entry system.
   b. generally accepted accounting principles.
   c. users' needs.
   d. the need to present historical and verifiable data.

6. Management accounting reports and analyses are usually heavily subjective, which means that
   a. much of the data have been estimated.
   b. the reports and analyses ignore inflation.
   c. the data are verifiable.
   d. the units of measurement used are historical dollars.

7. Managers compare actual performance with expectations of performance at which stage of the management cycle?
   a. Planning
   b. Executing
   c. Reviewing
   d. Reporting

8. Which of the following is *not* based on nonfinancial data?
   a. Analysis of deliveries
   b. Operating budgets
   c. Customer surveys
   d. Analysis of labor hours worked

APPLYING YOUR KNOWLEDGE

Exercises

1. Each item in the lettered list below describes a characteristic of management accounting or financial accounting and falls into one of the categories in the numbered list that follows. Write the appropriate letter in the blanks beneath the columns for financial accounting and management accounting.

   a. Business entity as a whole
   b. No restrictions on reporting format other than the usefulness of the information presented
   c. Managers and employees
   d. Historical, objective, and verifiable
   e. Persons and organizations outside the business
   f. Whenever needed; might not be on a regular basis
   g. Double-entry system
   h. Various segments of the business entity
   i. Dollars at historical and market values
   j. Subjective and future-oriented for planning purposes, but objective and verifiable for decision making
   k. On a periodic and regular basis
   l. Not restricted to double-entry system; may use any appropriate system
   m. Adherence to GAAP
   n. Any useful monetary or physical measurement

		Financial Accounting	Management Accounting
1.	Primary users of information	_____	_____
2.	Accounting systems used	_____	_____
3.	Restrictive guidelines	_____	_____
4.	Units of measurement	_____	_____
5.	Focal point of analysis	_____	_____
6.	Frequency of reporting	_____	_____
7.	Nature of information	_____	_____

2. Dom Lucia is the owner of Dom's Pizza Palace in upstate New York. The restaurant is always very busy. Over the years, Dom has developed the following measures of efficiency for his employees:

Number of Pizzas Served per Hour	Employee Rating
Over 20	Excellent
17–19	Good
14–16	Average
10–13	Lazy
Under 10	The Pits

During March, Dom's generated the following information about labor hours:

Employee	Hours Worked	Number of Pizzas Served
P. Sanchez	130	2,860
S. Wang	140	2,520
R. Scotti	145	1,885
E. Butterfield	136	2,176
B. Jolita	168	3,192
B. Warner	154	2,310
G. Cohen	150	1,350

Using Dom's Rating scale, evaluate the performance of these employees.

3. Sun Factory is implementing a total quality management system. It has found that the factors listed below have an impact on profits. Use an *a* to indicate that the costs related to each factor achieve quality and a *b* to indicate that they are the costs of poor quality.

1. Rework _____

2. Warranty repairs _____

3. Employee training _____

4. Inspection of materials _____

5. Customer complaints _____

CHAPTER 16 COST CONCEPTS AND COST ALLOCATION

REVIEWING THE CHAPTER

Objective 1: Describe how managers use information about costs in the management cycle.

1. Because costs affect profitability, having accurate and up-to-date cost information is important to managers in all types of for-profit organizations. During the management cycle, managers in manufacturing, retail, and service businesses use information about operating costs to plan, execute, review, and report on operating activities.
   a. In the planning stage, managers develop budgets and estimate selling prices for goods or services based on estimates of operating costs.
   b. In the executing stage, managers use cost information in several ways, including estimating the profitability of a product or service, deciding whether to drop a product line or service, and determining selling prices.
   c. In the reviewing stage, managers want to know about significant variances between estimated costs and actual costs. Such variances help them ascertain the reasons for cost overruns, which may enable them to avoid such problems in the future.
   d. In the reporting stage, managers expect to see financial statements that show the actual costs of operating activities, as well as performance reports that summarize the variance analyses done in the reviewing stage.

Objective 2: Explain how managers classify costs and how they use these cost classifications.

2. A single cost can be classified in several ways: by cost traceability, by cost behavior, by whether it is value-adding or nonvalue-adding, and by whether it is a product cost or a period cost.

3. By tracing costs to cost objects, such as products or services, managers can obtain a fairly accurate cost measurement on which to base decisions about pricing and about reallocating resources to other cost objects.
   a. **Direct costs** are costs that can be conveniently or economically traced to a specific cost object. The wages of production workers, which can be directly traced to an individual product, are an example.
   b. **Indirect costs** are costs that cannot be conveniently or economically traced to a cost object. Rivets used in the production of airplanes and glue used in the production of furniture are examples. Although difficult to trace, indirect costs must be included in the cost of a product or service; to do so, managers use a formula to assign them to a cost object.

4. Cost behavior is the way costs respond (or do not respond) to changes in volume or activity. A cost that changes in direct proportion to a change in productive output (or to any other measure of volume) is a **variable cost**. A **fixed cost** is one that remains constant within a defined range of activity or time period. By analyzing cost behavior, managers can calculate the number of units that must be sold to obtain a certain level of profit.

5. A **value-adding cost** is the cost of an activity that increases the market value of a product or service—that is, the value as perceived by the

customer. For example, if customers are willing to pay more for a product made of a better material, the company's cost of using that material in its product is a value-adding cost. A **nonvalue-adding cost** is the cost of an activity that adds cost to a product or service but does not increase its market value. Such a cost may, however, be necessary. For example, the accounting department is necessary for the operation of a business, but it does not add value to a business's product or service. By classifying costs as adding value or not adding value, managers can eliminate the costs of nonvalue-adding activities that are not essential to the business and try to reduce the costs of those that are essential.

6. For financial reporting purposes, managers classify costs as product costs or period costs.
   a. **Product costs** (also known as *inventoriable costs*) are costs assigned to inventory. They include the three elements of manufacturing cost: direct materials, direct labor, and manufacturing overhead. Product costs appear on the income statement as cost of goods sold and on the balance sheet as finished goods inventory.
   b. **Period costs** (also called *noninventoriable costs*) are the costs of resources used during the period that do not benefit future periods; selling and administrative expenses are an example. Period costs are classified as expenses in the period in which they are incurred and appear on the income statement as operating expenses.

Objective 3: Define and give examples of the three elements of product cost and compute the unit cost of a product.

7. The three elements of product cost are the costs of direct materials, direct labor, and manufacturing overhead. **Direct materials costs** are costs that can be conveniently and economically traced to specific products, such as the cost of the wood used in making a desk. **Direct labor costs** are the costs of the labor needed to make a product that can be conveniently and economically traced to specific units of the product (e.g., the wages of production workers). **Manufacturing overhead costs** (also called *factory overhead, factory burden,* or *indirect manufacturing costs*) are costs of production that cannot be practically or conveniently traced directly to an end product. They include the costs of indirect materials and indirect labor.
   a. **Indirect materials costs** are costs that are too insignificant to assign to direct materials—for example, the costs of nails, rivets, lubricants, and small tools.
   b. **Indirect labor costs** are labor costs for production-related activities that cannot be conveniently traced to a product, such as the costs of maintenance, inspection, engineering design, supervision, and materials handling.
   c. Other indirect manufacturing costs include the costs of building maintenance, property taxes, property insurance, rent, utilities, and depreciation on plant and equipment.

8. **Product unit cost** is the cost of manufacturing a single unit of product. It is computed either by dividing the total cost of direct materials, direct labor, and manufacturing overhead by the total number of units produced, or by determining the cost per unit for each element of the product cost and adding those per-unit costs. Product unit cost can be calculated by using the actual, normal, or standard costing methods.
   a. **Actual costing** uses the costs of direct materials, direct labor, and manufacturing overhead at the end of the accounting period, or when actual costs are known, to calculate the product unit cost.
   b. **Normal costing** can be used when the actual manufacturing overhead costs are not yet known. It combines *actual* direct materials and direct labor costs with *estimated* manufacturing overhead costs to calculate the product unit cost.
   c. **Standard costing** allows managers to use estimates (*standards*) of direct materials, direct labor, and manufacturing overhead costs to determine the product unit cost. Managers use standard costs as a benchmark for pricing decisions and for controlling product costs.

9. **Prime costs** are the primary costs of production; they are the sum of a product's direct materials costs and direct labor costs. **Conversion costs** are the costs of converting raw materials into finished goods; they are the sum of the direct labor and manufacturing overhead costs incurred in turning direct materials into a finished product.

Objective 4: Describe the flow of costs through a manufacturer's inventory accounts.

10. A manufacturer maintains a **Materials Inventory account,** a **Work in Process Inventory account,** and a **Finished Goods Inventory account.** The balance in the Materials Inventory account shows the cost of goods purchased but unused. The balance in the Work in Process Inventory account shows the costs assigned to partially completed

products. The balance in the Finished Goods Inventory account shows the costs of products completed but not yet sold.

11. Accountants track manufacturing costs and make changes in account balances by referring to the source documents that accompany the flow of costs through the production process.

   a. The purchasing process begins with a *purchase request* for materials. If the materials are not on hand, the purchasing department sends a *purchase order* to a supplier. A *receiving report* documents the arrival of the materials. The company then receives a *vendor's invoice* for payment for the materials. The costs of these materials increase the balance in the Materials Inventory account.

   b. As production begins, the storeroom clerk receives an authorized *materials request form* specifying which materials are to be sent to the production area. The cost of the direct materials transferred to production increases the balance of the Work in Process Inventory account, and the cost of the indirect materials transferred increases the balance of the Manufacturing Overhead account. The costs of both types of materials decrease the balance of the Materials Inventory account. *Time cards* are used to record production employees' hours; the cost of their labor increases the Work in Process Inventory account. A *job order cost card* records all costs incurred as the products move through production.

   c. The cost of completed products decreases the balance of the Work in Process Inventory account and increases the balance of the Finished Goods Inventory account. When a product is sold, a clerk prepares a *sales invoice*. A *shipping document* shows the quantity of goods shipped and gives a description of them. As products are sold, the balance in the Finished Goods Inventory account decreases, and the balance in the Cost of Goods Sold account increases.

12. **Manufacturing cost flow** is the flow of manufacturing costs (direct materials, direct labor, and manufacturing overhead) through the Materials Inventory, Work in Process Inventory, and Finished Goods Inventory accounts into the Cost of Goods Sold account. Manufacturing costs flow first into the Materials Inventory account, which is used to record the costs of materials when they are received and again when they are issued for use in production. As the production process begins, all manufacturing-related costs (direct materials, direct labor, and manufacturing overhead) are recorded in the Work in Process Inventory account. The total costs of direct materials, direct labor, and manufacturing overhead incurred and transferred to Work in Process Inventory during an accounting period are called **total manufacturing costs.** When products are completed, their costs move from the Work in Process Inventory account to the Finished Goods Inventory account. The **cost of goods manufactured** is the cost of all units completed and moved to finished goods storage. Costs remain in the Finished Goods Inventory account until the products are sold. They are then transferred to the Cost of Goods Sold account.

Objective 5: Compare how service, retail, and manufacturing organizations report costs on their financial statements and how they account for inventories.

13. A manufacturer prepares a **statement of cost of goods manufactured** so that the cost of goods sold can be summarized in the income statement. The example that follows illustrates the three steps involved in preparing a statement of cost of goods manufactured.

   a. First, the cost of direct materials used must be found.

Beginning balance, materials inventory	$100
Add direct materials purchased (net)	350
Cost of direct materials available for use	$450
Less ending balance, materials inventory	200
Cost of direct materials used	$250 (1)

   b. Second, total manufacturing costs must be computed.

Cost of direct materials used (computed in section **a**)	$ 250 (1)
Add direct labor costs	900
Add total manufacturing overhead costs	750
Total manufacturing costs	$1,900 (2)

   c. Third, the cost of goods manufactured must be computed.

Total manufacturing costs (computed in section **b**)	$1,900 (2)
Add beginning balance, work in process inventory	400
Total cost of work in process during the period	$2,300
Less ending balance, work in process inventory	700
Cost of goods manufactured	$1,600 (3)

14. When the figure for the cost of goods manufactured has been computed, it can be transferred to

the cost of goods sold section of the income statement, as follows:

Beginning balance, finished goods inventory	$1,250
Add cost of goods manufactured (computed in section **c**)	1,600 (3)
Total cost of finished goods available for sale	$2,850
Less ending balance, finished goods inventory	300
Cost of goods sold	$2,550

15. Because the operations of service, retail, and manufacturing organizations differ, their financial statements differ as well. Because a service organization sells services, not products, it has no inventory account on its balance sheet. The cost of sales on its income statement reflects the net cost of the services sold. A retail organization, which purchases products ready for resale, maintains only one inventory account on its balance sheet. Called the Merchandise Inventory account, it reflects the costs of goods held for resale. The cost of goods sold on a retail organization's income statement is simply the difference between the cost of goods available for sale and the ending merchandise inventory. A manufacturing organization, because it creates a product, maintains three inventory accounts on its balance sheet: Materials Inventory, Work in Process Inventory, and Finished Goods Inventory. Its cost of goods sold equals the cost of goods available for sale minus ending finished goods inventory.

Objective 6: Define *cost allocation* and explain how cost objects, cost pools, and cost drivers are used to assign manufacturing overhead costs.

16. Manufacturing overhead costs are indirect costs that must be collected and allocated in some manner. **Cost allocation** is the process of assigning a collection of indirect costs to a specific **cost object,** such as a product or service, using an allocation base known as a **cost driver.** A cost driver is an activity base representing a major business function, such as direct labor hours, direct labor costs, or units produced. As the cost driver increases in volume, it causes the **cost pool**—the collection of indirect costs assigned to a cost object—to increase in amount.

17. Allocating manufacturing overhead costs is a four-step process that corresponds to the four stages of the management cycle. In the first step (the planning stage), managers estimate manufacturing overhead costs and calculate a **predetermined overhead rate** (in traditional settings) or an activity pool rate (in activity-based costing settings) at which they will assign overhead costs to products. In the second step (the executing stage), the *estimated* overhead costs are applied to the product's costs as units are manufactured. In the third step (the reviewing stage), the actual manufacturing overhead costs are recorded. In the fourth step (the reporting stage), the difference between the estimated and actual overhead costs is calculated and reconciled. The Cost of Goods Sold account is corrected if the amount of **overapplied overhead costs** or **underapplied overhead costs** is immaterial. If the amount is material, adjustments are made not only to the Cost of Goods Sold account, but also to the Work in Process Inventory and Finished Goods Inventory accounts.

18. Because managers use predetermined overhead rates to make pricing decisions and to control costs, the rates should be calculated as accurately as possible. The successful allocation of manufacturing overhead costs depends on two factors: a careful estimate of the total manufacturing overhead costs and a good forecast of the activity level of the cost driver.

Objective 7: Using the traditional method of allocating manufacturing overhead costs, calculate product unit cost.

19. The traditional approach to applying manufacturing overhead costs is to use a single predetermined overhead rate. The total manufacturing overhead costs constitute one cost pool, and a traditional activity base, such as direct labor hours, direct labor costs, or machine hours, is the cost driver.

20. The first step in calculating product unit cost when using the traditional method is to compute a predetermined overhead rate. The second step is to apply overhead costs to the products by multiplying the predetermined rate by the actual cost driver level. For example, assume that total manufacturing overhead is estimated at $100,000 and that the cost driver (direct labor hours) is estimated at 5,000 hours. Actual direct labor hours total 4,500. Of the 4,500 hours, 2,000 were spent on the production of 6,000 units of Product A, and 2,500 were spent on the production of 7,000

units of Product B. The predetermined overhead rate would be calculated as follows:

$$\frac{\$100,000}{5,000} = \$20 \text{ per Direct Labor Hour}$$

Manufacturing overhead would then be applied to both products as follows:

A: 2,000 D.L. Hours × $20 Rate = $40,000
B: 2,500 D.L. Hours × $20 Rate = 50,000

Total Applied $90,000

Thus, manufacturing overhead cost per unit is

A: $\frac{\$40,000 \text{ Applied}}{6,000 \text{ Units}}$ = $6.67 per Unit

B: $\frac{\$50,000 \text{ Applied}}{7,000 \text{ Units}}$ = $7.14 per Unit

Objective 8: Using activity-based costing to assign manufacturing overhead costs, calculate product unit cost.

21. **Activity-based costing (ABC)** is a more accurate method of assigning overhead costs to products than the traditional method. It categorizes all indirect costs by activity, traces the indirect costs to those activities, and assigns activity costs to products using a cost driver related to the cause of the cost.

22. The first step in calculating product unit cost when using activity-based costing is to estimate the total manufacturing overhead costs and then group these costs into appropriate activity pools related to specific activities. After identifying the appropriate number of activity pools and a cost driver, estimated activity pool amounts and estimated cost driver levels must be determined. The next step is to calculate a predetermined activity cost rate for each activity pool, as shown in Table 1. The cost pool rate is the estimated activity pool amount divided by the estimated cost driver level. As shown in Table 2 (on the next page), manufacturing overhead costs are then applied to the products by using the cost driver levels for each cost driver multiplied by the appropriate rate.

23. The example in Table 2 shows that Product B's manufacturing overhead cost was lower than Product A's. The primary reason for this difference is that Product A requires more setups and inspections than Product B. The information about production requirements and the accuracy of the product unit cost that the ABC costing method yields provide managers with valuable insights.

Objective 9: Apply costing concepts to a service organization.

24. Because no products are manufactured in the course of providing services, service organizations have no materials costs. They do, however, have both direct labor costs and overhead costs, which are similar to those in manufacturing organizations. To determine the cost of performing a service, direct labor and service overhead costs are included in the computation.

TABLE 1

Activity Pool	Estimated Total Activity Pool Costs	Cost Driver	Estimated Total Cost Driver Level	Predetermined Activity Cost Rate
Setup	$10,000	Number of setups	100 setups	$100 per setup
Inspection	8,000	Number of inspections	400 inspections	$20 per inspection
Building	7,000	Machine hours	3,500 machine hours	$2 per machine hour
Packaging	5,000	Packaging hours	1,000 packaging hours	$5 per packaging hour
	$30,000			

TABLE 2

Activity Pool	Activity Cost Rate	*Product A* Actual Cost Driver Level	Cost Applied	*Product B* Actual Cost Driver Level	Cost Applied
Setup	$100	70	$ 7,000	30	$ 3,000
Inspection	20	250	5,000	150	3,000
Building	2	1,500	3,000	2,000	4,000
Packaging	5	300	1,500	700	3,500
Total			$16,500		$13,500
÷ by Number of units			1,000		2,000
= Manufacturing overhead cost per unit			$16.50		$6.75

SELF-TEST

Test your knowledge of the chapter by choosing the best answer for each item below.

1. Manufacturing overhead costs include all of the following *except*
   a. direct labor.
   b. indirect labor.
   c. indirect materials.
   d. other indirect manufacturing costs.

2. Total product cost includes
   a. direct labor.
   b. indirect labor.
   c. manufacturing overhead.
   d. all of the above.

3. Which of the following statements is *false?*
   a. Service organizations do not maintain inventory levels.
   b. Service organizations use accounting information to make better decisions.
   c. A service organization's income statement reports cost of sales rather than cost of goods sold.
   d. A service organization's balance sheet includes an inventory account called Cost of Service.

4. Which of the following documents starts the purchasing process?
   a. Purchase order
   b. Purchase request
   c. Materials request
   d. Vendor's invoice

5. All manufacturing costs incurred and assigned to products currently in production are classified as
   a. work in process inventory costs.
   b. materials inventory costs.
   c. finished goods inventory costs.
   d. costs of goods sold.

6. Given estimated total manufacturing overhead costs of $100,000, estimated total direct labor hours (the cost driver) of 10,000, and units produced of 6,000, the predetermined overhead rate under the traditional approach to allocating overhead is
   a. 10 percent.
   b. 6 percent.
   c. $6.
   d. $10.

7. If the beginning balance in the Materials Inventory account was $4,200, the ending balance was $3,940, and $21,560 of materials were used during the month, what was the cost of the materials purchased during this period?
   a. $21,600
   b. $21,820
   c. $21,790
   d. $21,300

8. At Price Company, the month-end cost of goods sold was $393,910, the beginning finished goods inventory was $40,410, and the ending finished goods inventory was $42,900. What was the total cost of completed goods transferred to finished goods inventory during the month?
   a. $396,400
   b. $391,120
   c. $391,420
   d. $393,400

9. Underapplied manufacturing overhead results when
   a. actual manufacturing overhead is less than estimated manufacturing overhead.
   b. applied overhead is less than actual manufacturing overhead.
   c. applied overhead is greater than actual manufacturing overhead.
   d. the cost of indirect materials is less than estimated.

10. A key difference between the activity-based costing (ABC) and traditional costing methods is that
    a. the traditional costing method uses multiple activity pools.
    b. ABC uses multiple activity pools.
    c. ABC uses a single activity pool.
    d. ABC uses a single cost driver.

TESTING YOUR KNOWLEDGE

*Matching**

Match each term with its definition by writing the appropriate letter in the blank.

_____ 1. Time card

_____ 2. Manufacturing overhead costs

_____ 3. Direct materials

_____ 4. Indirect materials

_____ 5. Direct labor costs

_____ 6. Indirect labor costs

_____ 7. Cost driver

_____ 8. Cost pool

_____ 9. Standard costing

_____ 10. Total product costs

_____ 11. Work in Process Inventory account

_____ 12. Finished Goods Inventory account

_____ 13. Cost of goods manufactured

_____ 14. Total manufacturing costs

_____ 15. Cost allocation

a. Materials that cannot be conveniently and economically traced to specific products

b. Materials that can be conveniently and economically traced to specific products

c. All indirect manufacturing costs

d. Wages, salaries, and related costs that cannot be conveniently and economically traced to specific products

e. The total cost charged to completed units during a period

f. Direct labor, direct materials, and manufacturing overhead costs

g. Wages, salaries, and related costs that can be conveniently and economically traced to specific products

h. A record of the number of hours worked by an employee

i. The assignment of a cost to a specific cost object

j. An activity that causes the activity pool to increase in amount

k. A collection of overhead costs or other indirect costs related to a cost object

l. An account that holds the costs assigned to all completed units that have not yet been sold

m. A method of cost measurement that uses the estimated costs of direct materials, direct labor, and manufacturing overhead to calculate a product unit cost

n. Total costs charged to production during a period

o. An account that records all manufacturing costs incurred and assigned to partially completed units of product

Short Answer

Use the lines provided to answer each item.

1. List the three types of inventory accounts that manufacturers maintain.

_____

_____

_____

2. What are the three main components of manufacturing costs?

_____

_____

_____

_____

Note to student: The matching quiz might be completed more efficiently by starting with the definition and searching for the corresponding term.

3. When is a materials cost considered a direct materials cost?

_____

_____

4. List four ways in which managers use information about costs.

_____

_____

_____

_____

5. Show how the cost of direct materials used is computed.

_____

+ _____

= _____

− _____

= _____

6. Indicate the way in which total manufacturing costs are computed.

_____

+ _____

+ _____

= _____

7. Show how the cost of goods manufactured is computed.

_____

+ _____

= _____

− _____

= _____

8. Explain how a predetermined overhead rate is computed.

_____

_____

_____

_____

9. What is overapplied manufacturing overhead?

_____

_____

_____

_____

10. What is cost of goods manufactured?

_____

_____

_____

_____

_____

_____

True-False

Circle T if the statement is true, F if it is false. Provide explanations for the false answers, using the blank lines at the end of the section.

T F **1.** A product cost should not appear in the income statement until the period in which the product is sold.

T F **2.** The Work in Process Inventory account does not contain any period costs (expenses).

T F **3.** Activity-based costing uses multiple cost pools.

T F **4.** *Factory burden* is another term for manufacturing overhead.

T F **5.** The Materials Inventory account decreases as materials are used in production.

T F **6.** Most of the product costs incurred by a manufacturer are also incurred by a service organization.

T F **7.** Number of inspections is an example of a cost driver used in ABC costing.

T F **8.** A purchase order is prepared before a purchase request.

T F 9. The costs of factory supervision are classified as direct labor.

T F 10. The statement of cost of goods manufactured must be prepared after the income statement.

T F 11. To compute the cost of goods sold for a manufacturer, the beginning balance of Finished Goods Inventory must be known.

T F 12. Cost of goods manufactured minus total manufacturing costs equals the change in Work in Process Inventory during a period.

T F 13. Cost of goods manufactured must be computed before total manufacturing costs.

T F 14. Cost of direct materials used must be computed before cost of goods manufactured.

T F 15. Activity-based costing calculates a more accurate product cost than the traditional costing method.

T F 16. An increase in the amount of an activity pool indicates that the cost driver has increased.

T F 17. The smaller a cost object, the easier it is to trace manufacturing costs to the object.

T F 18. Depreciation on plant and equipment is a direct cost.

_____

_____

_____

_____

_____

_____

_____

_____

_____

_____

_____

_____

_____

_____

_____

Circle the letter of the best answer.

1. Which of the following is a direct materials cost?
   a. The cost of glue used in making a bookcase
   b. A janitor's salary
   c. The cost of legs used in making a chair
   d. The cost of rags used in cleaning a machine

2. Documents relating to materials must be processed in a specific order. Which of the following lists those documents in their proper order?
   a. Materials request, purchase request, purchase order, receiving report
   b. Purchase order, purchase request, receiving report, materials request
   c. Purchase request, purchase order, receiving report, materials request
   d. Receiving report, purchase order, materials request, purchase request

3. Which of the following would probably be considered a period cost?
   a. Salaries of salespeople
   b. Wages of an assembly-line worker
   c. Freight in
   d. Materials used in the manufacture of a product

4. Which of the following documents does a purchasing department send to a vendor?
   a. Purchase request
   b. Materials request
   c. Receiving report
   d. Purchase order

5. Which of the following documents does a storeroom clerk receive before releasing materials to production?
   a. Materials request
   b. Purchase request
   c. Job order cost card
   d. Purchase order

6. "Activities" in activity-based costing are analogous to
   a. cost objects.
   b. activity pools.
   c. cost drivers.
   d. manufacturing overhead.

7. Activity pools in activity-based costing are
   a. usually fewer in number than in traditional costing.
   b. used to accumulate costs.
   c. the products being manufactured.
   d. the same as overapplied manufacturing overhead costs.

8. How many cost drivers does the traditional costing method typically use?
   a. One
   b. Two
   c. Three
   d. Four

9. In which stages of the management cycle do managers use product cost information?
   a. Planning
   b. Executing
   c. Reviewing
   d. All of the above

APPLYING YOUR KNOWLEDGE

Exercises

1. Kue Corporation has provided the following data for 20xx:

Cost of goods manufactured	$450,000
Finished goods, Jan. 1	75,000
Finished goods, Dec. 31	80,000
Direct materials, Jan. 1	92,000
Direct materials, Dec. 31	70,000
Work in process, Jan. 1	55,000
Work in process, Dec. 31	64,000

In the space provided at the right, compute the cost of goods sold.

2. Using the data below, calculate the activity cost rates, costs applied to Product A and Product B, total costs applied, and the overhead cost per unit.

Activity Pool	Estimated Total Activity Pool Costs	Cost Driver	Estimated Total Cost Driver Level	Predetermined Activity Cost Rate
Setup	$10,000	Number of setups	200 setups	$
Inspection	6,000	Number of inspections	300 inspections	$
Building	8,000	Machine hours	4,000 machine hours	$
Packaging	4,000 $28,000	Packaging hours	1,000 packaging hours	$

			Product A		Product B	
Activity Pool	Activity Cost Rate	Actual Cost Driver Level	Cost Applied	Actual Cost Driver Level	Cost Applied
Setup	$	70	$	30	$
Inspection		250		150	
Building		1,500		2,000	
Packaging		300	_____	700	_____
Total			$		$
÷ by Number of units			1,000		2,000
= Manufacturing overhead cost per unit			$		$

3. Using the following data, prepare a statement of cost of goods manufactured for Specialty Company in the form provided below:

Depreciation, factory building and equipment	$ 31,800
Direct labor	142,900
Factory insurance	2,300
Factory utilities expense	26,000
Finished goods inventory, Jan. 1	82,400
Finished goods inventory, Dec. 31	71,000
General and administrative expenses	163,000
Indirect labor	42,800
Net sales	855,100
Other factory costs	12,600
Materials inventory, Jan. 1	8,700
Materials inventory, Dec. 31	32,600
Materials purchased (net)	168,300
Selling expenses	88,500
Work in process inventory, Jan. 1	34,200
Work in process inventory, Dec. 31	28,700

Specialty Company
Statement of Cost of Goods Manufactured
For the Year Ended December 31, 20xx

4. Classify the costs of each of the following as direct materials (DM), direct labor (DL), or manufacturing overhead (OH) costs:

_____ **a.** Sandpaper

_____ **b.** Worker who assembles a product

_____ **c.** Worker who cleans machinery and sets it up

_____ **d.** Steel plates used in production

_____ **e.** Glue and nails

_____ **f.** Worker who sands a product before it is painted

_____ **g.** Wheels attached to a product

_____ **h.** Depreciation of machinery

_____ **i.** Paint used to touch up finished products

Crossword Puzzle
for Chapters 15 and 16

ACROSS

4. Document sent to a supplier (2 words)
7. Not traceable to specific products
8. Normal inventory account balance
10. _____ goods manufactured (2 words)
12. What managers do as they begin the management cycle
13. _____ (noninventoriable) cost
14. An indirect material
16. Audience for a management report
18. Activity that increases cost pool
19. Traceable to specific products
20. _____ (estimated) cost
21. The "T" of "TQM"

DOWN

1. Expenditure traceable to goods (2 words)
2. Predetermined overhead _____
3. Order, as materials
5. _____ report (prepared when goods arrive)
6. Partially completed goods (3 words)
9. Indirect manufacturing costs
11. _____ goods (ready-for-sale inventory)
15. Employee _____ cards
17. Example of 9-Down

CHAPTER 17 COSTING SYSTEMS: JOB ORDER COSTING

REVIEWING THE CHAPTER

Objective 1: Discuss the role information about costs plays in the management cycle and explain why unit cost is important.

1. The role of the management accountant is to develop a management information system that provides managers with the cost information they need. Information about costs is essential at each stage of the management cycle.

2. During the planning stage, managers use cost information to set performance expectations, estimate product or service costs, and establish selling prices. During the executing stage, they use cost information to make decisions about controlling costs, managing the company's volume of activity, ensuring quality, and negotiating prices. During the reviewing stage, managers analyze actual and targeted total and unit costs to evaluate performance and adjust planning and decision-making strategies. During the reporting stage, they use unit costs to prepare financial statements and internal performance reports.

Objective 2: Distinguish between the two basic types of product costing systems and identify the information each provides.

3. A **product costing system** is a set of procedures used to account for an organization's product costs. A product costing system should provide timely and accurate unit cost information for pricing, cost planning and control, inventory valuation, and financial statement preparation. The two basic types of product costing systems are the job order costing system and the process costing system.

4. Companies that make large, unique, or special-order products (e.g., ships, wedding invitations, or custom-made drapes) typically use a **job order costing system**. Such a system traces the costs of direct materials, direct labor, and manufacturing overhead to a specific batch of products or a specific **job order** (i.e., a customer order for a specific number of specially designed, made-to-order products). Job order costing measures the cost of each complete unit and summarizes the cost of all jobs in a single Work in Process Inventory account that is supported by job order cost cards. A **job order cost card** is the document on which all costs incurred in the production of a particular job order are recorded.

5. Companies that produce large amounts of similar products or liquid products or that have long, continuous production runs of identical products typically use a **process costing system.** Makers of paint, breakfast cereal, and paper would use such a system. A process costing system first traces the costs of direct materials, direct labor, and manufacturing overhead to processes, departments, or work cells and then assigns the costs to the products manufactured by those processes, departments, or work cells. Process costing uses several Work in Process Inventory accounts, one for each process, department, or work cell.

6. Few production processes are a perfect match for a job order costing or process costing system. The typical product costing system therefore combines parts of job order costing and process costing to create a hybrid system designed specifically for a company's production process.

Objective 3: Explain the cost flow in a manufacturer's job order costing system.

7. A job order costing system is designed to gather the costs of materials, labor, and manufacturing overhead for a specific order or batch of products. It provides timely, accurate cost information and facilitates the smooth and continuous flow of that information. This cost flow, along with the job order cost cards and the subsidiary ledgers for materials and finished goods inventories, is the core of the job order costing system. Because a job order costing system emphasizes cost flow, it is important to understand how costs are incurred, recorded, and transferred within the system.

  a. The purchase of materials or supplies is recorded by increasing Materials Inventory and decreasing Cash or increasing Accounts Payable.

  b. When materials or supplies are issued into production, Work in Process Inventory is increased for the direct materials portion, Manufacturing Overhead is increased for the indirect materials portion, and Materials Inventory is reduced.

  c. The total cost of wages earned during the period is debited to the Factory Payroll account. The factory payroll is distributed to the production accounts by increasing the Work in Process Inventory for direct labor, increasing Manufacturing Overhead for indirect labor, and decreasing Factory Payroll for the amount of direct labor.

  d. Manufacturing overhead costs, other than indirect materials and indirect labor, increase the Manufacturing Overhead account and decrease an appropriate account, such as Cash or Accounts Payable.

  e. Manufacturing overhead is applied to specific jobs by increasing the Work in Process Inventory account and reducing the Manufacturing Overhead account.

  f. Upon the completion of a job, Finished Goods Inventory is increased, and Work in Process Inventory is decreased.

  g. When finished goods are sold, the sale is first recorded by increasing Cash or Accounts Receivable and increasing Sales for the total sales price. Cost of Goods Sold is then recog-

nized and Finished Goods Inventory is reduced for the cost attached to the goods sold.

  h. At the end of the period, an adjustment must be made for under- or overapplied overhead.

Objective 4: Prepare a job order cost card and compute a job order's product unit cost.

8. In a job order costing system, all manufacturing costs are accumulated in one Work in Process Inventory account. Job order cost cards are used to connect those costs to specific jobs. Each job has its own job order cost card, which becomes part of the subsidiary ledger for the Work in Process Inventory account. The job cost card includes the costs of direct materials used, direct labor, and manufacturing overhead assigned to the job. When the job is completed, the product unit cost is computed by dividing the total costs for the job by the number of goods units produced.

Objective 5: Apply job order costing to a service organization.

9. Many service organizations use job order costing to compute the cost of rendering services. Because service organizations do not manufacture products, their materials costs are usually negligible.

10. Job order cost cards are used to track the costs of labor, materials and supplies, and service overhead for each job. To cover these costs and earn a profit, many service companies base jobs on **cost-plus contracts**, which require the customer to pay all costs plus a predetermined amount of profit.

11. When a job is finished, the costs on the completed job order cost card become the cost of services. The cost of services is adjusted at the end of the accounting period for the difference between the applied and actual service overhead costs.

Objective 6: Distinguish between job order costing and project costing.

12. **Projects** are broader and more complex than jobs. They require a multidisciplinary approach to the development and delivery of a product or service. Examples include the construction of a large-scale retail and residential complex and the development of a computer software program.

13. In contrast to job order costing, which focuses on a specific job order, project costing links many different job orders and processes by transferring costs from one job or process to another, collecting and summarizing costs in a variety of ways, and providing appropriate internal controls.

Test your knowledge of the chapter by choosing the best answer for each item below.

1. Which of the following companies is *most* likely to use a job order costing system?
   a. Jet aircraft manufacturer
   b. Paint manufacturer
   c. Soft drink producer
   d. Oil-refining company

2. An approach to product costing that assigns all manufacturing costs to specific job orders or batches of products is
   a. job order costing.
   b. process costing.
   c. total costing.
   d. activity-based costing.

3. The document used for tracking product costs in a job order costing system is a job order
   a. materials receiving report.
   b. cost card.
   c. request form.
   d. materials request card.

4. A job order cost card does *not* include costs for
   a. manufacturing overhead.
   b. direct materials used.
   c. direct materials purchased.
   d. direct labor.

5. During February, gross pay was $36,400 for direct labor and $45,600 for indirect labor. How much labor cost should have been entered directly into the Work in Process Inventory account during the month?
   a. $36,400
   b. $45,600
   c. $0
   d. $82,000

6. Job order costing in a service organization differs from job order costing in a manufacturing organization in that
   a. a job order cost card is not used.
   b. no overhead is applied.
   c. services cannot be inventoried.
   d. service costs include direct labor.

7. For complex tasks that require multiple departments, experts, and procedures, which costing technique is *most* appropriate?
   a. Job order costing
   b. Process costing
   c. Full costing
   d. Project costing

8. In which step(s) of the management cycle is product cost information useful?
   a. Planning
   b. Executing
   c. Reviewing
   d. All of the above

9. Project costing is used by companies that
   a. develop computer software programs.
   b. bottle soft drinks.
   c. produce made-to-order draperies.
   d. process milk.

10. In the planning stage of the management cycle, managers use product cost information to
    a. evaluate performance.
    b. make changes to improve quality.
    c. forecast product costs.
    d. determine whether production goals have been achieved.

TESTING YOUR KNOWLEDGE

Matching*

Match each term with its definition by writing the appropriate letter in the blank.

_____ **1.** Cost-plus contract

_____ **2.** Project costing

_____ **3.** Process costing system

_____ **4.** Job order costing system

_____ **5.** Job order cost cards

_____ **6.** Job order

_____ **7.** Manufacturing Overhead account

a. An accounting record that contains indirect manufacturing costs incurred and applied

b. The accounting method used by a manufacturer of one-of-a-kind or special-order products

c. An arrangement that requires a customer to pay for all costs incurred on a job plus a predetermined amount of profit

d. Records of the accumulation of job costs

e. A customer order for a specific number of special-order products

f. The accounting method used by a manufacturer of a large number of similar products

g. A broad, complex, multidisciplinary approach to the production of a good or delivery of a service

Short Answer

Use the lines provided to answer each item.

1. What are a service organization's three job costs ?

_____

_____

_____

2. What are the three components of work in process inventory?

_____

_____

_____

3. After all data have been recorded on a job order cost card, how is product unit cost computed?

_____

_____

4. List three products for which a job order costing system should be used.

_____

_____

_____

Note to student: The matching quiz might be completed more efficiently by starting with the definition and searching for the corresponding term.

True-False

Circle T if the statement is true, F if it is false. Provide explanations for the false answers, using the blank lines below.

T F **1.** A manufacturer that mass-produces toys would be likely to use a process costing system.

T F **2.** A job order costing system uses a single Work in Process Inventory account.

T F **3.** Indirect manufacturing costs bypass Work in Process Inventory and are charged directly to Finished Goods Inventory.

T F **4.** As soon as work begins on a job, a job order cost card is created.

T F **5.** The product unit cost can be calculated before a job is completed.

T F **6.** When overhead costs are applied to specific jobs, Work in Process Inventory increases, and Manufacturing Overhead decreases.

T F **7.** When goods are shipped to a customer, Cost of Goods Sold increases, and Work in Process Inventory decreases.

T F **8.** A manufacturer of custom-made clothing would probably use a job order costing system.

T F **9.** The cost information needed to compute product unit cost can be found on the completed job order cost cards.

T F **10.** Product cost information is used in all stages of the management cycle.

T F **11.** Product costing in a service organization is exactly the same as in a manufacturing organization.

T F **12.** A project costing system is the same as a process costing system.

T F **13.** A brewery would probably use a process costing system.

_____

_____

_____

_____

_____

_____

_____

_____

_____

_____

_____

_____

_____

_____

_____

_____

_____

_____

_____

_____

Multiple Choice

Circle the letter of the best answer.

1. A job order costing system would most likely be used by a manufacturer of
   a. paper clips.
   b. gasoline.
   c. supersonic jets.
   d. electric clocks.

2. In a job order costing system, which of the following does *not* require an increase in Manufacturing Overhead?
   a. Indirect materials
   b. Applied overhead
   c. Depreciation expense
   d. Indirect labor

3. The Work in Process Inventory account would *not* be increased for
   a. actual factory overhead.
   b. direct labor.
   c. applied factory overhead.
   d. direct materials used.

4. The Manufacturing Overhead account decreases when
   a. recording actual manufacturing overhead costs.
   b. assigning the manufacturing overhead costs to production.
   c. paying for indirect labor.
   d. transferring indirect materials from the Materials Inventory account.

5. A process costing system does *not*
   a. contain several Work in Process Inventory accounts.
   b. accumulate costs by job or batch of products.
   c. base costing on weekly or monthly time periods.
   d. apply to goods produced in a continuous flow.

6. Materials Inventory is reduced when
   a. materials are purchased.
   b. the related manufactured goods are sold.
   c. payment is made for materials.
   d. materials are issued into production.

7. Which of the following managerial uses of cost information is *most* likely to occur in the reviewing stage of the management cycle?
   a. Determining the cost of a product or service
   b. Reporting the cost of goods sold and inventory balances
   c. Computing unit costs based on actual costs incurred and units produced
   d. Evaluating performance by comparing budgeted costs with actual costs

8. Which of the following would *not* be included in the cost of a manufactured product?
   a. Advertising costs
   b. Materials
   c. Direct labor
   d. Factory foreperson's salary

APPLYING YOUR KNOWLEDGE

Exercises

1. Located in Las Cruces, New Mexico, Melvin's Septic Service Company employs 15 people. It uses job order cost cards to track the costs incurred on each of its jobs. Job costs include materials and supplies, labor, and service overhead. Melvin's categorizes these costs as septic design, septic tank installation, and job site cleanup. The company has tracked costs for the Gonzales job, and now that it has finished the job, it needs to complete the cost accounting. The service overhead charge for septic design is 30 percent of design labor cost, and the service overhead charge for septic tank installation is 50 percent of installation labor cost. The cost-plus contract has a 25 percent profit guarantee. The costs for the Gonzales job are as follows:

Beginning balances:

Septic design	$ 5,270
Septic tank installation	28,500
Job site cleanup	150

Costs during October:

Septic design	
Supplies	0
Design labor	500
Septic tank installation	
Materials and supplies	4,300
Direct labor	12,800
Job site cleanup	
Janitorial service	1,050

Complete the job cost card for the Gonzales job.

Job Order Cost Card
Melvin's Septic Service Company

Customer:	Gonzales
Contract Type:	Cost-plus
Type of Service:	Septic Services

Cost Summary:

Costs Charged to Job	Total
Septic design	
Beginning balance	
Design labor	
Service overhead (30% of	
design labor)	————
Totals	————
Septic tank installation	
Beginning balance	
Materials and supplies	
Installation labor	
Service overhead (50% of	
installation labor)	————
Totals	————
Job site cleanup	
Beginning balance	
Janitorial service cost	————
Totals	————
Totals	════
Cost of job	
Markup (25% of cost)	————
Amount billed	════

2. Watchung Shoe Company manufactures shoes of unusual lengths and widths on special order. It uses a job order costing system. For each item described below, enter increases or decreases in the T accounts on the next page.

Dec. 23 Purchased (on credit) materials that cost $2,950.

26 Issued materials costing $850 into production. Of this amount, $50 was for indirect materials.

26 Paid the following bills:

Utilities	$350
Rent	700
Telephone	150

27 The week's gross payroll of $1,500 was distributed to production accounts. Of this amount, 80 percent represents direct labor. (Do not prepare the entries when the payroll is *paid*.)

27 The week's overhead costs are applied to production based on direct labor dollars. Estimated overhead for the year is $165,000, and estimated direct labor dollars are $55,000.

29 Goods costing $3,900 were completed.

30 Finished goods costing $2,000 were shipped to a customer. The selling price was 70 percent greater than the cost, and payment for the goods is expected next month.

31 Applied overhead for the year was $132,500, and actual overhead was $130,000. The difference is closed into Cost of Goods Sold.

Materials Inventory

Accounts Payable

Work In Process Inventory

Manufacturing Overhead

Factory Payroll

Cash

Finished Goods Inventory

Cost of Goods Sold

Sales

Accounts Receivable

CHAPTER 18 COSTING SYSTEMS: PROCESS COSTING

REVIEWING THE CHAPTER

Objective 1: Describe the process costing system, identify the reasons for its use, and discuss its role in the management cycle.

1. A **process costing system** is a product costing system used by companies that produce large amounts of similar products or liquid products or that have a continuous production flow. Companies that produce paint, beverages, bricks, canned foods, milk, and paper are typical users of a process costing system.

2. A process costing system accumulates the costs of direct materials, direct labor, and manufacturing overhead for each process, department, or work cell and assigns those costs to products as they are produced during a particular period.

3. In the planning stage of the management cycle, managers use product cost information to decide what a product should cost and to determine the targeted number of units to be sold. All product-related costs for that targeted number can then be computed and used in the budget. During the executing stage, actual costs are incurred as units are produced, so managers are able to compute actual unit costs. In the reviewing stage, managers evaluate performance by comparing targeted costs with actual costs. If costs have exceeded expectations, they analyze why this has occurred and recommend changes. In the reporting stage, they use actual units produced and costs incurred to value inventory on the balance sheet and cost of goods sold on the income statement.

Objective 2: Relate the patterns of product flows to the cost flow methods in a process costing environment.

4. Before a product is completed, it usually must go through several processes, departments, or work cells. For example, a bookcase might go through the cutting, assembling, and staining departments. A process costing system accumulates costs by process, department, or work cell and passes them along to each subsequent process, department, or work cell as the product is being made. At the end of every accounting period, a process cost report assigns the costs that have accumulated during the period to the units that have transferred out of the process, department, or work cell and to the units that are still work in process.

5. A process cost report may use the FIFO costing method or the average costing method to assign the accumulated costs.
   a. With the **FIFO costing method,** the cost flow follows the logical flow of production; the costs assigned to the first materials processed are the first costs transferred out when the materials flow to the next process, department, or work cell.
   b. The **average costing method** does not attempt to match cost flow with product flow;

instead, it assigns an average cost to all products made during an accounting period.

Objective 3: Explain the role of the Work in Process Inventory accounts in a process costing system.

6. A process costing system maintains a separate Work in Process Inventory account for each process, department, or work cell. As products move from one process, department, or work cell to the next, the costs associated with them flow to the Work in Process Inventory account of that process, department, or work cell. Once the products are completed and ready for sale, their costs are transferred out of the Work in Process Inventory account to the Cost of Goods Sold account.

7. The process cost report prepared at the end of each period assigns the costs that have accumulated in each Work in Process Inventory account to the units transferred out and to the units still in process. The costs from all processes, departments, or work cells are used in computing the product unit cost.

Objective 4: Define *equivalent production* and compute equivalent units.

8. A process costing system assigns the costs incurred in a process, department, or work cell to the units worked on during an accounting period by computing an average cost per unit—that is, by dividing the total manufacturing costs by the total number of units worked on during the period. **Equivalent production** (also called *equivalent units*) is calculated to measure the number of equivalent whole units produced during the period. It expresses partially completed units in terms of completed whole units. The number of equivalent units produced is the sum of (a) total units started and completed during the period and (b) an amount representing the work done on partially completed products in both the beginning and the ending work in process inventories. A percentage of completion factor is applied to partially completed units to calculate the number of equivalent whole units.

9. Equivalent production must be computed separately for direct materials and conversion costs. Direct materials are usually added to the production process at the beginning of the process; therefore, equivalent units for materials typically reflect 100 percent completion. **Conversion costs,** which are the combined total costs of direct labor and manufacturing overhead, are often incurred uniformly throughout the production process. The computation of equivalent production for conversion costs consists of three components: the cost to finish the beginning work in process inventory, the cost to begin and finish the completed units, and the cost to begin work on the units in the ending work in process inventory.

Objective 5: Prepare a process cost report using the FIFO costing method.

10. A **process cost report** helps managers track and analyze costs in a process costing system. In a process cost report that uses the FIFO costing method, the cost flow follows the logical physical flow of production—that is, the costs assigned to the first materials processed are the first costs transferred when those materials flow to the next process, department, or work cell.

11. Preparation of a process cost report involves five steps:
   a. Steps 1 and 2 account for the physical flow of products and compute equivalent production for both direct materials costs and conversion costs.
   b. In Step 3, all direct materials and conversion costs for the current period are added to the costs of beginning inventory to arrive at the total costs to be accounted for.
   c. In Step 4, the cost per equivalent unit for both direct materials and conversion costs is found by dividing those costs by their respective equivalent units. These unit costs are then added to yield the total cost per equivalent unit for the period.
   d. In Step 5, costs are assigned to the units completed and transferred out during the period, as well as to the ending work in process inventory. The information needed to perform this step is provided by the equivalent units computed in Step 2 and the cost per equivalent unit computed in Step 4. When figures for the cost of ending work in process inventory and the cost of goods transferred out of the department are determined, they are totaled and compared with the total costs to be accounted for (computed in Step 3). If the figures do not agree, the difference is due to rounding or to an error in arithmetic.

12. When a company has more than one production process, department, or work cell, it must have a Work in Process Inventory account for each.

Objective 6: Prepare a process cost report using the average costing method.

13. A process cost report that uses the average costing method involves the same five steps as a

process report prepared with the FIFO costing method. However, the procedures for completing some of the steps differ.

a. Step 1 is the same under both the average and FIFO costing methods: the physical units in beginning inventory are added to the physical units started during the period to arrive at total units to be accounted for.

b. In Step 2, the number of units completed and transferred out and the number of units in ending inventory are added to arrive at units accounted for, and the equivalent units for direct materials and conversion costs are computed.

c. In Step 3, all direct materials costs and conversions costs for beginning inventory and the current period are added to arrive at the total costs to be accounted for.

d. In Step 4, the total of the costs in beginning inventory and the current period are divided by the equivalent units to determine the cost per equivalent unit.

e. In Step 5, the costs of the units completed and transferred out are assigned by multiplying the equivalent units for direct materials and conversion (computed in Step 2) by their respective cost per equivalent unit (computed in Step 4) and then totaling these assigned values. The costs of the units in ending work in process inventory are assigned in the same way.

Objective 7: Evaluate operating performance using information about product cost.

14. Product costing systems provide information that managers can use to evaluate an organization's operating performance. Such an analysis may include consideration of the cost trends of a product or product line, units produced per time period, materials usage per unit produced, labor cost per unit produced, special needs of customers, and the cost-effectiveness of changing to a more advanced production process.

Test your knowledge of the chapter by choosing the best answer for each item below.

1. Which of the following companies is *most* likely to use a process costing system?
   a. Bridge-building company
   b. Oil-refining company
   c. Highway construction company
   d. Made-to-order boat company

2. When a company uses a process costing system, how many Work in Process Inventory accounts does it maintain?
   a. Depends on the number of products produced
   b. One
   c. One for each process, department, or work cell
   d. Three

3. In a recent accounting period, a department that uses a process costing system and the FIFO costing method had 1,400 units in beginning Work in Process Inventory, 40 percent complete; started and completed 4,900 units; and had 1,200 units in ending Work in Process Inventory, 60 percent complete. What is the number of equivalent units for materials costs, assuming materials are added at the beginning of the process?
   a. 6,100
   b. 7,500
   c. 6,300
   d. 4,900

4. Assuming the same facts as in **3,** what is the number of equivalent units for conversion costs if those costs are incurred uniformly throughout the process?
   a. 6,180
   b. 7,120
   c. 6,460
   d. 7,500

5. Hood Corporation uses a process costing system and the FIFO costing method. In its production process, materials are added at the outset, and conversion costs are incurred uniformly throughout the process. The following information pertains to Hood's operations in May:

   Beginning work in process inventory: 1,000 units, 50 percent complete; materials costs, $14,700; conversion costs, $13,550

   Units started and completed: 8,000

Ending work in process inventory: 640 units, 80 percent complete

Current period costs: materials, $127,872; conversion, $243,324

Equivalent units: materials costs, 8,640 units; conversion costs, 9,012 units

Given this information, what was the unit cost for materials in May?
   a. $27.10
   b. $27.00
   c. $14.70
   d. $14.80

6. Assuming the same facts as in **5,** what was the unit cost for conversion costs in May?
   a. $27.10
   b. $27.00
   c. $14.70
   d. $14.80

7. Assuming the same facts as in **5,** what were the total costs transferred to Finished Goods Inventory during May?
   a. $23,296
   b. $41,750
   c. $334,400
   d. $376,150

8. Assuming the same facts as in **5,** what was the ending balance of Work in Process Inventory?
   a. $23,296
   b. $41,750
   c. $334,400
   d. $376,150

9. A process cost report includes all of the following *except* the
   a. unit cost for conversion costs.
   b. equivalent production (units).
   c. schedule of finished goods.
   d. unit cost for direct materials.

10. A process costing system provides information about all of the following *except*
   a. sales revenue.
   b. product cost trends.
   c. material usage per unit.
   d. units produced per period.

TESTING YOUR KNOWLEDGE

Matching*

Match each term with its definition by writing the appropriate letter in the blank.

_____ 1. Process costing system

_____ 2. Step 2: accounting for equivalent units

_____ 3. Step 4: computing cost per equivalent unit

_____ 4. Step 5: assigning costs

_____ 5. Equivalent production

_____ 6. Conversion costs

_____ 7. FIFO costing method

_____ 8. Average costing method

a. A costing method that assumes that beginning work in process was started and completed during the accounting period

b. Combined direct labor and manufacturing overhead costs

c. The step in a process cost report in which costs are distributed to ending Work in Process Inventory and to units transferred out during the period

d. The product costing system used by companies that make large quantities of identical products

e. A costing method in which cost flow follows product flow

f. The step in a process cost report in which a cost per unit is computed

g. A measure that expresses partially completed units in terms of completed whole units

h. The step in a process cost report in which equivalent production is computed

Short Answer

Use the lines provided to answer each item.

1. List the five steps involved in preparing a process cost report in the order in which the steps are performed.

   _____

   _____

   _____

   _____

2. Using the FIFO costing approach, show the computation for equivalent units.

   _____

   + _____

   + _____

   = _____

3. What two costs are computed in Step 5 of a process cost report?

   _____

   _____

4. Using the FIFO costing approach, show the computation for the cost of goods completed and transferred out of a process, department, or work cell.

   _____

   + _____

   + _____

   = _____

Note to student: The matching quiz might be completed more efficiently by starting with the definition and searching for the corresponding term.

Costing Systems: Process Costing

Circle T if the statement is true, F if it is false. Provide explanations for the false answers, using the blank lines below. (For all statements, assume a process costing system.)

T F **1.** Because process costing is used when large quantities of identical items are produced, only one Work in Process Inventory account is ever needed.

T F **2.** Manufacturing overhead must be applied to production for the period.

T F **3.** The finished units of one department become, in effect, the materials input of the next department.

T F **4.** Product unit cost is made up of cost elements used in all departments.

T F **5.** Equivalent units produced equal the number of units that were started and completed during the period.

T F **6.** Conversion costs equal direct labor plus manufacturing overhead.

T F **7.** Separate unit cost figures are normally computed for direct labor and manufacturing overhead.

T F **8.** When the average costing method is used to compute equivalent production, beginning inventory is multiplied by the percentage completed as of the beginning of the period.

T F **9.** Cost per equivalent unit must be determined before costs are assigned to units.

T F **10.** Ending Work in Process Inventory is determined by multiplying total units by total cost per unit.

T F **11.** Units completed minus units in beginning inventory equal units started and completed (assuming that all units in beginning inventory have been completed).

T F **12.** Process costing information is used in all stages of the management cycle.

T F **13.** A FIFO costing approach follows the logical product flow.

_____

_____

_____

_____

_____

_____

_____

_____

_____

_____

_____

Circle the letter of the best answer.

1. A department started and completed 10,000 units during the period. Beginning inventory of 5,000 units was 60 percent complete for conversion costs, and ending inventory of 7,000 units was 30 percent complete for conversion costs. What is equivalent production for conversion costs for the period under the FIFO costing method?
   a. 4,000 units
   b. 14,100 units
   c. 15,000 units
   d. 17,100 units

2. Assuming the same facts as in **1**, what is equivalent production for conversion costs for the period under the average costing method?
   a. 4,000 units
   b. 14,100 units
   c. 15,000 units
   d. 17,100 units

3. Which of the following is *not* a component of cost of goods manufactured and transferred out?
   a. Costs necessary to complete units in beginning inventory
   b. Costs attached to units in beginning inventory
   c. Costs of units started and completed
   d. Costs necessary to complete units in ending inventory

4. In which step of a process cost report do equivalent units *not* appear?
   a. Step 2
   b. Step 4
   c. Step 5
   d. Step 1

5. A department began the period with 5,000 units that were 80 percent complete, started and completed 12,000 units, and ended with 2,000 units that were 30 percent complete. Under the average costing method, equivalent units produced would equal
   a. 13,600.
   b. 14,400.
   c. 17,600.
   d. 19,000.

6. Conversion costs are the sum of
   a. direct materials and direct labor.
   b. direct labor and manufacturing overhead.
   c. manufacturing overhead and direct materials.
   d. direct materials, direct labor, and manufacturing overhead.

7. The cost of ending work in process inventory is computed in
   a. Step 2 of a process cost report.
   b. Step 5 of a process cost report.
   c. Step 4 of a process cost report.
   d. the income statement.

8. The cost of goods transferred to finished goods inventory is computed in
   a. Step 2 of a process cost report.
   b. Step 5 of a process cost report.
   c. Step 3 of a process cost report.
   d. the balance sheet.

9. In which stage of the management cycle do managers use process costing information to forecast unit costs?
   a. Executing
   b. Planning
   c. Reviewing
   d. Reporting

10. A process costing system would be used by companies that produce all of the following *except*
   a. beverages.
   b. computers.
   c. custom-made suits.
   d. vacuum cleaners.

APPLYING YOUR KNOWLEDGE

Exercises

1. Data for Department 1 of Jaquette Manufacturing Company for the month of May are as follows:

   Beginning Work in Process Inventory
   Units = 2,000
   Direct materials = 100% complete
   Conversion costs = 30% complete
   Direct materials costs = $12,000
   Conversion costs = $3,000

   Ending Work in Process Inventory
   Direct materials = 100% complete
   Conversion costs = 30% complete

   Operations for May
   Units started = 24,000
   Direct materials costs = $114,000
   Conversion costs = $30,750
   Units completed and transferred to the next department
      = 19,000

   Using the FIFO costing approach, complete the process cost report on the next page. Round off unit cost computations to two decimal places.

Jaquette Manufacturing Company
Process Cost Report: FIFO Costing Method
For the Month Ended May 31, 20xx

Crossword Puzzle
for Chapters 17 and 18

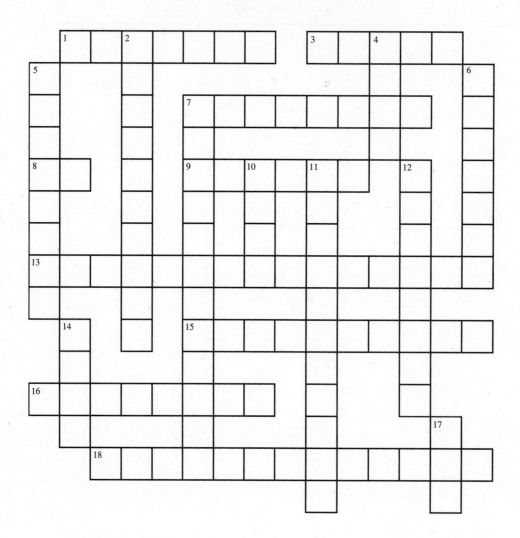

ACROSS

1. _____ Payroll account
3. Management _____ (a process divided into stages)
7. Outlay per manufactured item (2 words)
8. Cost _____ goods sold
9. Cost that can be traced to a specific job or product
13. Productive output of 6-Down (2 words)
15. Manufacturing output
16. First stage of 3-Across
18. With 10-Down, used in applying overhead to jobs

DOWN

2. _____ costs (combined total costs of direct labor and manufacturing overhead)
4. _____-plus contract
5. Costing system for batches of products (2 words)
6. Costing system for mass production
7. Term for actual overhead that exceeds allocated overhead
10. See 18-Across
11. Component of a job order cost card (2 words)
12. Manufacturing task or function
14. Work center
17. For each, as in cost for each unit

CHAPTER 19   ACTIVITY-BASED SYSTEMS: ABM AND JIT

REVIEWING THE CHAPTER

Objective 1: Explain the role of activity-based systems in the management cycle.

1. **Activity-based systems** are information systems that provide quantitative information about an organization's activities. These systems help managers view the organization as a collection of related activities. The cost information they provide enables managers to improve operating processes and make better pricing decisions.

2. In the planning stage of the management cycle, activity-based systems help managers identify value-adding activities, determine the resources required for those activities, and estimate product costs. In the executing and reviewing stages, activity-based systems help managers determine the **full product cost** (which includes not only the costs of direct materials and direct labor, but also the costs of all production and nonproduction activities), identify actions that may reduce product cost, and determine if cost-reduction goals for nonvalue-adding activities were achieved. In the reporting stage, managers report the cost of inventory and determine the degree to which product goals were achieved.

Objective 2: Define *activity-based management (ABM)* and discuss its relationship to the supply chain and the value chain.

3. **Activity-based management (ABM)** is an approach to managing an organization that identifies all major operating activities, determines the resources consumed by each activity and the cause of the resource usage, and categorizes the activities as either adding value to a product or service or not adding value. ABM focuses on reducing or eliminating nonvalue-adding activities. Because it provides financial and performance information at the activity level, ABM is useful both for strategic planning and for making operational decisions about business segments, such as product lines, market segments, and customer groups. It also helps managers eliminate waste and inefficiencies and redirect resources to activities that add value to a product or service.

4. A **value chain** is a sequence of activities, or primary processes, that add value to a company's product or service; the value chain also includes support services, such as management accounting, that facilitate the primary processes. ABM enables managers to see their organization's value chain as part of a larger system that includes the value chains of suppliers and customers. This larger system is the **supply chain** (also called the *supply network*)—the path that leads from the suppliers of the materials from which a product is made to the final customer. Managers who understand the supply chain and how their company's value-adding activities fit into their suppliers' and customers' value chains can see their company's role in the overall process of creating and delivering products or services. Such an understanding can make a company more profitable. When organizations work cooperatively with others in their

supply chain, they can develop new processes that reduce the total costs of their products or services.

Objective 3: Distinguish between value-adding and nonvalue-adding activities, and describe process value analysis.

5. A **value-adding activity** adds value to a product or service as perceived by the customer. Examples include assembling a car, painting it, and installing seats and airbags. A **nonvalue-adding activity** is an activity that adds cost to a product or service but does not increase its market value. ABM focuses on eliminating nonvalue-adding activities that are not essential to an organization and on reducing the costs of those that are essential, such as legal services, materials handling, and building maintenance. It thus enables managers to redirect resources to value-adding activities.

6. **Process value analysis (PVA)** is a technique that managers use to identify and link all the activities involved in the value chain. It analyzes business processes by relating activities to the events that prompt the activities and to the resources that the activities consume. PVA forces managers to look critically at all phases of their operations. It improves cost traceability and results in significantly more accurate product costs, which in turn improves management decisions and increases profitability.

Objective 4: Define *activity-based costing* and explain how a cost hierarchy and a bill of activities are used.

7. **Activity-based costing (ABC)** is a method of assigning costs that calculates a more accurate product cost than traditional methods. It does so by categorizing all indirect costs by activity, tracing the indirect costs to those activities, and assigning those costs to products using a cost driver related to the cause of the cost. Implementing ABC involves five steps: (a) identifying and classifying each activity, (b) estimating the cost of resources for each activity, (c) identifying a cost driver for each activity and estimating the quantity of each cost driver, (d) calculating an activity cost rate for each activity, and (e) assigning costs to cost objects based on the level of activity required to make the product or provide the service.

8. Two tools that help managers implement ABC are a cost hierarchy and a bill of activities. A **cost hierarchy** is a framework for classifying activities according to the level at which their costs are incurred. In a manufacturing company, a cost hierar-chy typically has four levels. **Unit-level activities** are performed each time a unit is produced. **Batch-level activities** are performed each time a batch of goods is produced. **Product-level activities** are performed to support the diversity of products in a manufacturing plant. **Facility-level activities** are performed to support a facility's general manufacturing process. A cost hierarchy includes both value-adding and nonvalue-adding activities; the frequency of activities varies across levels. Service organizations can also use a cost hierarchy to group activities.

9. After managers have created a cost hierarchy, they prepare a summary in the form of a bill of activities. A **bill of activities** is a list of activities and related costs that is used to compute the costs assigned to activities and the product unit cost. A bill of activities may be used as the primary document or as a supporting schedule for calculating product unit cost in both job order and process costing systems and in both manufacturing and service organizations.

Objective 5: Define the *just-in-time (JIT) operating philosophy* and identify the elements of a JIT operating environment.

10. The **just-in-time (JIT) operating philosophy** is one of the management philosophies that evolved to help companies stay competitive in today's business environment. It requires that all resources—materials, personnel, and facilities—be acquired and used only as needed. Its objectives are to enhance productivity, eliminate waste, reduce costs, and improve product quality. To meet the objectives of this management philosophy, a company must redesign its operating systems, plant layout, and management methods to conform to several basic concepts.

11. The elements in a JIT operating environment that support the concepts of the JIT philosophy are (a) maintaining minimum inventory levels; (b) using **pull-through production,** in which production is triggered by a customer order (as opposed to the traditional **push-through method,** in which products are manufactured in long production runs and stored in anticipation of customers' orders); (c) performing quick, inexpensive machine setups by using a cluster of machinery known as a **work cell,** an autonomous production line that can efficiently and continuously perform all required operations; (d) developing a multiskilled work force; (e) maintaining high levels of product quality; (f) enforcing a system of effective pre-

ventive maintenance; and (g) encouraging continuous improvement of the work environment.

Objective 6: Identify the changes in product costing that result when a firm adopts a JIT operating environment.

12. The traditional operating environment divides the production process into five time frames: (a) **processing time,** the actual time required to work on a product; (b) **inspection time,** the time spent detecting product flaws or reworking defective units; (c) **moving time,** the time needed to transfer a product from one operation or department to another; (d) **queue time,** the time a product waits to be worked on once it reaches the next operation or department; and (e) **storage time,** the time a product spends in materials storage, work in process inventory, or finished goods inventory.

13. In product costing under JIT, costs associated with processing time are categorized as either direct materials costs or conversion costs. **Conversion costs** are the sum of the direct labor costs and manufacturing overhead costs incurred by a production department, JIT work cell, or other work center. According to the JIT philosophy, product costs associated with inspection, moving, queue, and storage time should be reduced or eliminated because they do not add value to the product.

14. The key measure in a JIT operating environment is **throughput time,** the time it takes to move a product through the entire production process. Measures of product movement are used to apply conversion costs to products. With computerized monitoring of the JIT work cells, many costs that are treated as indirect costs in traditional manufacturing settings, such as the costs of utilities and operating supplies, can be traced directly to work cells. The only costs that remain indirect costs of the work cells are those associated with building occupancy, insurance, and property taxes.

Objective 7: Define and apply *backflush costing,* and compare the cost flows in traditional and backflush costing.

15. A JIT environment can reduce waste of resources and time not only in production operations, but in other areas as well, including the accounting process. Because materials arrive just in time to be used in the production process, there is little reason to maintain a separate Materials Inventory account, and because a JIT environment reduces labor costs, the accounting system can add direct labor costs and allocated manufacturing costs into the Work in Process Inventory account. Thus, by simplifying cost flows through the accounting records, a JIT environment makes it possible to reduce the time it takes to record and account for the costs of the manufacturing process.

16. A JIT organization can also streamline its accounting process by using **backflush costing.** When backflush costing is used, all product costs are first accumulated in the Cost of Goods Sold account, and at the end of the accounting period, they are "flushed back," or worked backward, into the appropriate inventory accounts. By having all product costs flow straight to a final destination and working back to determine the proper balances for the inventory accounts at the end of the period, backflush costing saves recording time.

17. When direct materials arrive at a factory in which traditional costing methods are used, their costs flow into the Materials Inventory account. Then, when the direct materials are requisitioned into production, their costs flow into the Work in Process Inventory account. When direct labor is used, its costs are added to the Work in Process Inventory account. Manufacturing overhead is then applied and is added to the other costs in the Work in Process Inventory account. At the end of the manufacturing process, the costs are transferred to the Finished Goods Inventory account, and when the units are sold, their costs are transferred to the Cost of Goods Sold account.

18. In a JIT setting in which backflush costing is used, the direct materials costs and the conversion costs (direct labor and manufacturing overhead) are immediately charged to the Cost of Goods Sold account. At the end of the period, the costs of goods in work in process inventory and in finished goods inventory are determined, and those costs are flushed back to the Work in Process Inventory account and the Finished Goods Inventory account. Once those costs have been flushed back, the Cost of Goods Sold account contains only the costs of units completed and sold during the period.

Objective 8: Compare ABM and JIT as activity-based systems.

19. ABM and JIT are similar in that as activity-based systems, both analyze processes and identify value-adding and nonvalue-adding activities. Both seek to eliminate waste, reduce costs, improve product or service quality, and enhance an

organization's efficiency and productivity. Both also improve the quality of the information managers use in making decisions.

20. ABM and JIT differ in their approaches to the calculation of product cost and cost assignment. Using ABC, ABM calculates product cost by using cost drivers to assign indirect manufacturing overhead costs to cost objects. ABC is used with job order and process costing systems.

21. JIT reorganizes activities so that they are performed within work cells. The costs of those activities become direct costs of the work cell. The total production costs within the work cell can be assigned by using simple cost drivers, such as process hours or direct materials cost. This approach focuses on the output at the end of the production process and simplifies the accounting system.

SELF-TEST

Test your knowledge of the chapter by choosing the best answer for each item below.

1. Which of the following is *not* a basic concept underlying just-in-time operations?
   a. An emphasis on quality and continuous improvement
   b. Producing goods only as they are needed
   c. Maintaining inventory levels to support probable demand
   d. The belief that simple is better

2. A switch to a just-in-time operating environment is facilitated by
   a. creating production work cells that comprise several different types of operations.
   b. enhancing a factory's storage capabilities.
   c. concentrating on areas of possible cost reduction rather than on the reduction of processing time.
   d. increasing inventories so that customers' demands can always be met.

3. Pull-through production means that
   a. the size of production runs is determined by how much can be pulled through the production process.
   b. production processes rely on long production runs to reduce the number of machine setups.
   c. it is very difficult to pull products through the production process.
   d. a customer order triggers the purchase of materials and the scheduling of production for the required products.

4. An activity that adds costs to a product or service but does not increase its market value is a
   a. cost-adding activity.
   b. cost driver.
   c. nonvalue-adding activity.
   d. value-adding activity.

5. In what stage of the management cycle are activity-based systems used?
   a. Executing
   b. Planning
   c. Reviewing
   d. All of the above

6. In a backflush costing system, all product costs are first charged to the
   a. Materials Inventory account.
   b. Finished Goods Inventory account.
   c. Cost of Goods Sold account.
   d. Work in Process Inventory account.

7. Which of the following would most likely be a value-adding cost in the production of a table?
   a. Salary of job foreman
   b. Electric utility cost
   c. The cost of using solid mahogany rather than a veneer
   d. Depreciation of factory building

8. Which of the following is *not* an activity level in a cost hierarchy?
   a. Cost level
   b. Batch level
   c. Unit level
   d. Product level

9. Processing time is the time
   a. spent detecting product flaws.
   b. required to work on a product.
   c. a product waits to be worked on once it reaches the next operation or department.
   d. a product spends in materials storage, work in process inventory, or finished goods inventory.

10. When direct materials arrive at the factory in which a traditional costing system is used, their costs flow first into the
    a. Cost of Goods Sold account.
    b. Finished Goods Inventory account.
    c. Materials Inventory account.
    d. Work in Process Inventory account.

TESTING YOUR KNOWLEDGE

Matching*

Match each term with its definition by writing the appropriate letter in the blank.

_____ **1.** Conversion costs

_____ **2.** Inspection time

_____ **3.** Activity-based system

_____ **4.** Just-in-time (JIT) operating philosophy

_____ **5.** Value chain

_____ **6.** Pull-through production

_____ **7.** Supply chain

_____ **8.** Nonvalue-adding activity

_____ **9.** Work cell

_____ **10.** Cost hierarchy

_____ **11.** Push-through method

_____ **12.** Bill of activities

_____ **13.** Unit-level activities

a. The time spent looking for product flaws or reworking defective units

b. A concept of management in which all resources are acquired and used only as needed

c. An activity that adds costs to a product or service but does not increase its market value

d. A sequence of activities that add value to a company's product or service

e. An interdependent web of organizations that supplies materials, products, or services to a customer

f. A system in which a customer order triggers the purchase of materials and the scheduling of production for the required products

g. An information system that provides quantitative information about an organization's activities

h. An autonomous production line that can perform all required operations efficiently and continuously

i. Direct labor and manufacturing overhead costs incurred by a department, work cell, or other work center

j. A framework for classifying activities according to the level at which their costs are incurred

k. A production system in which products are manufactured in long production runs and stored in anticipation of customers' orders

l. Activities performed each time a unit is produced

m. A list of activities and related costs that is used to compute the costs assigned to activities and the product unit cost

---

*Note to student: The matching quiz might be completed more efficiently by starting with the definition and searching for the corresponding term.

Short Answer

Use the lines provided to answer each item.

1. Briefly define the just-in-time operating philosophy.

_____

_____

_____

_____

_____

_____

_____

2. List the five steps involved in implementing an activity-based costing system.

_____

_____

_____

_____

3. Define *process value analysis (PVA)* and explain how it can be helpful to managers.

_____

_____

_____

_____

_____

_____

4. Just-in-time is not an inventory system. Explain why.

_____

_____

_____

_____

_____

_____

True-False

Circle T if the statement is true, F if it is false. Provide explanations for the false answers, using the blank lines at the end of the section.

T F **1.** Activity-based management and just-in-time have different primary goals.

T F **2.** Eliminating waste is a key concept of the just-in-time operating philosophy.

T F **3.** In a JIT environment, materials and other resources are acquired and used only as needed in order to eliminate waste.

T F **4.** Pull-through production means that a customer order triggers the purchase of materials and the scheduling of production.

T F **5.** A primary goal of the JIT operating philosophy is to reduce processing time.

T F **6.** Product inspections are not performed in a just-in-time operating environment.

T F **7.** Queue time is the time spent moving a product from one operation or department to another.

T F **8.** Processing time is the actual time required to work on a product.

T F **9.** Service organizations can use a cost hierarchy to group activities.

T F **10.** A service organization's cost hierarchy includes only unit-level and batch-level activities.

T F **11.** A bill of activities is used in traditional costing systems.

T F **12.** When an organization uses a backflush costing system, it backs costs out of the Cost of Goods Sold account.

T F **13.** A nonvalue-adding activity adds costs to a product but does not increase its market value.

T F **14.** Installing an airbag in an automobile is an example of a value-adding activity.

T F **15.** Activity-based systems can be used in all stages of the management cycle.

_____

_____

_____

_____

_____

_____

_____

_____

Multiple Choice

Circle the letter of the best answer.

1. Which of the following activities is *not* a batch-level activity?
   a. Production-line setup
   b. Production-line inspection
   c. Installation of a vehicle's engine
   d. Scheduling

2. Which of the following is *not* an element of the just-in-time operating philosophy?
   a. Maintaining minimum inventory levels
   b. Developing a multiskilled labor force
   c. Emphasizing direct labor variance analysis
   d. Encouraging continuous improvement in the work environment

3. Pull-through production means that
   a. automated machinery is used to pull products through the production process.
   b. a customer order triggers the purchase of materials and the scheduling of production.
   c. a customer complaint triggers the scheduling of rework on a defective product.
   d. production and scheduling are not functioning properly and a special device must be used to correct the situation.

4. Maintaining minimum inventory levels is a goal of JIT because
   a. carrying inventory is a waste of resources.
   b. carrying inventory maximizes the use of factory floor space.
   c. customer needs are not a major consideration in the JIT operating philosophy.
   d. doing so increases a company's current ratio.

5. Unit costs in a JIT operating environment are minimized by
   a. using inexpensive materials and supplies.
   b. performing quick, inexpensive machine setups.
   c. sacrificing quality for high-speed processes.
   d. using unskilled labor whenever possible.

6. Which of the following is *not* part of the traditional production process?
   a. Storage time
   b. Processing time
   c. Queue time
   d. Decision time

7. Which of the following would be a nonvalue-adding activity for a pizzeria?
   a. Home delivery
   b. Buying fresh pepperoni
   c. Recording daily cash receipts
   d. Preparing thick pizza dough

8. When backflush costing is used in a JIT environment, which of the following costs would *not* initially flow into the Cost of Goods Sold account?
   a. Sales salaries
   b. Manufacturing overhead
   c. Direct materials
   d. Direct labor

9. In the planning stage of the management cycle, an activity-based system can provide information that helps managers
   a. estimate product costs.
   b. attain production goals.
   c. determine inventory cost on the balance sheet.
   d. do all of the above.

10. Processing time is
    a. the time spent looking for product flaws or reworking defective units.
    b. the actual time spent working on a product.
    c. the time a product waits to be worked on.
    d. none of the above.

APPLYING YOUR KNOWLEDGE

Exercises

1. Puffy Corporation produces ten types of bicycles. The fully suspended titanium model is the most expensive and the most difficult to produce. The rigid-frame steel model is the easiest to produce and is the company's leading seller. Other models range from a fully suspended aluminum frame to a front-suspension steel frame; they become more complex as suspension is added and frame materials change. Bikes Incorporated recently ordered 350 of the front-suspended aluminum bicycles. Paula Jas, Puffy Corporation's controller, has decided to use this order to compare activity-based costing with the traditional costing approach. Costs directly traceable to the order are as follows:

Direct materials	$28,645
Purchased parts	$38,205
Direct labor hours	660
Average direct labor pay rate per hour	$7.00

With the traditional costing approach, Jas applies manufacturing overhead costs at a rate of 160 percent of direct labor dollars.

  a. Use a traditional costing approach to compute the total cost and the product unit cost of the Bikes Incorporated order.

  b. Use activity-based costing to compute the total cost and the product unit cost of the order.

Activity-based costing approach:

Activity	Activity Cost Rate	Cost Driver Level
Unit level:		
Parts production	$19 per machine hour	190 machine hours
Assembly	$9.50 per direct labor hour	42 direct labor hours
Packaging and shipping	$13 per unit	350 units
Batch level:		
Work cell setup	$45 per setup	8 setups
Product level:		
Product design	$31 per engineering hour	38 engineering hours
Product simulation	$45 per testing hour	14 testing hours
Facility level:		
Building occupancy	125% of direct labor costs	$4,620 direct labor costs

2. Listed below are several costs commonly incurred in a manufacturing environment:

Direct labor	Operating supplies
Depreciation, machinery	Fire insurance, plant
Raw materials	Setup labor
Product design costs	Rework costs
President's salary	Supervisory salaries
Small tools	Utilities costs, machinery

Classify each cost as direct or indirect when it is incurred in (a) a traditional manufacturing setting and (b) a JIT operating environment. Explain why some of these cost classifications differ between settings.

3. Kim Lazar is adapting UCF Manufacturing Company's accounting system to the company's new JIT environment. The Work in Process Inventory account has been installed. The following transactions took place last week:

Dec. 22 Metal brackets for Jobs 213 and 216 were ordered and received, $4,890.

23 Steel castings for the product's body were received, $13,300.

23 Work began on both jobs.

24 Both jobs were completed. Total costs for Job 213 were $14,870; for Job 216, they were $17,880.

26 Job 216 was shipped to customer.

The company uses a 60 percent markup over cost to price its products. Use the T accounts that follow to record the above transactions.

Work in Process Inventory	Finished Goods Inventory	Cost of Goods Sold

Accounts Payable	Accounts Receivable	Sales

CHAPTER 20 COST BEHAVIOR ANALYSIS

REVIEWING THE CHAPTER

Objective 1: Define *cost behavior* **and explain how managers use this concept in the management cycle.**

1. **Cost behavior**—the way costs respond to changes in volume or activity—affects decisions that managers make in all stages of the management cycle. In the planning stage, managers use cost behavior to determine how many units must be sold to generate a targeted amount of profit and how changes in operating, investing, and financing activities will affect operating income. During the executing stage, managers must understand cost behavior to determine the impact of their decisions on operating income. When reviewing operations and preparing reports, managers use cost behavior to analyze how changes in cost and sales affect the profitability of various business segments, as well as to make decisions about whether to eliminate a product line, accept a special order, or outsource certain activities.

Objective 2: Identify variable, fixed, and mixed costs, and separate mixed costs into their variable and fixed components.

2. Total costs that change in direct proportion to changes in productive output (or any other measure of volume) are **variable costs.** Examples include hourly wages and the costs of direct materials and operating supplies.
   a. Because variable costs change in relation to volume or output, it is important to know an organization's **operating capacity**—that is, its upper limit of productive output, given its

existing resources. There are three common measures of operating capacity. **Theoretical (ideal) capacity** is the maximum productive output for a given period in which all machinery is operating continuously at optimal speed. **Practical capacity** is theoretical capacity reduced by normal and expected work stoppages. Theoretical capacity and practical capacity are useful when estimating maximum production levels, but they are unrealistic measures when planning operations. In contrast, **normal capacity**—the average annual level of operating capacity needed to meet expected sales demand—is a realistic measure of what an organization is likely to produce, not what it *can* produce.
   b. The traditional definition of variable cost assumes a linear relationship between costs and activity levels. However, many variable costs behave in a nonlinear fashion; for example, an additional hourly rental rate for computer usage may be higher than the previous hour's rental rate. *Linear approximation* is a method of converting nonlinear variable costs into linear variable costs. It relies on the concept of **relevant range,** which is range of volume or activity in which a company's actual operations are likely to occur.

3. **Fixed costs** are total costs that remain constant within a relevant range of volume or activity. Salaries, annual property taxes, and depreciation expense are examples. Fixed costs change only

when volume or activity exceeds the relevant range—for example, when additional supervisory personnel must be hired to accommodate increased activity. Fixed *unit* costs vary inversely with activity or volume. If more units are produced than anticipated, the fixed costs are spread over more units, thus decreasing the fixed cost per unit; if fewer units are produced than anticipated, the fixed costs are spread over fewer units, thus increasing the fixed cost per unit. (Note, however, that fixed costs are usually considered as a total rather than on a per unit basis.)

4. **Mixed costs** have both fixed and variable cost components. For example, monthly electricity charges include both a fixed service charge and a per kilowatt-hour charge. For planning and control purposes, mixed costs must be broken down into their fixed and variable components. The following four methods are commonly used to do this:

   a. The **engineering method** (sometimes called a *time and motion study*) separates costs into their fixed and variable components by performing a step-by-step analysis of the tasks, costs, and processes involved in completing an activity or product.

   b. A **scatter diagram**—a chart of plotted points representing past costs and related measures of volume—helps determine whether a linear relationship exists between a cost item and the related measure. If the diagram suggests a linear relationship, a cost line drawn through the points can provide an approximate representation of the relationship.

   c. The **high-low method** is a three-step approach to separating a mixed cost into its variable and fixed components. It calculates the variable cost per activity base, the total fixed costs, and a formula to estimate the total costs (fixed and variable) within the relevant range.

   d. Statistical methods, such as **regression analysis,** mathematically describe the relationship between costs and activities. Because these methods use all data observations, their results are more representative of cost behavior than that those produced by either the high-low or scatter diagram methods.

Objective 3: Define *cost-volume-profit (C-V-P) analysis* and discuss how managers use it as a tool for planning and control.

5. **Cost-volume-profit (C-V-P) analysis** is an examination of the cost behavior patterns that underlie the relationships among cost, volume of output, and profit. The techniques and problem-solving procedures involved in the analysis express relationships among revenue, sales mix, cost, volume, and profit. Those relationships provide a general model of financial activity that managers use for short-range planning, evaluating performance, and analyzing alternative courses of action. For example, managers use C-V-P analysis to project profit at different activity levels, to develop budgets, to evaluate a department's performance, and to measure the effects of alternative courses of action, such as the effects of changes in variable or fixed costs, selling prices, and sales volume. C-V-P analysis is also useful in making decisions about product pricing, product mix, adding or dropping a product line, and accepting special orders.

6. C-V-P analysis is, however, useful only under certain conditions and only when certain assumptions hold true. If any of the following are absent, C-V-P analysis can be misleading:

   a. The behavior of variable and fixed costs can be measured accurately.

   b. Costs and revenues have a close linear relationship (e.g., when costs rise, revenues rise proportionately).

   c. Efficiency and productivity hold steady within the relevant range of activity.

   d. Cost and price variables also hold steady during the period being planned.

   e. The sales mix does not change during the period being planned.

   f. Production and sales volume are roughly equal.

Objective 4: Define *breakeven point* and use contribution margin to determine a company's breakeven point for multiple products.

7. The **breakeven point** is the point at which sales revenues equal the sum of all variable and fixed costs. A company can earn a profit only by surpassing the breakeven point. The breakeven point is useful in assessing the likelihood that a new venture will succeed. If the margin of safety is low, the profitability of the venture is unlikely. The **margin of safety** is the number of sales units or the amount of sales dollars by which actual sales can fall below planned sales without resulting in a loss.

8. Sales (S), variable costs (VC), and fixed costs (FC) are used to compute the breakeven point, as follows:

$$S - VC - FC = 0.$$

A rough estimate of the breakeven point can also be made by using a scatter, or breakeven, graph. Although less exact, this method does yield meaningful data. A breakeven graph has (a) a horizontal axis for units of output, (b) a vertical axis for dollars of revenue, (c) a horizontal fixed-cost line, (d) a sloping line representing total cost that begins where the fixed-cost line crosses the vertical axis, and (e) a sloping line representing total revenue that begins at the origin. At the point at which the total revenue line crosses the total cost line, revenues equal total costs.

9. **Contribution margin** (CM) is the amount that remains after all variable costs have been subtracted from sales:

$$S - VC = CM$$

A product's contribution margin represents its net contribution to paying off fixed costs and earning a profit (P):

$$CM - FC = P$$

Using the contribution margin, the breakeven point (BE) can be expressed as the point at which contribution margin minus total fixed costs equals zero. Stated another way, the BE is at the point at which the contribution margin equals total fixed costs.

10. The breakeven point for multiple products can be computed in three steps:
    a. Compute the weighted-average contribution margin by multiplying the contribution margin for each product by its percentage of the sales mix. The **sales mix** is the proportion of each product's unit sales relative to the company's total unit sales.
    b. Calculate the weighted-average breakeven point by dividing total fixed costs by the weighted-average contribution margin.
    c. Calculate the breakeven point for each product by multiplying the weighted-average breakeven point by each product's percentage of the sales mix.

Objective 5: Use C-V-P analysis to project the profitability of products and services.

11. The primary goal of a business venture is not to break even; it is to generate a profit. A targeted profit can be factored into the C-V-P analysis to estimate a new venture's profitability. This approach is excellent for "what-if" analyses, in which managers select several scenarios and compute the profit that may be anticipated from each.

12. Managers in a manufacturing business can estimate the profitability of a product by using the following equation, in which P is the targeted profit, and solving for the number of unit sales needed to achieve the desired profit:

$$S - VC - FC = P$$

The contribution margin approach is also useful for profit planning. For example, it can be used to project operating income given a change in one or more of the income statement components. In contribution income statements, all variable costs related to production, selling, and administration are subtracted from sales to determine the total contribution margin; all fixed costs related to those functions are subtracted from the total contribution margin to determine operating income.

13. C-V-P analysis can also be used to estimate the profitability of a service. In this case, managers do the following:
    a. Estimate service overhead costs by calculating (1) the variable service overhead cost per service, (2) the total fixed service overhead costs, (3) the total service overhead costs for a period, and (4) the total service overhead costs for that period assuming a certain number services will be performed.
    b. Determine the breakeven point by using the following formula, in which x = number of services (e.g., number of tax returns prepared by an accountant):

$$Sx = VCx + FC$$

    c. Determine the effect of a change in operating costs (i.e., the effect on profitability if fixed or variable costs change).
    d. Compute targeted profit for a given number of services by using the following formula, in which x = targeted sales in units:

$$Sx = VCx + FC + P$$

Test your knowledge of the chapter by choosing the best answer for each item below.

1. "The way that costs respond to changes in volume or activity" is the definition of
   a. cost flow.
   b. cost behavior.
   c. period costs.
   d. product costs.

2. An operating unit's ideal capacity reduced by normal and expected work stoppages is called
   a. theoretical capacity.
   b. excess capacity.
   c. practical capacity.
   d. normal capacity.

3. The records of Technology Company reveal the following data about electrical costs:

Month	Activity Level	Cost
April	960 machine hours	$ 8,978
May	940 machine hours	8,842
June	1,120 machine hours	10,066

   If the high-low method is applied to these figures, the variable cost per machine hour for the quarter would be
   a. $6.80.
   b. $8.60.
   c. $7.40.
   d. $4.70.

4. Assuming the same facts as in 3, the monthly fixed costs would be
   a. $2,230.
   b. $2,450.
   c. $2,540.
   d. $1,890.

5. Product AB has a suggested selling price of $27 per unit and a projected variable cost per unit of $15. Fixed costs are expected to increase by $197,040 per month. The breakeven point in sales units per month is
   a. 16,240.
   b. 11,590.
   c. 11,950.
   d. 16,420.

6. Assuming the same facts as in 5, the breakeven point in sales dollars per month is
   a. $443,340.
   b. $322,650.
   c. $312,930.
   d. $438,480.

7. Assuming the same facts as in 5, how many units must be sold each month to earn a profit of $6,000 per month?
   a. 12,450
   b. 16,740
   c. 16,920
   d. 12,090

8. Assuming the same facts as in 5, how many units must be sold each month to support an additional fixed monthly cost of $15,000 for advertising and earn a profit of $9,000 per month?
   a. 18,240
   b. 18,420
   c. 13,590
   d. 13,950

9. Products A, B, and C have contribution margins of $3, $5, and $4 per unit, respectively. Granada Company intends to manufacture one of the products and expects sales to be $30,000 regardless of which product it manufactures. If the same machinery and workers are used to produce each product, which one will yield the highest profit?
   a. A
   b. B
   c. C
   d. More information is needed.

10. Which of the following statements is *true*?
   a. Fixed costs vary within the relevant range.
   b. Fixed costs vary directly with activity levels.
   c. Fixed unit costs vary inversely with activity.
   d. Fixed unit costs are constant in the relevant range.

TESTING YOUR KNOWLEDGE

Matching*

Match each term with its definition by writing the appropriate letter in the blank.

_____ 1. Cost behavior

_____ 2. Variable costs

_____ 3. Fixed costs

_____ 4. Relevant range

_____ 5. Mixed costs

_____ 6. Theoretical (ideal) capacity

_____ 7. Practical capacity

_____ 8. Normal capacity

_____ 9. Cost-volume-profit (C-V-P) analysis

_____ 10. Breakeven point

_____ 11. Contribution margin

a. The operating level needed to satisfy expected sales demand

b. The maximum productive output possible over a given period

c. The point at which total revenues equal total costs

d. The way costs respond to changes in volume or activity

e. Sales minus total variable costs

f. A method of determining profit at different levels of volume

g. Costs that vary in direct proportion to volume

h. Costs that remain constant within a relevant range of volume or activity

i. Ideal capacity reduced by normal work stoppages

j. Costs with both fixed and variable components

k. The span of activity in which actual operations are likely to occur

Short Answer

Use the lines provided to answer each item.

1. What is the breakeven formula?

   _____

   _____

2. Define *mixed cost* and give three examples of such a cost.

   _____

   _____

   _____

   _____

3. Briefly explain the purpose of the high-low method.

   _____

   _____

   _____

4. Distinguish between the concepts of sales and contribution margin.

   _____

   _____

   _____

   _____

   _____

   _____

5. Show how profit is calculated using the contribution margin format.

   _____

   − _____

   = _____

   − _____

   = _____

Note to student: The matching quiz might be completed more efficiently by starting with the definition and searching for the corresponding term.

6. Briefly describe how managers in a service business use C-V-P analysis to estimate the profitability of a service.

_____

_____

_____

_____

_____

_____

True-False

Circle T if the statement is true, F if it is false. Provide explanations for the false answers, using the blank lines below.

T F **1.** On a per unit basis, variable costs remain constant with changes in volume.

T F **2.** On a breakeven graph, fixed costs are represented by a horizontal line.

T F **3.** A fixed cost may change when it is outside the relevant range.

T F **4.** Factory insurance is an example of a variable cost.

T F **5.** The most realistic measure of plant capacity is practical capacity.

T F **6.** At the breakeven point, sales equal total costs.

T F **7.** A contribution margin cannot occur until the breakeven point has been surpassed.

T F **8.** The breakeven point in dollars can be determined by multiplying breakeven units by the selling price.

T F **9.** Property taxes are a fixed cost.

T F **10.** An assumption of C-V-P analysis is that the sales mix does not change during the period being planned.

T F **11.** A mixed cost has both variable and fixed cost components.

T F **12.** On a breakeven graph, the horizontal axis represents dollars of cost or revenue.

T F **13.** At the breakeven point, the total contribution margin equals fixed costs.

T F **14.** A reduction in sales dollars reduces the contribution margin per unit.

T F **15.** At the point at which the total revenue line crosses the total cost line on a breakeven graph, revenues equal total costs.

T F **16.** C-V-P analysis does not apply to service industries.

_____

_____

_____

_____

_____

_____

_____

_____

_____

_____

_____

_____

_____

_____

Multiple Choice

Circle the letter of the best answer.

1. A taxi fare with a base price plus a mileage charge would be an example of a
   a. fixed cost.
   b. variable cost.
   c. mixed cost.
   d. standard cost.

2. When fixed costs are $10,000, variable cost is $8 per unit, and selling price is $10 per unit, the breakeven point is
   a. 1,000 units.
   b. 1,250 units.
   c. 5,000 units.
   d. 10,000 units.

3. When volume equals zero units,
   a. fixed cost equals $0.
   b. variable cost equals $0.
   c. total cost equals $0.
   d. net income equals $0.

4. At the breakeven point,
   a. total contribution margin equals fixed cost.
   b. sales equal variable cost.
   c. total cost equals contribution margin.
   d. profit equals total cost.

5. In graph form, the breakeven point is at the intersection of the
   a. total-revenue and variable-cost lines.
   b. total-cost line and vertical axis.
   c. variable-cost and fixed-cost lines.
   d. total-cost and total-revenue lines.

6. The operating capacity required to satisfy anticipated sales demand is
   a. normal capacity.
   b. excess capacity.
   c. practical capacity.
   d. theoretical capacity.

7. As volume decreases,
   a. variable cost per unit decreases.
   b. fixed cost in total decreases.
   c. variable cost in total remains the same.
   d. fixed cost per unit increases.

8. When both the selling price and the variable cost per unit are increased by $5,
   a. more units need to be sold to break even.
   b. fewer units need to be sold to break even.
   c. the contribution margin per unit also increases by $5.
   d. the breakeven point remains the same.

9. Product X has a selling price of $50 and a variable cost per unit of 70 percent of the selling price. If fixed costs total $30,000, how many units must be sold to earn a profit of $45,000?
   a. 900
   b. 1,500
   c. 2,143
   d. 5,000

10. Product Y has a variable cost per unit of $10 and requires a fixed investment of $40,000. If sales are anticipated at 10,000 units, what selling price must be established to earn a profit of $26,000?
    a. $16.60
    b. $14.00
    c. $12.60
    d. $6.60

11. When calculating the breakeven point for multiple products, a weighted-average contribution margin is computed by
    a. multiplying variable costs of each product by units of each product.
    b. multiplying the contribution margin for each product by its percentage of the sales mix.
    c. multiplying total number of units of each product by sales price for each product.
    d. adding total fixed costs and total variable costs for each product.

12. Which of the following is a step in calculating the breakeven point for a service business?
    a. Estimating service overhead costs
    b. Computing variable overhead cost per service
    c. Computing total overhead cost, based on an estimated number of services
    d. All of the above

APPLYING YOUR KNOWLEDGE

Exercises

1. Leisure Manufacturing Company is planning to introduce a new line of bowling balls. Annual fixed costs are estimated to be $80,000. Each ball will be sold to retailers for $13 and requires $9 of variable costs.

   a. The breakeven point in units is

   _____.

   b. The breakeven point in dollars is

   _____.

   c. If 12,000 balls are sold per year, the overall profit or loss will be

   _____.

   d. The number of balls that must be sold for an annual profit of $50,000 is

   _____.

2. Using the letters listed below, identify the elements on the breakeven graph that follows. The *a* has already been used to indicate volume.
   a. Volume
   b. Cost or revenue
   c. Breakeven point
   d. Profit area
   e. Loss area
   f. Fixed cost
   g. Total cost
   h. Contribution margin
   i. Sales

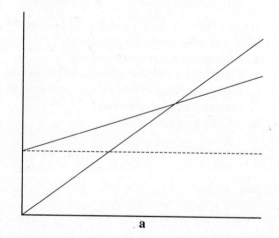

3. Chess Cab Company assembled the following figures for repairs to company vehicles during the first four months of 20xx:

Month	Activity Level	Cost
January	10,000 miles	$3,400
February	12,400	3,900
March	11,200	3,550
April	9,600	3,200

   a. Using the high-low method, produce a total cost formula that describes the cost behavior of the company's vehicle repairs.

   b. Based on your answer to **a**, approximately what repair cost should the company expect to have at an activity level of 16,000 miles?

4. Evans Corporation sold 20,000 units of Product Z last year. Each unit sold for $40 and had a variable cost of $26. Annual fixed costs totaled $300,000. This year, management is thinking of reducing the selling price by 15 percent, purchasing less expensive material to save $2 per unit, and spending $50,000 more on advertising. It is expected that with the proposed changes, sales will double.

   a. What was the corporation's profit or loss last year?

   b. What would the corporation's per unit contribution margin be after the proposed changes are made?

   c. If the projections are accurate, what would the corporation's profit be after the changes are made?

Crossword Puzzle
for Chapters 19 and 20

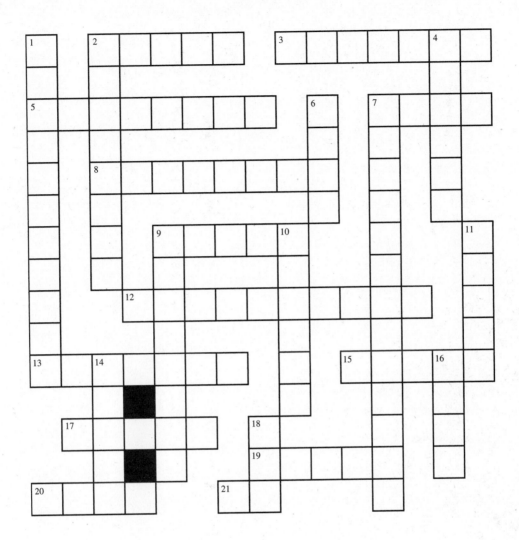

ACROSS

2. See 2-Down
3. _____ value analysis (PVA)
5. Proportion of each product's unit sales relative to total unit sales (2 words)
7. Full product _____
8. Cost affected by volume change
9. Cost not affected by volume change
12. Value-adding and nonvalue-adding _____
13. Method of separating mixed costs (hyphenated)
15. _____ chain
17. Common accounting period
19. _____-level activities (by job)
20. The "J" of JIT
21. S – VC = _____

DOWN

1. Method of long production runs (hyphenated)
2. With 2-Across, expected span of activity
4. Activity-based _____ (such as JIT or ABM)
6. Break _____
7. Framework for classifying activities by level (2 words)
9. _____-level activities (by plant)
10. Cost causer
11. _____ (waiting) time
14. _____ margin
16. _____-level activities (by item)
18. Kin to JIT, for short

CHAPTER 21 THE BUDGETING PROCESS

REVIEWING THE CHAPTER

Objective 1: Define *budgeting* and explain its role in the management cycle.

1. **Budgeting** is the process of identifying, gathering, summarizing, and communicating financial and nonfinancial information about an organization's future activities. It is an essential part of the continuous planning all types of organizations must do to accomplish their long-term goals. **Budgets**—plans of action based on forecasted transactions, activities, and events—are synonymous with managing an organization. They are used for a variety of purposes, including communicating information, coordinating activities, and resource usage, motivating employees, and evaluating performance.

2. **Strategic planning** is the process by which management establishes an organization's long-term goals. These goals define the strategic direction an organization will take over a five- to ten-year period and are the basis for making annual operating plans and preparing budgets. Annual operating plans involve every part of an enterprise and are much more detailed than long-term strategic plans. To formulate an annual operating plan, an organization must restate its long-term goals in terms of what it needs to accomplish during the next year. The short-term goals identified in an annual operating plan are the basis of an organization's operating budgets for the year.

3. The key to a successful budget is **participative budgeting.** This is a process in which personnel at all levels of an organization take an active and meaningful part in the creation of the budget.

4. Budgeting is helpful to managers at each stage of the management cycle.
   a. During the planning stage, budgeting helps managers relate long-term strategic goals to short-term activities, distribute resources and workloads, communicate responsibilities, select performance measures, and set standards for bonuses and rewards.
   b. In the executing stage, managers use budget information to communicate expectations, measure performance and motivate employees, coordinate activities, and allot resources.
   c. In the reviewing stage, budgets helps managers evaluate performance, including its timeliness; find variances between planned and actual performance; and create solutions to any significant variances that they detect.
   d. To provide continuous feedback about an organization's financing, investing, and operating activities, managers issue reports based on budget information throughout the year.

Objective 2: Identify the elements of a master budget in different types of organizations and the guidelines for preparing budgets.

5. A **master budget** consists of a set of *operating* budgets and a set of *financial* budgets that detail an organization's financial plans for a specific accounting period, generally a year. **Operating budgets** are plans used in daily operations. They

are also the basis for preparing the **financial budgets,** which are projections of financial results for the accounting period. Financial budgets include a budgeted income statement, a capital expenditures budget, a cash budget, and a budgeted balance sheet. The budgeted income statement and budgeted balance sheet are also called **pro forma statements,** meaning that they show projections rather than actual results.

6. The process of preparing a master budget is similar in manufacturing, retail, and service organizations in that each prepares a set of operating budgets that serve as the basis for preparing the financial budgets. The process differs mainly in the kinds of operating budgets that each type of organization prepares.

   a. Manufacturing organizations prepare operating budgets for sales, production, direct materials purchases, direct labor, manufacturing overhead, selling and administrative expenses, and cost of goods manufactured.

   b. Retail organizations prepare operating budgets for sales, purchases, selling and administrative expenses, and cost of goods sold.

   c. Service organization prepare operating budgets for service revenue, labor, services overhead, and selling and administrative expenses.

   d. The sales budget (or in service organizations, the service revenue budget) is prepared first because it is used to estimate sales volume and revenues. Once managers know the quantity of products or services to be sold and how many sales dollars to expect, they can develop other budgets that will enable them to manage their organization's resources so that they generate profits on those sales.

7. No standard format for budget preparation exists. The only universal requirement is that budgets communicate the appropriate information to the reader in a clear and understandable manner. General guidelines for preparing budgets include identifying the purpose of the budget, the user group and its information needs, and appropriate sources of budget information; establishing a clear format for the budget; using suitable formulas and calculations to derive the quantitative information; and revising the budget until it includes all planning decisions.

Objective 3: Prepare the operating budgets that support the financial budgets.

8. A **sales** (or service revenue) **budget** is a detailed plan, expressed in both units and dollars, that identifies expected product (or service) sales for a future period. The following equation is used to determine budgeted sales:

$$\text{Total Budgeted Sales} = \text{Estimated Selling Price per Unit} \times \text{Estimated Sales in Units}$$

Estimated sales volume is very important because it will affect the level of operating activities and the amount of resources needed for operations. A sales forecast can help in making this estimate. A **sales forecast** is a projection of sales demand (the estimated sales in units) based on an analysis of external and internal factors.

9. Once the sales budget has been established, managers can prepare a production budget. A **production budget** shows how many units a company must produce to meet budgeted sales and inventory needs. The production budget is based on the following formula:

$$\text{Total Production Units} = \text{Budgeted Sales in Units} + \text{Desired Units of Ending Finished Goods Inventory} - \text{Desired Units of Beginning Finished Goods Inventory}$$

10. After the production budget has been prepared, managers can prepare a **direct materials purchases budget**. This budget is a detailed plan that identifies the quantity of purchases required to meet budgeted production and inventory needs and the costs associated with those purchases. The first step in preparing a direct materials purchases budget is to calculate the total production needs in units of materials. In the second step, the following formula is used to determine the quantity of direct materials to be purchased during each accounting period in the budget:

$$\text{Total Units of Direct Materials to Be Purchased} = \text{Total Production Needs in Units of Direct Materials} + \text{Desired Units of Ending Direct Materials Inventory} - \text{Desired Units of Beginning Direct Materials Inventory}$$

The third step is to calculate the cost of the direct materials purchases by multiplying the total number of unit purchases by the direct materials cost per unit.

11. A **direct labor budget** is a detailed plan that estimates the direct labor needed in an accounting period and the associated costs. The first step in preparing a direct labor budget is to estimate the total direct labor hours by multiplying the estimated direct labor hours per unit by the antici-

pated units of production. The second step is to calculate the total budgeted direct labor cost by multiplying the estimated total direct labor hours by the estimated direct labor cost per hour. A company's human resources department provides an estimate of the hourly labor wage.

12. A **manufacturing overhead budget** is a detailed plan of anticipated manufacturing costs, other than direct materials and direct labor costs, that must be incurred to meet budgeted production needs. It has two purposes: to integrate the overhead cost budgets of the production department and production-related departments, and to group information for the calculation of manufacturing overhead rates for the forthcoming period.

13. A **selling and administrative expense budget** is a detailed plan of operating expenses, other than those related to production, that are needed to support sales and overall operations in a future accounting period.

14. A **cost of goods manufactured budget** is a detailed plan that summarizes the costs of production in a future period. The sources of information for this budget are the direct materials, direct labor, and manufacturing overhead budgets. (See Exhibit 7 in the text for an example of a cost of goods manufactured budget.)

Objective 4: Prepare a budgeted income statement, a cash budget, and a budgeted balance sheet.

15. After revenues and expenses have been itemized in the operating budgets, the budgeted income statement can be prepared. A **budgeted income statement** projects an organization's net income in an accounting period based on the revenues and expenses estimated for that period. Data related to projected sales and costs come from several of the operating budgets.

16. A **capital expenditures budget** is a detailed plan outlining the anticipated amount and timing of capital outlays for long-term assets in an accounting period. Managers rely on the capital expenditures budget when making decisions about such matters as buying equipment or building a new facility. The information in this budget affects the cash budget and the budgeted balance sheet.

17. A **cash budget** is a projection of the cash an organization will receive and the cash it will pay out in an accounting period. It summarizes all planned cash transactions found in the operating budgets and the budgeted income statement. The information it provides enables managers to plan for short-term loans when the cash balance is low and for short-term investments when the cash balance is high. The components of a cash budget are estimated cash receipts, cash payments, beginning cash balance, and ending cash balance. The ending cash balance is computed as follows:

Estimated		Total		Total		Estimated
Ending	=	Estimated	−	Estimated	+	Beginning
Cash		Cash		Cash		Cash
Balance		Receipts		Payments		Balance

Estimates of cash receipts and cash payments are based on information from several sources, including the operating budgets. For example, the sales budget may be the main source of data for predicting cash receipts.

18. A **budgeted balance sheet** projects an organization's financial position of at the end of an accounting period. It uses the estimated data compiled in the course of preparing a master budget and is the final step in that process. (See Exhibit 12 in the text for a complete list of the data sources.)

Objective 5: Describe management's role in budget implementation.

19. A **budget committee** made up of top management has overall responsibility for budget implementation. The committee oversees each stage in the preparation of the master budget, decides any departmental disputes that may arise in the process, and gives final approval to the budget. After the committee approves the master budget, periodic reports from department managers enable it to monitor the progress the company is making in attaining budget targets. To ensure the cooperation of personnel in implementing the budget, top managers must clearly communicate performance expectations and budget targets. They must also show their support for the budget and encourage its implementation.

SELF-TEST

Test your knowledge of the chapter by choosing the best answer for each item below.

1. Which of the following is *not* a guideline for preparing a budget?
   a. Know the purpose of the budget.
   b. Identify the user group and their information needs.
   c. Provide a clearly stated heading.
   d. All of the above are guidelines.

2. Participative budgeting is the key to a successful budgeting process because
   a. senior executives set goals and expect all employees to implement them.
   b. the budget director prepares the master budget and its supporting budgets.
   c. middle managers prepare the budgets; top managers are involved only with strategic planning.
   d. personnel at all levels of the organization take a meaningful and active part in the creation of the budget.

3. Costabile Enterprises uses three gallons of material 2D, two gallons of material 4R, five gallons of material 6T, and ten gallons of material 8K to make each of the twenty-gallon barrels of plant food that it produces. Expected costs per gallon are as follows: 2D, $2.40; 4R, $1.80; 6T, $10.50; and 8K, $3.30. The production budget indicates that 12,400 barrels will be produced in April; 10,800 barrels, in May; and 9,800 barrels, in June. Materials are purchased one month ahead of production. What is the total dollar value of budgeted materials purchases in April?
   a. $1,040,040
   b. $1,194,120
   c. $549,040
   d. $449,620

4. Which of the following cannot be prepared until after a cash budget has been prepared?
   a. Capital expenditures budget
   b. Sales budget
   c. Budgeted balance sheet
   d. Budgeted income statement

5. Which of the following are needed to prepare a cash budget?
   a. Total estimated cash receipts
   b. Total estimated cash payments
   c. Estimated beginning cash balance
   d. All of the above

6. A retail organization would *not* have which of the following operating budgets?
   a. Direct materials purchases budget
   b. Service revenue budget
   c. Cost of goods sold budget
   d. Selling and administrative expense budget

7. The initial step in developing a master budget is to prepare the
   a. cash budget.
   b. capital expenditures budget.
   c. cost of goods sold budget.
   d. sales budget.

8. Which of the following budgets has inputs from essentially all other budgets?
   a. Sales budget
   b. Direct materials purchases budget
   c. Budgeted balance sheet
   d. Production budget

9. Using budgets to evaluate performance is usually done in which stage of the management cycle?
   a. Reviewing
   b. Planning
   c. Reporting
   d. None of the above

10. Which of the following summarizes the costs of production in a future period?
    a. Direct materials purchases budget
    b. Cost of goods manufactured budget
    c. Budgeted balance sheet
    d. Manufacturing overhead budget

TESTING YOUR KNOWLEDGE

Matching*

Match each term with its definition by writing the appropriate letter in the blank.

_____ **1.** Operating budgets

_____ **2.** Master budget

_____ **3.** Cash budget

_____ **4.** Sales budget

_____ **5.** Budget committee

_____ **6.** Production budget

_____ **7.** Budgeted income statement

_____ **8.** Cost of goods manufactured budget

_____ **9.** Sales forecast

_____ **10.** Direct materials purchases budget

_____ **11.** Budgeted balance sheet

a. A statement that projects an organization's financial position at the end of an accounting period

b. A projection of sales demand based on an analysis of internal and external factors

c. A detailed plan that summarizes the costs of production in a future period

d. A projection of net income in an accounting period based on revenues and expenses estimated for that period

e. A detailed plan that identifies the purchases required for budgeted production

f. The basis for all operating budgets

g. A consolidation of operating budgets and financial budgets that establishes a company's financial plans for an accounting period

h. The basis for the direct materials, direct labor, and manufacturing overhead budgets

i. The group with overall responsibility for budget implementation

j. The budget that is prepared after the budgeted income statement

k. Plans used in daily operations

Short Answer

Use the lines provided to answer each item.

1. Briefly define *budgeting*.

_____

_____

_____

_____

2. Define the two categories of budgets that constitute a master budget.

_____

_____

_____

_____

3. How is a cash budget useful to managers?

_____

_____

_____

_____

4. What are the three steps in preparing a direct materials purchases budget?

_____

_____

_____

_____

Note to student: The matching quiz might be completed more efficiently by starting with the definition and searching for the corresponding term.

Circle T if the statement is true, F if it is false. Provide explanations for the false answers, using the blank lines below.

T F **1.** A master budget covers a period of five to ten years.

T F **2.** A master budget applies to just one business segment.

T F **3.** A projection of sales must be made before a production budget can be prepared.

T F **4.** A service organization does not have a direct materials budget.

T F **5.** Depreciation expense is listed as a cash payment in the cash budget.

T F **6.** An annual operating plan identifies a company's short-term goals.

T F **7.** A capital expenditures budget estimates capital outlays for long-term assets.

T F **8.** Total sales for an accounting period are included in that period's cash budget as part of cash receipts.

T F **9.** Preparation of a selling and administrative expense budget relies on information from the cash budget.

T F **10.** The first step in preparing a direct labor budget is to calculate the estimated total direct labor hours for the period.

T F **11.** External factors have no influence on a sales forecast.

T F **12.** A sales budget must be prepared before a production budget can be prepared.

T F **13.** The first step in developing a master budget is to prepare a budgeted balance sheet.

_____

_____

_____

_____

_____

_____

_____

_____

_____

_____

_____

_____

_____

_____

Multiple Choice

Circle the letter of the best answer.

1. The first step in developing a master budget is to prepare
   a. a budgeted income statement.
   b. pro forma statements.
   c. a budgeted balance sheet.
   d. detailed operating budgets.

2. Which of the following components of a master budget must be prepared before the others?
   a. Direct labor budget
   b. Manufacturing overhead budget
   c. Production budget
   d. Direct materials purchases budget

3. The cash budget is prepared
   a. before all operating budgets are prepared.
   b. after the budgeted income statement but before the budgeted balance sheet.
   c. as the last step in preparing the master budget.
   d. only if a company has doubts about its debt-paying ability.

4. Which of the following data would *not* be found in a direct labor budget?
   a. Direct labor hours per unit
   b. Total budgeted direct labor cost
   c. Estimated total direct labor hours
   d. Forecasted sales in dollars

5. Which of the following would *not* be a source of data for estimates of cash payments in the cash budget?
   a. Sales budget
   b. Capital expenditures budget
   c. Selling and administrative expense budget
   d. Direct labor budget

6. The cash budget consists of
   a. projected cash receipts.
   b. the ending cash balance.
   c. projected cash payments.
   d. all of the above.

7. Woodley Company has the following budget information for the first three quarters of its fiscal year:

Quarter	1	2	3
Units produced	23,000	24,000	21,000

Each finished unit requires three pounds of material. The inventory of material at the end of each quarter should equal 10 percent of the following quarter's production needs. How many pounds of material should be purchased for the second quarter?
   a. 71,100 pounds
   b. 72,000 pounds
   c. 74,400 pounds
   d. 75,000 pounds

8. A service organization would prepare all of the following budgets *except* the
   a. direct labor budget.
   b. services overhead budget.
   c. cash budget.
   d. direct materials budget.

9. Timbo Company typically pays 40 percent of its purchases on account in the month of purchase and 60 percent in the month following purchase. Given the following projections of expenditures for direct materials, what would Timbo's expected cash payments be in March 20xx?

	Purchases on Account	Cash Purchases
February 20xx	$10,000	$ 5,000
March 20xx	15,000	20,000
April 20xx	4,000	8,000

   a. $35,000
   b. $30,000
   c. $32,000
   d. $20,000

10. To determine total budgeted direct labor costs, estimated direct labor cost per hour must be multiplied by the
   a. predetermined manufacturing overhead rate.
   b. unit sales projection.
   c. total estimated units of production.
   d. estimated total direct labor hours.

APPLYING YOUR KNOWLEDGE

Exercises

1. Donlevy Company produces and sells a single product. Expected sales for the next four months are as follows:

Month	Units
April	10,000
May	12,000
June	15,000
July	9,000

The company needs a production budget for the second quarter. Experience indicates that end-of-month finished goods inventory must equal 10 percent of the following month's sales in units. At the end of March, 1,000 units were on hand. Compute production needs for the second quarter by preparing a production budget.

Donlevy Company
Production Budget
For the Quarter Ended June 30, 20xx

2. Monahan Enterprises needs a cash budget for the month of June. The following data are available:

   a. The cash balance on June 1 is $7,000.
   b. Sales for May and June are $80,000 and $60,000, respectively. Cash collections on sales are 30 percent in the month of the sale, 65 percent in the following month, and 5 percent uncollectible.
   c. General and administrative expenses are budgeted at $24,000 for June. Depreciation represents $2,000 of this amount.
   d. Inventory purchases totaled $40,000 in May and will total $30,000 in June. Half of inventory purchases are always paid for in the month of the purchase. The remainder are paid for in the following month.
   e. Office furniture costing $3,000 will be purchased for cash in June, and selling expenses (exclusive of $2,000 in depreciation) are budgeted at $14,000.
   f. The company must maintain a minimum ending cash balance of $4,000 and can borrow from the bank in multiples of $100. All loans are repaid after 60 days.

In the space provided below, prepare a cash budget for Monahan Enterprises for the month of June.

Monahan Enterprises
Cash Budget
For the Month Ended June 30, 20xx

3. Jeppo Titanium Company manufactures three products in a single plant with two departments: Bending and Welding. The company has estimated costs for products X and Y and is currently analyzing direct labor hour requirements for the budget year 20xx. The departmental data are as follows:

	Estimated Hours per Unit	
	Bending	Welding
Product X	1	2
Product Y	.6	3
Hourly labor rate	$10	$15

Budgeted unit production in 20xx of Product X is 10,000 and of Product Y, 20,000. Prepare a direct labor budget for 20xx that shows the budgeted direct labor costs for each department and for the company as a whole.

Jeppo Titanium Company
Direct Labor Budget
For the Year Ended December 31, 20xx

4. Explain the role of budgeting in each stage of the management cycle.

_____

_____

_____

_____

_____

_____

_____

_____

_____

_____

_____

CHAPTER 22 STANDARD COSTING AND VARIANCE ANALYSIS

REVIEWING THE CHAPTER

Objective 1: Define *standard costs* and describe how managers use standard costs in the management cycle.

1. **Standard costs** are realistic estimates of costs based on analyses of both past and projected costs and operating conditions. They provide a standard, or predetermined, performance level for use in **standard costing,** a method of cost control that also includes a measure of actual performance and a measure of the difference, or **variance,** between standard and actual performance. This method of measuring and controlling costs differs from the actual and normal costing methods in that it uses estimated costs only to compute all three elements of product cost—direct materials, direct labor, and manufacturing overhead.

2. In the planning stage of the management cycle, managers use standard costs to develop budgets for direct materials, direct labor, and variable manufacturing overhead. These estimated costs not only serve as targets for product costing; they are also useful in making decisions about product distribution and pricing. During the executing stage, managers use standard costs to measure expenditures and to control costs as they occur. At the end of an accounting period, they compare actual costs with standard costs and compute the variances. The variances provide measures of performance that can be used to control costs. Managers also use standard costs to report on operations and managerial performance. A variance report tailored to a manager's responsibilities provides useful information about how well operations are proceeding and how well the manager is controlling them.

Objective 2: Explain how standard costs are developed and compute a standard unit cost.

3. A fully integrated standard costing system uses standard costs for all the elements of product cost. Inventory accounts for materials, work in process, and finished goods, as well as the Cost of Goods Sold account, are maintained and reported in terms of standard costs, and standard unit costs are used to compute account balances. Actual costs are recorded separately so that managers can compare what should have been spent (the standard costs) with the actual costs incurred.

4. A standard unit cost for a manufactured product has six elements: (a) a direct materials price standard, (b) a direct materials quantity standard, (c) a direct labor rate standard, (d) a direct labor time standard, (e) a standard variable overhead rate, and (f) a standard fixed overhead rate. (A standard unit cost for a service includes only the elements that relate to labor and overhead.)

5. To compute a standard cost per unit of output, the following amounts must be identified:
   a. **Standard Direct Materials Cost** = Direct Materials Price Standard × Direct Materials Quantity Standard
      (1) The **direct materials price standard** is the estimated cost of a specific direct material to be used in the next accounting period.

(2) The **direct materials quantity standard** is the estimated amount of direct materials to be used in the period.

b. **Standard Direct Labor Cost** = Direct Labor Rate Standard × Direct Labor Time Standard

   (1) The **direct labor rate standard** is the hourly direct labor cost expected to prevail during the next accounting period for each function or job classification.

   (2) The **direct labor time standard** is the expected time required for each department, machine, or process to complete the production of one unit or one batch of output.

c. **Standard Manufacturing Overhead Cost** = Standard Variable Overhead Rate + Standard Fixed Overhead Rate

   (1) The **standard variable overhead rate** is the total budgeted variable overhead costs divided by an appropriate application base, such as standard machine hours or standard direct labor hours.

   (2) The **standard fixed overhead rate** is the total budgeted fixed overhead costs divided by an expression of capacity, usually normal capacity in terms of standard hours or units.

6. A product's standard unit cost is determined by adding the standard direct materials cost, the standard direct labor cost, and the standard manufacturing overhead cost.

Objective 3: Prepare a flexible budget and describe how variance analysis is used to control costs.

7. **Variance analysis** is the process of computing the differences between standard (or budgeted) costs and actual costs and identifying the causes of those differences.

8. The accuracy of variance analysis depends to a large extent on the type of budget managers use when comparing variances. A **flexible budget** (also called a *variable budget*) is a summary of expected costs for a range of activity levels. Unlike a static budget, which forecasts revenues and expenses for just one level of sales and just one level of output, a flexible budget provides forecasted data that can be adjusted for changes in the level of output. It presents budgeted fixed and variable costs and their totals, as well as the budgeted variable cost per unit. The variable cost per unit and total fixed costs are components of the **flexible budget formula,** an equation that can be used to determine the expected, or budgeted, cost

for any level of output. The formula is as follows: (Variable Cost per Unit × Number of Units Produced) + Budgeted Fixed Costs = Total budgeted Costs. The total budgeted costs can be compared with actual costs to measure the performance of individuals and departments.

9. A flexible budget improves the accuracy of variance analysis, which is a four-step approach to controlling costs. First, managers compute the amount of the variance. If the amount is insignificant, no corrective action is needed. If the amount is significant, managers analyze the variance to identify its cause. In identifying the cause, they are usually able to pinpoint the activities that need to be monitored. They then select performance measures that will enable them to track those activities, analyze the results, and determine the action needed to correct the problem. Their final step is to take the appropriate corrective action.

Objective 4: Compute and analyze direct materials variances.

10. The **total direct materials cost variance** is the difference between the standard cost and actual cost of direct materials. When standard costs exceed actual costs, the variance is favorable (F). When the reverse is true, the variance is unfavorable (U). The total direct materials cost variance is broken down into the direct materials price variance and direct materials quantity variance.

a. **Direct Materials Price Variance** = (Standard Price – Actual Price) × Actual Quantity

b. **Direct materials quantity variance** = Standard Price × (Standard Quantity Allowed – Actual Quantity)

Objective 5: Compute and analyze direct labor variances.

11. The **total direct labor cost variance** is the sum of the direct labor rate variance and the direct labor efficiency variance.

a. **Direct Labor Rate Variance** = (Standard Rate – Actual Rate) × Actual Hours

b. **Direct Labor Efficiency Variance** = Standard Rate × (Standard Hours Allowed – Actual Hours)

Objective 6: Compute and analyze manufacturing overhead variances.

12. **Total manufacturing overhead variance** is the difference between actual overhead costs and standard overhead costs. The latter costs are ap-

plied to production by using a standard overhead rate. A standard overhead rate has two parts: a variable rate and a fixed rate. The standard fixed rate is calculated by dividing total budgeted fixed overhead by normal capacity. The total manufacturing overhead variance can be broken down into variable overhead variances and fixed overhead variances.

a. The **total variable overhead variance** is the difference between the variable overhead spending variance and the variable overhead efficiency variance. The **variable overhead spending variance** is computed by multiplying the actual hours worked by the difference between actual variable overhead costs and the standard variable overhead rate. The **variable overhead efficiency variance** is the difference between the standard direct labor hours allowed for good units produced and the actual hours worked multiplied by the standard variable overhead rate per hour.

b. The **total fixed overhead variance** is the difference between actual fixed overhead costs and the standard fixed overhead costs that are applied to good units produced using the standard fixed overhead rate. For effective performance evaluation, managers break down the total fixed overhead cost variance into two additional variances: the fixed overhead budget variance and the fixed overhead volume variance. The **fixed overhead budget variance** is the difference between budgeted and actual fixed overhead costs. The **fixed overhead volume variance** is the difference between budgeted fixed overhead costs and the overhead costs that are applied to production using the

standard fixed overhead rate. Because the fixed overhead volume variance gauges the use of existing facilities and capacity, a volume variance will occur if more or less than normal capacity is used.

c. The total manufacturing overhead variance is also the amount of over- or underapplied overhead, which must be computed and reconciled at the end of each accounting period. By breaking down the total manufacturing overhead variance into variable and fixed variances, managers can more accurately control costs and reconcile their causes. An analysis of these two overhead variances will help explain why the amount of manufacturing overhead applied to units produced differs from the actual manufacturing overhead costs incurred.

Objective 7: Explain how variances are used to evaluate managers' performance.

13. To ensure that performance evaluation is effective and fair, a company's evaluation policies should be based on input from managers and employees and should be specific about the procedures managers are to follow. The evaluation process becomes more accurate when managerial performance reports include variances from standard costs. A managerial performance report based on standard costs and related variances should identify the causes of each significant variance, as well as the personnel involved, and the corrective actions taken. It should be tailored to the manager's specific areas of responsibility. Managers should be held accountable only for the cost areas under their control.

SELF-TEST

Test your knowledge of the chapter by choosing the best answer for each item below.

1. In which of the following stages of the management cycle do managers use standard costs?
   a. Planning
   b. Reviewing
   c. Executing
   d. All of the above

2. The direct labor efficiency variance is the difference between standard direct labor hours allowed for the good units produced and the
   a. standard hours allowed and standard rate per hour.
   b. actual direct labor hours worked, multiplied by the standard direct labor rate.
   c. direct labor rate per hour.
   d. none of the above.

3. An unfavorable fixed overhead volume variance exists when
   a. budgeted fixed overhead for the level of production is less than fixed overhead applied.
   b. total fixed overhead is less than the predetermined overhead rate.
   c. budgeted fixed overhead for the level of production is greater than standard fixed overhead applied.
   d. none of the above obtain.

4. Which of the following is the correct formula for determining the direct materials price variance?
   a. (Standard Price ÷ Actual Price) × Actual Quantity
   b. (Standard Price − Actual Price) × Standard Quantity
   c. (Standard Price − Actual Price) × Actual Quantity
   d. (Standard Quantity − Actual Quantity) × Actual Price

5. Which of the following is *not* an element of a standard unit cost?
   a. Direct materials price standard
   b. Actual direct labor costs
   c. Direct labor rate standard
   d. All of the above are included in a standard unit cost.

6. Product engineering specifications, the quality of direct materials, and the age and productivity of machinery influence the direct
   a. materials quantity standard.
   b. labor rate standard.
   c. materials price standard.
   d. labor time standard.

7. To compute the standard fixed overhead rate, total budgeted fixed overhead costs are divided by the
   a. flexible budget formula.
   b. actual hours worked.
   c. standard hours allowed.
   d. normal capacity.

8. The Sahlen Company uses a standard costing system in its glass division. The standard cost of making one glass windshield is as follows:

Direct materials (60 lb @ $1/lb)	$ 60.00
Direct labor (3 hr @ $10/hr)	30.00
Manufacturing overhead (3 hr @ $8/hr)	24.00
Total standard unit cost	$114.00

The current variable overhead rate is $3 per labor hour, and the budgeted fixed overhead is $27,000. During January, the division produced 1,650 windshields; normal capacity is 1,800 windshields. The actual cost per windshield was as follows:

Direct materials (58 lb @ $1.10/lb)	$ 63.80
Direct labor (3.1 hr @ $10/hr)	31.00
Manufacturing overhead ($39,930/1,650 products)	24.20
Total actual unit cost	$119.00

The total direct materials quantity variance for January is
   a. $9,570 (U).
   b. $9,570 (F).
   c. $3,300 (F).
   d. $3,300 (U).

9. Assuming the same facts as in **8,** the direct labor rate variance for January is
   a. 0.
   b. $1,650 (U).
   c. $1,920 (F).
   d. $1,650 (F).

10. In the flexible budget formula, the variable cost per unit is multiplied by the
   a. standard hours worked.
   b. number of units produced.
   c. standard hours allowed.
   d. number of units planned.

TESTING YOUR KNOWLEDGE

*Matching**

Match each term with its definition by writing the appropriate letter in the blank.

_____ **1.** Fixed overhead budget variance

_____ **2.** Variance

_____ **3.** Direct materials price standard

_____ **4.** Variance analysis

_____ **5.** Standard costs

_____ **6.** Favorable variance

_____ **7.** Unfavorable variance

_____ **8.** Direct materials price variance

_____ **9.** Direct materials quantity variance

_____ **10.** Direct labor rate variance

_____ **11.** Direct labor efficiency variance

_____ **12.** Performance report

_____ **13.** Flexible budget

a. The difference between the standard direct labor rate and the actual direct labor rate, times actual direct labor hours worked

b. A variance in which actual costs exceed standard costs

c. A summary of expected costs for various levels of production

d. The difference between standard price and actual price, times actual quantity of material purchased

e. A written comparison between actual costs and budgeted costs for a business segment

f. The difference between standard quantity and quantity of material used, times standard price

g. A variance in which standard costs exceed actual costs

h. The difference between standard direct labor hours allowed and actual direct labor hours worked, times standard direct labor rate

i. Predetermined costs that are expressed as a cost per unit of finished product

j. The difference between actual fixed overhead incurred and the fixed overhead budgeted

k. The difference between a standard cost and an actual cost

l. A standard based on a careful estimate of the cost of a specific direct material in the next accounting period

m. The process of computing the difference between standard costs and actual costs and identifying the causes of those differences

---

Note to student: The matching quiz might be completed more efficiently by starting with the definition and searching for the corresponding term.

Use the lines provided to answer each item.

1. Briefly describe how managers use standard costs in each stage of the management cycle.

   _____

   _____

   _____

   _____

   _____

   _____

2. When does a favorable fixed overhead volume variance exist?

   _____

   _____

   _____

   _____

3. List the six standards used to compute total standard unit cost.

   _____

   _____

   _____

   _____

   _____

4. When does a favorable direct materials quantity variance exist?

   _____

   _____

5. When does an unfavorable direct labor rate variance exist?

   _____

   _____

True-False

Circle T if the statement is true, F if it is false. Provide explanations for the false answers, using the blank lines at the end of the section.

T F 1. Time and motion studies of workers are used in establishing direct labor rate standards.

T F 2. In a standard costing system, all costs that flow through the inventory accounts are standard costs.

T F 3. Computing variances is an essential part of the managerial planning function.

T F 4. When direct materials price and quantity variances are unfavorable, it is impossible to have a favorable total direct materials cost variance.

T F 5. The flexible budget includes both budgeted fixed costs and budgeted variable costs for each level of anticipated activity.

T F 6. The total direct labor cost variance is the sum of the direct labor rate variance and the direct labor efficiency variance.

T F 7. The standard overhead rate consists of the standard variable rate only.

T F 8. Computing the total direct labor cost variance is more important than computing the direct labor rate and direct labor efficiency variances.

T F 9. A managerial performance report should contain only cost items controllable by the manager who is being evaluated.

T F 10. A flexible budget is also known as a *fixed budget.*

T F **11.** It is possible to have both an unfavorable fixed overhead volume variance and a favorable total manufacturing overhead variance.

T F **12.** Once an unfavorable variance has been calculated, it is unnecessary to determine its cause.

T F **13.** The flexible budget formula is an equation that determines the budgeted cost for any level of output.

_____

_____

_____

_____

_____

_____

_____

_____

_____

_____

_____

_____

_____

_____

_____

_____

_____

_____

_____

_____

_____

_____

_____

_____

Multiple Choice

Circle the letter of the best answer.

1. Workers' wages paid during a period are all that is needed to compute the
   a. actual direct labor cost.
   b. direct labor rate standard.
   c. standard direct labor cost.
   d. direct labor cost variance.

2. Which of the following would *not* be a cause of a direct materials price variance?
   a. Increases or decreases in vendors' prices
   b. Inaccurate direct materials price standards
   c. Differences between expected quantity discounts and the actual discounts received
   d. Each of the above could be a cause.

3. If an organization is not using a flexible budget that adjusts with changes in activity, it is probably using a
   a. master budget.
   b. production budget.
   c. cash disbursements budget.
   d. static budget.

4. When a company's actual manufacturing overhead is $140,000 and the standard overhead applied to good units produced is $100,000, the company has a(n)

  a. unfavorable variance of $40,000.
  b. favorable variance of $40,000.
  c. error in calculation.
  d. none of the above.

5. Given the following information, what would be the total budgeted costs at 10,000 units of output?

Variable costs:	
Direct materials	$4.00 per unit
Direct labor	$1.00 per unit
Variable manufacturing overhead	$3.00 per unit
Fixed manufacturing overhead	$20,000

  a. $80,000
  b. $100,000
  c. $40,000
  d. Undeterminable without more data

6. Assuming the same facts as in 5, what would be the total budgeted costs at a production level of 20,000 units?

  a. $180,000
  b. $160,000
  c. $20,000
  d. Undeterminable without more data

7. Which of the following variances could be used to evaluate a purchasing manager's performance?

  a. Direct materials price variance
  b. Direct labor rate variance
  c. Direct labor efficiency variance
  d. Direct materials quantity variance

8. If employees take more time to achieve a given level of production than the standard allows, there will be a(n)

  a. favorable direct labor rate variance.
  b. unfavorable direct labor rate variance.
  c. favorable direct labor efficiency variance.
  d. unfavorable direct labor efficiency variance.

9. In a flexible budget, which total costs would *not* change, given different levels of production?

  a. Fixed manufacturing overhead
  b. Variable manufacturing overhead
  c. Direct labor costs
  d. Direct materials costs

10. Managers can use standard costing for

  a. evaluating performance.
  b. identifying inefficiencies.
  c. product pricing.
  d. all of the above.

APPLYING YOUR KNOWLEDGE

Exercises

1. Goethe Company employs a standard costing system in the manufacture of hand-painted dishes. The standards for the current year are as follows:

Direct materials price standards
Porcelain	$.80/pound
Red paint	$1.00/tube
Blue paint	$1.00/tube

Direct materials quantity standards
Porcelain	½ pound/dish
Red paint	1 tube/20 dishes
Blue paint	1 tube/50 dishes

Direct labor time standards
Molding department	.03 hour/dish
Painting department	.05 hour/dish

Direct labor rate standards
Molding department	$4.00/hour
Painting department	$6.00/hour

Standard manufacturing overhead rates
Standard variable overhead rate	$3.00/direct labor hour
Standard fixed overhead rate	$2.00/direct labor hour

Compute the standard cost per dish.

Porcelain	$_____
Red paint	_____
Blue paint	_____
Molding department wages	_____
Painting department wages	_____
Variable overhead	_____
Fixed overhead	_____
Standard cost of one dish	$_____

2. Sturchio Company expects fixed overhead for 20xx to total $50,000. Variable costs per unit are expected to be as follows: direct labor, $4.50; direct materials, $1.25; and variable overhead, $2.75. Using these data, prepare a flexible budget for volumes of 10,000 units, 15,000 units, and 20,000 units. In addition, determine the flexible budget formula.

Sturchio Company
Flexible Budget
For the Year Ended December 31, 20xx

---

3. Mississippi Sporting Goods Company uses a standard costing system in its manufacture of 10-pound steel dumbbells. The standard cost for steel is $.60 per pound, and each dumbbell should require .3 standard direct labor hours. The standard direct labor rate is $4.50 per hour. During March, the company produced 65,000 dumbbells, and it purchased and used 657,000 pounds of steel; the steel cost $381,060. Direct labor hours totaled 22,100; direct labor cost was $100,555. Using these data, compute the following variances for March; indicate whether each variance is favorable or unfavorable by putting an F or a U in the parentheses after each amount:

a. Direct materials price variance =

   $_____ ( )

b. Direct materials quantity variance =

   $_____ ( )

c. Direct labor rate variance =

   $_____ ( )

d. Direct labor efficiency variance =

   $_____ ( )

Crossword Puzzle
for Chapters 21 and 22

ACROSS

5. Type of budget disclosing receipts and payments
6. Direct materials _____ variance
7. Purchase made with idle cash
9. Item in 5-Across
10. _____ expenditures budget
12. _____ and administrative expense budget
13. Opposite of "less" in a budget
14. Short-term _____ (a budget objective)
18. Operating, investing, or financing _____
19. Cash movement
20. Type of budget expressed in hours and dollars
21. Direct labor _____ standard
22. Business plans based on forecasted transactions, activities, or events

DOWN

1. Difference between standard performance and actual performance
2. Part of "JIT"
3. Estimated amount to be paid for materials, labor, or overhead (2 words)
4. Budgeted _____ sheet
8. Capable of being contained, as a cost
11. Type of budget covering a range of volumes
15. _____ Costs (column head in a performance report)
16. Static, like some budgets
17. Management _____ (a four-stage process)

Standard Costing and Variance Analysis

CHAPTER 23 PERFORMANCE MANAGEMENT AND EVALUATION

REVIEWING THE CHAPTER

Objective 1: Describe how the balanced scorecard aligns performance with organizational goals, and explain the role of the balanced scorecard in the management cycle.

1. The **balanced scorecard** is a framework that links the perspectives of an organization's four basic stakeholder groups with the organization's mission and vision, performance measures, strategic plan, and resources. The four groups are investors, employees, internal business processes, and customers. To add value for these groups, an organization determines each group's objectives and translates them into performance measures that have specific, quantifiable targets.

2. During the planning stage of the management cycle, managers use the balanced scorecard to translate their organization's vision and strategy into operational objectives that will benefit all stakeholder groups. Once they have established these objectives, they set performance targets and select performance measures. In the executing stage, managers use the organization's operational objectives as the basis for decision making within their individual areas of responsibility. In the reviewing stage, they evaluate their strategies in meeting the performance targets set during the planning stage and compare planned performance with actual results. The reports prepared during the reporting stage enable managers to monitor and evaluate performance measures that add value for the stakeholder groups.

Objective 2: Discuss performance measurement, and state the issues that affect management's ability to measure performance.

3. A **performance management and evaluation system** is a set of procedures that account for and report on both financial and nonfinancial performance. Such a system enables a company to identify how well it is doing, the direction it is taking, and what improvements will make it more profitable.

4. **Performance measurement** is the use of quantitative tools to gauge an organization's performance in relation to a specific goal or an expected outcome. Each organization must develop a unique set of performance measures appropriate to its specific situation that will help managers distinguish between what is being measured and the actual measures used to monitor performance.

Objective 3: Define *responsibility accounting,* **and describe the role responsibility centers play in performance management and evaluation.**

5. **Responsibility accounting** is an information system that classifies data according to areas of responsibility and reports each area's activities by including only the revenue, cost, and resource categories that the assigned manager can control.

6. A **responsibility center** is an organizational unit whose manager has been assigned the responsibility of managing a portion of the organization's

resources. The five types of responsibility centers are as follows:

a. A **cost center** is a responsibility center whose manager is accountable only for controllable costs that have well-defined relationships between the center's resources and products or services.

b. A **discretionary cost center** is a responsibility center whose manager is accountable only for costs in which the relationship between resources and products or services produced is not well defined. These centers, like cost centers, have approved budgets that set spending limits.

c. A **revenue center** is a responsibility center whose manager is accountable primarily for revenue and whose success is based on its ability to generate revenue.

d. A **profit center** is a responsibility center whose manager is accountable for both revenue and costs and for the resulting operating income.

e. An **investment center** is a responsibility center whose manager is accountable for profit generation; the manager can also make significant decisions about the resources the center uses. The manager can control revenues, costs, and the investments of assets to achieve the organization's goals.

7. An **organization chart** is a visual representation of an organization's hierarchy of responsibility for the purposes of management control. A responsibility accounting system establishes a communications network within an organization that is ideal for gathering and reporting information about the operations of each these areas of responsibility. The system is used to prepare budgets by responsibility area and to report on the actual performance of each responsibility center. The performance report for a responsibility center should contain only **controllable costs and revenues**—that is, the costs, revenues, and resources that the manager of the center can control.

Objective 4: Prepare performance reports for cost centers using flexible budgets and for profit centers using variable costing.

8. Performance reports allow comparisons between actual performance and budget expectations. Such comparisons enable management to evaluate an individual's performance with respect to responsibility center objectives and companywide objectives and to recommend changes. The con-

tent and format of a performance report depend on the nature of the responsibility center.

9. The performance of a cost center can be evaluated by comparing its actual costs with the corresponding amounts in the flexible and master budgets. A flexible budget is a cost control tool used to evaluate performance and is derived by multiplying actual unit output by standard unit costs for each cost item in the report. Variances between actual costs and the flexible budget can be examined further by using standard costing to compute specific variances for direct materials, direct labor, and manufacturing overhead.

10. A profit center's performance is usually evaluated by comparing its actual income statement with its budgeted income statement. When **variable costing** is used, the profit center manager's controllable costs are classified as variable or fixed. The variable cost of goods sold and the variable selling and administrative expenses are subtracted from sales to arrive at the center's contribution margin; all controllable fixed costs are subtracted from the contribution margin to determine operating income. The variable costing income statement takes the form of a contribution income statement rather than a traditional income statement. A traditional income statement (also called a *full costing* or *absorption costing income statement*) assigns all manufacturing costs to cost of goods sold. A variable costing income statement uses only direct materials, direct labor, and variable manufacturing overhead to compute variable cost of goods sold. Fixed manufacturing overhead is considered a cost of the current accounting period and is listed with fixed selling expenses.

Objective 5: Prepare performance reports for investment centers using traditional measures of return on investment and residual income and the newer measure of economic value added.

11. **Return on investment (ROI)** is a performance measure that takes into account both operating income and the assets invested to earn that income. It is computed as follows:

$$\text{Return on Investment (ROI)} = \frac{\text{Operating Income}}{\text{Assets Invested}}$$

In this formula, assets invested are the average of the beginning and ending asset balances for the period. Return on investment can also be examined in terms of profit margin and asset turnover.

Profit margin is the ratio of operating income to sales; it represents the percentage of each sales dollar that results in profit. **Asset turnover** is the ratio of sales to average assets invested; it indicates the productivity of assets, or the number of sales dollars generated by each dollar invested in assets. Return on investment is equal to profit margin multiplied by asset turnover:

$$\text{ROI} = \text{Profit Margin} \times \text{Asset Turnover}$$

or

$$\text{ROI} = \frac{\text{Operating Income}}{\text{Sales}} \times \frac{\text{Sales}}{\text{Assets Invested}} = \frac{\text{Operating Income}}{\text{Assets Invested}}$$

12. **Residual income (RI)** is the operating income that an investment center earns above a minimum desired return on invested assets. The formula for computing residual income is

$$\text{Residual Income} = \text{Operating Income} - (\text{Desired ROI} \times \text{Assets Invested})$$

13. **Economic value added (EVA)** is an indicator of performance that measures the shareholder wealth created by an investment center. A manager can improve the economic value of an investment center by increasing sales, decreasing costs, decreasing assets, or lowering the cost of capital. The **cost of capital** is the minimum desired rate of return on an investment. The formula for computing economic value added is as follows:

$$\text{Economic Value Added} = \text{After-Tax Operating Income} - \text{Cost of Capital in Dollars}$$

or

$$\text{Economic Value Added} = \text{After-Tax Operating Income} - [\text{Cost of Capital} \times (\text{Total Assets} - \text{Current Liabilities})]$$

Objective 6: Explain how properly linked performance incentives and measures add value for all stakeholders in performance management and evaluation.

14. The effectiveness of a performance management and evaluation system depends on how well it coordinates the goals of responsibility centers, managers, and the entire company. Performance can be optimized by linking goals to measurable objectives and targets and by tying appropriate compensation incentives to the achievement of those targets through **performance-based pay.** Cash bonuses, awards, profit-sharing plans, and stock option programs are common types of incentive compensation. Each organization's unique circumstances will determine its correct mix of performance measures and compensation incentives. If management values the perspectives of all stakeholder groups, its performance management and evaluation system will balance and benefit all interests.

SELF-TEST

Test your knowledge of the chapter by choosing the best answer for each item below.

1. During the planning stage of the management cycle, the balanced scorecard provides
   a. reports that enable managers to monitor performance measures.
   b. performance measures for evaluating managers' strategies.
   c. a framework that enables managers to translate their organization's vision and strategy into operational objectives.
   d. objectives that managers use as a basis for decision making within their individual areas of responsibility.

2. A responsibility center whose manager is accountable for both revenues and costs and for the resulting operating income is a(n)
   a. investment center.
   b. profit center.
   c. cost center.
   d. discretionary cost center.

3. The difference between a variable costing income statement and a traditional income statement is that in a variable statement, cost of goods sold includes
   a. all expenses.
   b. only fixed costs.
   c. all variable costs.
   d. fixed overhead but not fixed selling costs.

4. Operating income divided by assets invested is the formula for which of the following performance measures?
   a. Return on investment
   b. Residual income
   c. Economic value added
   d. Cost of capital

5. An accounting, personnel, or legal department is a(n)
   a. discretionary cost center.
   b. cost center.
   c. profit center.
   d. investment center.

6. The standard cost for producing a bottle of mustard is as follows:

Direct materials	$.35
Direct labor	$.10
Variable overhead	$.05
Total fixed overhead	$3,000

   The company estimated that it would produce 10,000 bottles during April. The actual number of bottles produced was 11,000. The amount in the flexible budget will equal
   a. $5,000.
   b. $3,000.
   c. $8,000.
   d. $8,500.

7. Which of the following would *not* be included as a variable cost in a candy manufacturer's flexible budget?
   a. Sugar
   b. Depreciation expense
   c. Candy wrappers
   d. Sales commissions

8. The minimum desired rate of return on an investment is called
   a. cost of capital.
   b. return on investment.
   c. operating income.
   d. profit margin.

9. The objective of performance-based pay is to
   a. give all employees an annual bonus.
   b. guarantee that all employees get a pay raise each year.
   c. link compensation to an employee's measurable performance targets.
   d. link an employee's overtime with the production for a given period.

TESTING YOUR KNOWLEDGE

*Matching**

Match each term with its definition by writing the appropriate letter in the blank.

_____ 1. Profit center

_____ 2. Organization chart

_____ 3. Residual income

_____ 4. Cost center

_____ 5. Balanced scorecard

_____ 6. Cost of capital

_____ 7. Profit margin

_____ 8. Asset turnover

_____ 9. Performance-based pay

_____ 10. Economic value added

a. Minimum desired rate of return on an investment

b. A framework that links the perspectives of an organization's four basic stakeholder groups with the organization's mission and vision, performance measures, strategic plan, and resources

c. The ratio of operating income to sales

d. An indicator of performance that measures the shareholder wealth created by an investment center

e. A responsibility center whose manager is accountable only for controllable costs that have well-defined relationships between the center's resources and products or services

f. The operating income that an investment center earns above a minimum desired return on invested assets

g. A responsibility center whose manager is accountable for both revenue and costs and for the resulting operating income

h. A visual representation of an organization's hierarchy of responsibility for the purposes of management control

i. The ratio of sales to average assets invested

j. Compensation based on the achievement of measurable performance targets

Short Answer

Use the lines provided to answer each item.

1. What is the formula for economic value added?

_____

_____

_____

2. What are the five types of responsibility centers?

_____

_____

_____

_____

3. Explain the difference between a variable costing income statement and a traditional income statement.

_____

_____

_____

_____

4. What is the purpose of a balanced scorecard?

_____

_____

_____

_____

Note to student: The matching quiz might be completed more efficiently by starting with the definition and searching for the corresponding term.

Circle T if the statement is true, F if it is false. Provide explanations for the false answers, using the blank lines below.

T F **1.** Responsibility accounting is an information system that classifies data according to areas of responsibility.

T F **2.** The manager of a discretionary cost center is accountable for costs in which the relationship between resources and products or services is well defined.

T F **3.** Return on investment is equal to profit margin divided by asset turnover.

T F **4.** Performance reports should contain all costs, revenues, and resources, regardless of whether managers can control them.

T F **5.** The traditional income statement, the variable income statement, and the contribution income statement produce the same net income.

T F **6.** An organization's four basic stakeholder groups are investors, customers, employees, and creditors.

T F **7.** Asset turnover is the ratio of sales to current assets.

T F **8.** The manager of an investment center is accountable for profit generation and can make significant decisions about the resources the center uses.

T F **9.** The reports prepared during the reporting stage of the management cycle should be designed to give managers a standard format for comparing performance among departments.

_____

_____

_____

_____

_____

_____

_____

_____

_____

_____

_____

_____

_____

_____

Circle the letter of the best answer.

1. In a flexible budget, which total costs would *not* change for different levels of production?
   a. Fixed manufacturing overhead
   b. Variable manufacturing overhead
   c. Direct labor costs
   d. Direct materials costs

2. Given the following information, what would the total dollar amount in a flexible budget be at 20,000 units of output?

   Variable costs:
Direct materials	$4 per unit
Direct labor	1 per unit
Variable overhead	3 per unit
Fixed overhead	$20,000

   a. $160,000
   b. $20,000
   c. $180,000
   d. $80,000

3. The four basic stakeholder groups are
   a. investors, employees, internal business processes, and customers.
   b. employees, lenders, customers, and managers.
   c. investors, employees, creditors, and customers.
   d. investors, government tax agencies, employees, and customers.

4. Which of the following equations is used to compute return on investment?
   a. Operating Income ÷ Assets Invested
   b. Operating Income − (Desired ROI × Assets Invested)
   c. Operating Income × Assets Invested
   d. Operating Income + (Desired ROI × Assets Invested)

5. Which of the following represents the percentage of each sales dollar that results in profit?
   a. Cost of capital
   b. Profit margin
   c. Net sales
   d. Net income after taxes

6. A responsibility center that is accountable primarily for revenue and whose success is judged on its ability to generate revenue is a(n)
   a. profit center.
   b. investment center.
   c. revenue center.
   d. discretionary cost center.

7. In a variable income statement, which of the following costs are included in the cost of goods sold?
   a. Direct materials, direct labor, and all manufacturing overhead
   b. Direct materials, direct labor, and fixed manufacturing overhead
   c. Direct materials, direct labor, and variable manufacturing overhead
   d. Manufacturing overhead only

8. All of the following are responsibility centers *except*
   a. cost centers.
   b. operating centers.
   c. profit centers.
   d. investment centers.

9. Managers use the asset turnover ratio to determine the
   a. productivity of assets, or the number of sales dollars generated by each dollar invested in assets.
   b. productivity of liabilities, or the number of sales dollars generated by each dollar owed.
   c. productivity of sales by the number of asset dollars generated by each dollar of sales.
   d. None of the above.

APPLYING YOUR KNOWLEDGE

Exercises

1. Corwin Company manufactures scented candles. For the year ended December 31, 20xx, it expects its fixed manufacturing overhead to be $135,000. Variable costs are expected to be as follows: direct materials, $1.80; direct labor, $.35; and variable manufacturing overhead, $.60. Using these data and assuming the production of 350,000 candles, prepare a flexible budget for Corwin.

Corwin Company
Flexible Budget
For the Year Ended December 31, 20xx

---

2. The following report compares Cazuelas Company's budgeted costs and actual costs for 20xx and presents the variances:

Cazuelas Company
Budgeted Versus Actual Costs
For the Year Ended December 31, 20xx

	Budgeted	Actual	Variance
Sales	$120,000	$125,000	$5,000
Cost of goods sold	70,000	79,000	(9,000)
Gross margin	50,000	46,000	(4,000)
Operating expenses	30,000	28,000	2,000
Net income	20,000	18,000	(2,000)

Cazuelas sells each unit for $100. The standard cost per unit is $62.50. What is the amount of variance that each of the following responsibility centers would be accountable for?

a. Revenue center

b. Profit center

c. Cost center (Production Department)

CHAPTER 24 SHORT-RUN DECISION ANALYSIS

REVIEWING THE CHAPTER

Objective 1: Explain how managers make short-run decisions during the management cycle.

1. **Short-run decision analysis** is the systematic examination of any decision whose effects will be felt over the course of the next year. To perform this type of analysis, managers need both historical and estimated quantitative and qualitative information. The information should be relevant, timely, and presented in a format that is easy to use in decision making.

2. Short-run decision analysis is an important component of the management cycle.
   a. Analyzing short-run decisions in the planning stage involves discovering a problem or need, identifying alternative courses of action to solve the problem or meet the need, analyzing the effects of each alternative on business operations, and selecting the best alternative. Short-run decisions should support the company's strategic plan and objectives and take into consideration not only quantitative factors, such as projected costs and revenues, but also qualitative factors, such as the competition, economic conditions, social issues, product or service quality, and timeliness.
   b. In the executing stage, managers make and implement many decisions that affect their organization's profitability and liquidity in the short run. For example, they may decide to outsource a product or service, accept a special order, or change the sales mix. All these decisions affect operations in the current period.

   c. In the reviewing stage, managers analyze each decision to determine if it produced the desired results, and, if necessary, they identify and prescribe corrective action.
   d. Managers prepare reports related to short-run decisions throughout the management cycle. In addition to developing budgets and compiling analyses of data that support their decisions, they issue reports that measure the effects their decisions had on the organization.

Objective 2: Define *incremental analysis* and describe how it applies to short-run decision analysis.

3. **Incremental analysis** (also called *differential analysis*) is a technique that helps managers compare alternative courses of action by focusing on differences in the projected revenues and costs. Only data that differ among the alternatives are included in the analysis. A cost that differs among alternatives is called a **differential** (or *incremental*) **cost**.

4. The first step in incremental analysis is to eliminate irrelevant revenues and costs—that is, those that do not differ among the alternatives. Also eliminated are sunk costs. A **sunk cost** is a cost that was incurred because of a previous decision and cannot be recovered through the current decision. Once all irrelevant revenues and costs have been identified, the incremental analysis can be prepared using only projected revenues and expenses that differ for each alternative. The alternative that results in the highest increase in net income or

cost savings is the one that managers generally choose.

5. Incremental analysis simplifies the evaluation of a decision and reduces the time needed to choose the best course of action. However, it is only one input to the final decision. Managers also need to consider other issues, such as **opportunity costs,** which are the benefits forfeited or lost when one alternative is chosen over another.

Objective 3: Perform incremental analysis for outsourcing decisions.

6. **Outsourcing** is the use of suppliers outside the organization to perform services or produce goods that could be performed or produced internally. **Make-or-buy decisions** are decisions about whether to make a part internally or to buy it from an external supplier. Such decisions may also be concerned with the outsourcing of operating activities.

7. To focus their resources on their core competencies (i.e., the activities they perform best), many companies outsource nonvalue-adding activities, especially those that involve relatively low levels of skill (such as payroll processing or storage and distribution) or highly specialized knowledge (such as information management).

8. Incremental analysis of the costs and revenues of outsourcing a product or service as opposed to producing or performing it internally helps managers identify the best alternative.

Objective 4: Perform incremental analysis for special order decisions.

9. **Special order decisions** are decisions about whether to accept or reject special orders at prices below the normal market prices. A special order should be accepted only if it maximizes operating income. Like all short-run decisions, a special order decision should support the organization's strategic plan and objectives and be based on the relevant costs and revenues, as well as qualitative factors.

10. One approach to analyzing a special order decision is to compare its price with the costs of producing, packaging, and shipping the order to see if a profit can be generated. Another approach is to prepare a bid price by calculating the minimum selling price for the special order; the bid price equals the relevant costs plus an estimated profit.

11. Qualitative factors that can influence a special order decision are the special order's impact on

sales to regular customers, its potential to lead the company into new sales areas, and the customer's ability to maintain an ongoing relationship with the company that includes good ordering and paying practices.

Objective 5: Perform incremental analysis for segment profitability decisions.

12. The objective of analyzing a decision about segment profitability is to identify segments that have a negative segment margin. A **segment margin** is a segment's sales revenue minus its direct costs (direct variable costs and direct fixed costs traceable to the segment). These direct costs are **avoidable costs** because if management decides to drop the segment, they will be eliminated; because they vary among segments, they are relevant to the decision. If a segment has a positive segment margin (i.e., if the segment's revenue is greater than its direct costs), the segment should be kept. If a segment has a negative segment margin (i.e., if its revenue is less than its direct costs), it should be dropped. Certain costs will occur regardless of the decision; because these costs are unavoidable and are common to all alternatives, they are excluded from the calculation of the segment margin.

13. An analysis of segment profitability includes the preparation of a segmented income statement using variable costing to identify variable and fixed costs.

Objective 6: Perform incremental analysis for sales mix decisions involving constrained resources.

14. **Sales mix decisions** arise when limited resources, such as machine time or labor, restrict the types or quantities of products that a company can manufacture or the services it can deliver. The objective of a sales mix decision is to select the alternative that maximizes the contribution margin per constrained resource, as well as operating income.

15. Incremental analysis of a sales mix decision involves two steps:
    a. Calculate the contribution margin per unit for each product or service line affected by the constrained resource. The contribution margin per unit equals the selling price per unit less the variable costs per unit.
    b. Calculate the contribution margin per unit of the constrained resource. The contribution margin per unit of the constrained resource equals the contribution margin per unit divided

by the quantity of the constrained resource required per unit.

Objective 7: Perform incremental analysis for sell or process-further decisions.

16. A **sell or process-further decision** is a decision about whether to sell a joint product or service at the split-off point or to sell it after further processing. **Joint products** are two or more products or services composed of a common material or process that cannot be identified as separate during some or all of the production process. Only at a specific point, called the **split-off point,** do joint products or services become separate and identifiable. At that point, a company may decide to sell the product or service as is, or it may decide to process it into another form for sale to a different market. The objective of a sell or process-further decision is to select the alternative that maximizes operating income.

Test your knowledge of the chapter by choosing the best answer for each item below.

1. In which stage of the management cycle do managers estimate cost and revenue information that can be used to make short-run decisions during the coming year?
   a. Reviewing stage
   b. Executing stage
   c. Reporting stage
   d. Planning stage

2. An approach to decision analysis that considers only revenue and cost items that differ among alternatives is known as
   a. contribution margin analysis.
   b. incremental analysis.
   c. outsourcing decision analysis.
   d. special order decision analysis.

3. Which of the following costs are considered when using incremental analysis?
   a. Sunk costs
   b. Relevant costs
   c. Opportunity costs
   d. Irrelevant costs

4. Likely candidates for outsourcing include all of the following *except*
   a. information management.
   b. storage and distribution.
   c. payroll processing.
   d. a company's core competencies.

5. A management decision to accept or reject a sizable but unusual order at a price below the market price is
   a. an outsourcing decision.
   b. a special order decision.
   c. a sell or process-further decision.
   d. a segment profitability decision.

6. Products A and B can be sold at the split-off point for $27.50 and $32.50, respectively. Each unit of Product A can be sold for $45.00 if the company spends an additional $15.20 per unit on the product. Product B can be sold for $50.25 per unit if an additional $18.00 is spent processing each unit. Joint product costs are $12.40 per unit of Product A and $14.40 per unit of Product B. The company should
   a. process only Product A further.
   b. process only Product B further.
   c. process both products further.
   d. sell both products at the split-off point.

7. Short-run decision making requires
   a. information about relevant variable costs.
   b. relevant estimated nonfinancial information.
   c. relevant estimated financial information.
   d. all of the above.

8. A service organization may use short-term decision analysis for all of the following decisions *except* whether to
   a. outsource a service.
   b. accept or bid on a special order.
   c. allow more floor space for a product.
   d. drop an unprofitable service.

9. Costs incurred because of previous decisions that *cannot* be recovered through the current decision are called
   a. relevant costs.
   b. fixed costs.
   c. variable costs.
   d. sunk costs.

TESTING YOUR KNOWLEDGE

Matching*

Match each term with its definition by writing the appropriate letter in the blank.

_____ 1. Sunk costs

_____ 2. Incremental analysis

_____ 3. Sales mix decision

_____ 4. Avoidable costs

_____ 5. Irrelevant costs

_____ 6. Contribution margin

_____ 7. Special order decision

_____ 8. Sell or process-further decision

_____ 9. Opportunity costs

_____ 10. Outsourcing

a. The benefits forfeited or lost when one alternative is chosen over another

b. Relevant costs in short-run decisions

c. Sunk costs and costs that do not differ among alternatives

d. Costs incurred because of a previous decision that cannot be recovered through the current decision

e. The use of suppliers outside the organization to perform services or produce goods that could be performed or produced internally

f. A method of comparing alternative courses of action by focusing on differences in their projected revenues and costs

g. A decision to sell a joint product or service at split-off or to subject it to additional processing

h. A decision concerning the most profitable combination of product or service sales

i. Sales revenue minus all variable costs

j. A decision to accept or reject a large, one-time order at a price below the normal market price

Short Answer

Use the lines provided to complete each item.

1. List the four steps involved in analyzing short-run decisions in the planning stage of the management cycle.

   _____

   _____

   _____

   _____

2. Distinguish between relevant and irrelevant decision information.

   _____

   _____

   _____

3. List three possible benefits of outsourcing.

   _____

   _____

   _____

4. Identify five types of short-run decisions.

   _____

   _____

   _____

   _____

   _____

_____

*Note to student: The matching quiz might be completed more efficiently by starting with the definition and searching for the corresponding term.

True-False

Circle T if the statement is true, F if it is false. Provide explanations for the false answers, using the blank lines below.

T F **1.** Irrelevant costs are costs that do not differ among alternatives.

T F **2.** When applying incremental analysis to a special order decision, a service company considers only sunk costs.

T F **3.** Managers use cost information in each stage of the management cycle.

T F **4.** The main concern in incremental analysis is to project the operating income that each alternative will produce.

T F **5.** Incremental analysis is very useful for outsourcing decisions.

T F **6.** In a special order decision, the only relevant costs are those that vary because of the decision.

T F **7.** Management decisions require that a course of action be selected from a defined set of alternatives.

T F **8.** A segment that has a positive contribution margin and a negative segment margin should not be eliminated.

T F **9.** When decision alternatives involve both costs and revenues, the typical objective is to maximize annual operating income.

T F **10.** Joint products are two or more products or services that cannot be identified as separate during some or all of the production process.

T F **11.** Avoidable costs are sunk costs.

T F **12.** A special order decision requires a determination of the most profitable combination of product or service sales.

T F **13.** Only quantitative factors should be considered in special order decisions.

_____

_____

_____

_____

_____

_____

_____

_____

_____

Multiple Choice

Circle the letter of the best answer.

1. When a service business is deciding on a sales mix involving constrained resources, the approach that it uses focuses on
   a. fixed costs.
   b. contribution margin.
   c. sunk costs.
   d. full costs.

2. The best method to use in deciding whether to outsource a product is
   a. variable costing.
   b. equivalent unit analysis.
   c. incremental analysis.
   d. opportunity costing.

3. The Machining Department of Onufer Company has a total capacity of 2,400 machine hours per month. The company makes three different products. Data for the products are as follows:

	Machine Hours Required per Unit	Contribution Margin per Unit	Current Unit Sales Demand
Superior	2	$6.00	1,000
Deluxe	1	4.00	1,500
Standard	½	2.50	2,000

   To produce the highest operating income, the sales mix should be as follows:
   a. Produce 1,000 units of Superior, 800 units of Standard, and 0 units of Deluxe.
   b. Produce 500 units of Superior, 750 units of Deluxe, and 1,300 units of Standard.
   c. Produce 1,500 units of Deluxe, 450 units of Superior, and 0 units of Standard.
   d. Produce 2,000 units of Standard, 1,400 units of Deluxe, and 0 units of Superior.

4. Which of the following would *not* be a valid reason to outsource a product?
   a. To improve cash flows
   b. To capitalize on the fact that manufacturing the product requires only unskilled labor
   c. To increase operating income
   d. To share critical information with competitors

5. A make-or-buy decision would be classified as
   a. an outsourcing decision.
   b. a sales mix decision.
   c. a segment profitability decision.
   d. a special order decision.

6. Estimated costs that differ among alternative courses of action are called
   a. relevant costs.
   b. opportunity costs.
   c. irrelevant costs.
   d. sunk costs.

7. For several years, a company has produced a joint product that is processed after split-off. The product is salable at the split-off point. To justify the additional processing, a decision analysis should demonstrate that
   a. ultimate revenues exceed all joint and separable costs.
   b. additional processing increases the revenue potential.
   c. the costs of further processing are less than incremental revenues.
   d. unit production costs are lower after additional processing.

8. The point in the production process at which a joint product or service becomes separate and identifiable is the
   a. breakeven point.
   b. split-off point.
   c. point of indifference.
   d. point of inflection.

9. Costs that can be eliminated if a segment is discontinued are called
   a. avoidable costs.
   b. fixed costs.
   c. historical costs.
   d. unnecessary costs.

10. In a sell or process-further decision,
    a. the method chosen to allocate joint costs is a critical factor.
    b. the assignment of joint costs can be influenced by the final decision.
    c. joint costs are irrelevant to the decision and should be ignored.
    d. joint costs must be minimized.

APPLYING YOUR KNOWLEDGE

Exercises

1. A company must decide whether to purchase machine A for $10,000 or machine B for $17,000. Both machines are expected to have a life of only one year. Machine A would require the use of two operators, each of whom earns $8,000 per year, and maintenance of $300 per year. However, it would cost $50 per year less for electricity than the machine currently in use. Machine B would require only one part-time operator at $8,000 per year. It would require maintenance of $500 per year, but it would cost $80 per year more for electricity than the machine currently in use. Each machine would generate the same amount of revenue. Prepare an incremental analysis to determine which machine the company should purchase.

2. On June 30, 20xx, Time, LLP, had 100,000 unsold 20xx calendars. The director of marketing thinks these calendars can no longer be sold to the company's regular customers at the normal selling price. Direct materials cost is $3 per calendar, direct labor cost is $2 per calendar, variable overhead is $.50 per calendar, and fixed overhead (based on a production volume of 300,000 calendars) is $1 per calendar. The cost of shipping and packaging (paid by the company) is $1.75 per calendar. The normal selling price is $12 per calendar. What is the *minimum* special price that the company could set for the unsold calendars?

3. Houses for the Needy, a not-for-profit organization, has offered Matt Printing Company $600 to prepare a custom brochure to be used in soliciting funds. The brochure is to be multicolored and contain a number of graphic designs. Matt estimates that it would take ten hours of design labor at $40 per hour and four printing hours at $15 per hour to produce the brochures. Fixed costs are already covered by regular business. Prepare an incremental analysis of costs to determine whether Matt should accept the order. In addition, briefly discuss other factors that may influence the decision to accept or reject the special order.

Crossword Puzzle
for Chapters 23 and 24

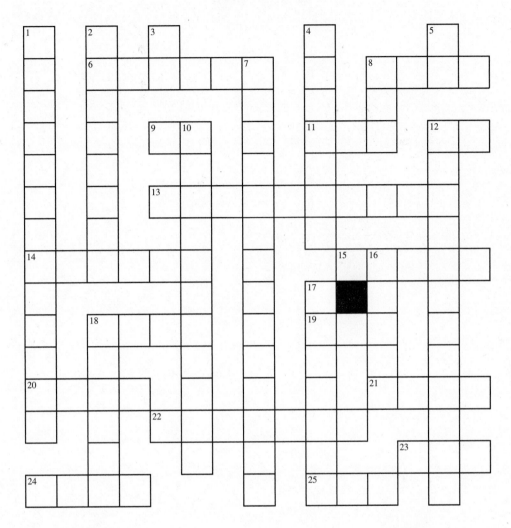

ACROSS

6. Investment or profit _____
8. Measures of short-_____ success
9. 14-Across, for short
11. Sales _____ decision
12. Cost _____ goods sold
13. See 7-Down
14. Residual _____
15. _____ products (products made from the same material)
18. _____-or-buy decision
19. Cause-_____-effect relationships
20. Example of a fixed cost
21. Minimum desired _____ of return
22. Cost of _____ (see 21-Across)
23. 3-Down, for short
24. Discovering a _____ (first step in short-run decision analysis)
25. 2-Down, for short

DOWN

1. Type of cost center
2. _____ value added
3. Return _____ investment
4. _____ margin (sales minus direct costs)
5. Sell _____ process further decision
7. With 13-Across, information system emphasizing assignment of control
8. After-_____ operating income
10. Type of analysis emphasizing cost and revenue differences
12. _____ chart (visual representation of a company's hierarchy)
16. Special _____ decision
17. _____ (residual or scrap) value
18. Supervise

CHAPTER 25 PRICING DECISIONS, INCLUDING TARGET COSTING AND TRANSFER PRICING

REVIEWING THE CHAPTER

Objective 1: Identify the objectives and rules used to establish prices of goods and services, and relate pricing issues to the management cycle.

1. A company's long-term objectives should include a pricing policy. Possible pricing objectives include (a) identifying and adhering to short-run and long-run pricing strategies; (b) maximizing profits; (c) maintaining or gaining market share; (d) setting socially responsible prices; (e) maintaining a minimum rate of return on investment; and (f) being customer focused.

2. Pricing strategies depend on many factors and conditions. Identifying the market being served and meeting the needs of that market are of primary importance. Companies that make standard products for a competitive market have different pricing strategies from firms that make products to customers' specifications.

3. For a company to stay in business, the selling price of its product or service must (a) be equal to or lower than the competition's price, (b) be acceptable to the customer, (c) recover all costs incurred in bringing the product or service to market, and (d) return a profit. If a manager deviates from any of these four selling rules, there must be a specific short-run objective that accounts for the change. Breaking these pricing rules for a long period will force a company into bankruptcy.

4. Pricing issues are addressed at each stage of the management cycle. During the planning stage, managers must decide how much to charge for each product or service. During the executing stage, the product or service is sold at the specified price or on the auction market. During the reviewing stage, managers evaluate sales to determine which pricing strategies were successful and which failed. During the reporting stage, analyses of actual and targeted prices and profits are prepared for use inside the organization.

5. When making and evaluating pricing decisions, managers must consider many factors, some relating to the market and others to internal constraints. Factors related to the market include the demand for the product, customer needs, competition, and the quantity and quality of competing products or services. Internal constraints include the cost of the product or service, the desired return on investment, the quality and quantity of materials and labor, and the allocation of scarce resources.

Objective 2: Describe economic pricing concepts including the auction-based pricing method used on the Internet.

6. Economic pricing concepts are based on microeconomic theory. A product's total revenue and total costs are plotted against units produced. Initially, because of fixed costs, the cost line is above the revenue line, illustrating a loss. When enough products are produced and sold to cover both variable and fixed costs, the lines cross, illustrating a profit. However, the lines are destined to

cross again. Price competition will eventually bend the revenue line down; as more units are sold at a lower price, total revenue will decrease. The cost line will eventually bend upward as production exceeds capacity, causing an increase in fixed costs. Another way of stating this is that the **marginal revenue** (the change in total revenue caused by a one-unit change in output) is decreasing as more units are produced, while the **marginal cost** (the change in total cost caused by a one-unit change in output) is increasing.

7. The point at which the total revenue line and the total cost line are farthest apart (maximum profit) is also the point at which marginal revenue equals marginal cost. Graphs of marginal revenue and marginal cost would cross at this point. Projecting this point onto the product's demand curve indicates the optimal price the market will bring at that level of output and the optimal number of units to produce. However, implementation is difficult and uncertain. An analysis of this type is useful but should not be the only approach relied on when establishing a price.

8. Because of the increasing amount of business conducted over the Internet by both companies and individuals, auction-based pricing has become an important pricing mechanism. The Internet allows sellers and buyers to solicit bids and transact exchanges in an open market environment. A willing buyer and seller set an auction-based price in a sales transaction.

Objective 3: Use cost-based pricing methods to develop prices.

9. Managers may use any of several pricing methods to establish a selling price. Two methods based on the cost of producing a product or service are gross margin pricing and return on asset pricing.

10. **Gross margin pricing** is a cost-based pricing method that establishes a selling price at a percentage above an item's total production costs. The following formulas are used:

$$\text{Markup Percentage} = \frac{\text{Desired Profit} + \text{Total Selling, General, and Administrative Expenses}}{\text{Total Production Costs}}$$

$$\begin{array}{l}\text{Gross} \\ \text{Margin-} \\ \text{Based} \\ \text{Price}\end{array} = \begin{array}{l}\text{Total Production Costs per Unit} + \\ \text{(Markup Percentage} \times \text{Total Production} \\ \text{Costs per Unit)}\end{array}$$

11. Whereas gross margin pricing is based on a percentage above total costs, **return on assets pricing** is based on a specific rate of return on assets

employed in the generation of a product or service. Assuming that a company has a specified minimum rate of return, the following formula is used to calculate the selling price:

$$\begin{array}{l}\text{Return on} \\ \text{Assets-} \\ \text{Based} \\ \text{Price}\end{array} = \begin{array}{l}\text{Total Costs and Expenses per Unit} + \\ \text{[Desired Rate of Return} \times \text{(Total Costs} \\ \text{of Assets Employed} \div \text{Anticipated Units} \\ \text{to Be Produced)]}\end{array}$$

12. **Time and materials pricing** is common practice in service businesses. The two primary types of costs used in this method are the cost of actual materials and parts and the cost of actual direct labor. An overhead rate, which includes a profit factor, is computed for each of these cost categories. When preparing a billing, the two overhead percentages are added to the two major cost categories.

13. Although managers may depend on traditional, objective, formula-driven pricing methods to set prices, they must at times deviate from those approaches and rely on their own experience.

Objective 4: Describe target costing and use that concept to analyze pricing decisions and evaluate a new product opportunity.

14. **Target costing** is a pricing method that (a) uses market research to identify the price at which a new product will be competitive in the marketplace, (b) defines the desired profit to be made on the product, and (c) computes the target cost for the product by subtracting the desired profit from the competitive market price. The following formula is used to determine the target cost:

$$\text{Target Price} - \text{Desired Profit} = \text{Target Cost}$$

The company's engineers use the target cost as the maximum amount to be incurred in designing and manufacturing the product. If this cost goal cannot be met, the product is not manufactured.

15. Target costing gives managers the ability to control the costs of a new product in the planning stage of the product's life cycle. The pricing decision is made as soon as market research has revealed the potential demand for the product and the maximum price that customers would be willing to pay for it. In contrast, when traditional cost-based pricing methods are used, the pricing decision must wait until production has taken place and costs have been incurred and analyzed. At that point, a profit factor is added to the product's cost, and the product is ready to be offered to customers. Because target costing enables managers to analyze a product's potential before

they commit resources to its production, it enhances a company's ability to compete, especially in new or emerging markets. The philosophy underlying target costing is that a product should be designed and built so that it produces a profit as soon as it is introduced to the marketplace.

16. Two types of cost patterns are involved as a new product moves through its life cycle. **Committed costs** are design, development, engineering, testing, and production costs that are engineered into a product or service at the design stage of development; these costs should be incurred if all design specifications are followed. **Incurred costs** are the actual costs of making the product. When cost-based pricing is used, controlling the costs of a new product from the planning phase through the production phase is very difficult; management has a hard time setting realistic targets because the product is being produced for the first time. Because customers are expected to pay whatever amount cost-based pricing identifies, the focus is on sales rather than on design and manufacture, and efforts at cost control focus on costs incurred after the product has been introduced to the marketplace. With target costing, committed costs are minimized because the product has been designed and built to a specific cost goal. Target costing allows profitability to be built into the selling price from the outset.

17. A company's engineers sometimes determine that a product cannot be manufactured at or below its target cost. In this case, the company should try to adjust the product's design and the approach to production. If those attempts fail, it should either invest in new equipment and procedures or abandon its plans to market the product.

Objective 5: Describe how transfer pricing is used for transferring goods and services and evaluating performance within a division or segment.

18. A **decentralized organization** has several divisions or operating segments. These divisions or segments sell their goods and services both inside and outside the organization. The price a division or segment charges for exchanging goods and services with another division or segment is called a **transfer price**. This internal pricing mechanism enables an organization to assess both the internal and external profitability of its products or services. There are three basic kinds of transfer prices:

a. A **cost-plus transfer price** is the sum of costs incurred by the producing division plus an agreed-on profit percentage. The weakness of cost-plus pricing is that it guarantees that the selling division will recover its costs. Guaranteed cost recovery does not take into account any inefficiencies in a division's operations or the incurrence of excessive costs.

b. A **market transfer price** is based on the price a product could command on the open market. The danger in using market prices as transfer prices is that a decision to sell to outside customers at the market price may cause an internal shortage of critical materials; the selling division may realize a profit, but the overall profitability of the company will suffer. Market prices are therefore usually used only as a basis for negotiation.

c. A **negotiated transfer price** is reached through bargaining between the managers of the buying and selling divisions. This approach allows the selling division to recover its costs and still earn a profit. To develop a negotiated transfer price, the managers should compute the unit cost of the item being transferred and an appropriate profit markup. If the item has an external market or if the buying division can purchase the same item from an outside source, the market price should be included in the negotiations. The transfer price on which the managers ultimately agree should be beneficial to the company as a whole.

19. Because transfer prices include an estimated amount of profit, they can be used as a basis for measuring performance. Even divisions that sell their products only within the company can be evaluated as profit centers by using transfer prices to simulate revenues.

SELF-TEST

Test your knowledge of the chapter by choosing the best answer for each item below.

1. Setting socially responsible prices means
   a. the customer should have the final word on price setting.
   b. the price should not be so high that people with average incomes cannot afford the product or service.
   c. a company's pricing policy takes into consideration social concerns, such as environmental factors, legal constraints, and ethical issues.
   d. the buyer no longer has to beware.

2. A company is still increasing its profit margin when
   a. marginal revenue equals marginal cost.
   b. marginal cost is greater than marginal revenue.
   c. marginal revenue is less than marginal cost.
   d. marginal revenue is greater than marginal cost.

3. Which of the following is *not* an external factor affecting a pricing decision?
   a. The company's profit markup percentage
   b. Demand for the product or service
   c. Prices of competing products or services
   d. Seasonal demand or continual demand

4. Desired profit plus total selling, general, and administrative expenses divided by total production costs is the formula for the markup percentage used in
   a. gross margin pricing.
   b. total cost pricing.
   c. target costing.
   d. return on asset pricing.

5. Time and materials pricing would most likely be used by a
   a. manufacturing company.
   b. jewelry store.
   c. plumbing company.
   d. government agency.

6. Which of the following is *not* true about target costing?
   a. Target costing identifies the price at which a product will be competitive in the marketplace.
   b. Target costing defines the minimum desired profit for a product.
   c. Target costing allows managers to assess a product's potential for success before committing resources to its production.
   d. Target costing is a cost-based method used to make pricing decisions.

7. Transfer prices are normally used by
   a. major league ballparks.
   b. city bus companies.
   c. decentralized companies whose divisions use internally produced products.
   d. companies that have divisions in several different countries.

8. A transfer price is
   a. an artificial price used only within a firm.
   b. a fee charged every time a product is transferred between departments.
   c. a price derived through time and materials pricing.
   d. a fee that bus companies charge for transfers among bus lines.

9. A transfer price is negotiated by the
   a. purchasing agent and store clerk.
   b. managers of the buying and selling divisions.
   c. management accountant and the buying department's manager.
   d. selling department's manager and the production superintendent.

TESTING YOUR KNOWLEDGE

*Matching**

Match each term with its definition by writing the appropriate letter in the blank.

_____ 1. Marginal revenue

_____ 2. Target costing

_____ 3. Committed costs

_____ 4. Gross margin–based price

_____ 5. Return on assets–based price

_____ 6. Time and materials pricing

_____ 7. Transfer price

_____ 8. Cost-plus transfer price

_____ 9. Negotiated transfer price

_____ 10. Marginal cost

a. A pricing approach often used by service firms

b. Total production costs per unit plus the markup percentage times total production costs per unit

c. A price reached through bargaining between the managers of the buying and selling divisions

d. A pricing method that determines a maximum production cost by subtracting the desired profit from the competitive market price

e. The change in total revenue caused by a one-unit change in output

f. Total costs and expenses per unit plus the desired rate of return times total costs of assets employed divided by anticipated units to be made

g. The costs of design, development, engineering, testing, and production that are engineered into a product at the design stage of development

h. The change in total cost caused by a one-unit change in output

i. The sum of costs incurred by the producing division plus an agreed-on profit percentage

j. The price at which goods are exchanged between a company's divisions

Short Answer

Use the lines provided to answer each item.

1. Explain the economic approach to determining a price.

_____

_____

_____

_____

2. List four external factors that can influence a pricing decision.

_____

_____

_____

_____

3. List four internal factors that can influence a pricing decision.

_____

_____

_____

_____

4. Explain the time and materials pricing calculation.

_____

_____

_____

_____

_____

Note to student: The matching quiz might be completed more efficiently by starting with the definition and searching for the corresponding term.

5. List and explain the three basic kinds of transfer prices.

_____   _____

_____   _____

_____   _____

_____   _____

_____   _____

True-False

Circle T if the statement is true, F if it is false. Provide explanations for the false answers, using the blank lines below.

T F **1.** Because pricing decisions are short-run decisions, a pricing policy does not need to be included in a company's long-term objectives.

T F **2.** The process of establishing a correct price is more of a science than an art.

T F **3.** Total revenue is defined as the change in revenue caused by a one-unit change in output.

T F **4.** Demand for a product or service is an external factor that affects a pricing decision.

T F **5.** Maintaining or gaining market share is an internal factor that influences a pricing decision.

T F **6.** One of the benefits of target costing is that a product is not produced if it cannot be designed to be profitable.

T F **7.** The markup percentage for gross margin pricing is applied to total production costs per unit.

T F **8.** Service companies often use the return on assets pricing method.

T F **9.** Managers of the buying and selling divisions bargain for a cost-plus transfer price.

T F **10.** Market transfer prices are usually used only as a basis for negotiations between managers.

T F **11.** When intracompany transfers are priced in excess of cost to the selling division, the total profits of the company increase.

_____   _____

_____   _____

_____   _____

_____   _____

_____   _____

_____   _____

_____   _____

_____   _____

Multiple Choice

Circle the letter of the best answer.

1. Which of the following is *not* an objective of a pricing policy?
   a. Maintaining or gaining market share
   b. Setting socially responsible prices
   c. Being customer focused
   d. Charging unrealistically low prices to eliminate competition

2. Establishing a price for a product or service is more of an art than a science because
   a. the pricing process must be properly displayed.
   b. it takes a creative person with experience in pricing to arrive at a just and fair price.
   c. prices developed without supporting analysis are as good as those backed up by cost studies.
   d. prices are developed on an easel.

3. In the economic pricing concept, a product's sales show more than one breakeven point because
   a. start-up costs double.
   b. after the first breakeven point, marginal costs equal marginal revenues.
   c. after the initial breakeven point, increased competition and volume tend to increase costs and decrease selling prices.
   d. total revenue always equals marginal cost.

4. Which of the following is *not* an external factor influencing a pricing decision?
   a. Return on investment
   b. Total demand for product or service
   c. Prices of competing products or services
   d. Seasonal demand or continual demand

5. Which of the following is *not* true about target costing?
   a. The price of a product is determined before the product is produced.
   b. Committed costs are minimized because the product is designed and built to a specific cost goal.
   c. The product is expected to produce a profit as soon as it is marketed.
   d. After the product is marketed, the production procedure is analyzed to determine a way to reduce costs so the product can be made at a profitable "target" cost.

6. Total production costs per unit plus the markup percentage times total production costs per unit is the formula used in
   a. target costing.
   b. gross margin pricing.
   c. time and materials pricing.
   d. return on assets pricing.

7. Service businesses commonly use
   a. target costing.
   b. gross margin pricing.
   c. time and materials pricing.
   d. transfer pricing.

8. An internal price bargained for by managers of the buying and selling divisions is called a
   a. normal transfer price.
   b. cost-plus transfer price.
   c. market transfer price.
   d. negotiated transfer price.

9. Transfer prices allow a decentralized company to
   a. evaluate individual departments' contributions to the company's profitability.
   b. increase overall profits.
   c. decrease prices to outside customers.
   d. increase company morale.

10. In pricing decisions,
    a. external prices are easier to develop than transfer prices.
    b. the objectives of external pricing and transfer pricing are much the same.
    c. transfer pricing policies are taken more seriously than external pricing policies.
    d. the gross margin and profit margin pricing methods are used to develop both external prices and transfer prices.

APPLYING YOUR KNOWLEDGE

Exercises

1. Gomez Corporation is in the process of developing a price for a new product called Bioderm. Anticipated production data revealed the following cost information:

Direct materials costs	$680,000
Direct labor costs	552,500
Variable manufacturing overhead costs	204,000
Fixed manufacturing overhead costs	263,500
Selling expenses	238,000
General and administrative expenses	510,000
Minimum desired profit	382,500

Management predicts that 850,000 bottles of Bioderm will be produced and sold during the coming year. From the data presented, compute the selling price per bottle using the gross margin pricing method.

2. Zeriscape Landscaping Company has just completed a major job. Costs were $46,500 for materials and $32,800 for labor. Overhead and profit percentages developed at the beginning of the year were 40 percent for materials and supplies and 60 percent for labor. Prepare the billing for the customer using the time and materials pricing method. Show the breakdown of all costs involved.

3. Steel Components Company is considering the development of a new all-steel workbench. After conferring with the design engineers, the accountant's staff put together the information that appears below, which is directly linked to the decision to produce this product.

a. Compute the product's target cost.
b. Compute the product's projected cost based on the design engineer's estimates.
c. What decision should the company make about producing the all-steel workbench? Explain your answer.

Targeted selling price	$575	per unit
Desired profit percentage	25%	of total unit cost
Anticipated unit demand	25,000	units
Per unit data for the workbench		
Raw materials cost	$120	
Purchased parts cost	$80	
Manufacturing labor		
Hours	2	hours
Hourly labor rate	$14	
Assembly labor		
Hours	4	hours
Hourly labor rate	$15	
Machine hours	8	hours
Activity-based cost rates		
Materials and parts handling activity	5%	of raw materials and purchased parts cost
Engineering activity	$20	per workbench unit
Production and assembly activity	$15	per machine hour
Packaging and delivery activity	$33	per workbench unit
Sales and marketing activity	$14	per workbench unit

4. Electra Division and Ohms Division belong to the same company. For several years, Electra Division has produced an electronic component that it sells to Ohms Division at the prevailing market price of $20. Electra manufactures the component only for Ohms Division and has not previously sold this product to outside customers. The product is available from outside suppliers, who would charge Ohms Division $20 per unit. Electra currently produces and sells 20,000 of these components each year and also manufactures several other products. The following annual cost information was compiled for the electronic component after the close of 20xx operations, during which time Electra operated at full capacity.

Electra Division—20xx

Cost Category	Unit Cost
Direct materials	$ 6.50
Direct labor (hourly basis)	8.60
Variable manufacturing overhead	4.50
General fixed overhead of plant	5.20
Traceable fixed overhead	
($60,000 ÷ 20,000)	3.00
Variable shipping expenses	.25
	$28.05

General fixed overhead represents allocated joint fixed costs, such as building depreciation, property taxes, and salaries of production executives. If production of the components were discontinued, $50,000 of the annual traceable fixed overhead costs could be eliminated. The balance of traceable fixed overhead is equipment depreciation on machinery that could be used elsewhere in the plant.

a. Compute the cost per unit of the electronic component made by Electra Division.
b. The division manager contends that producing the component to accommodate other divisions is a sound company policy as long as variable costs are recovered by the sales. Should Electra Division continue to produce the component for Ohms Division?

CHAPTER 26 CAPITAL INVESTMENT ANALYSIS

REVIEWING THE CHAPTER

Objective 1: Define *capital investment analysis* and describe its relation to the management cycle.

1. **Capital investment decisions** are decisions about when and how much to spend on capital facilities and other long-term projects. They are among the most significant decisions that management must make. They involve such matters as installing new equipment, replacing old equipment, expanding a production area by renovating or adding to a building, buying or building a new factory or office building, and acquiring another company.

2. **Capital investment analysis** (also called *capital budgeting*) is the process of identifying the need for a capital investment, analyzing courses of action to meet that need, preparing reports for managers, choosing the best alternative, and allocating funds among competing needs. Personnel from all parts of an organization participate in this decision-making process.

3. Managers pay close attention to capital investments throughout the management cycle.
   a. Decisions about capital investments are vitally important because they involve a large amount of money and may commit a company to a course of action for many years. Most of the analysis of these investments takes place in the planning stage of the management cycle. The analysis involves six steps: (1) identification of capital investment needs; (2) formal requests for capital investments, (3) preliminary screening, (4) establishment of an acceptance-

   rejection standard, (5) evaluation of proposals, and (6) final decisions on the proposals.
   b. Capital investment decisions are implemented during the executing stage of the management cycle. This involves scheduling projects and overseeing their development, construction, or purchase.
   c. During the reviewing stage, each project undergoes a postcompletion audit to determine if it is meeting the goals and targets set forth in the planning stage.
   d. In the reporting stage, reports on the results of capital investment decisions are prepared and distributed within the company. They include comparisons of budgeted expenditures with actual expenditures, as well as comparisons of projected net cash flows or cost savings with actual results.

Objective 2: State the purpose of the minimum rate of return and identify the methods used to arrive at that rate.

4. In most companies, management sets a minimum rate of return on investments, and any capital expenditure proposal that predicts a rate of return below that minimum is automatically refused. The most commonly used measures of rate of return are cost of capital, corporate return on investment, industry average return on investment, and bank interest rates.

5. The **cost of capital** is the weighted-average rate of return a company must pay its long-term creditors

and shareholders for the use of their funds. The components of cost of capital are the cost of debt, the cost of preferred stock, the cost of common stock, and the cost of retained earnings.

Objective 3: Identify the types of projected costs and revenues used to evaluate alternatives for capital investment.

6. Managers use a variety of measures to estimate the benefits to be derived from a proposed capital investment.

   a. *Net income and net cash inflows:* Estimating the net income that a capital investment will produce is one way of measuring its benefits. A more widely used measure is projected cash flow. **Net cash inflows** are the balance of increases in projected cash receipts over increases in projected cash payments. They are used when the analysis involves cash receipts. When the analysis involves only cash outlays, **cost savings** are used as the measure.

   b. *Equal versus unequal cash flows:* Projected cash flows may be the same for each year of an asset's life, or they may vary from year to year. Unequal cash flows are common and must be analyzed for each year of the asset's life.

   c. *Carrying value of assets:* **Carrying value** is the undepreciated portion of the original cost of a fixed asset. When analyzing a decision to replace an old asset, carrying value is irrelevant because it is a past, or historical, cost. However, net proceeds from the asset's sale or disposal are relevant.

   d. *Depreciation expense and income taxes:* Depreciation is a noncash expense requiring no cash outlay during the period. However, because depreciation expense is deductible when determining income taxes, it can result in significant savings. Thus, depreciation expense is relevant to evaluations based on after-tax cash flows.

   e. *Disposal or residual values:* Proceeds from the sale of an old asset are current cash inflows and are relevant to evaluating a proposed capital investment. Projected disposal or residual values of replacement equipment are also relevant because they represent future cash inflows and usually differ among alternatives.

Objective 4: Apply the concept of the time value of money.

7. A key question in capital investment analysis is how to measure the return on a fixed asset. When the asset has a long useful life, managers usually analyze the cash flows that it will generate in terms of the time value of money. The **time value of money** is the concept that cash flows of equal dollar amounts separated by an interval of time have different present values because of the effect of compound interest. The notions of interest, present value, future value, and ordinary annuity are all related to the time value of money.

8. **Interest** is the cost associated with the use of money for a specific period. **Simple interest** is the interest cost for one or more periods when the amount on which the interest is computed stays the same from period to period. **Compound interest** is the interest cost for two or more periods when the amount on which interest is computed changes in each period to include all interest paid in previous periods.

9. **Future value** is the amount an investment will be worth at a future date if invested today at compound interest. **Present value** is the amount that must be invested today at a given rate of compound interest to produce a given future value.

10. An **ordinary annuity** is a series of equal payments or receipts that will begin one time period from the current date. The present value of an ordinary annuity is equal to the present value of equal amounts equally spaced over time.

Objective 5: Analyze capital investment proposals using the net present value method.

11. The **net present value method** evaluates a capital investment by discounting its future cash flows to their present values and subtracting the amount of the initial investment from their sum. The advantage of this method is that it incorporates the time value of money into the analysis of proposed capital investments by discounting future cash inflows and outflows by the company's minimum rate of return. If the net present value is positive, the rate of return on the investment will exceed the company's minimum rate of return, and the project can be accepted.

Objective 6: Analyze capital investment proposals using the the payback period method and the accounting rate-of-return method.

12. The **payback period method** of evaluating a capital investment focuses on the minimum length of time needed to recover the initial investment. When two or more investment alternatives are being considered, the one with the shortest payback period should be selected. The payback period is computed as follows:

$$\text{Payback Period} = \frac{\text{Cost of Investment}}{\text{Annual Net Cash Inflows}}$$

The projected annual net cash inflows are found by determining the increase in cash revenue resulting from the investment and subtracting the cash expenses. The advantage of the payback period method is that it is easy to understand and apply. Its disadvantages are that it does not measure profitability; it ignores the time value of money; and by disregarding cash flows after the payback period is reached, it fails to consider long-term returns on the investment.

13. The **accounting rate-of-return method** uses a net income approach. Two variables—estimated annual net income from the investment and the average cost of the investment—are used to measure performance. The basic equation is as follows:

$$\text{Accounting Rate of Return} = \frac{\text{Project's Average Annual Net Income}}{\text{Average Investment Cost}}$$

Average investment in a proposed capital investment is calculated as follows:

$$\text{Average Investment Cost} = \left(\frac{\text{Total Investment} - \text{Residual Value}}{2}\right) + \text{Residual Value}$$

If the rate of return is higher than the desired minimum rate, management may decide to make the investment. Like the payback period method, the accounting rate-of-return method is easy to apply and understand. Its disadvantages are that it averages net income over the life of the investment, it is unreliable if estimated annual income differs from year to year, it ignores cash flows, and it does not consider the time value of money.

SELF-TEST

Test your knowledge of the chapter by choosing the best answer for each item below.

1. The process of identifying the need for a capital investment, analyzing different courses of action to meet that need, preparing reports for managers, choosing the best alternative, and allocating funds among competing needs is the definition of
   a. special order budgeting.
   b. capital investment analysis.
   c. capital budgeting.
   d. flexible budgeting.

2. Future value is
   a. the amount an investment will be worth at a future date if invested today at compound interest.
   b. the amount an investment will be worth at a future date if invested today at simple interest.
   c. the amount an investment will be worth in today's dollars if invested now at compound interest.
   d. a series of equal payments or receipts that will begin one time period at a future date.

3. Which of the following is *not* relevant when evaluating a capital investment proposal?
   a. Residual value of the new capital asset
   b. Carrying value of the capital asset that is being replaced
   c. Net cash flows from the proposal
   d. Cost savings from the proposal

4. Annual net cash inflows are
   a. annual cash inflows minus annual cash outflows.
   b. annual cash inflows minus the amount of capital investment.
   c. annual revenues minus expenses.
   d. annual cash inflows minus annual cash outflows minus total depreciation expense.

5. Which of the following is *not* a method used in capital investment analysis?
   a. Make-or-buy method
   b. Payback period method
   c. Accounting rate-of-return method
   d. Net present value method

6. JLT Enterprises is contemplating a major investment in a new flexible manufacturing system. The company's minimum desired rate of return is 16 percent. The total investment is $2,500,000. The system is expected to have an eight-year useful life and a 10 percent residual value at the end of that time. The company uses straight-line depreciation. The system should produce $1,400,000 of revenue annually. Annual cash operating costs are expected to be $776,375. Using the accounting rate-of-return method, what is the expected rate of return from the proposed investment?
   a. 37.7 percent
   b. 26.6 percent
   c. 24.9 percent
   d. 19.2 percent

7. Assuming the same facts as in **6** and using the net present value method, what is the expected net present value of the proposed investment?
   a. Positive net present value of $1,051,450
   b. Negative net present value of $12,455
   c. Positive net present value of $285,277
   d. Negative net present value of $62,235

8. Assuming the same facts as in **6** and using the payback period method, what is the expected payback period for the proposed investment?
   a. 4.009 years
   b. 3.954 years
   c. 3.125 years
   d. 3.625 years

9. The accounting rate-of-return is calculated as
   a. average investment cost divided by average annual net income from investment.
   b. average cash flows from investment divided by average investment cost.
   c. average annual net income from investment divided by average investment cost.
   d. average investment cost minus average annual net income from investment.

10. That cash flows of equal dollar amounts separated by an interval of time have different values is the concept of the
    a. money value of time.
    b. time value of money.
    c. cost of capital.
    d. residual value.

TESTING YOUR KNOWLEDGE

*Matching**

Match each term with its definition by writing the appropriate letter in the blank.

_____ 1. Capital investment analysis

_____ 2. Cost of capital

_____ 3. Accounting rate-of-return method

_____ 4. Payback period method

_____ 5. Net present value method

_____ 6. Capital investment decision

_____ 7. Compound interest

_____ 8. Time value of money

_____ 9. Carrying value

_____ 10. Present value

a. The amount that must be invested today at a given rate of compound interest to produce a given future value

b. The concept that cash flows of equal dollar amounts separated by an interval of time have different current values

c. A determination of when and how much to spend on capital facilities

d. The process of identifying the need for a capital investment, analyzing different courses of action, preparing reports, choosing the best alternative, and allocating funds among competing needs

e. A method of evaluating capital investments that determines the minimum length of time it would take to recover an asset's initial cost in net cash inflows

f. A method of evaluating capital investments that divides a proposed project's net income by the average investment cost

g. The weighted-average rate of return a company must pay its long-term creditors and shareholders for the use of their funds

h. The undepreciated portion of the original cost of a fixed asset

i. The interest cost for two or more periods when the amount on which interest is computed changes in each period to include all interest paid in previous periods

j. A method of evaluating capital investments that discounts all net cash inflows back to the present

---

Note to student: The matching quiz might be completed more efficiently by starting with the definition and searching for the corresponding term.

Short Answer

Use the lines provided to complete each item.

1. List the six steps involved in analyzing a capital investment in the planning stage of the management cycle.

_____

_____

_____

_____

_____

_____

2. Identify the four components used to compute cost of capital.

_____

_____

_____

_____

3. List three methods frequently used to evaluate capital expenditure proposals.

_____

_____

_____

True-False

Circle T if the statement is true, F if it is false. Provide explanations for the false answers, using the blank lines at the end of the section.

T F **1.** Capital investment analysis involves obtaining cash for business operations.

T F **2.** The simplest method to apply in evaluating a capital investment proposal is the net present value method.

T F **3.** Both the accounting rate-of-return and payback period methods ignore the time value of money.

T F **4.** The payback period is the maximum length of time it should take to recover in cash the cost of an investment.

T F **5.** The payback period equals the cost of the capital investment divided by the annual net cash inflows.

T F **6.** A minimum rate of return is not a factor when the net present value method is used.

T F **7.** When the net present value method shows that a proposed project has a negative net present value, the project should probably be rejected.

T F **8.** Carrying values of existing assets are relevant considerations when analyzing capital expenditure proposals to replace facilities.

T F **9.** Managers screen, evaluate, and select capital investment proposals during the executing stage of the management cycle.

T F **10.** Disposal or residual values are not relevant to capital investment decisions.

_____

_____

_____

_____

_____

_____

_____

_____

_____

_____

_____

_____

_____

_____

_____

_____

_____

_____

_____

_____

_____

_____

Multiple Choice

Circle the letter of the best answer.

1. Under the accounting rate-of-return method, which of the following is irrelevant?
   a. Residual value of the asset
   b. Net cash inflows
   c. Cost of the asset
   d. Project's average annual net income

2. The average cost of capital is
   a. the cost of each source of available capital.
   b. the Federal Reserve's current lending rate.
   c. an average of the cost of debt, equity, and retained earnings multiplied by the prime rate.
   d. the sum of the products of each financing source's percentage multiplied by its cost rate.

3. The method of capital investment evaluation that brings the time value of money into the analysis is
   a. the net present value method.
   b. the accounting rate of return on initial investment method.
   c. the payback period method.
   d. the accounting rate of return on average investment method.

4. The time value of money is considered in long-range investment decisions by
   a. investing only in short-term projects.
   b. assigning greater value to more immediate cash flows.
   c. using subjective probabilities to weight cash flows.
   d. assuming equal annual cash-flow patterns.

5. The payback period method measures
   a. the time needed to recover investment dollars.
   b. the cash flows from an investment.
   c. the economic life of an investment.
   d. the probability of an investment's success.

6. In which stage of the management cycle does a postcompletion audit determine if a capital investment project is meeting the goals and targets set for it?
   a. Planning stage
   b. Reviewing stage
   c. Executing stage
   d. Reporting stage

7. The net present value method of evaluating proposed capital investments
   a. measures an investment's time-adjusted rate of return.
   b. ignores cash flows beyond the payback period.
   c. applies only to mutually exclusive proposals.
   d. discounts cash flows at a company's minimum rate of return.

8. Cost analysis for capital investment decisions is best accomplished by techniques that
   a. accrue, defer, and allocate costs to short time periods.
   b. emphasize the liquidity of invested costs.
   c. measure total cash flows over a project's life.
   d. clearly distinguish between different equivalent unit computations.

9. Pine Industries is considering a $500,000 capital investment project that has the following projected cash flows:

Year	Net Cash Inflows
1	$160,000
2	140,000
3	120,000
4	80,000
5	60,000
6	30,000

The payback period is
a. 3.2 years.
b. 3.0 years.
c. 4.0 years.
d. 6.0 years.

APPLYING YOUR KNOWLEDGE

Exercises

1. A company is considering the purchase of a machine to produce the plastic chin protectors used in ice hockey. The machine costs $70,000 and will have a five-year life (no residual value). It is expected to produce $8,000 per year in net income (after depreciation). The company's desired rate of return is 25 percent, and the minimum payback period is three years. The company uses straight-line depreciation.

   a. Determine the accounting rate of return.

   b. Using the payback period method, determine whether the company should invest in the machine. Show all your work.

2. A machine that costs $20,000 (no residual value) will produce net cash inflows of $8,000 in the first year of operations and $6,000 in the remaining four years of use. The company's desired rate of return is 16 percent. Present value information for the 16 percent rate of return is as follows:

   Present value of $1 due in 1 year = .862
   Present value of $1 due in 2 years = .743
   Present value of $1 due in 3 years = .641
   Present value of $1 due in 4 years = .552
   Present value of $1 due in 5 years = .476

   Using the net present value method, determine whether the company should purchase the machine.

3. Quality Donut Company is considering the acquisition of a new automatic donut dropper machine that will cost $400,000. The machine will have a life of five years and produce a cash savings from operations of $160,000 per year. The asset is to be depreciated using the straight-line method and will have a residual value of $40,000 at the end of its useful life. The company's management expects a 20 percent minimum rate of return on all investments and a maximum payback period of three years.

   a. What is the amount of depreciation per year?

   b. What is the accounting rate of return on the machine?

   c. What will the payback period on this machine be?

   d. What is the present value of future net cash inflows?

   e. Should the company invest in this machine?

Crossword Puzzle
for Chapters 25 and 26

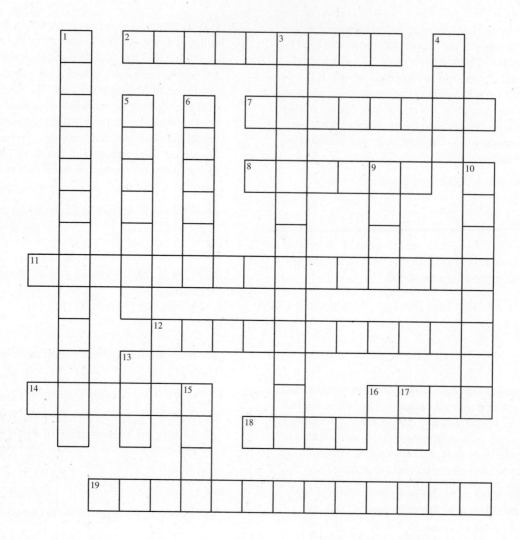

ACROSS

2. Type of cost engineered into a product at the design stage

7. _____ value (undepreciated balance)

8. Return on _____ pricing

11. Change caused by a one-unit change in output (2 words)

12. Amount of an investment at a later date (2 words)

14. _____ cost (competitive market price minus desired profit)

16. With 5-Down, benefits, such as reduced costs

18. Equity or _____ financing

19. Having several operating segments

DOWN

1. Weighted-average rate of return paid for use of funds (3 words)

3. Amount charged when goods or services are exchanged between a company's divisions (2 words)

4. _____-run pricing strategy

5. See 16-Across

6. Accounting rate-of-_____ method

9. _____ value of money

10. Cost of using money

13. Supervisor, e.g. (abbreviation)

15. _____ and materials pricing method

17. Present value _____ a single sum

CHAPTER 27 QUALITY MANAGEMENT AND MEASUREMENT

REVIEWING THE CHAPTER

Objective 1: Describe a management information system and explain how it enhances the management cycle.

1. A **management information system (MIS)** is a reporting system that identifies, monitors, and maintains continuous, detailed analyses of a company's activities and provides managers with timely measures of operating results. An MIS captures both financial and nonfinancial information. It is designed to support total quality management, the just-in-time operating philosophy, activity-based costing and activity-based management, and other management philosophies. The primary focus of an MIS is on activities, not costs. By focusing on activities, it provides managers with improved knowledge of the processes under their control. The MIS pinpoints resource usage for each activity and fosters management decisions that lead to continuous improvement throughout the organization.

2. A management information system can be designed as a customized, informally linked series of systems for specific purposes, such as financial reporting, product costing, and process measurement, or as a fully integrated database system known as an **enterprise resource planning (ERP) system.** An ERP system manages all major business functions through one easy-to-access centralized data warehouse.

3. A management information system supplies managers with relevant, reliable information through-out the management cycle. During the planning stage, managers use the MIS database to obtain the information they need for for formulating strategic plans, making forecasts, and preparing budgets. During the executing stage, managers use the financial and nonfinancial information in the MIS database to implement decisions about personnel, resources, and activities that will minimize waste and improve quality. As managers evaluate all major business functions during the reviewing stage, they use the system to track financial and nonfinancial measures of performance. During the reporting stage, an MIS helps managers generate customized reports that evaluate performance and provide useful information for decision making.

Objective 2: Define *total quality management (TQM)* and identify financial and nonfinancial measures of quality.

4. **Total quality management (TQM)** is an organizational environment in which all business functions work together to build quality into a firm's products or services. The first step in creating a total quality environment is to identify and manage the financial measures of quality, or the costs of quality. The second step is to analyze operating performance using nonfinancial measures and to require that all business processes and products or services be improved continuously.

5. **Quality** is the result of an operating environment in which a company's product or service meets a

customer's specifications the first time it is produced or delivered. **Costs of quality** are costs associated with the achievement or nonachievement of product or service quality. The costs of quality have two components: the costs of conformance and the costs of nonconformance.

    a. **Costs of conformance** are the costs incurred to produce a quality product or service. They include **prevention costs** (the costs of preventing failures) and **appraisal costs** (the costs of measuring quality).

    b. **Costs of nonconformance** are the costs incurred to correct the defects of a product or service. They include **internal failure costs** (costs resulting from defects discovered before shipment) and **external failure costs** (costs resulting from defects discovered after shipment).

    c. There is an inverse relationship between the cost of conformance and the cost of nonconformance; if the cost of one is low, the cost of the other is likely to be high. An organization's overall goal is to avoid the costs of nonconformance because these costs affect customer satisfaction. High initial costs of conformance can be justified if they minimize the total costs of quality over a product's or service's life cycle.

6. Measuring the costs of quality helps a company track how much it has spent in its efforts to improve product or service quality. Nonfinancial measures of quality are used to supplement the cost-based measures. By monitoring and controlling nonfinancial measures, managers can maximize the financial return from operations. Nonfinancial measures of quality include measures of product design, vendor performance, production performance, delivery cycle time, and customer satisfaction.

    a. To improve the quality of product design, many businesses use **computer-aided design (CAD).** CAD is a computer-based engineering system that can detect flaws in product design before production begins.

    b. To ensure that high-quality materials are available when needed, managers monitor the performance of vendors by using measures of quality (such as defect-free materials as a percentage of total deliveries) and measures of delivery (such as on-time deliveries as a percentage of total deliveries).

    c. To improve production performance by reducing waste caused by defective products,

scrapped parts, machine maintenance, and downtime, many companies use **computer integrated manufacturing (CIM) systems.** In these systems, production and its support activities are coordinated by computers. Most direct labor hours are replaced by machine hours.

    d. To evaluate their responsiveness to customers, companies measure **delivery cycle time**—the time between acceptance of an order and final delivery of the product or service. The delivery cycle time consists of the **purchase order lead** time (the time it takes for materials to be ordered and received so that production can begin), **production cycle time** (the time it takes to make a product), and **delivery time** (the time between the product's completion and the customer's receipt of the product).

    e. Measures of customer satisfaction include the number and types of customer complaints, the number and causes of warranty claims, and the percentage of shipments returned as a percentage of total shipments.

7. Many measures of the costs of quality and several of the nonfinancial measures of quality apply directly to services and can be used by any type of service organization. For example, a service business can measure customer satisfaction by tracking the number of services accepted or rejected, the number of customer complaints, and the number of returning customers.

Objective 3: Use measures of quality to evaluate operating performance.

8. In analyzing the costs of quality, managers examine the costs of conformance to customer standards, including prevention costs and appraisal costs, and the costs of nonconformance to customer standards, including internal failure costs and external failure costs. By analyzing the costs of quality, as well as nonfinancial measures of quality, managers help a firm meet its goal of continuously improving the production process and product or service quality.

Objective 4: Discuss the evolving concept of quality.

9. Over the years, to meet customers' needs and the demands of a changing business environment, the concept of quality has been constantly evolving. Among the concepts that preceded TQM was re**turn on quality (ROQ). ROQ** is the trade-off between the costs and benefits of improving quality; the high costs of consistent quality are weighed against the expected higher returns. In the 1980s, companies emphasized **kaizen,** the continual improvement of quality and processes and the reduction of costs. By the end of the 1980s, companies that applied these concepts had achieved high levels of product reliability.

10. Among the techniques that evolved to help managers understand and measure quality improvements are benchmarking and process mapping. **Benchmarking** is the measurement of the gap between the quality of a company's process and the quality of a parallel process at the best-in-class company. **Process mapping** is a method of diagramming process inputs, outputs, constraints, and flows to help managers identify unnecessary efforts and inefficiencies in a business process.

Objective 5: Recognize the awards and organizations that promote quality.

11. Many awards have been established to recognize and promote the importance of quality. In 1951, the Japanese Union of Scientists and Engineers created the Deming Prize to honor individuals or groups who contribute to the development and dissemination of total quality control. This organization also created the **Deming Application Prize,** which honors companies that achieve distinctive results by carrying out total quality control. In 1987, the U.S. Congress established the **Malcolm Baldrige Quality Award** to recognize U.S. organizations for their achievements in quality and business performance and to raise awareness about the importance of these factors.

12. The International Organization for Standardization (ISO) promotes standardization with a view to facilitating the international exchange of goods and services. To standardize quality management and quality assurance, the ISO developed **ISO 9000,** a set of guidelines covering the design, development, production, final inspection and testing, installation, and servicing of products, processes, and services. To become ISO-certified, an organization must pass a rigorous audit of its manufacturing and service processes.

SELF-TEST

Test your knowledge of the chapter by choosing the best answer for each item below.

1. A management information system
   a. identifies nonvalue-adding activities.
   b. supports just-in-time and activity-based management philosophies.
   c. relies on the concept of continuous improvement to reduce costs and increase quality.
   d. does all of the above.

2. A management information system focuses primarily on
   a. costs.
   b. activities.
   c. net income.
   d. departments.

3. The costs of quality are the total costs of
   a. prevention and appraisal.
   b. internal and external failures.
   c. conformance and nonconformance.
   d. conformance and appraisal.

4. The commitment to quality that underlies TQM operations would justify
   a. prevention costs in excess of internal failure costs.
   b. costs of nonconformance in excess of the costs of conformance.
   c. internal failure costs in excess of appraisal costs.
   d. prevention and appraisal costs in excess of the costs of conformance.

5. The rate of defects per million units produced is a nonfinancial measure of
   a. raw materials input.
   b. product design.
   c. customer acceptance.
   d. production quality.

6. Which of the following costs of quality is a cost of nonconformance?
   a. Cost of inspecting materials
   b. Cost of technical support for vendors
   c. Cost of inspecting rework
   d. Cost of design review

7. Which of the following are prevention costs?
   a. Cost of quality training for employees
   b. Cost of developing an integrated system
   c. Cost of technical support for vendors
   d. All of the above

8. Which of the following is *not* a nonfinancial measure of product quality?
   a. Inventory turnover rate
   b. Number of warranty claims
   c. Data on vendor deliveries
   d. Trend in number of customer complaints

9. The time between acceptance of an order and final delivery of the product or service is called
   a. delivery time.
   b. purchase order lead time.
   c. production cycle time.
   d. delivery cycle time.

10. Which of the following is a set of standards for quality management and quality assurance?
    a. Malcolm Baldrige Quality Award
    b. Deming Application Prize
    c. ISO 9000
    d. None of the above

TESTING YOUR KNOWLEDGE

*Matching**

Match each term with its definition by writing the appropriate letter in the blank.

_____ 1. Computer-aided design (CAD)

_____ 2. Total quality management (TQM)

_____ 3. Costs of conformance

_____ 4. Appraisal costs

_____ 5. Internal failure costs

_____ 6. Management information system (MIS)

_____ 7. Prevention costs

_____ 8. External failure costs

_____ 9. Delivery cycle time

_____ 10. Benchmarking

a. The costs of activities that measure, evaluate, or audit products, processes, or services to ensure conformance to quality standards and performance requirements

b. A computer-based engineering system that can detect design flaws

c. A reporting system that identifies, monitors, and maintains continuous, detailed analyses of a company's activities and provides managers with timely measures of operating results

d. The costs incurred to produce a quality product or service

e. The costs incurred when defects are discovered after a product or service has been delivered to a customer

f. The measurement of the gap between the quality of a company's process and the quality of a parallel process at the best-in-class company

g. The costs incurred when defects are discovered before a product or service is delivered to a customer

h. Time between acceptance of an order and final delivery of the product or service to the customer

i. The costs associated with the prevention of defects and failures in products and services

j. An organizational environment in which all business functions work together to build quality into a firm's products or services

---

Note to student: The matching quiz might be completed more efficiently by starting with the definition and searching for the corresponding term.

Short Answer

Use the lines provided to answer each item.

1. Briefly explain how a management information system enhances the management cycle.

   _____

   _____

   _____

   _____

   _____

2. Identify the costs of conformance and the costs of nonconformance, and give two examples of each of these cost categories.

   _____

   _____

   _____

   _____

   _____

   _____

3. Identify the nonfinancial measures of quality, and explain why they are important in maximizing profits.

   _____

   _____

   _____

   _____

   _____

   _____

True-False

Circle T if the statement is true, F if it is false. Provide explanations for the false answers, using the blank lines at the end of the section.

T F   **1.** CAD is the acronym for commonly adjusted defects.

T F   **2.** The only valid measurements of quality are financial in nature.

T F   **3.** The costs of quality are the costs associated with the achievement or nonachievement of product or service quality.

T F   **4.** As the costs of conformance increase, the costs of nonconformance generally also increase.

T F   **5.** Benchmarking is a method of diagramming process inputs, outputs, constraints, and flows to help managers identify unnecessary efforts and inefficiencies in a business process.

T F   **6.** Over the long run, the costs of conformance are less expensive than the costs of nonconformance.

T F   **7.** Without an effective system of performance measurement, a company is unable to identify the improvements needed to increase profitability.

T F   **8.** Reductions in delivery cycle time have a negative impact on income.

T F   **9.** Prevention costs and appraisal costs are components of the costs of conformance.

T F   **10.** The Malcolm Baldrige Quality Award honors U.S. organizations for achieving high net profits.

_____

_____

_____

_____

_____

_____

_____

_____

_____

_____

_____

_____

_____

_____

_____

_____

_____

_____

Multiple Choice

Circle the letter of the best answer.

1. Which of the following is *not* characteristic of a management information system?
   a. Fosters continuous improvement
   b. Provides only historical cost information
   c. Supports total quality management
   d. Focuses on managing activities

2. Which of the following would *not* be considered a cost of conformance?
   a. Cost of inspecting rework
   b. Cost of vendor audits and sample testing
   c. Cost of product simulation and development
   d. Cost of design review

3. The overall objective of controlling the costs of quality is to eliminate
   a. appraisal costs.
   b. costs of nonconformance.
   c. costs of quality.
   d. costs of conformance.

4. SafeWorld Corporation produces custom-designed safety gear for police vehicles. During April 20xx, the company had the following costs of quality:

Product testing costs	$11,200
Product warranty claims	13,000
Scrap and rework costs	10,500
Product design costs	18,900
Employee training costs	10,100
Product simulation costs	16,400

Total costs of conformance for the month were
   a. $80,100.
   b. $56,600.
   c. $40,200.
   d. $42,400.

5. Assuming the same facts as in **4**, total costs of nonconformance for the month were
   a. $42,400.
   b. $40,200.
   c. $23,500.
   d. $13,000.

6. Nonfinancial measures of quality are important to TQM operations because
   a. cost drivers are identified.
   b. reporting nonfinancial measures encourages continuous improvement of production processes, which results in products of higher quality.
   c. to ensure high-quality products or services, managers need both nonfinancial and financial information
   d. All of the above

7. Production cycle time is the time
   a. between a product's completion and the customer's receipt of the product.
   b. it takes to make a product.
   c. it takes for materials to be ordered and received so that production can begin.
   d. between receipt of a customer's order and shipment to the customer.

8. What are the two components of the costs of quality?
   a. Conformance and nonconformance costs
   b. Appraisal and prevention costs
   c. Prevention and conformance costs
   d. Internal and external costs

9. Delivery cycle time consists of
   a. production cycle time and delivery time.
   b. delivery time and purchase order lead time.
   c. purchase order lead time, production cycle time, and delivery time.
   d. none of the above.

10. Company A and Company B generate the same amount of annual revenues and incurred the following costs of quality during the past year:

Company A:

Conformance costs	$1,750,000
Nonconformance costs	1,650,000
Total	$3,400,000

Company B:

Conformance costs	$1,000,000
Nonconformance costs	200,000
Total	$1,200,000

Based on this information, which company is likely to have a higher level of product quality?

a. Company A, because it spends more on the costs of quality
b. Company B, because it spends less on the costs of quality
c. Company A, because its costs of conformance exceed those of Company B
d. Company B, because its costs of conformance far exceed its costs of nonconformance

APPLYING YOUR KNOWLEDGE

Exercises

1. At the beginning of the year, Cline Industries initiated a quality improvement program. The program was successful in reducing scrap and rework costs. To help assess the impact of the quality improvement program, the following data were collected for the past two years:

	20x4	20x5
Sales	$1,200,000	$1,500,000
Scrap	20,000	15,000
Rework	50,000	35,000
Prototype design	38,000	42,000
Product simulation	6,000	9,000
Quality training	20,000	30,000
Materials testing	4,000	6,000
Product warranty	40,000	25,000

   a. What were the total costs of conformance for the two years?

   b. What were the total costs of nonconformance for the two years?

   c. Was the quality improvement program successful? Defend your answer.

2. The lab department of Shamrock Hospital is in the process of evaluating its costs of quality. Identify each of the following items as related to the costs of conformance (CC) or the costs of nonconformance (CN):

   _____ a. Preventive maintenance on equipment

   _____ b. Patient complaints

   _____ c. Training of lab technicians

   _____ d. Redoing of lab tests

   _____ e. Inspection of processes and machines

   _____ f. Machine downtime

   _____ g. Monitoring of the quality of lab supplies received from vendors

CHAPTER 28 FINANCIAL PERFORMANCE EVALUATION

REVIEWING THE CHAPTER

Objective 1: Describe and discuss financial performance evaluation by internal and external users.

1. **Financial performance evaluation,** or *financial statement analysis,* comprises all the techniques users of financial statements employ to show important relationships in an organization's financial statements and to relate them to important financial objectives. Internal users of financial statements include top managers, who set and strive to achieve financial performance objectives; middle-level managers of business processes; and employee stockholders. External users are creditors and investors who want to assess how well management has accomplished its financial objectives, as well as customers who have cooperative agreements with the company.

2. During the planning phase of the management cycle, managers set financial performance objectives that will achieve the company's strategic goals. In the executing phase, they carry out plans designed to achieve those objectives. In the reviewing phase, they monitor financial performance measures to determine causes for deviations in the measures and propose corrective actions. In the reporting phase, they develop reports that compare actual performance with planned performance in achieving key business objectives.

3. Most creditors and investors put their funds into a **portfolio** to average the returns and risks of making loans and investments. However, they must still make decisions about which loans or stocks to put in their portfolios. In doing so, they use finan-cial performance evaluation to judge a company's past performance and current financial position, as well as its future potential and the risk associated with that potential.

   a. In judging a company's past performance and current status, investors and creditors look at trends in past sales, expenses, net income, cash flows, and return on investment. They also look at a company's assets and liabilities, its debt in relation to equity, and its levels of inventories and receivables.

   b. Information about a company's past and present enables creditors and investors to make more accurate projections about its future—and the more accurate their projections are, the lower their risk of realizing a loss will be. In return for assuming a higher risk, creditors may charge higher interest rates or demand security on their loans; stock investors look for a higher return in the form of dividends or an increase in market price.

4. To bolster investor confidence in the financial reporting systems of public companies, the U.S. Congress passed broad legislation known as the **Sarbanes-Oxley Act**. In addition to establishing a Public Oversight Board for the accounting profession, the act requires top executives to attest to the accuracy of financial statements filed with the SEC and imposes criminal penalties for fraudulent financial reporting. It also specifies the composition and qualifications of audit committee members and requires the audit committee to appoint an auditor who does not consult for the company.

Objective 2: Describe and discuss the standards for financial performance evaluation.

5. When analyzing financial statements, decision makers commonly use three standards of comparison: rule-of-thumb measures, past performance of the company, and industry norms.
   a. Rule-of-thumb measures for key financial ratios are helpful but should not be the only basis for making a decision. For example, a company may report high earnings per share but lack the assets needed to pay current debts.
   b. Analysis of a company's past performance is helpful in showing current trends and may also indicate future trends. However, trends reverse at times, so projections based on past performance should be made with care.
   c. Using industry norms to compare a company's performance with the performance of other companies in the same industry has advantages, but it also has three limitations. First, the operations of two companies in the same industry may be so different that the companies cannot be compared. Second, **diversified companies,** or *conglomerates,* operate in many unrelated industries, which makes it difficult if not impossible to use industry norms as standards. (The FASB requirement that financial information be reported by segments has provided a partial solution to this problem.) Third, companies may use different acceptable accounting procedures for recording similar items.

Objective 3: Identify the sources of information for financial performance evaluation.

6. The major sources of information about publicly held corporations are reports published by the company, SEC reports, business periodicals, and credit and investment advisory services.
   a. A corporation's annual report provides much useful financial information. Its main sections are management's analysis of the past year's operations; the financial statements; the notes to the financial statements, which include a summary of significant accounting policies; the auditors' report; and financial highlights for a five- or ten-year period. Most public companies also publish **interim financial statements** each quarter. These reports present limited financial information in the form of condensed financial statements and may indicate significant trends in a company's earnings.
   b. Publicly held corporations must file an annual report with the SEC on Form 10-K, a quarterly report on Form 10-Q, and a current report of significant events on Form 8-K. These reports are available to the public and are a valuable source of financial information.
   c. Financial analysts obtain information from such sources as *The Wall Street Journal, Forbes, Barron's, Fortune,* the *Financial Times,* Moody's, Standard & Poor's, and Dun & Bradstreet.

Objective 4: Apply horizontal analysis, trend analysis, vertical analysis, and ratio analysis to financial statements.

7. The most widely used tools of financial analysis are horizontal analysis, trend analysis, vertical analysis, and ratio analysis.
   a. **Horizontal analysis** is commonly used to study comparative financial statements, which present data for the current year and previous year side by side. Horizontal analysis computes both dollar and percentage changes in specific items from one year to the next. The first year is called the **base year,** and the percentage change is computed by dividing the amount of the change by the base year amount.
   b. **Trend analysis** is like horizontal analysis, except that it calculates percentage changes for several consecutive years. To show changes in related items over time, trend analysis uses an **index number**, which is calculated by setting the base year equal to 100 percent.
   c. **Vertical analysis** uses percentages to show the relationship of individual items on a statement to a total within the statement (e.g., cost of goods sold as a percentage of net sales). The result is a **common-size statement.** On a common-size balance sheet, total assets are set at 100 percent, as are total liabilities and stockholders' equity; on a common-size income statement, net sales or net revenues are set at 100 percent. Comparative common-size statements enable analysts to identify changes both within a period and between periods They also make it easier to compare companies.
   d. **Ratio analysis** identifies meaningful relationships between the components of the financial statements. The primary purpose of ratios is to identify areas needing further investigation.

Objective 5: Apply ratio analysis to financial statements in a comprehensive evaluation of a company's financial performance.

8. The ratios used in ratio analysis provide information about a company's liquidity, profitability, long-term solvency, cash flow adequacy, and market strength. The most common ratios are shown in the table that follows.

Ratio	Components	Use
Liquidity Ratios		
Current ratio	$\dfrac{\text{Current Assets}}{\text{Current Liabilities}}$	Measure of short-term debt-paying ability
Quick ratio	$\dfrac{\text{Cash + Marketable Securities + Receivables}}{\text{Current Liabilities}}$	Measure of short-term debt-paying ability
Receivable turnover	$\dfrac{\text{Net Sales}}{\text{Average Accounts Receivable}}$	Measure of relative size of accounts receivable and effectiveness of credit policies
Average days' sales uncollected	$\dfrac{\text{Days in Year}}{\text{Receivable Turnover}}$	Measure of average days taken to collect receivables
Inventory turnover	$\dfrac{\text{Cost of Goods Sold}}{\text{Average Inventory}}$	Measure of relative size of inventory
Average days' inventory on hand	$\dfrac{\text{Days in Year}}{\text{Inventory Turnover}}$	Measure of average days taken to sell inventory
Payables turnover	$\dfrac{\text{Cost of Goods Sold +/– Change in Inventory}}{\text{Average Accounts Payable}}$	Measure of relative size of accounts payable
Average days' payable	$\dfrac{\text{Days in Year}}{\text{Payables Turnover}}$	Measure of average days taken to pay accounts payable

(**Note:** The **operating cycle** is the time taken to sell and collect for products sold. It equals average days' inventory on hand plus average days' sales uncollected.)

Ratio	Components	Use
Profitability Ratios		
Profit margin	$\dfrac{\text{Net Income}}{\text{Net Sales}}$	Measure of net income produced by each dollar of sales
Asset turnover	$\dfrac{\text{Net Sales}}{\text{Average Total Assets}}$	Measure of how efficiently assets are used to produce sales
Return on assets	$\dfrac{\text{Net Income}}{\text{Average Total Assets}}$	Measure of overall earning power or profitability
Return on equity	$\dfrac{\text{Net Income}}{\text{Average Stockholders' Equity}}$	Measure of the profitability of stockholders' investments
Long-Term Solvency Ratios		
Debt to equity ratio	$\dfrac{\text{Total Liabilities}}{\text{Stockholders' Equity}}$	Measure of capital structure and leverage
Interest coverage ratio	$\dfrac{\text{Income Before Income Taxes + Interest Expense}}{\text{Interest Expense}}$	Measure of creditors' protection from default on interest payments
Cash Flow Adequacy Ratios		
Cash flow yield	$\dfrac{\text{Net Cash Flows from Operating Activities}}{\text{Net Income}}$	Measure of the ability to generate operating cash flows in relation to net income
Cash flows to sales	$\dfrac{\text{Net Cash Flows from Operating Activities}}{\text{Net Sales}}$	Measure of the ability of sales to generate operating cash flows
Cash flows to assets	$\dfrac{\text{Net Cash Flows from Operating Activities}}{\text{Average Total Assets}}$	Measure of the ability of assets to generate operating cash flows
Free cash flow	Net Cash Flows from Operating Activities – Dividends – Net Capital Expenditures	Measure of cash generated or cash deficiency after providing for commitments
Market Strength Ratios		
Price/earnings (P/E) ratio	$\dfrac{\text{Market Price per Share}}{\text{Earnings per Share}}$	Measure of investor confidence in a company
Dividends yield	$\dfrac{\text{Dividends per Share}}{\text{Market Price per Share}}$	Measure of a stock's current return to an investor

SELF-TEST

Test your knowledge of the chapter by choosing the best answer for each of the following items.

1. A general rule in choosing among alternative investments is that the higher the risk involved, the
   a. greater the return expected.
   b. lower the profits expected.
   c. lower the potential expected.
   d. greater the price of the investment.

2. Which of the following is the most useful in evaluating whether a company has improved its position in relation to its competitors?
   a. Rule-of-thumb measures
   b. A company's past performance
   c. A company's past performance and current financial position
   d. Industry averages

3. One of the best places to look for early signals of change in a firm's profitability is the firm's
   a. interim financial statements.
   b. year-end financial statements.
   c. annual report sent to stockholders.
   d. annual report sent to the SEC.

4. Cash flow yield equals net cash flows from operating activities divided by
   a. average stockholders' equity.
   b. net income.
   c. average total assets.
   d. net sales.

5. In trend analysis, each item is expressed as a percentage of the
   a. net income figure.
   b. retained earnings figure.
   c. base year figure.
   d. total assets figure.

6. In a common-size balance sheet for a wholesale company, which of the following could represent the 100 percent figure?
   a. Merchandise inventory
   b. Total current assets
   c. Total property, plant, and equipment
   d. Total assets

7. The best way to study the changes in financial statements between two years is to prepare
   a. common-size statements.
   b. a trend analysis.
   c. a horizontal analysis.
   d. a ratio analysis.

8. A common measure of liquidity is
   a. return on assets.
   b. profit margin.
   c. inventory turnover.
   d. interest coverage ratio.

9. Asset turnover is most closely related to
   a. profit margin and return on assets.
   b. profit margin and debt to equity ratio.
   c. interest coverage ratio and debt to equity ratio.
   d. earnings per share and profit margin.

10. Which of the following describes the computation of the interest coverage ratio?
    a. Net income minus interest expense divided by interest expense
    b. Net income plus interest expense divided by interest expense
    c. Income before income taxes plus interest expense divided by interest expense
    d. Net income divided by interest expense

TESTING YOUR KNOWLEDGE

Matching*

Match each term with its definition by writing the appropriate letter in the blank.

_____ 1. Financial performance evaluation

_____ 2. Portfolio

_____ 3. Diversified companies (conglomerates)

_____ 4. Interim financial statements

_____ 5. Horizontal analysis

_____ 6. Base year

_____ 7. Trend analysis

_____ 8. Index number

_____ 9. Vertical analysis

_____ 10. Common-size statement

_____ 11. Ratio analysis

_____ 12. Operating cycle

a. The time it takes to sell and collect for products sold

b. A group of investments or loans

c. A means of identifying significant relationships between the components of financial statements

d. A statement produced by vertical analysis in which components of a total figure are stated as percentages of that total

e. Statements presenting financial information for periods of less than a year

f. The first year considered in horizontal analysis

g. All the techniques used to show important relationships in financial statements and to relate them to important financial objectives

h. A technique for showing percentage changes in specific items over several years

i. A number used in trend analysis to show changes in related items over time

j. A technique for showing dollar and percentage changes in specific items between two years

k. A technique that uses percentages to show the relationships of individual items on a financial statement to a total within the statement

l. Large companies that operate in many unrelated industries

Short Answer

Use the lines provided to answer each item.

1. List four ratios that measure profitability.

_____

_____

_____

_____

2. Briefly distinguish between horizontal analysis and vertical analysis.

_____

_____

_____

3. List the three standards that decision makers use in assessing a company's performance.

_____

_____

_____

4. It is usually wiser to acquire a portfolio of small investments than to make one large investment. Why is this so?

_____

_____

_____

---

*Note to student: The matching quiz might be completed more efficiently by starting with the definition and searching for the corresponding term.

5. List four measures of cash flow adequacy.

_____

_____

_____

_____

True-False

Circle T if the statement is true, F if it is false. Provide explanations for the false answers, using the blank lines below.

T F **1.** Horizontal analysis is applicable to both an income statement and a balance sheet.

T F **2.** Common-size statements show the dollar amount of changes in specific items from one year to the next.

T F **3.** A company with a 2.0 current ratio experiences a decline in the current ratio when it pays a short-term liability.

T F **4.** Inventory is not a component in the computation of the quick ratio.

T F **5.** Inventory turnover equals average inventory divided by cost of goods sold.

T F **6.** The price/earnings ratio must be computed before earnings per share can be determined.

T F **7.** In computing return on equity, interest expense is added back to net income.

T F **8.** When a company has no debt, its return on assets equals its return on equity.

T F **9.** A company with a low debt to equity ratio is a high-risk investment.

T F **10.** Receivable turnover measures the time taken to collect an average receivable.

T F **11.** A low interest coverage ratio would be of concern to a company's bondholders.

T F **12.** Average days' inventory on hand is a liquidity ratio.

T F **13.** Dividends yield is a profitability ratio.

T F **14.** On a common-size income statement, net income is set at 100 percent.

T F **15.** Interim financial statements may provide early signals of significant changes in a company's earnings trend.

T F **16.** _The Wall Street Journal_ is the most complete financial newspaper in America.

T F **17.** Return on assets equals the profit margin times asset turnover.

T F **18.** The higher the payables turnover is, the longer the average days' payable is.

T F **19.** The Sarbanes-Oxley Act prohibits auditors from acting as consultants for the companies they audit.

_____

_____

_____

_____

_____

_____

_____

_____

_____

_____

_____

_____

Multiple Choice

Circle the letter of the best answer.

1. Which of the following is a measure of long-term solvency?
   a. Current ratio
   b. Interest coverage ratio
   c. Asset turnover
   d. Profit margin

2. Short-term creditors would probably be *most* interested in which of the following ratios?
   a. Current ratio
   b. Average days' inventory on hand
   c. Debt to equity ratio
   d. Quick ratio

3. Net income is irrelevant in computing which of the following ratios?
   a. Cash flow yield
   b. Return on assets
   c. Asset turnover
   d. Return on equity

4. A high price/earnings ratio indicates
   a. investor confidence in future earnings.
   b. that the stock is probably overvalued.
   c. that the stock is probably undervalued.
   d. lack of investor confidence in future earnings.

5. Index numbers are used in
   a. trend analysis.
   b. ratio analysis.
   c. vertical analysis.
   d. common-size statements.

6. The principal internal users of financial statements are
   a. SEC administrators.
   b. managers.
   c. investors.
   d. creditors.

7. Using industry norms to evaluate a company's financial performance is complicated by
   a. the existence of diversified companies.
   b. the use of different accounting procedures by different companies.
   c. the fact that companies in the same industry usually differ in some respect.
   d. all of the above.

8. A low receivable turnover indicates that
   a. few customers are defaulting on their debts.
   b. the company's inventory is moving slowly.
   c. the company is slow in making collections from its customers.
   d. a small proportion of the company's sales are credit sales.

9. In a common-size income statement, net income is set at
   a. 0 percent.
   b. the percentage that it is in relation to net sales.
   c. the percentage that it is in relation to operating expenses.
   d. 100 percent.

10. Which of the following is a measure of cash generated or cash deficiency after providing for commitments?
    a. Cash flows to assets
    b. Cash flow yield
    c. Free cash flow
    d. Cash flows to sales

APPLYING YOUR KNOWLEDGE

Exercises

1. Complete the horizontal analysis for the comparative income statements shown below. Round percentages to the nearest tenth of a percent.

	20x6	20x5	Increase (Decrease)	
			Amount	Percentage
Sales	$250,000	$200,000		
Cost of goods sold	144,000	120,000		
Gross margin	$106,000	$ 80,000		
Operating expenses	62,000	50,000		
Income before income taxes	$ 44,000	$ 30,000		
Income taxes	16,000	8,000		
Net income	$ 28,000	$ 22,000		

2. The following is financial information for Norton Corporation for 20xx. Current assets consist of cash, accounts receivable, marketable securities, and inventory.

Average accounts receivable	$100,000
Average (and ending) inventory	180,000
Cost of goods sold	350,000
Current assets, Dec. 31	500,000
Current liabilities, Dec. 31	250,000
Market price, Dec. 31, on	
21,200 shares	40/share
Net income	106,000
Net sales	600,000
Average stockholders' equity	480,000
Average total assets	880,000
Net cash flows from operating activities	75,000

Compute the following ratios as of December 31. Round off to the nearest tenth of a whole number.

a. Current ratio = _____

b. Quick ratio = _____

c. Inventory turnover = _____

d. Average days' inventory on hand = _____

e. Return on assets = _____

f. Return on equity = _____

g. Receivable turnover = _____

h. Average days' sales uncollected = _____

i. Profit margin = _____

j. Cash flow yield = _____

k. Cash flows to sales = _____

l. Cash flows to assets = _____

m. Asset turnover = _____

n. Price/earnings ratio = _____

Crossword Puzzle
for Chapters 27 and 28

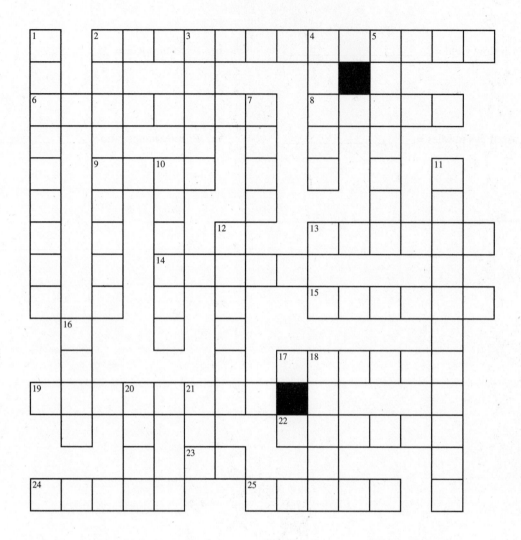

ACROSS

2. Ratio indicating investor confidence in a company (2 words)
6. Analysis resulting in 15-Across
8. The "T" of TQM
9. _____ cash flow
13. _____ Application Prize
14. Number used in trend analysis
15. _____-size statement
17. The "S" of MIS
19. Malcolm _____ Quality Award
22. _____ on assets
23. The "O" of ROQ
24. Internal failure _____
25. The "A" of CAD

DOWN

1. _____ turnover
2. Group of investment or loans
3. Operating _____
4. Current _____
5. Quarterly financial statements, e.g.
7. Purchase order _____ time
10. Return on _____
11. Costs of _____ (prevention and appraisal costs)
12. Nonvalue-_____ activity
16. Base _____
18. Dividends _____
20. _____ to equity ratio
21. _____ 9000 (quality management guidelines) activities

APPENDIX A THE MERCHANDISING WORK SHEET AND CLOSING ENTRIES

REVIEWING THE APPENDIX

1. The work sheet for a merchandising company is basically the same as for a service firm. However, it includes the additional accounts needed to handle merchandising transactions (e.g., Merchandise Inventory, Sales, and Freight In). The treatment of these accounts differs depending on whether the periodic or perpetual inventory system is used.

2. Under the periodic inventory system, the objectives of dealing with inventory at the end of a period are to (a) remove the beginning balance from the Merchandise Inventory account, (b) enter the ending balance into the Merchandise Inventory account, and (c) enter the beginning inventory as a debit and the ending inventory as a credit to the Income Summary account to calculate net income.

3. Under the periodic inventory system, beginning inventory appears as a debit in the Income Statement column. Ending inventory appears as a credit in the Income Statement column and as a debit in the Balance Sheet column. A Cost of Goods Sold account does *not* appear on the work sheet, though it does under the perpetual inventory system. Under either inventory system, an Adjusted Trial Balance column may be eliminated if only a few adjustments are necessary.

4. Data for closing entries can be obtained from the completed work sheet. Below is a summary of the closing entries prepared when using the periodic inventory system.

Income Summary	XX	(sum of credits)
Merchandise Inventory	XX	(beginning amount)
Sales Returns and Allowances	XX	(current debit balance)
Sales Discounts	XX	(current debit balance)
Purchases	XX	(current debit balance)
Freight In	XX	(current debit balance)
All other expenses	XX	(current debit balances)

Closing entry 1: To close temporary expense and revenue accounts with debit balances and to remove the beginning inventory

Merchandise Inventory	XX (ending amount)	
Sales	XX (current credit balance)	
Purchases Returns and Allowances	XX (current credit balance)	
Purchases Discounts	XX (current credit balance)	
Income Summary		XX (sum of debits)

       Closing entry 2: To close temporary expense and revenue accounts
       with credit balances and to establish the ending inventory

Income Summary	XX (current credit balance)	
Retained Earnings		XX (net income amount)

       Closing entry 3: To close the Income Summary account

Retained Earnings	XX (amount declared)	
Dividends		XX (amount declared)

       Closing entry 4: To close the Dividends account

---

5. Under the perpetual inventory system, the Merchandise Inventory account is updated whenever a purchase, sale, or return occurs. It is therefore up to date at the end of the accounting period and is not involved in the closing process. On the work sheet, both the Trial Balance and Balance Sheet columns reflect the ending balance.

6. As inventory is sold under the perpetual inventory system, the cost is transferred from the Merchandise Inventory account to Cost of Goods Sold. Cost of Goods Sold therefore appears on the work sheet and in the closing entries along with all the other expenses.

7. Data for closing entries can be obtained from the completed work sheet. Below is a summary of the closing entries prepared when using a perpetual inventory system.

Income Summary	XX (sum of credits)	
Sales Returns and Allowances		XX (current debit balance)
Sales Discounts		XX (current debit balance)
Cost of Goods Sold		XX (current debit balance)
Freight In		XX (current debit balance)
All other expenses		XX (current debit balances)

       Closing entry 1: To close temporary expense and revenue accounts
       with debit balances

Sales	XX (current credit balance)	
Income Summary		XX (sales amount)

       Closing entry 2: To close temporary revenue account with credit balance

Income Summary	XX (current credit balance)	
Retained Earnings		XX (net income amount)

       Closing entry 3: To close the Income Summary account

Retained Earnings	XX (amount declared)	
Dividends		XX (amount declared)

       Closing entry 4: To close the Dividends account

APPLYING YOUR KNOWLEDGE

Exercises

1. A partially complete work sheet for Mammoth Mart, Inc., appears on the next page. Use the following information to complete the work sheet (remember to key the adjustments). Assume that the company uses the periodic inventory system. Notice that the Adjusted Trial Balance column has been provided, even though it is not absolutely necessary.

   a. Expired rent, $250
   b. Accrued salaries, $500
   c. Depreciation on equipment, $375
   d. Ending merchandise inventory, $620
   e. Accrued income taxes expense, $180

Mammoth Mart, Inc.
Work Sheet
For the Month Ended March 31, 20xx

Account Name	Trial Balance		Adjustments		Adjusted Trial Balance		Income Statement		Balance Sheet	
	Debit	Credit	Debit	Credit	Debit	Credit	Debit	Credit	Debit	Credit
Cash	1,000									
Accounts Receivable	700									
Merchandise Inventory	400									
Prepaid Rent	750									
Equipment	4,200									
Accounts Payable		900								
Common Stock		3,000								
Retained Earnings		1,200								
Sales		9,800								
Sales Discounts	300									
Purchases	3,700									
Purchases Returns and Allowances		150								
Freight In	400									
Salaries Expense	3,000									
Advertising Expense	600									
	15,050	15,050								

2. Following are the accounts and data needed to prepare the 20xx closing entries for Renick Manufacturing Company. Assume a normal balance for each account, as well as use of the perpetual inventory system. Use the journal provided below. Omit explanations.

Cost of Goods Sold	$52,700
Freight In	3,200
General and Administrative Expenses	24,800
Income Taxes Expense	6,500
Sales	244,100
Sales Returns and Allowances	5,300
Selling Expenses	39,400

The company declared and paid dividends of $50,000 during the year.

General Journal				
Date		Description	Debit	Credit

The Merchandising Work Sheet and Closing Entries

APPENDIX B   SPECIAL-PURPOSE JOURNALS

REVIEWING THE APPENDIX

1. Although companies can record all their transactions in the general journal, those with a large number of transactions also use special-purpose journals to promote efficiency, economy, and control.

2. Most business transactions fall into one of four categories and are recorded in one of four special-purpose journals:
   a. Sales of merchandise on credit are recorded in the sales journal.
   b. Purchases on credit are recorded in the purchases journal
   c. Receipts of cash are recorded in the cash receipts journal.
   d. Disbursements of cash are recorded in the cash payments journal.

3. The *sales journal,* used only to record credit sales, saves time because (a) each entry requires only one line, (b) account names do not need to be written out since frequently occurring accounts are used as column headings, (c) no explanation is needed, and (d) only total sales for the month, not each individual sale, are posted to the Sales account in the general ledger. (However, postings are made daily to the accounts receivable subsidiary ledger.) Similar time-saving principles apply to the other special-purpose journals.
   a. Most companies that sell to customers on credit keep an accounts receivable record for each customer, which enables the company to determine how much a customer owes at any given time. All customer accounts are filed al-

phabetically or by account number in the accounts receivable *subsidiary ledger.* Postings are made daily to the customer accounts in this ledger.
   b. The general ledger contains a *controlling* (or *control*) *account* for the accounts receivable in the subsidiary ledger. The controlling account is updated at the end of each month. Its end-of-month balance must equal the sum of all the accounts in the accounts receivable subsidiary ledger (determined by preparing a schedule of accounts receivable).
   c. Most companies also maintain a subsidiary ledger and controlling account for accounts payable, which function in much the same way as the subsidiary ledger and controlling account for accounts receivable.

4 The *purchases journal* is used to record purchases on credit. A single-column purchases journal records only purchases of merchandise on credit. A multicolumn purchases journal can accommodate other purchases on credit, such as those for supplies and freight. Only total purchases for the month are posted to the Purchases account. However, postings are made daily to creditor accounts in the accounts payable subsidiary ledger.

5. All receipts of cash are recorded in the *cash receipts journal.* A cash receipts journal typically includes debit columns for Cash, Sales Discounts, and Other Accounts and credit columns for Accounts Receivable, Sales, and Other Accounts. Postings to customer accounts and Other Accounts

are made daily. All column totals, except for Other Accounts, are posted to the general ledger at the end of the month.

6. All payments of cash are recorded in the *cash payments journal* (also called a *cash disbursements journal*). A cash payments journal typically includes debit columns for Accounts Payable and Other Accounts and credit columns for Cash, Purchases Discounts, and Other Accounts. Postings to credit accounts and Other Accounts are made daily.

All column totals, except for Other Accounts, are posted to the general ledger at the end of the month.

7. Transactions that cannot be recorded in a special-purpose journal, such as a return of merchandise bought on account, are recorded in the general journal. Closing entries and adjusting entries are also recorded in the general journal. Postings are made at the end of each day; for accounts receivable and accounts payable, they are made to both the controlling and subsidiary accounts.

TESTING YOUR KNOWLEDGE

Matching*

Match each term with its definition by writing the appropriate letter in the blank.

_____ **1.** Special-purpose journal

_____ **2.** Subsidiary ledger

_____ **3.** Subsidiary account

_____ **4.** Controlling account

_____ **5.** Schedule of accounts receivable

a. Any journal except the general journal

b. A formal listing of customers' account balances

c. A customer's or creditor's record in a subsidiary ledger

d. A ledger separate from the general ledger that contains a group of related accounts

e. Any general ledger account that has a related subsidiary ledger

---

**Note to student:* The matching quiz might be completed more efficiently by starting with the definition and searching for the corresponding term.

APPLYING YOUR KNOWLEDGE

Exercises

1. Use the following abbreviations to indicate the journal in which Davis Appliance Store should record the transactions described below:

S = Sales journal
P = Purchases journal (single-column)
CR = Cash receipts journal
CP = Cash payments journal
J = General journal

_____ a. Returns goods that it purchased on credit.
_____ b. Returns goods that it purchased for cash for a cash refund.
_____ c. Purchases toasters on credit.
_____ d. Pays for the toasters.
_____ e. Sells a blender on credit.
_____ f. Pays the electric bill.
_____ g. Makes adjusting entries.
_____ h. Purchases office furniture on credit.
_____ i. Makes closing entries.
_____ j. Pays for half of the office furniture.
_____ k. Receives payment from a customer and allows a discount.

2. Enter the following transactions of Wallace Liquidators, Inc., into the cash receipts journal provided below. Make the posting notations as if the end-of-month postings had been made, and fill in the Post. Ref. column as if the entries had been posted daily. Accounts Receivable is account no. 114, Sales is account no. 411, Sales Discounts is account no. 412, and Cash is account no. 111.

Feb. 3 Received payment of $500 less a 2 percent discount from Don Morris for merchandise purchased on credit.
9 Sold land (account no. 135) for $8,000 cash.
14 Issued $10,000 more in common stock (account no. 311).
23 Sue O'Neill paid Wallace $150 for merchandise she had purchased on credit.
28 Cash sales for the month totaled $25,000.

Cash Receipts Journal									Page 1
			Post. Ref.	Debits			Credits		
Date		Account Debited/Credited		Cash	Sales Disc.	Other Accts.	Accts. Receiv.	Sales	Other Accts.

3. A page from a special-purpose journal appears below.

Date	Ck. No.	Payee	Account Credited/ Debited	Post. Ref.	Credits			Debits	
					Cash	Purchases Discounts	Other Accounts	Accounts Payable	Other Accounts
May 1	114	DePasquale Supply Co.		✓	784	16		800	
7	115	Monahan Bus Equip.	Office Equipment	167	2,000				2,000
13	116	Celestial News	Advertising Expense	512	350				350
19	117	Denecker Motors		✓	420			420	
					3,554	16		1,220	2,350
					(111)	(413)		(211)	(315)

a. What type of journal is this? _____
_____

b. What error was made in this journal? _____
_____
_____

c. Provide an explanation for each of the four transactions.

May 1 _____
_____

May 7 _____
_____

May 13 _____
_____

May 19 _____
_____

d. Explain the following:

1. The check marks in the Post. Ref. column
_____

2. The numbers 167 and 512 in the Post. Ref. column _____
_____

3. The numbers below the column totals ____
_____
_____
_____
_____
_____
_____

APPENDIX C ACCOUNTING FOR UNINCORPORATED BUSINESSES

REVIEWING THE APPENDIX

1. A *sole proprietorship* is a business owned by one person. In accounting, a sole proprietorship is treated as an entity separate from its owner, but for legal purposes, the owner and proprietorship are considered one and the same (i.e., the owner is personally liable for all debts of the business). When the owner makes a cash investment in the business, it is recorded as a debit to Cash and a credit to the owner's Capital account. A cash withdrawal is recorded as a debit to the owner's Withdrawals account and a credit to Cash. Closing entries for a sole proprietorship are the same as for a corporation, except that Income Summary is closed to the owner's capital account, as is the owner's Withdrawals account.

2. The Uniform Partnership Act defines a *partnership* as "an association of two or more persons to carry on as co-owners of a business for profit." The chief characteristics of a partnership are as follows:
   a. Voluntary association: Partners choose each other when they form their business.
   b. *Partnership agreement:* Partners may have either an oral or a written agreement.
   c. *Limited life:* Certain events may dissolve the partnership.
   d. *Mutual agency:* Each partner may bind the partnership to outside contracts.
   e. *Unlimited liability:* Each partner is personally liable for all debts of the partnership.
   f. Co-ownership of partnership property: Business property is jointly owned by all partners.

   g. Participation in partnership income: Each partner shares income and losses of the business.

3. The owners' equity section of a partnership's balance sheet is called *partners' equity.* Separate Capital and Withdrawals accounts must be maintained for each partner. When a partner makes an investment in the business, the assets contributed are debited at their fair market value, and the partner's Capital account is credited.

4. The method of distributing partnership income and losses should be specified in the partnership agreement. If the agreement does not mention the distribution of income and losses, the law requires that they be shared equally. The most common methods base distribution on a stated ratio only, a capital balance ratio only, or a combination of salaries, interest on each partner's capital, and the stated ratio. Net income is distributed to partners' equity by debiting Income Summary and crediting each partner's Capital account; the reverse is done for a net loss.
   a. When income and losses are based on a stated ratio only, partnership income or loss for the period is multiplied by each partner's ratio (stated as a fraction or percentage) to arrive at each partner's share.
   b. When income and losses are based on a *capital balance* ratio only, partnership income or loss for the period is multiplied by each partner's proportion of the capital balance at the beginning of the period.

c. When income and losses are based on salaries, interest, and a stated ratio, salaries and interest must be allocated to the partners regardless of whether the business has a net income or loss for the period. Any net income left over after the salaries and interest are paid must be allocated to the partners according to the stated ratio. If salaries and interest are greater than net income, the excess must be deducted from each partner's allocation according to the stated ratio.

5. The admission of a new partner, the withdrawal of a partner, or the death of a partner results in the *dissolution* of the partnership. When a partnership is dissolved, the partners lose the authority to continue the business as a going concern.

6. A person can be admitted to a partnership by either purchasing an interest in the partnership from one or more of the original partners or by investing assets in the partnership.

   a. When a person purchases an interest from a partner, the selling partner's Capital account is debited and the buying partner's Capital account is credited for the interest in the business sold. The purchase price is ignored in making this entry.

   b. When a person becomes a partner by investing assets in the partnership, the contributed assets are debited and the new partner's Capital account is credited. The amount of the debit and credit may or may not equal the value of the contributed assets; it depends on the value of the business and the method applied. When the partners feel that a share of their business is worth more than the value of the assets being contributed, they generally ask the entering partner to pay them a *bonus*. When the value of the contributed assets is greater than the value of the share in the business, the partnership may give the new partner a bonus by transferring part of the original partners' capital to the new partner's Capital account.

7. A partner can withdraw from a partnership by selling his or her interest to new or existing partners or by withdrawing assets that are equal to his or her capital balance, less than his or her capital balance (in this case, the remaining partners receive a bonus), or greater than his or capital balance (the withdrawing partner receives a bonus).

8. When a partner dies, the partnership automatically is dissolved, and immediate steps must be taken to settle with the heirs of the deceased partner.

9. *Liquidation* of a partnership is the process of ending the business by selling the partnership's assets, paying off its liabilities, and distributing any remaining assets among the partners. As cash becomes available, it must be applied first to outside creditors, then to loans from partners, and finally to the partners' capital balances.

TESTING YOUR KNOWLEDGE

*Matching**

Match each term with its definition by writing the appropriate letter in the blank.

_____ **1.** Sole proprietorship

_____ **2.** Partnership

_____ **3.** Voluntary association

_____ **4.** Partnership agreement

_____ **5.** Limited life

_____ **6.** Mutual agency

_____ **7.** Unlimited liability

_____ **8.** Dissolution

_____ **9.** Liquidation

_____ **10.** Partners' equity

a. A form of dissolution in which a partnership ends by selling assets, paying creditors, and distributing any remaining assets to the partners

b. A characteristic of a partnership resulting from the fact that any change in partners will cause the business to dissolve

c. The power of each partner to enter into contracts that are within the normal scope of the business

d. The balance sheet section that lists the partners' Capital accounts

e. A business owned by one person

f. An association of two or more persons to carry on as co-owners of a business for profit

g. The personal liability of each partner for the debts of the partnership

h. The end of a partnership as a going concern

i. The partners' understanding about how the partnership will operate

j. A phrase describing the consensual nature of a partnership

---

Note to student: The matching quiz might be completed more efficiently by starting with the definition and searching for the corresponding term.

APPLYING YOUR KNOWLEDGE

Exercises

1. Partners A, B, and C each receive a $10,000 salary, as well as 5 percent interest on their respective investments of $60,000, $40,000, and $50,000. If they share income and losses in a 3:2:1 ratio, how much net income or loss would be allocated to each partner under the following circumstances?

   a. A net income of $40,500

   A = $ _____

   B = $ _____

   C = $ _____

   b. A net income of $25,500

   A = $ _____

   B = $ _____

   C = $ _____

   c. A net loss of $4,500

   A = $ _____

   B = $ _____

   C = $ _____

2. Partners G, H, and I have capital balances of $10,000 each and share income and losses in a 2:2:1 ratio. They agree to allow J to purchase a one-third interest in the business, and they use the bonus method to record the transaction. Provide the proper journal entry under each of the following assumptions:

   a. J contributes $12,000 in cash.
   b. J contributes $15,000 in cash.
   c. J contributes $21,000 in cash.

General Journal				
Date		**Description**	**Debit**	**Credit**

APPENDIX D INTERNATIONAL ACCOUNTING

REVIEWING THE APPENDIX

1. Today, many *multinational* or *transnational corporations* conduct business in countries throughout the world. International business has two major effects on accounting. First, foreign transactions involve different currencies, which must be translated into the domestic currency by means of an *exchange rate*. Second, financial standards differ from country to country, making comparisons among companies difficult.

2. No accounting problem arises when the domestic company bills and receives payment from the foreign company in the domestic currency. However, when a transaction involves foreign currency, the domestic company will probably realize and record an *exchange gain or loss*. This exchange gain or loss reflects the change in the exchange rate between the transaction date and the date of payment. When financial statements are prepared between the transaction date and the date of payment, GAAP requires that an unrealized gain or loss be recorded if the exchange rate has changed.

3. A foreign subsidiary that a parent company controls should be included in the parent company's consolidated financial statements. The subsidiary's financial statements must therefore be restated in the parent's *reporting currency*. The method of *restatement* depends on the foreign subsidiary's *functional currency*—that is, the currency in which it transacts most of its business. There are two basic types of foreign subsidiaries.

   a. Type I subsidiaries are self-contained within a foreign country. Their financial statements must be restated from the local currency to the reporting currency.

   b. Type II subsidiaries are an extension of the parent company's operations. As a rule, their functional currency is the currency of the parent company.

   c. When a Type I subsidiary of a U.S. company operates in a country where there is hyperinflation (more than 100 percent cumulative inflation over three years), it is treated as a Type II subsidiary, with the functional currency being the U.S. dollar.

4. At present, few standards of accounting are recognized worldwide. Although the International Accounting Standards Board (IASB) and the International Federation of Accountants (IFAC) have made considerable progress in promoting uniform international accounting standards, there are still serious inconsistencies in financial statements among countries, and comparison remains a difficult task. Obstacles to establishing international standards include disagreement between accountants and users of financial information on the goals of financial statements, inconsistencies in accounting practices, differences in the laws regulating companies, and the influence of tax laws on financial reporting. More and more countries, however, are recognizing the importance of uniform international accounting standards.

A. Accounts Receivable, foreign company   XX (amount billed)
    Sales   XX (amount billed)
        Credit sale made, fixed amount billed in foreign currency,
        recorded in U.S. dollars

B. Cash   XX (amount received)
    Exchange Gain or Loss   XX (the difference)
        Accounts Receivable, foreign company   XX (amount billed)
            Received payment in foreign currency, exchange loss
            arose from weakening of foreign currency in relation
            to U.S. dollar

C. Purchases   XX (amount billed)
        Accounts Payable, foreign company   XX (amount billed)
            Credit purchase made, fixed amount billed in foreign
            currency

D. Accounts Payable, foreign company   XX (amount billed)
    Exchange Gain or Loss   XX (the difference)
    Cash   XX (amount paid)
        Made payment in foreign currency, exchange gain
        arose from weakening of foreign currency in relation
        to U.S. dollar

E. Accounts Payable, foreign company   XX (amount of gain)
    Exchange Gain or Loss   XX (amount of gain)
        Made adjusting entry to record unrealized exchange
        gain on outstanding payable to be settled in a foreign
        currency

Note: When a U.S. company transacts business entirely in U.S.
dollars, no exchange gain or loss will occur. The simple journal
entries to record those transaction are not duplicated here.

TESTING YOUR KNOWLEDGE

*Matching**

Match each term with its definition by writing the appropriate letter in the blank.

_____	**1.** Restatement	
_____	**2.** Exchange rate	
_____	**3.** Reporting currency	
_____	**4.** Functional currency	
_____	**5.** Multinational corporation	

a. A business that operates in more than one country

b. The currency in which a set of consolidated financial statements is presented

c. The expression of one currency in terms of another

d. The currency which a company transacts most of its business

e. The value of one currency in terms of another

Note to student: The matching quiz might be completed more efficiently by starting with the definition and searching for the corresponding term.

APPLYING YOUR KNOWLEDGE

Exercise

1. Ison Corporation, an U.S. company, sold merchandise on credit to a Mexican company for 100,000 pesos. On the sale date, the exchange rate was $.05 per peso. On the date of receipt, the value of the peso had declined to $.045. In the journal below, prepare entries to record Ison's sale and receipt of payment. (Leave the date column empty, as no dates have been specified.)

General Journal				
Date		Description	Debit	Credit

APPENDIX E LONG-TERM INVESTMENTS

REVIEWING THE APPENDIX

1. Companies make long-term investments in stocks and bonds for a variety of reasons. For example, they may buy stock in another company whose operations are critical to the distribution of their own products, or they may invest in bonds to ensure that an affiliate company has sufficient long-term capital.

2. Long-term investments in bonds are recorded at cost, which is the price of the bonds plus the broker's commission. When bonds are purchased between interest dates, the investor must also pay for the accrued interest (which will be returned to the investor on the next interest payment date). Most long-term bonds are classified as *available-for-sale securities* because investors usually sell them before they mature. Such securities are valued at fair (market) value. Long-term bonds are classified as *held-to-maturity securities* when an early sale is not intended. Such securities are valued at cost, adjusted by discount or premium amortization.

3. All long-term investments in the stock of other companies are initially recorded at cost. After purchase, the accounting treatment depends on the extent of influence exercised by the investing company. If it can affect the operating and financing policies of the company in which it has invested, even though it owns 50 percent or less of that company's voting stock, the investing company has *significant influence;* if it owns more than 50 percent of the voting stock and can therefore decide operating and financing policies, it has

control. The extent of an investing company's influence can be difficult to measure accurately. However, unless there is evidence to the contrary, long-term investments in stock are classified as (a) noninfluential and noncontrolling (less than 20 percent ownership), (b) influential but noncontrolling (20 to 50 percent ownership), or (c) controlling (over 50 percent ownership).

4. The cost adjusted to market method should be used in accounting for noninfluential and noncontrolling investments. The equity method should be used in accounting for the other two categories of investments. In addition, consolidated financial statements are prepared when a controlling relationship exists.

   a. Under the *cost adjusted to market method,* the investor credits Dividend Income as dividends are received. In addition, the securities are recorded on the balance sheet and in comprehensive income disclosures at the lower of cost or market. Unrealized Loss on Long-Term Investments is debited for the excess of total cost over total market, and Allowance to Adjust Long-Term Investments to Market is credited. For available-for-sale equity securities, the Unrealized Loss on Long-Term Investments appears in the stockholders' equity section of the balance sheet as a negative amount (and as a component of other comprehensive income); the Allowance to Adjust Long-Term Investments to Market appears there as a contra account to Long-Term Investments. An adjusting entry opposite to the one described above would be made when market value relative to cost has increased.

b. Under the *equity method,* the investor records its share of the periodic net income of the company in which it has invested as a debit to the Investment account and makes a corresponding credit to an investment income account. The amount recorded is the periodic net income multiplied by the investor's ownership percentage. When the investor receives a cash divi-

dend, the Cash account is debited, and the Investment account is credited.

5. When a company has a controlling interest in another company, it is called the *parent company,* and the other company is called the *subsidiary.* Companies in a parent-subsidiary relationship must prepare *consolidated financial statements* (combined statements of a parent and its subsidiaries).

A. Long-Term Investments   XX (purchase price)
    Cash   XX (purchase price)
        Purchased long-term investment in stock

B. Unrealized Loss on Long-Term Investments   XX (amount of decline)
    Allowance to Adjust Long-Term Investments to Market   XX (amount of decline)
        Recorded reduction of long-term investment to market

C. Cash   XX (amount received)
    Loss on Sale of Investments   XX (the difference)
        Long-Term Investments   XX (purchase price)
        Sold shares of stock
        (Note: Had a gain on the sale arisen, Gain on Sale of
        Investment would have been credited.)

D. Cash   XX (amount received)
    Dividend Income   XX (amount received)
        Received cash dividend (cost adjusted to market
        method assumed)

E. Allowance to Adjust Long-Term Investments to Market   XX (amount of recovery)
    Unrealized Loss on Long-Term Investments   XX (amount of recovery)
        Recorded the adjustment in long-term investment so it is
        reported at market (market below cost)

F. Investment in XYZ Corporation   XX (amount paid)
    Cash   XX (amount paid)
        Invested in XYZ Corporation common stock

G. Investment in XYZ Corporation   XX (equity percentage of income)
    Income, XYZ Corporation Investment   XX (equity percentage of income)
        Recognized percentage of income reported by XYX
        (equity method assumed)

H. Cash   XX (amount received)
    Investment in XYZ Corporation   XX (amount received)
        Received cash dividend (equity method assumed)

TESTING YOUR KNOWLEDGE

Matching*

Match each term with its definition by writing the appropriate letter in the blank.

_____ 1. Available-for-sale securities

_____ 2. Held-to-maturity securities

_____ 3. Cost adjusted to market method

_____ 4. Equity method

_____ 5. Parent

_____ 6. Subsidiary

_____ 7. Consolidated financial statements

_____ 8. Influential but noncontrolling investment

_____ 9. Controlling investment

a. Ownership of more than 50 percent of a corporation's voting stock

b. The method used to account for noninfluential and noncontrolling investments

c. Investments that a business may at some point decide to sell

d. The method used to account for influential but noncontrolling investments

e. A company controlled by another company

f. A company that has a controlling interest in another company

g. Combined statements of a parent company and its subsidiaries

h. Investments in bonds that a business intends to keep until their maturity date

i. Ownership of 20 to 50 percent of another company's voting stock

---

Note to student: The matching quiz might be completed more efficiently by starting with the definition and searching for the corresponding term.

APPLYING YOUR KNOWLEDGE

Exercise

1. Jamal Corporation owns 15 percent of the voting stock of Tewa Company and 30 percent of the voting stock of Rorris Company. Both are long-term investments. During a recent year, Tewa earned $110,000 and paid total dividends of $80,000, and Rorris earned $65,000 and paid total dividends of $50,000. In the journal below, prepare Jamal's entries to reflect these facts. (Leave the date column empty, as no dates have been specified.)

General Journal				
Date		Description	Debit	Credit

APPENDIX F   THE TIME VALUE OF MONEY

REVIEWING THE APPENDIX

1. *Interest,* the cost of using money for a specific period, should be a consideration in any business decision. Interest can be calculated on a simple or compound basis.
   a. When *simple interest* is computed for one or more periods, the amount on which interest is computed does not increase each period—that is, interest is not computed on principal plus accrued interest.
   b. When *compound interest* is computed for two or more periods, the amount on which interest is computed *does* increase each period—that is, interest is computed on principal plus accrued interest.

2. *Future value* is the amount an investment will be worth at a future date if invested now at compound interest.
   a. Future value may be computed on a single sum invested at compound interest. Table 1 in Appendix G of the text facilitates this computation.
   b. Future value may also be computed on an *ordinary annuity* (i.e., a series of equal payments made at the end of equal intervals of time) at compound interest. Table 2 in Appendix G of the text facilitates this computation.

3. *Present value* is the amount that must be invested now at a given rate of interest to produce a given future value.
   a. Present value may be computed on a single sum due in the future. Table 3 in Appendix G of the text facilitates this computation.
   b. Present value may also be computed on an ordinary annuity. Table 4 in Appendix G of the text facilitates this computation.

4. All four tables facilitate both annual compounding and compounding for less than a year. For example, when computing 12 percent annual interest that is compounded quarterly, one would refer to the 3 percent column for four periods per year.

5. Present value can be used in accounting to (a) impute interest on noninterest-bearing notes, (b) determine the value of an asset that is being considered for purchase, (c) calculate deferred payments for the purchase of an asset, (d) account for the investment of idle cash, (e) accumulate funds needed to pay off a loan, and (f) determine numerous other accounting quantities, such as the a bond's value, pension and lease obligations, and depreciation.

A.   Purchases   XX (present value of note)
     Discount on Notes Payable   XX (imputed interest)
          Notes Payable   XX (face amount)
              Purchased merchandise, non-interest-bearing note issued

B.   Interest Expense   XX (amount accrued)
     Discount on Notes Payable   XX (amount accrued)
              Recorded interest expense for one year (see Entry A)

C.   Interest Expense   XX (interest for period)
     Notes Payable   XX (face amount)
          Discount on Notes Payable   XX (interest for period)
          Cash   XX (face amount)
              Paid note (see Entry A)

D.   Notes Receivable   XX (face amount)
     Discount on Notes Receivable   XX (imputed interest)
     Sales   XX (present value of note)
          Sold merchandise, non-interest-bearing note received

E.   Discount on Notes Receivable   XX (amount accrued)
     Interest Income   XX (amount accrued)
          Recorded interest income for one year (see Entry D)

F.   Discount on Notes Receivable   XX (interest for period)
     Cash   XX (face amount of note)
          Interest Income   XX (interest for period)
          Notes Receivable   XX (face amount)
          Received interest on note (see Entry D)

G.   Tractor   XX (present value of payment)
     Accounts Payable   XX (present value of payment)
          Purchased tractor, payment deferred

H.   Accounts Payable   XX (present value of payment)
     Interest Expense   XX (imputed amount)
          Cash   XX (amount paid)
          Paid on account, including imputed interest expense
          (see Entry G)

I.   Accounts Receivable   XX (present value of payment)
     Sales   XX (present value of payment)
          Sold tractor, payment deferred

J.   Cash   XX (amount received)
     Accounts Receivable   XX (present value of payment)
     Interest Income   XX (imputed amount)
          Received payment on account, including imputed interest
          earned (see Entry I)

K. Short-Term Investments   XX (amount invested)

Cash   XX (amount invested)

     Invested idle cash

L. Short-Term Investments   XX (interest for period)

Interest Income   XX (interest for period)

     Earned interest income for period

M. Loan Repayment Fund   XX (amount contributed)

Cash   XX (amount contributed)

     Recorded annual contribution to loan repayment fund

TESTING YOUR KNOWLEDGE

*Matching**

Match each term with its definition by writing the appropriate letter in the blank.

_____ **1.** Interest

_____ **2.** Simple interest

_____ **3.** Compound interest

_____ **4.** Future value

_____ **5.** Present value

_____ **6.** Ordinary annuity

a. The amount that must be invested now at a given rate of interest to produce a given future value

b. Interest computed without considering accrued interest

c. A series of equal payments made at the end of each period

d. The cost of using money for a specific period

e. The amount an investment will be worth at a future date if invested now at compound interest

f. Interest computed on the principal plus accrued interest

**Note to student:* The matching quiz might be completed more efficiently by starting with the definition and searching for the corresponding term.

APPLYING YOUR KNOWLEDGE

Exercises

1. Use Appendix G of the text to answer the following questions:

   a. What amount received today is equivalent to $1,000 receivable at the end of five years, assuming a 6 percent annual interest rate compounded annually?

      $_____

   b. If payments of $1,000 are invested at 8 percent annual interest at the end of each quarter for one year, what amount will accumulate by the time the last payment is made?

      $_____

   c. If $1,000 is invested on June 30, 20x5, at 6 percent annual interest compounded semiannually, how much will be in the account on June 30, 20x7?

      $_____

   d. Compute the equal annual deposits required to accumulate a fund of $100,000 at the end of 20 years, assuming a 10 percent interest rate compounded annually.

      $_____

2. The manager of City Center Bowling is considering replacing the existing automatic pinsetters with improved ones that cost $10,000 each. It is estimated that each new pinsetter will save $2,000 annually and will last for ten years. Using an interest rate of 18 percent and Appendix G of the text, compute the present value of the savings of each new pinsetter.

   $_____

   Should City Center Bowling make the purchase?

3. On January 1, 20x6, Douglas Corporation purchased equipment from Courtright Sales by signing a two-year, non-interest-bearing note for $10,000. Douglas currently pays 10 percent interest on money borrowed. In the journal below, prepare Douglas's journal entries to (a) to record the purchase and the note, (b) adjust the accounts after one year, and (c) record payment of the note after two years. Use Appendix G of the text for information on the time value of money information. Omit explanations.

General Journal				
Date		Description	Debit	Credit

ANSWERS

Chapter 1

Self-Test

1. d	(LO 1)	**6.** d	(LO 5)
2. a	(LO 2)	**7.** a	(LO 5)
3. b	(LO 3)	**8.** d	(LO 6)
4. b	(LO 4)	**9.** a	(LO 7)
5. b	(LO 5)	**10.** c	(LO 8)

Matching

1. h	**7.** s	**13.** u	**19.** d
2. f	**8.** c	**14.** e	**20.** g
3. o	**9.** j	**15.** l	**21.** a
4. r	**10.** v	**16.** q	**22.** p
5. w	**11.** i	**17.** m	**23.** k
6. n	**12.** b	**18.** t	**24.** x

Short Answer

1. (LO 6)
   Nolan Corporation
   Income Statement
   For the Year Ended August 31, 20xx
2. (LO 1) Bookkeeping deals only with the mechanical and repetitive recordkeeping process. Accounting involves bookkeeping as well as the design of an accounting system, its use, and the analysis of its output.

3. (LO 8)
   a. *Integrity*—The accountant is honest, regardless of consequences.
   b. *Objectivity*—The accountant is impartial in performing his or her job.
   c. *Independence*—The accountant avoids all relationships or situations that could impair or appear to impair his or her objectivity.

    d. *Due care*—The accountant carries out his or her responsibilities with competence and diligence.

4. (LO 2) Management, outsiders with a direct financial interest, and outsiders with an indirect financial interest

5. (LO 1) Profitability (earning enough income to attract and hold investment capital) and liquidity (keeping sufficient funds on hand to pay debts as they fall due)

6. (LO 6)

Statement
  a. Income statement
  b. Statement of retained earnings
  c. Balance sheet
  d. Statement of cash flows

Purpose
  a. Measures net income during a certain period
  b. Shows how retained earnings changed during the period
  c. Shows financial position at a point in time
  d. Discloses the cash flows that result from the business's operating, investing, and financing activities during the period

True-False

1. F (LO 6) It is the balance sheet that shows financial position.

2. F (LO 7) The IRS interprets and enforces tax laws.

3. T (LO 5)

4. T (LO 5)

5. F (LO 5) It indicates that the company has one or more debtors.

6. T (LO 5)

7. F (LO 3) The measurement stage refers to the recording of business transactions.

8. F (LO 6) Dividends are a deduction on the statement of retained earnings.

9. T (LO 7)

10. T (LO 4)

11. T (LO 6)

12. T (LO 6)

13. F (LO 7) That is the GASB's responsibility.

14. F (LO 4) A corporation is managed by its board of directors.

15. T (LO 7)

16. F (LO 5) Net assets equal assets *minus* liabilities.

17. F (LO 6) Balance sheets do not list revenues and expenses.

18. F (LO 3) Nonexchange transactions, such as the accumulation of interest, do exist.

19. T (LO 1)

20. T (LO 6)

21. T (LO 3)

22. F (LO 2) Economic planners have an indirect financial interest in accounting information.

23. T (LO 5)

24. F (LO 1) Cash flow is a measure of liquidity.

Multiple Choice

1. a (LO 6) The income statement reports revenues and expenses. Wages Expense would therefore appear on that statement rather than on the balance sheet.

2. c (LO 7) Public corporations must file various reports containing specific financial information with the SEC (Securities and Exchange Commission), the agency that regulates the issuance and trading of stock in the United States. The SEC makes these reports available to the public, thus helping to ensure that investors have complete and accurate information on which to base their decisions.

3. b (LO 4) The owners of a corporation—the stockholders—can easily transfer their shares to other investors.

4. b (LO 6) The balance sheet is in a sense a "snapshot" of a business on a given date. The account balances on the statement are a report of the ultimate effect of financial transactions during an accounting period, not a report of the actual transactions.

5. a (LO 7) The principal purpose of an audit is to verify the quality of the information that a company's management presents in its financial statements. *Fairness* refers to the ability of users of the financial statements to rely on the information as presented.

6. d (LO 5) Collection on an account receivable is simply an exchange of one asset (the account receivable) for another asset (cash). It has no effect on the accounting equation.

7. d (LO 4) The partners *are* the partnership (i.e., there is no separate legal entity in this form of business organization). When a partner leaves the partnership, the original partnership is dissolved, although a new partnership may then be formed by replacing the exiting partner.

8. a (LO 6) "Assets" is a major heading found on the balance sheet; Accounts Receivable is a type of asset.

9. c (LO 5) The payment of a liability reduces both sides of the accounting equation (assets and liabilities) in equal amounts.

10. d (LO 5) The purchase of an asset for cash is an exchange of one asset for another. It results in an increase and a decrease, in equal amounts, on one side of the accounting equation. It therefore has no effect on total assets, liabilities, or stockholders' equity.

11. b (LO 6) The statement of cash flows does not list any "funding" activities.

Exercises

1. (LO 2)
   a. Potential investors need all recent financial statements to assess the future profitability of a company to determine whether they should invest in it.
   b. The principal goal of the SEC is to protect the investing public. Insisting that Atlantic make its statements public as well as examining the statements for propriety certainly will help the public make decisions regarding Atlantic.
   c. The bank would have difficulty in determining Atlantic's ability to repay the loan if it does not have access to Atlantic's most recent financial statements.
   d. Present stockholders will wish to see the statements in order to decide whether to sell, maintain, or increase their investments.
   e. Management will want to see the statements because the statements should help them pinpoint the weaknesses that caused the year's loss.

2. (LO 5) $35,000

3. (LO 6)

Farnsworth's TV Repair Corporation
Balance Sheet
December 31, 20xx

Assets	
Cash	$ 950
Accounts receivable	1,500
Equipment	850
Land	1,000
Building	10,000
Truck	4,500
Total assets	$18,800
Liabilities	
Accounts payable	$ 1,300
Stockholders' Equity	
Common stock	14,500
Retained earnings	3,000
Total liabilities and stockholders' equity	$18,800

4. (LO 5)

Transaction	Cash	Accounts Receivable	Supplies and Equipment	Trucks	Accounts Payable	Common Stock	Retained Earnings
			Assets		**Liabilities**	**Stockholders' Equity**	
a	+$20,000					+$20,000	
b	−650		+$650				
c				+$5,200	+$5,200		
d	+525						+$525
e	−2,600				−2,600		
f		$150					+150
g	−250						−250
h	+150	−150					
i		+20					+20
j	−200						−200
Balance at end of month	$16,975	$20	$650	$5,200	$2,600	$20,000	$245

Solution to Crossword Puzzle
(Chapter 1)

Chapter 2

1. a	(LO 1)		**6.** a	(LO 4)
2. b	(LO 2)		**7.** c	(LO 4)
3. d	(LO 3)		**8.** c	(LO 6)
4. b	(LO 3)		**9.** a	(LO 7)
5. c	(LO 3)		**10.** a	(LO 5)

Matching

1. k		**8.** m		**14.** n
2. f		**9.** l		**15.** p
3. q		**10.** s		**16.** h
4. o		**11.** j		**17.** c
5. b		**12.** r		**18.** i
6. g		**13.** e		**19.** d
7. a				

Short Answer

1. (LO 3) Determine the transaction's effect on the accounts, apply the rules of double entry, make the entry (journalize), post the entry to the ledger, and prepare a trial balance.
2. (LO 1)
   a. July 14
   b. $150
   c. Cash and Accounts Receivable

3. (LO 4) One example is the purchase of an asset for cash. Another example is the collection of an account receivable.
4. (LO 4) One example is the payment of an account payable.
5. (LO 2) Revenues, expenses, and dividends
6. (LO 3) Liabilities, stockholders' equity, and revenues are credited when increased.

True-False

1. F (LO 1) A sale should be recorded when it takes place.
2. T (LO 1)
3. T (LO 2)
4. F (LO 3) The credit side of an account does not imply anything favorable or unfavorable.
5. F (LO 3) Only accounts with zero balances have equal debits and credits.
6. F (LO 7) One can quickly determine cash on hand by referring to the ledger.
7. T (LO 2)

8. F (LO 2) Notes Payable is the proper account title; the liability is evidenced by the existence of a promissory note.
9. T (LO 2)
10. T (LO 3)
11. F (LO 3) It is possible to have only increases or only decreases in a journal entry.
12. F (LO 6) Journal entries are made before transactions are posted to the ledger.
13. F (LO 6) Liabilities and stockholders' equity accounts are indented only when credited.

14. T (LO 6)
15. T (LO 7)
16. T (LO 7)
17. T (LO 3, LO 7)
18. F (LO 2) It is a table of contents to the general ledger.
19. F (LO 5) Unearned Revenue has a normal credit balance.

20. F (LO 2) Retained earnings is not cash and should be shown in the stockholders' equity section.
21. T (LO 2)
22. F (LO 5) They would be divisible by 9.
23. T (LO 5)
24. F (LO 1) It is not a recordable transaction because the product has not been received.

Multiple Choice

1. c (LO 1) Summarization of accounting data occurs at the end of the accounting cycle.

2. d (LO 4) When a liability is paid, each side of the accounting equation is reduced by the same amount. The transaction results in a reduction in an asset and a corresponding reduction in a liability.

3. c (LO 6) The explanation accompanying a journal entry is a brief statement about the entire transaction. Debits and credits are elements of the recorded transaction. The explanation is entered after all debit and credit entries have been made.

4. d (LO 7) The final step in the posting process is the transfer of the ledger account number to the Post. Ref. column of the general journal. It is an indication that all other steps in the process are complete.

5. c (LO 5) If only part of a journal entry has been posted, the information omitted would usually be either a debit or a credit. As a result, total debits would not equal total credits in the general ledger accounts. The trial balance would therefore be out of balance.

6. b (LO 4) When cash is received in payment of an account receivable, one asset is being exchanged for another. Total assets would therefore remain unchanged.

7. a (LO 3) Increasing the Dividends account ultimately causes a reduction in Retained Earnings, a stockholders' equity account. A decrease in stockholders' equity is recorded with a debit.

8. b (LO 2) Of the accounts listed, Prepaid Rent is the only one that is classified as an asset. Unearned Revenue is a liability account, Retained Earnings is a stockholders' equity account, and Fees Earned is a revenue account.

9. a (LO 2) Of the accounts listed, only Interest Payable would represent an amount owed.

10. b (LO 4) Unearned Rent would represent a liability on the accounting records of the *lessor.* The question refers to the possible entries of the *lessee,* which include entries for Prepaid Rent, Rent Payable, and Rent Expense.

11. c (LO 5) Sales is a revenue account. Revenues increase with a credit entry, and therefore Sales is referred to as having a *normal credit balance.* Revenues ultimately cause an increase in Retained Earnings, which also has a normal credit balance.

12. d (LO 5) The use of an incorrect account will not cause a trial balance to be out of balance. However, in this case, both Accounts Receivable and Accounts Payable will be overstated.

Exercises

1. (LO 6)

		General Journal		
Date		**Description**	**Debit**	**Credit**
May	2	Cash	28,000	
		Common Stock		28,000
		Recorded the stockholders' original investment		
	3	Prepaid Rent	900	
		Cash		900
		Paid three months' rent in advance		
	5	Printing Equipment	10,000	
		Photographic Equipment	3,000	
		Cash		2,000
		Accounts Payable		11,000
		Purchased a press and equipment from Irvine Press, Inc.		
	8	No entry		
	9	Cash	1,200	
		Unearned Revenue		1,200
		Received payment in advance from Raymond's Department Store for brochures to be printed		
	11	Printing Supplies	800	
		Notes Payable		800
		Purchased paper from Pacific Paper Co.		
	14	Cash	250	
		Accounts Receivable	250	
		Revenue from Services		500
		Completed job for Sunrise Shoes		
	14	Salaries Expense	200	
		Cash		200
		Paid the pressman his weekly salary		
	15	Accounts Payable	1,000	
		Cash		1,000
		Paid on account amount owed to Irvine Press, Inc.		
	18	Cash	250	
		Accounts Receivable		250
		Sunrise Shoes paid its debt in full		
	20	Dividends	700	
		Cash		700
		The board of directors declared and paid a $700 cash dividend		
	24	Utilities Expense	45	
		Accounts Payable		45
		Recorded electric bill		
	30	Accounts Payable	45	
		Cash		45
		Recorded payment of electric bill		

2. (LO 3)
   a. debit balance of $1,750
   b. credit balance of $1,000
   c. debit balance of $14,600

3. (LO 7)

General Journal					Page 7
Date		**Description**	**Post. Ref.**	**Debit**	**Credit**
Apr.	3	Cash	11	1,000	
		Revenue from Services	41		1,000
		Received payment from Woodley Company for services			
	5	Accounts Payable	21	300	
		Cash	11		300
		Paid Valley Supply Company for supplies purchased			
		on March 31 on credit			

Cash   Account No. 11

						Balance	
Date		**Item**	**Post. Ref.**	**Debit**	**Credit**	**Debit**	**Credit**
Apr.	3		J7	1,000		1,000	
	5		J7		300	700	

Accounts Payable   Account No. 21

						Balance*	
Date		**Item**	**Post. Ref.**	**Debit**	**Credit**	**Debit**	**Credit**
Apr.	5		J7	300		300	

Revenue from Services   Account No. 41

						Balance*	
Date		**Item**	**Post. Ref.**	**Debit**	**Credit**	**Debit**	**Credit**
Apr.	3		J7		1,000		1,000

*Previous postings have been omitted, resulting in an improbable debit balance in Accounts Payable.

Chapter 3

Self-Test

1. a	(LO 1)	**6.** c	(LO 4)
2. d	(LO 4)	**7.** b	(LO 4)
3. d	(LO 2)	**8.** a	(LO 4)
4. c	(LO 2)	**9.** d	(SO 6)
5. a	(LO 3)	**10.** c	(LO 5)

Matching

1. i	**6.** q	**11.** a	**16.** j
2. d	**7.** f	**12.** h	**17.** b
3. n	**8.** k	**13.** m	**18.** g
4. r	**9.** e	**14.** p	
5. c	**10.** o	**15.** l	

Short Answer

1. (LO 4) Dividing recorded expenses between two or more accounting periods; dividing recorded revenues between two or more accounting periods; recording unrecorded expenses; and recording unrecorded revenues
2. (LO 2) The matching rule means that revenues should be recorded in the period in which they are earned and that all expenses related to those revenues also should be recorded in that period.
3. (LO 4) Depreciation is the allocation of the cost of a long-lived asset to the periods benefiting from the asset.

4. (LO 4) Prepaid expenses are expenses paid in advance; they initially are recorded as assets. Unearned revenues represent payments received in advance of providing goods or services; they initially are recorded as liabilities.
5. (LO 3)
   a. A purchase or sale arrangement exists.
   b. Goods have been delivered or services rendered.
   c. The price is fixed or determinable.
   d. Collectibility is reasonably assured.

True-False

1. T (LO 4)
2. T (LO 1)
3. F (LO 2) The calendar year is the period from January 1 to December 31.
4. T (LO 2)
5. F (LO 3) Under accrual accounting, the timing of cash exchanges is irrelevant in recording revenues and expenses.
6. F (LO 5) Adjusting entries are made before the financial statements are prepared.
7. T (LO 4)
8. F (LO 4) It is debited for the amount consumed during the period (the amount available during the period less ending inventory).

9. F (LO 4) Accumulated Depreciation (a contra account) has a credit balance, even though it appears in the asset section of the balance sheet.
10. T (LO 4)
11. F (LO 4) The Unearned Revenues account is a liability account.
12. F (LO 4) The credit is to a liability account.
13. T (LO 5)
14. F (LO 4) If payment has not yet been received, the debit is to Accounts Receivable.
15. T (LO 4)
16. T (LO 2, LO 4)

Multiple Choice

1. c (LO 4) An adjusting entry normally contains at least one balance sheet account and at least one income statement account. Choice **c** does not, nor does it fit the description for any adjusting entry.

2. b (LO 4) Office supplies are not considered long-lived assets subject to periodic depreciation, as are the other items listed. Instead, they are expensed once they have been consumed (used up).

3. b (LO 4) Unearned Fees is used to record a firm's liability for amounts received but not yet earned. This recognition is required so that revenue amounts can be represented properly and allocated in the appropriate accounting period. As the revenues are earned, the proper amounts are transferred from liabilities to revenues. Between the time the revenues are received and the time they actually are earned, one accounting period may have ended and another accounting period may have begun.

4. a (LO 4) Depreciation is the allocation of the cost of an asset over the asset's expected useful life. The matching rule requires the allocation of the cost while the asset is being used in a firm's revenue-generating activities.

5. c (LO 5) Net income is the result of the calculation that nets revenues and expenses. The adjusted trial balance contains summary balances of each general ledger account after adjusting entries have been made.

6. d (LO 4) The adjustment debiting Interest Receivable and crediting Interest Income is required so that interest income for the period is recorded, even though the interest has not yet been received.

7. a (LO 2) Estimates are involved in the preparation of account balances used to report net income. An example of this kind of estimate is the recording of depreciation expense. Although not exact, the reported net income of one accounting period can be compared with the net income of other accounting periods, providing a basis for conclusions about the firm.

8. d (LO 4) Until Prepaid Rent is expired and is recorded as an expense through adjustments, it remains an asset on a firm's books.

9. b (LO 4) Because of the nature of accruals and deferrals, Cash is *never* involved in the end-of-period adjustments.

10. c (LO 5) After preparation of the trial balance, but before preparation of the adjusted trial balance, an adjusting entry is made to record office supplies consumed. This entry reduces the Office Supplies account and increases the Office Supplies Expense account.

Exercises

1. (LO 5)

Norton Transit Company
Partial Balance Sheet
December 31, 20x5

Assets		
Cash		$ 5,000
Accounts receivable		3,000
Company vehicles	$24,000	
Less accumulated depreciation,		
Company vehicles	9,000	15,000
Total assets		$23,000

---

2. (LO 4)
  a. $970 ($510 + $800 − $340)
  b. $1,750 [($14,000 ÷ 4 yrs.) × ½ yr.]
  c. $450 ($600 × ¾)

3. (LO 4)

General Journal				
Date*		**Description**	**Debit**	**Credit**
a.		Supplies Expense	125	
		Supplies		125
		Recorded supplies consumed during the period		
b.		Wages Expense	2,000	
		Wages Payable		2,000
		Recorded accrued wages		
c.		Unearned Revenues	600	
		Revenues from Services		600
		Recorded earned revenues		
d.		Depreciation Expense, Buildings	4,500	
		Accumulated Depreciation, Buildings		4,500
		Recorded depreciation on buildings		
e.		Advertising Expense	2,000	
		Prepaid Advertising		2,000
		Recorded advertising used during the year		
f.		Insurance Expense	250	
		Prepaid Insurance		250
		Recorded insurance expired during the year		
g.		Accounts Receivable	2,200	
		Revenues from Services		2,200
		Recorded revenues earned for which payment has not been received		
h.		Interest Expense	52	
		Interest Payable		52
		Recorded accrued interest on a note payable		
i.		Income Taxes Expense	21,700	
		Income Taxes Payable		21,700
		Recorded accrued income tax expense		

*In reality, all of the adjusting entries would be dated December 31.

4. (SO 6)

    a. $6,200 ($1,200 + $8,700 − $3,700)

    b. $35,400 ($900 + $35,000 − $500)

    c. $3,000 ($1,800 + $3,600 − $2,400)

Solution to Crossword Puzzle
(Chapters 2 and 3)

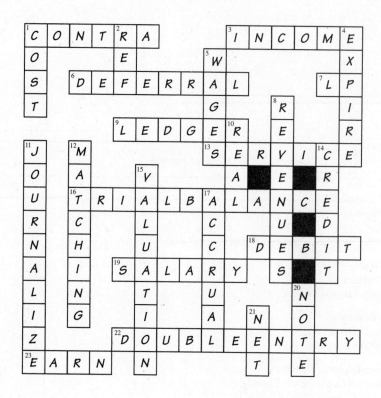

Chapter 4

Self-Test

1. b	(LO 2)	**6.** d	(SO 7)
2. c	(LO 5)	**7.** c	(SO 8)
3. d	(LO 5)	**8.** a	(LO 1)
4. c	(LO 5)	**9.** b	(LO 4)
5. b	(LO 6)	**10.** d	(LO 3)

Matching

1. h	**5.** i	**9.** b	**13.** e
2. o	**6.** f	**10.** l	**14.** k
3. g	**7.** j	**11.** d	**15.** n
4. m	**8.** p	**12.** c	**16.** a

Short Answer

1. (LO 5) Revenue accounts, expense accounts, Income Summary, Dividends
2. (SO 8) Trial Balance, Adjustments, Adjusted Trial Balance, Income Statement, Balance Sheet
3. (LO 6) Assets, liabilities, and stockholders' equity accounts will appear. Revenue and expense accounts, Income Summary, and the Dividends account will not appear.
4. (SO 7) Reversing entries enable the bookkeeper to make simple, routine journal entries and avoid more complicated ones.
5. (LO 2) The steps should be numbered as follows: 3, 5, 1, 4, 2, 6.
6. (LO 1)
   a. Cost-benefit principle: The benefits of the system must match or exceed its cost.
   b. Control principle: The system must provide good internal control.
   c. Compatibility principle: The system must be in harmony with the company and its personnel.
   d. Flexibility principle: The system must be able to accommodate change.

True-False

1. T (SO 8)
2. T (SO 8)
3. T (SO 8)
4. T (SO 8)
5. F (LO 5) Income Summary does not appear on any statement.
6. F (LO 5) Only nominal accounts are closed.
7. T (LO 5)
8. F (LO 5) The Dividends account is closed to Retained Earnings.
9. F (LO 5) When there is a net loss, Income Summary is credited.
10. T (SO 7)
11. F (SO 8) The work sheet is never published.
12. F (SO 8) A key letter is needed in the Adjustments columns to relate debits and credits of the same entry.
13. T (SO 8)
14. F (LO 6) It does not include Dividends because that account will have a zero balance.
15. F (SO 7) Reversing entries, dated the first day of the new accounting period, serve to simplify the bookkeeping process.
16. T (LO 5)
17. T (LO 3)
18. T (LO 4)
19. F (LO 4) Edgar is the SEC's online warehouse of financial information.

1. c (LO 6) Retained Earnings is the only account listed that would remain open after the closing procedures are complete at the end of the accounting cycle. The post-closing trial balance is a listing of such accounts, along with their account balances.

2. d (LO 5) Of the choices given, this is the only one that presents a sequence in which it would be possible to perform the tasks.

3. b (SO 7) By definition, reversing entries are the opposite of the related adjusting entries.

4. a (SO 8) The amount used to balance the Income Statement and Balance Sheet columns of the work sheet is the net income or net loss. When the amount required to bring the Balance Sheet columns into balance on the work sheet is an entry to the credit column, there had to have been a net income. The corresponding amount to bring the Income Statement columns into balance will be to the debit column.

5. a (LO 5) Of the accounts listed, Unearned Commissions is the only one not involved in the closing process. Unearned Commissions is a permanent balance sheet account and remains open from one period to the next if it contains a balance.

6. b (LO 5) When Income Summary has a debit balance after expenses and revenues have been closed, the account is closed by a credit entry equal to the debit balance. The corresponding debit is an entry to Retained Earnings, reducing the balance of that account by an amount equal to the net loss for the period.

7. c (LO 5) Updating the revenue and expense accounts is the purpose of the adjusting entries. The closing entries are prepared after the adjusting entries.

8. a (SO 8) The facts given include all the components of a statement of owner's equity except net income or loss. A net income of $55,000 will correctly answer the question.

9. c (LO 5) Temporary accounts are those that appear on the income statement. They also are referred to as *nominal accounts*.

10. c (LO 1) The design of a firm's accounting information system must anticipate changes in the business. This accommodation for potential change is called the *flexibility principle*.

Exercises

1. (LO 5)

General Journal

Date		Description	Debit	Credit
July	31	Revenue from Services	4,700	
		Income Summary		4,700
		Closed the revenue account		
	31	Income Summary	700	
		Rent Expense		500
		Telephone Expense		50
		Utilities Expense		150
		Closed the expense accounts		
	31	Income Summary	4,000	
		Retained Earnings		4,000
		Closed the Income Summary account		
	31	Retained Earnings	2,500	
		Dividends		2,500
		Closed the dividends account		

2. (SO 8)

Frank's Fix-It Services, Inc.
Statement of Retained Earnings
For the Month Ended July 31, 20xx

Retained Earnings, July 1, 20xx	$3,000
Net Income	4,000
Subtotal	$7,000
Less Dividends	2,500
Retained Earnings, July 31, 20xx	$4,500

3. (SO 8)

Mike's Maintenance, Inc.
Work Sheet
For the Year Ended December 31, 20xx

Account Name	Trial Balance Debit	Trial Balance Credit	Adjustments Debit	Adjustments Credit	Adjusted Trial Balance Debit	Adjusted Trial Balance Credit	Income Statement Debit	Income Statement Credit	Balance Sheet Debit	Balance Sheet Credit
Cash	2,560				2,560				2,560	
Accounts Receivable	880		(e) 50		930				930	
Prepaid Rent	750			(a) 550	200				200	
Lawn Supplies	250			(c) 150	100				100	
Lawn Equipment	10,000				10,000				10,000	
Accum. Deprec., Lawn Equipment		2,000		(b) 1,500		3,500				3,500
Accounts Payable		630				630				630
Unearned Landscaping Fees		300	(f) 120			180				180
Common Stock		5,000				5,000				5,000
Retained Earnings		1,000				1,000				1,000
Dividends	6,050				6,050				6,050	
Grass-Cutting Fees		15,000		(e) 50		15,050		15,050		
Wages Expense	3,300		(d) 280		3,580		3,580			
Gasoline Expense	140				140		140			
	23,930	23,930								
Rent Expense			(a) 550		550		550			
Depreciation Expense, Lawn Equipment			(b) 1,500		1,500		1,500			
Lawn Supplies Expense			(c) 150		150		150			
Landscaping Fees Earned				(f) 120		120		120		
Wages Payable				(d) 280		280				280
Income Taxes Expense			(g) 1,570		1,570		1,570			
Income Taxes Payable				(g) 1,570		1,570				1,570
			4,220	4,220	27,330	27,330	7,490	15,170	19,840	12,160
Net Income							7,680			7,680
							15,170	15,170	19,840	19,840

4. (SO 7)

		General Journal	Debit	Credit
Date		Description		
Dec.	1	Cash	20,000	
		Notes Payable		20,000
		Recorded 90-day bank note		
	31	Interest Expense	200	
		Interest Payable		200
		Recorded accrued interest on note ($20,000 × .12 × 1/12)		
	31	Income Summary	200	
		Interest Expense		200
		Closed interest expense account		
Jan.	1	Interest Payable	200	
		Interest Expense		200
		Reversed adjusting entry for interest expense		
Mar.	1	Notes Payable	20,000	
		Interest Expense	600	
		Cash		20,600
		Recorded payment of note plus interest		

Chapter 5

Self-Test

1. c	(LO 5)		**6.** b	(LO 5)
2. b	(LO 2)		**7.** a	(LO 6)
3. a	(LO 3)		**8.** c	(LO 7)
4. c	(LO 4)		**9.** c	(LO 7)
5. b	(LO 5)		**10.** d	(LO 5)

Matching

1. e	**6.** q	**10.** f	**14.** a
2. l	**7.** k	**11.** o	**15.** h
3. p	**8.** b	**12.** j	**16.** n
4. c	**9.** m	**13.** i	**17.** d
5. g			

Short Answer

1. (LO 5)

Business Organization	Name for Equity Section
Sole proprietorship	Owner's equity
Partnership	Partners' equity
Corporation	Stockholders' equity

2. (LO 7) *Profit margin* shows net income in relation to net sales.

Asset turnover shows how efficiently assets are used to produce sales.

Return on assets shows net income in relation to average total assets.

Return on equity shows net income in relation to average owner's investment.

Debt to equity ratio shows the proportion of a business financed by creditors and the proportion financed by owners.

3. (LO 7) *Working capital* equals current assets minus current liabilities.

Current ratio equals current assets divided by current liabilities.

4. (LO 3) *Consistency and comparability*—Applying the same accounting procedures from one period to the next

Materiality—The relative importance of an item or event

Cost-benefit—Ensuring that the cost of providing accounting information does not exceed the benefits gained from it

Conservatism—Choosing the accounting procedure that will be least likely to overstate assets and income

Full disclosure—Showing all relevant information in the financial statements or in the notes

1. F (LO 5) They are considered current assets if collection is expected within the normal operating cycle, even if that cycle is longer than one year.
2. T (LO 6)
3. T (LO 6)
4. F (LO 6) Operating expenses consist of selling expenses and general and administrative expenses only.
5. T (LO 2)
6. T (LO 7)
7. F (LO 5) Short-term investments in stock are included in the current assets section of a balance sheet.
8. F (LO 7) Liquidity is what is being defined.
9. F (LO 5) The operating cycle can be less than one year.

10. F (LO 5) *Net worth* is merely another term for owners' equity and would rarely equal the market value of net assets.
11. T (LO 6)
12. F (LO 6) The net income figures will be the same, although they are arrived at differently.
13. F (LO 7) Working capital equals current assets *minus* current liabilities.
14. T (LO 7)
15. F (LO 2) Reliability is what is being described.
16. F (LO 6) Earnings per share is a measure of profitability.
17. F (LO 3) The dividing line between material and immaterial is a judgment call and varies from company to company.

Multiple Choice

1. c (LO 5) The conversion of inventories to cash is the basis for a firm's operations. This conversion cycle (called the *normal operating cycle*) is frequently less than one year. However, if it is longer than one year, the inventory by definition is still classified as a current asset.
2. c (LO 6) The single-step income statement does not isolate gross margin from sales. Instead, cost of goods sold is combined with other operating expenses and then subtracted from total revenues to arrive at income from operations.
3. b (LO 7) The current ratio gives creditors information about a firm's liquidity—that is, its ability to pay its debts.
4. d (LO 5) The owner's capital account would appear on the balance sheet of a sole proprietorship or partnership only.
5. a (LO 7) The ratio described is profit margin, which shows the relationship between net income and net sales.

6. c (LO 6) *Operating expenses* is a broad term referring to all the expenses of running a company other than cost of goods sold and income taxes.
7. d (LO 1) Each choice except **d** describes an objective of FASB *Statement of Financial Accounting Concepts No. 1*. The FASB statement stresses *external* use of financial information, and management consists of internal users.
8. d (LO 7) One calculation of return on assets is profit margin times asset turnover, which in this case equals 12 percent.
9. b (LO 6) Because a service company does not sell merchandise, it does not use a cost of goods sold account. Thus, a gross margin figure could not be obtained.

Exercises

1. (LO 5)

1. d	**5.** a	**9.** f	**13.** *X*
2. e	**6.** c	**10.** e	**14.** a
3. c	**7.** a	**11.** d	**15.** e
4. g	**8.** b	**12.** a	

2. (LO 7)

   a. $40,000 ($60,000 − $20,000)

   b. 3 ($60,000/$20,000)

   c. 10% ($25,000/$250,000)

   d. 12.5% ($25,000/$200,000)

   e. 16.7% ($25,000/$150,000)

   f. 1.25 times ($250,000/$200,000)

3. (LO 6)

a.

Lassen Corporation
Income Statement (Multistep)
For the Year Ended December 31, 20xx

Net sales	$200,000
Less cost of goods sold	150,000
Gross margin	$ 50,000
Operating expenses	30,000
Income from operations	$ 20,000
Other revenues	
Interest income	2,000
Income before income taxes	$ 22,000
Income taxes	5,000
Net income	$ 17,000
Earnings per share	$4.86

b.

Lassen Corporation
Income Statement (Single-Step)
For the Year Ended December 31, 20xx

Revenues		
Net sales	$200,000	
Interest income	2,000	$202,000
Costs and expenses		
Cost of goods sold	$150,000	
Operating expenses	30,000	180,000
Income before income taxes		$ 22,000
Income taxes		5,000
Net income		$ 17,000
Earnings per share		$4.86

Solution to Crossword Puzzle
(Chapters 4 and 5)

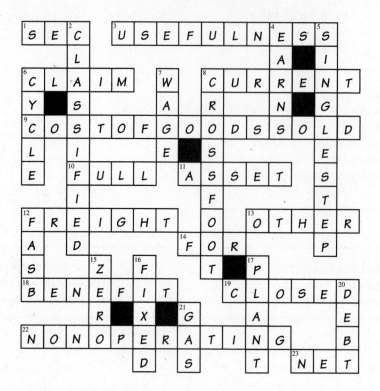

Chapter 6

Self-Test

1. a	(LO 1)	**6.** a	(LO 4)
2. d	(LO 3, LO 4)	**7.** d	(LO 3)
3. b	(LO 3, LO 4)	**8.** c	(LO 5)
4. a	(LO 4)	**9.** b	(LO 5)
5. c	(SO 7)	**10.** d	(LO 6)

Matching

1. h		**6.** k		**11.** m		**16.** r
2. e		**7.** c		**12.** a		**17.** j
3. q		**8.** g		**13.** f		**18.** o
4. b		**9.** i		**14.** p		
5. l		**10.** d		**15.** n		

Short Answer

1. (LO 5)

   Requiring authorization for certain transactions

   Recording all transactions

   Using well-designed documents

   Establishing physical controls over assets and records

   Making periodic independent checks of records and assets

   Separating duties

   Employing sound personnel procedures

2. (LO 6) Any six of the following would answer the question:

   Separating the authorization, recordkeeping, and custodianship of cash

   Limiting access to cash

   Designating a person to handle cash

   Maximizing the use of banking facilities and minimizing cash on hand

   Bonding employees who have access to cash

   Protecting cash on hand with safes, cash registers, and similar equipment

   Conducting surprise audits of the cash on hand

   Recording cash receipts promptly

   Depositing cash receipts promptly

   Paying by check

   Having someone who is not involved with cash transactions reconcile the Cash account

3. (LO 6) Purchase order, invoice, and receiving report

4. (LO 4)

   Beginning merchandise inventory

   + Net cost of purchases

   = Goods available for sale

   − Ending merchandise inventory

   = Cost of goods sold

5. (LO 4)

   Purchases

   − Purchases returns and allowances

   − Purchases discounts

   = Net purchases

   + Freight in

   = Net cost of purchases

1. F (LO 4) *Beginning* inventory is needed.
2. F (LO 2) It means that payment is due ten days *after* the end of the month.
3. T (LO 1)
4. T (LO 1, LO 3)
5. T (LO 2)
6. F (SO 7) It is a contra account to *sales*.
7. T (LO 4)
8. T (LO 4)
9. T (LO 1)
10. T (LO 4)
11. F (LO 3, LO 4) It normally has a debit balance.
12. F (LO 4) It requires a debit to Office Supplies (office supplies are not merchandise).
13. T (LO 3)
14. F (LO 2) They treat it as a selling expense.
15. F (LO 4) Both are done at the end of the period.
16. F (LO 2) A trade discount is a percentage off the list or catalogue price; 2/10, n/30 is a sales discount, offered for early payment.
17. F (LO 2) Title passes at the shipping point.
18. F (LO 5) It increases the probability of accuracy but will not guarantee it.
19. T (LO 5)
20. F (LO 6) This procedure could easily lead to theft.
21. F (LO 6) The company sends the supplier a purchase order.
22. F (LO 5) Rotating employees is good internal control because it might uncover theft.
23. T (LO 5)

Multiple Choice

1. d (SO 7) According to the terms, Dew would be entitled to a 2 percent purchases discount of $10. In this example (after allowing for the purchase returns), the discount would be entered as a credit to balance the journal entry, which would also include a debit to Accounts Payable for the balance due ($500) and a credit to Cash for the balance due less the discount ($490).
2. c (LO 4) Purchase Returns and Allowances is a contra account to the Purchases account. Purchases has a normal debit balance. Its corresponding contra accounts have normal credit balances.
3. b (LO 4) Freight Out Expense is a selling expense; it is not an element of cost of goods sold.
4. d (LO 6) The purchase requisition is the initial request for materials filed by the person or department that needs them.
5. a (LO 6) To prevent theft by employees, internal control procedures should separate recordkeeping from the handling of assets.
6. c (LO 3) Under the perpetual inventory system, purchases of merchandise are recorded in the Merchandise Inventory account, not in a Purchases account.
7. b (LO 1) When operating expenses are paid for has no bearing on the length of the operating cycle.
8. d (LO 2) The entry would also include a debit to Credit Card Discount Expense for $50 and a credit to Sales for $1,000.
9. a (LO 1) The financing period equals the number of days taken to sell inventory, plus the number of days to make collection, minus the number of days the company takes to pay its suppliers for the goods (45 + 60 − 30 = 75).

Exercises

1. (LO 4, SO 7)

<table>
<tr><td colspan="5" align="center">**General Journal**</td></tr>
<tr><td colspan="2" align="center">**Date**</td><td align="center">**Description**</td><td align="center">**Debit**</td><td align="center">**Credit**</td></tr>
<tr><td>May</td><td>1</td><td>Purchases
   Accounts Payable
      Purchased merchandise on credit, terms 2/10, n/60</td><td align="right">500</td><td align="right">500</td></tr>
<tr><td></td><td>3</td><td>Accounts Receivable
   Sales
      Sold merchandise on credit, terms 2/10, 1/20, n/30</td><td align="right">500</td><td align="right">500</td></tr>
<tr><td></td><td>4</td><td>Freight In
   Cash
      Paid for freight charges</td><td align="right">42</td><td align="right">42</td></tr>
<tr><td></td><td>5</td><td>Office Supplies
   Accounts Payable
      Purchased office supplies on credit</td><td align="right">100</td><td align="right">100</td></tr>
<tr><td></td><td>6</td><td>Accounts Payable
   Office Supplies
      Returned office supplies from May 5 purchase</td><td align="right">20</td><td align="right">20</td></tr>
<tr><td></td><td>7</td><td>Accounts Payable
   Purchases Returns and Allowances
      Returned merchandise from May 1 purchase</td><td align="right">50</td><td align="right">50</td></tr>
<tr><td></td><td>9</td><td>Accounts Receivable
   Sales
      Sold merchandise on credit, terms 2/10, 1/15, n/30</td><td align="right">225</td><td align="right">225</td></tr>
<tr><td></td><td>10</td><td>Accounts Payable
   Purchases Discounts
   Cash
      Paid for purchase of May 1</td><td align="right">450</td><td align="right">9
441</td></tr>
<tr><td></td><td>14</td><td>Sales Returns and Allowances
   Accounts Receivable
      Accepted return of merchandise from customer of May 9</td><td align="right">25</td><td align="right">25</td></tr>
<tr><td></td><td>22</td><td>Cash
Sales Discounts
   Accounts Receivable
      Received payment from customer of May 9 within discount period</td><td align="right">198
2</td><td align="right">200</td></tr>
<tr><td></td><td>26</td><td>Cash
   Accounts Receivable
      Received payment from customer of May 3</td><td align="right">500</td><td align="right">500</td></tr>
</table>

2. (LO 4, SO 7)

<table>
<tr><td colspan="4" align="center">**Gaviota Merchandising Company**
Partial Income Statement
For the Year 20xx</td></tr>
<tr><td>Gross sales</td><td></td><td></td><td>$100,000</td></tr>
<tr><td>Less sales discounts</td><td></td><td>$ 300</td><td></td></tr>
<tr><td>Less sales returns and allowances</td><td></td><td>200</td><td>500</td></tr>
<tr><td>Net sales</td><td></td><td></td><td>$ 99,500</td></tr>
<tr><td>Less cost of goods sold</td><td></td><td></td><td></td></tr>
<tr><td>   Merchandise inventory, January 1</td><td></td><td>$10,000</td><td></td></tr>
<tr><td>   Purchases</td><td>$50,000</td><td></td><td></td></tr>
<tr><td>   Less purchases discounts</td><td>500</td><td></td><td></td></tr>
<tr><td>   Less purchases returns and allowances</td><td>500</td><td></td><td></td></tr>
<tr><td>   Net purchases</td><td>$49,000</td><td></td><td></td></tr>
<tr><td>   Freight in</td><td>2,000</td><td></td><td></td></tr>
<tr><td>   Net cost of purchases</td><td></td><td>51,000</td><td></td></tr>
<tr><td>   Goods available for sale</td><td></td><td>$61,000</td><td></td></tr>
<tr><td>   Less merchandise inventory, December 31</td><td></td><td>8,000</td><td></td></tr>
<tr><td>   Cost of goods sold</td><td></td><td></td><td>53,000</td></tr>
<tr><td>Gross margin</td><td></td><td></td><td>$ 46,500</td></tr>
</table>

Chapter 7

Self-Test

1.	b	(LO 1)	**6.**	d	(LO 4)
2.	c	(LO 2)	**7.**	c	(LO 4)
3.	a	(LO 3)	**8.**	d	(LO 5)
4.	a	(LO 4)	**9.**	d	(LO 5)
5.	c	(LO 4)	**10.**	b	(SO 6)

Matching

1. j	**6.** e	**11.** c	**16.** n
2. g	**7.** r	**12.** o	**17.** q
3. f	**8.** l	**13.** s	**18.** a
4. m	**9.** i	**14.** h	**19.** b
5. p	**10.** t	**15.** d	**20.** k

Short Answer

1. (LO 4) Percentage of net sales method, accounts receivable aging method, and direct charge-off method
2. (LO 1) It means that the original payee, who discounts the note receivable, must make good on the note if the maker does not pay at maturity.
3. (LO 4) There would be a debit balance when more accounts are written off (in dollar amounts) than have been provided for in the adjusting entries for estimated uncollectible accounts.
4. (LO 3) Held-to-maturity securities, trading securities, and available-for-sale securities
5. (LO 1) Cash and cash equivalents, short-term investments, and accounts and notes receivable due within the current period.
6. (SO 6) Examples are a customer's NSF check; a bank's service charges; a bank's miscellaneous charges for collecting and paying notes, stopping payments, and printing checks; an error in recording a check (only if the amount is understated)

True-False

1. T (LO 4)
2. F (LO 4) It follows the matching rule.
3. F (LO 4) The balance must be taken into account.
4. T (LO 4)
5. T (LO 4)
6. T (LO 4)
7. F (LO 5) The computation is $700 \times 5/100 \times 90/360$.
8. T (LO 4)
9. F (LO 1) The payee must make good if the maker defaults.
10. F (LO 5) It has a duration of 62 days.
11. T (LO 1)
12. F (LO 4) Total assets remain the same.
13. T (LO 5)
14. F (LO 4) The debit is to Allowance for Uncollectible Accounts.
15. T (LO 5)

16. T (SO 6)

17. F (LO 2) Accounts Receivable are a short-term liquid asset but not a cash equivalent.

18. F (LO 1) Major credit cards involve factoring without recourse.

19. F (LO 1) It equals short-term liquid assets divided by current liabilities.

20. T (LO 2)

21. T (LO 3)

22. F (LO 3) They appear at market value.

23. T (LO 1)

Multiple Choice

1. b (LO 5) Principal × rate × time for *b* equals $12. Each of the other choices results in $6.

2. c (LO 4) Under the percentage of net sales method, the amount of the Uncollectible Accounts Expense is based on the sales during the period. Therefore, it is not netted with an existing balance in the allowance account.

3. a (LO 1) Because the discounting bank has the right to extract funds from a firm's account if a note is dishonored, the firm carries that liability until such time as the note is paid to the bank. Once the note is paid, the contingent liability is eliminated.

4. b (LO 4) Under this method, Uncollectible Accounts Expense equals the amount deemed uncollectible ($850) minus the credit balance in Allowance for Uncollectible Accounts ($300), or $550.

5. c (LO 4) When an allowance account is established to record anticipated uncollectible accounts, the expense is recorded at the time the adjusting entry is made. When the actual uncollectible account is known and written off, the allowance account is reduced, and Accounts Receivable is reduced by the same amount.

6. a (LO 5) The discount rate is used as an adjustment to the maturity value of a note to calculate the proceeds on discounting that note to the bank. A note would not show the discount rate because the rate is not known at the time the note is written. In addition, whether a note is going to be discounted or not is irrelevant in determining the note's specifications.

7. b (LO 4) The direct charge-off method of handling uncollectible accounts often postpones the uncollectible accounts expense of a given accounting period to subsequent accounting periods. Usually, a significant period of time elapses between a credit sale and the determination that the corresponding receivable is uncollectible.

8. c (LO 1) Short-term financial assets consist of cash or assets that can be converted quickly to cash to cover operating expenses and immediate cash requirements. Although a firm's ability to convert its inventory to cash is the basis of its operations, inventory is not considered a short-term financial asset.

9. c (LO 3) They are labeled accumulated other comprehensive income.

10. b (SO 6) The company presumably has already recorded the deposits in transit. However, it would not have learned of the bank's service charges, the note collected by the bank, or the bank error until it received its bank statement, and it must therefore adjust for those items.

Exercises

1. (LO 4, 5)

<table>
<tr><td colspan="5" align="center">General Journal</td></tr>
<tr><td colspan="2" align="center">Date</td><td align="center">Description</td><td align="center">Debit</td><td align="center">Credit</td></tr>
<tr><td>Dec.</td><td>31</td><td>Interest Receivable
    Interest Income
        To record accrued interest on Notes Receivable</td><td>75</td><td>75</td></tr>
<tr><td></td><td>31</td><td>Uncollectible Accounts Expense
    Allowance for Uncollectible Accounts
        To record estimated bad debts</td><td>24,000</td><td>24,000</td></tr>
<tr><td>Jan.</td><td>3</td><td>Notes Receivable
    Accounts Receivable, Kohn
        Kohn substituted a 30-day, 6 percent note for her debt</td><td>10,000</td><td>10,000</td></tr>
<tr><td></td><td>8</td><td>Allowance for Uncollectible Accounts
    Accounts Receivable, O'Brien
        To write off O'Brien's account</td><td>1,000</td><td>1,000</td></tr>
<tr><td></td><td>25</td><td>Accounts Receivable, O'Brien
    Allowance for Uncollectible Accounts
        To reinstate portion of O'Brien's account</td><td>600</td><td>600</td></tr>
<tr><td></td><td>28</td><td>Cash
    Accounts Receivable, O'Brien
        Collection from O'Brien</td><td>200</td><td>200</td></tr>
</table>

2. (LO 5)
    a. $16.00
    b. $910.00
    c. $43.17
    d. $4.00

3. (LO 3)

<table>
<tr><td colspan="5" align="center">General Journal</td></tr>
<tr><td colspan="2" align="center">Date</td><td align="center">Description</td><td align="center">Debit</td><td align="center">Credit</td></tr>
<tr><td>Nov.</td><td>17</td><td>Short-Term Investments
    Cash
        Purchased Welu stock for trading</td><td>60,000</td><td>60,000</td></tr>
<tr><td>Dec.</td><td>31</td><td>Unrealized Loss on Investments
    Allowance to Adjust Short-Term Investments to Market
        Year-end adjustment for market decline</td><td>4,000</td><td>4,000</td></tr>
<tr><td>Jan.</td><td>12</td><td>Cash
    Short-Term Investments
    Realized Gain on Investments
        To record sale of Welu stock</td><td>66,000</td><td>60,000
6,000</td></tr>
</table>

Solution to Crossword Puzzle
(Chapters 6 and 7)

						¹B			²F			
³A	⁴D	E	P	O	S	I	T		⁵O	R	D	E	R
G	I			L		R			R			
I	S		⁶C	O	L	L	U	S	I	⁷O	N	
N	C		A			A			N	N	
⁸G	O	O	D	S	S	O	L	D		L	B	
	U		H				⁹R	E	P	O	R	T
¹⁰D	N		¹¹T	■	¹²F					A	
¹³I	N	T	E	R	N	A	L	¹⁴C	O	N	T	R	O	¹⁵L
R	I		A		C		O			D		O
E	N		N		T		¹⁶L				S
C	G		¹⁷S	H	O	R	T	T	E	R	M	S
T			F	■	R	■	R	■	N		¹⁸A
¹⁹N	O	T	E	S		²⁰B	A	D	D	E	B	T	S
		R					S			M	

Chapter 8

Self-Test

1.	b	(LO 5)	**6.**	d	(LO 1)
2.	a	(LO 2)	**7.**	c	(LO 3)
3.	c	(LO 3)	**8.**	d	(LO 6)
4.	b	(LO 3)	**9.**	d	(SO 7)
5.	d	(LO 3)	**10.**	d	(SO 7)

Matching

1. m	**5.** j	**9.** c	**13.** k
2. h	**6.** n	**10.** l	**14.** a
3. d	**7.** o	**11.** e	**15.** f
4. g	**8.** p	**12.** b	**16.** i

Short Answer

1. (LO 3) Specific identification; average-cost; first-in, first-out; and last-in, first-out methods
2. (LO 6) Item-by-item and major category methods
3. (SO 7) Retail method and gross profit method
4. (LO 3, LO 4) The periodic system does not keep detailed records of inventory; the perpetual system does. Under the periodic system, physical inventory taken at the end of each period determines the cost of goods sold.
5. (LO 1) Raw materials, work in process, and finished goods

True-False

1. T (LO 1)
2. T (LO 5)
3. T (LO 5)
4. T (LO 5)
5. F (LO 2) They belong in the buyer's ending inventory if the buyer has title to the goods.
6. T (LO 3)
7. F (LO 3) This is not necessarily true. The actual flow of goods is not known; the flow of costs is assumed.
8. F (LO 3) It results in the highest income.
9. T (SO 7)
10. F (SO 7) The cost of goods sold is estimated by subtracting the gross profit percentage of sales from total sales.
11. F (LO 3) The average-cost method results in a higher income before income taxes.
12. F (LO 5) The requirement is for LIFO, not FIFO.
13. F (LO 2) The consignee has possession of the goods but does not have title to them.
14. T (LO 5)
15. F (LO 1) Very little money would be tied up in inventories.

Multiple Choice

1. **b** (LO 2) Because the cost of storing goods is usually too difficult to trace to specific items of inventory, it is expensed when incurred. The other costs listed are more closely related to the cost of acquiring inventory.

2. **a** (LO 5) The FIFO method matches current selling prices with the oldest, least expensive costs. In periods of rising prices, this method yields a higher income before income taxes than the other inventory costing methods.

3. **c** (LO 5) When an item in a warehouse is not included in inventory, it results in an understated ending inventory, which, in turn, produces an overstated cost of goods sold. An overstated cost of goods sold produces an understated income before income taxes and thus an understated stockholders' equity.

4. **c** (LO 3) With low-volume, high-priced goods, it is especially important to match the selling price of an item with its cost in order to avoid distortion in the financial statements. Only the specific identification method directly matches cost and selling price.

5. **b** (SO 7) In the retail method calculation, freight in is incorporated at cost, not at retail.

6. **a** (LO 1) The matching rule states that a cost must be expensed in the period in which it helps to generate revenue. Thus, the cost of inventory is expensed in the period in which the inventory is sold.

7. **d** (LO 2) Inventory should appear on the balance sheet of the company that has title to the goods even if the company does not have possession of them.

8. **d** (SO 7) The gross profit method is a simple way of estimating the amount of inventory lost or destroyed by fire, theft, or other hazards. It assumes a relatively consistent gross profit ratio over time.

9. **b** (LO 1) Unlike the other three choices, office wages are not factory-related and thus would not be included in the cost of a manufactured item.

Exercises

1. (LO 3)
   a. $6,600; $8,800
   b. $7,200; $8,200
   c. $6,820; $8,580

2. (SO 7)

	Cost	Retail	
Beginning inventory	$ 70,000	$125,000	
Net purchases	48,000	75,000	
Freight in	2,000	—	
Cost/retail	$120,000 ÷	$200,000	= 60%
Less sales		156,000	
Estimated ending inventory at retail		$ 44,000	
		× 60%	
Estimated cost of ending inventory		$ 26,400	

3. (SO 7)

Beginning inventory at cost	$150,000
Purchases at cost	120,000
Cost of goods available for sale	$270,000
Less estimated cost of goods sold	
($300,000 × 80%)	240,000
Estimated cost of ending inventory	$ 30,000

4. (LO 4)

May 1	Beginning Inventory	100 units @ $10				$1,000
4	Purchase	60 units @ $12				720
8	Sale	50 units @ $12				(600)
8	Balance	100 units @ $10	$1,000			
		10 units @$12	120		$1,120	
17	Purchase	70 units @ $11				770
31	Sale	70 units @ $11	($ 770)			
		10 units @ $12	(120)			
		20 units @ $10	(200)		(1,090)	
31	Ending Inventory	80 units @ $10			$ 800	

Cost of Goods Sold = $600 + $1,090 $1,690

5. (LO 4)

May 1	Beginning Inventory	100 units @ $10.00	$1,000.00	
4	Purchase	60 units @ $12.00	720.00	
4	Balance	160 units @ $10.75	$1,720.00	
8	Sale	50 units @ $10.75	(537.50)	
8	Balance	110 units @ $10.75	$1,182.50	
17	Purchase	70 units @ $11.00	770.00	
17	Balance	180 units @ $10.85*	$1,952.50	
31	Sale	100 units @ $10.85	(1,085.00)	
31	Ending Inventory	80 units @ $10.84*	$ 867.50	

Cost of Goods Sold = $537.50 + $1,085.00 $1,622.50

*Rounded.

Chapter 9

Self-Test

1. b	(LO 1)	**6.** a	(LO 2)
2. d	(LO 2)	**7.** c	(LO 2)
3. d	(LO 2)	**8.** c	(LO 3)
4. b	(LO 2)	**9.** c	(SO 4)
5. b	(LO 2)	**10.** c	(SO 4)

Matching

1. b	**6.** j	**11.** f	**16.** d
2. r	**7.** h	**12.** n	**17.** p
3. g	**8.** l	**13.** a	**18.** c
4. e	**9.** k	**14.** m	**19.** s
5. o	**10.** i	**15.** q	

Short Answer

1. (LO 2) Definitely determinable liabilities and estimated liabilities
2. (LO 3) Examples include pending lawsuits, tax disputes, discounted notes receivable, the guarantee of another company's debt, and failure to follow government regulations.
3. (LO 2) Examples include income taxes payable, property taxes payable, estimated warranty expense, and vacation pay.
4. (LO 2) Examples include accounts payable, bank loans and commercial paper, short-term notes payable, accrued liabilities, dividends payable, sales and excise taxes payable, the current portion of long-term debt, payroll liabilities, and deferred revenues.
5. (SO 4) Social security taxes, Medicare taxes, federal income taxes, and state income taxes
6. (SO 4) Social security taxes, Medicare taxes, federal unemployment taxes, and state unemployment taxes

True-False

1. F (LO 2) Deferred revenues are a liability representing an obligation to deliver goods or services. They are shown on the balance sheet.
2. T (LO 1)
3. T (LO 1)
4. T (LO 2)
5. F (LO 2) Sales tax payable is a definitely determinable liability.
6. F (LO 2) A warranty is an estimated liability.
7. T (SO 4)
8. T (SO 4)
9. F (SO 4) FUTA is assessed against employers only.
10. T (LO 3)
11. F (LO 2) The account is associated with notes whose interest is included in the face amount.
12. T (LO 1)
13. T (LO 2)
14. F (LO 2) An estimate should be recorded for Product Warranty Expense in year 1, the year of the sale.
15. T (SO 4)
16. F (LO 2, SO 4) They are borne by both the employee and the employer.
17. T (LO 2)
18. T (LO 1)

1. c. (LO 2) Property tax bills are usually not available to a firm until months after the liability exists. Thus, to adhere to the matching rule, the accountant usually must estimate the property taxes due for the accounting period and enter that estimate in the books as a liability. When the firm receives its property tax bill, the accountant makes the necessary adjustments.

2. d (LO 2) A pending lawsuit is an example of a *contingent* liability, which is recorded only if the outcome against the company can be estimated and is probable.

3. a (SO 4) FUTA is an expense borne solely by the employer.

4. d (SO 4) Withholding an employee's federal income tax creates a current liability on the employer's books. The employer withholds cash from the gross payroll and places it in a depository until the employee's ultimate tax liability is known. Until the employer makes such a deposit, the amount owing on behalf of the employee is recorded as a current liability.

5. c (LO 2) Under the matching rule, estimated liabilities for vacation pay must be recorded as an expense of the current period. Therefore, by the time the employee exercises the right to a paid vacation, the expense has been recorded in an allowance account, Estimated Liability for Vacation Pay. As the liability expires, it is reduced by a debit entry. The credit entry is to Cash for the disbursement of pay to the employee.

6. a (LO 2) Even though the note bears no interest, a rate must be applied. The method for doing this is to record the note discounted at an appropriate rate. The principal of the note less the discount is the actual cost of the equipment to Balboa.

7. b (LO 2) With the passage of time, Discount on Notes Payable becomes Interest Expense, in accordance with the matching rule.

Exercises

1. (LO 2)

General Journal				
Date		**Description**	**Debit**	**Credit**
Dec.	31	Product Warranty Expense	525	
		Estimated Product Warranty Liability		525
		To record estimated warranty expense for washing machines		
Apr.	9	Estimated Product Warranty Liability	48	
		Parts, Wages Payable, etc.		48
		To record the repair of a washing machine		

2. (SO 4)

<table>
<tr><td colspan="5" align="center">**General Journal**</td></tr>
<tr><td colspan="2" align="center">**Date**</td><td align="center">**Description**</td><td align="center">**Debit**</td><td align="center">**Credit**</td></tr>
<tr><td>May</td><td>11</td><td>Office Wages Expense</td><td>260.00</td><td></td></tr>
<tr><td></td><td></td><td>   Social Security Tax Payable</td><td></td><td>16.12</td></tr>
<tr><td></td><td></td><td>   Medicare Tax Payable</td><td></td><td>3.77</td></tr>
<tr><td></td><td></td><td>   Union Dues Payable</td><td></td><td>5.00</td></tr>
<tr><td></td><td></td><td>   State Income Tax Payable</td><td></td><td>8.00</td></tr>
<tr><td></td><td></td><td>   Federal Income Tax Payable</td><td></td><td>52.00</td></tr>
<tr><td></td><td></td><td>   Wages Payable</td><td></td><td>175.11</td></tr>
<tr><td></td><td></td><td>   To record payroll liabilities and wages expense for Pat Bauer</td><td></td><td></td></tr>
<tr><td></td><td>11</td><td>Payroll Tax Expense</td><td>36.01</td><td></td></tr>
<tr><td></td><td></td><td>   Social Security Tax Payable</td><td></td><td>16.12</td></tr>
<tr><td></td><td></td><td>   Medicare Tax Payable</td><td></td><td>3.77</td></tr>
<tr><td></td><td></td><td>   Federal Unemployment Tax Payable</td><td></td><td>2.08</td></tr>
<tr><td></td><td></td><td>   State Unemployment Tax Payable</td><td></td><td>14.04</td></tr>
<tr><td></td><td></td><td>   To record payroll taxes on Bauer's earnings</td><td></td><td></td></tr>
</table>

3. (LO 1)
   a. $60,000 ($100,000 − $40,000)
   b. 11 times

$$\left[(\$290,000 - \$15,000) \div \left(\frac{\$30,000 + \$20,000}{2}\right)\right]$$

   c. 33.2 days (365 ÷ 11)

Solution to Crossword Puzzle
(Chapters 8 and 9)

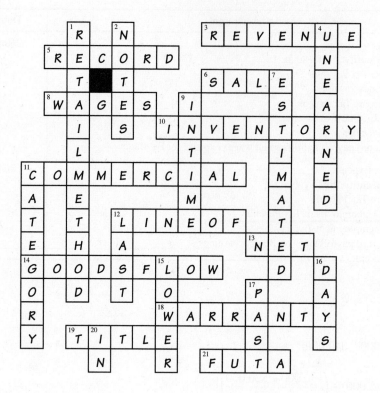

Chapter 10

Self-Test

1. b	(LO 1)	**6.** b	(LO 4)	
2. a	(LO 2)	**7.** c	(LO 5)	
3. a	(LO 3)	**8.** a	(LO 6)	
4. a	(LO 3)	**9.** d	(LO 6)	
5. b	(LO 4)	**10.** c	(SO 7)	

Matching

1. e	**7.** r	**13.** u	**18.** a
2. f	**8.** h	**14.** c	**19.** i
3. n	**9.** v	**15.** k	**20.** d
4. s	**10.** j	**16.** m	**21.** p
5. l	**11.** b	**17.** g	**22.** q
6. t	**12.** o		

Short Answer

1. (SO 7) Additions, such as a new building wing, expand a physical layout. Betterments, such as a new air-conditioning system, simply improve an existing layout.
2. (LO 4) When the cash received equals the carrying value of the asset sold
3. (LO 5) The cost of the well, the estimated residual value of the well, the estimated barrels to be extracted over the life of the well, and the actual barrels extracted and sold during the year
4. (SO 7) Ordinary repairs (e.g., painting or a tune-up) merely maintain an asset in good operating condition. Extraordinary repairs (e.g., a complete overhaul) increase an asset's estimated useful life or residual value.
5. (LO 1) Amortization, depreciation, and depletion
6. (LO 3) Physical deterioration and obsolescence

True-False

1. T (LO 2)
2. T (LO 4)
3. T (LO 1)
4. F (LO 3) Depreciation is a process of allocation, not of valuation.
5. F (LO 3) The physical deterioration of a machine is irrelevant in computing depreciation.
6. T (LO 2)
7. T (LO 3)
8. T (LO 3)
9. F (LO 3) Depreciation expense will be $1,000 in the second year also.
10. T (SO 7)
11. T (LO 4)
12. F (LO 3) It results in more net income.
13. F (LO 3) Depreciable cost equals cost minus residual value.
14. T (SO 7)
15. F (LO 6) A trademark is a name or symbol that can be used only by its owner.

16. T (LO 2)

17. F (SO 7) A betterment is a capital expenditure.

18. F (SO 7) The carrying value increases because the accumulated depreciation account is decreased (debited).

19. F (LO 4) The Accumulated Depreciation account always is debited when a depreciable asset is sold.

20. F (LO 2) *Capital expenditure* refers to the purchase of an asset; *expense* refers to the expiration of asset cost through the use or depreciation of an asset.

21. T (LO 4)

22. F (LO 4) Depreciation expense should be brought up to date before the sale is recorded.

23. T (LO 6)

24. T (LO 3)

25. T (LO 6)

26. F (LO 6) Research and development costs normally are charged as expenses in the year they are incurred.

27. T (LO 5)

28. T (LO 1)

Multiple Choice

1. c (LO 2) Because the relative values of the lump-sum purchase are known, a ratio can be determined and applied to the purchase price of both assets. The total appraised value of the land and building is $80,000. Of that $80,000, $20,000, or 25%, is apportioned to the land. So 25% of the purchase price for both assets, $16,500, would be allocated to land.

2. a (LO 3) The expired cost of an asset is its total accumulated depreciation to date. Depreciation is the allocation of the cost of an asset over its useful life.

3. d (LO 3) The declining-balance method would probably produce the greatest depreciation charge in the first year, but it is possible that the production method would. Thus, more information is needed to answer the question.

4. c (SO 7) The change requires an adjustment to the depreciation schedule of the asset. The remaining depreciable cost would be spread over the remaining (new) estimated useful life of the machine.

5. c (LO 6) When the fair value of goodwill drops below its carrying value, an impairment loss must be recorded.

6. b (LO 2) Although land is not a depreciable asset, improvements to land (buildings, street lights, pavement, etc.) are. Each improvement has an estimated useful life over which the costs will be allocated.

7. d (LO 4) To eliminate the asset from the company's accounting records, existing accounts pertaining to the asset must be removed from the books. Because the book value of the machine was $2,000 and the original cost was $9,000, accumulated depreciation must have been $7,000 (credit balance). To eliminate that account, a debit of $7,000 should be recorded to Accumulated Depreciation.

8. b (LO 2) A new roof has an economic life of more than a year. An expenditure for a new roof is therefore a capital expenditure.

9. d (LO 2) Understatement of net income results from expensing a capital expenditure. By definition, capital expenditures should be spread over the useful life of the acquisition (more than one period). If the entire cost is put into one period, expenses for that period will be overstated.

10. b (LO 5) Depletion costs assigned to a given period are the result of calculations based on expected total output over the life of an asset. Total costs divided by total expected units of output equal the depletion cost per unit. If the expected units of output are overestimated, the unit cost will be underestimated.

11. a (LO 6) Up to the point at which software is deemed technologically feasible, its costs are treated as research and development costs and are therefore expensed.

12. d (LO 6) Research and development costs are treated as revenue expenditures and are recognized in the period in which they are incurred.

Exercises

1. (LO 3)

	Depreciation Expense for 20x5	Accumulated Depreciation as of 12/31/x5	Carrying Value as of 12/31/x5
a.	$4,800	$ 9,600	$16,400
b.	$6,240	$16,640	$ 9,360

2. (LO 3)

$$\$2,250 = \left(\frac{\$35,000 - \$5,000}{100,000 \text{ toys}} \times 7,500 \text{ toys} \right)$$

3. (LO 2)

a. C	**d.** C	**f.** R	**h.** C
b. R	**e.** C	**g.** C	**i.** R
c. R			

4. (LO 1)

Acquisition cost ($22,000 × 1.000)	($22,000)
Present value of net annual cash flows ($4,000 × 4.623)	18,492
Present value of residual value ($3,000 × .630)	1,890
Net present value of equipment	($ 1,618)

The equipment should *not* be purchased because its net present value is negative.

5. (LO 4)

General Journal				
Date		**Description**	**Debit**	**Credit**
Jan.	2	Machinery (new)	23,000	
		Accumulated Depreciation, Machinery	17,000	
		Loss on Exchange of Machinery	500	
		Cash		15,500
		Machinery (old)		25,000
		To record exchange of machine, following GAAP		
	2	Machinery (new)	23,500	
		Accumulated Depreciation, Machinery	17,000	
		Cash		15,500
		Machinery (old)		25,000
		To record exchange of machine, following income tax rulings*		

*For income tax purposes, neither gains nor losses are recognized on the exchange of similar assets.

6. (LO 5)

		General Journal		
Date		**Description**	**Debit**	**Credit**
Dec.	31	Depletion Expense, Coal Deposits	40,000	
		Accumulated Depletion, Coal Deposits		40,000
		To record depletion of coal mine for 20xx		

Chapter 11

Self-Test

1. a	(LO 1)	**6.** d	(LO 5)
2. c	(LO 2)	**7.** c	(LO 5)
3. b	(LO 3)	**8.** b	(LO 6)
4. d	(LO 4)	**9.** d	(SO 7)
5. b	(LO 5)	**10.** c	(SO 8)

Matching

1. i	**7.** j	**12.** l	**17.** p
2. u	**8.** f	**13.** b	**18.** h
3. q	**9.** c	**14.** g	**19.** k
4. a	**10.** e	**15.** r	**20.** t
5. o	**11.** m	**16.** n	**21.** d
6. s			

Short Answer

1. (LO 2) A debenture bond is an unsecured bond; a bond indenture is a corporation's contract with bondholders.
2. (LO 3) When the face interest rate of bonds is higher than the market interest rate for similar bonds on the date of issue, a bond issue usually sells at a premium.
3. (LO 3) Interest = Principal × Rate × Time
4. (LO 4) The present value of periodic interest payments and the present value of the face value at maturity
5. (LO 1) Stockholders retain their level of control, interest is tax deductible, and stockholders' earnings may increase because of financial leverage.

True-False

1. F (LO 2) They are creditors.
2. T (LO 1)
3. F (LO 2) Bond interest must be paid on each interest date. It is not declared by the board of directors.
4. T (LO 3)
5. F (LO 5) It is less than the cash paid.
6. T (LO 5)
7. F (LO 6) Bond Interest Expense is credited.
8. T (LO 5)
9. F (LO 5) It equals interest payments *plus* the bond discount.
10. T (SO 7)
11. F (LO 5) The premium amortized increases each year.
12. T (LO 5)
13. F (SO 8) The statement describes capital leases.
14. T (SO 8)
15. F (SO 7) No gain or loss is recorded.
16. T (LO 3)
17. T (SO 8)
18. T (LO 1)
19. F (LO 1) It indicates a high risk of default.

Multiple Choice

1. **d** (LO 6) When bonds are issued between interest dates, the amount an investor pays for a bond includes the interest accrued since the last interest date. On the next interest date, the corporation pays the interest due for the entire period to all bondholders, including those who have held a bond for only a part of the period. The corporation maintains the abnormal balance in the Bond Interest Expense account until it pays the interest to the bondholders.

2. **a** (SO 8) Interest expense on a mortgage is based on the unpaid balance. As the principal of a mortgage is reduced over time, the interest portion of a fixed payment decreases, while the portion applied to the unpaid balance increases.

3. **d** (LO 3) Bonds issued at a premium have a carrying value above their face value. On the balance sheet, Unamortized Bond Premium is added to Bonds Payable to produce the carrying value.

4. **c** (LO 6) Interest expense for an accounting period must be recorded as an adjustment at year end. In recording interest expense for bonds sold at a discount, the calculation includes a reduction in Unamortized Bond Discount, which has a normal debit balance.

5. **b** (LO 5) When the effective interest method is used, the calculation of interest expense is based on the current carrying value of the bonds. As the bond discount is amortized, that value increases. As a result, the interest expense per period also increases.

6. **b** (SO 8) The lease described in **b** is not a capital lease because its terms do not resemble those of a purchase. It is therefore an operating lease.

7. **c** (SO 7) In the transaction described, the company paid $204,000 ($200,000 × 102%) for bonds outstanding that had a carrying value of $195,000. The difference between the carrying value and the amount paid—$9,000—is recorded as a loss.

8. **c** (SO 7) The carrying value of the bonds is $612,000. If one-third of the bonds are converted, the carrying value of the bonds payable will be reduced by $204,000 ($612,000/3).

Exercises

1. (LO 3, LO 5)
   a. $9,000 ($600,000 − $591,000)
   b. $21,000 ($600,000 × 7% × ½)

   c. $21,450 $\left(\$21,000 + \dfrac{\$9,000}{20}\right)$

   d. $593,700 ($600,000 − $6,300)

2. (LO 3, LO 5)
   a. $550,000 ($500,000 × 110%)
   b. $17,500 ($500,000 × 7% × ½)
   c. $16,500 ($550,000 × 6% × ½)
   d. $1,000 ($17,500 − $16,500)
   e. $549,000 ($550,000 − $1,000)

3. (LO 5)

Interest payments ($600,000 × 8% × 10)	$480,000
Premium on bonds payable ($600,000 × 6%)	36,000
Total interest cost	$444,000 ($44,400/year)

Solution to Crossword Puzzle
(Chapters 10 and 11)

```
P  E  N  S  I  O  N  P  L  A  N              N
R              R                    L  I  F  E
E        T  R  A  D  E  M  A  R  K  N        T
M        A     I                    T
I        N     I  N  S  T  A  L  L  M  E  N  T
U        G     A        C           R        R
M        I     F  R  A  N  C  H  I  S  E     A
         B     Y        E           S        D
C  A  L  L  S     V  A  L  U  E      T        E
A     E              E                       I
P           Z     B  R     T     F           N
I  S  S  U  E     L  E  A  S  E   I
T           R     D     T     R   X
A        L  O  N  G  T  E  R  M  D  E  B  T
L              S     D           D
```

Chapter 12

Self-Test

1. a	(LO 1)	**6.** c	(LO 4)
2. c	(LO 1)	**7.** a	(LO 5)
3. c	(LO 2)	**8.** b	(LO 5)
4. b	(LO 3)	**9.** a	(LO 6)
5. b	(LO 3)	**10.** a	(LO 1)

Matching

1. f	**6.** m	**11.** d	**16.** q
2. k	**7.** g	**12.** h	**17.** i
3. p	**8.** a	**13.** c	**18.** r
4. l	**9.** o	**14.** s	**19.** j
5. e	**10.** n	**15.** t	**20.** b

Short Answer

1. (LO 1) Separate legal entity, limited liability, ability to raise capital, ease of ownership transfer, lack of mutual agency, continuous existence, centralized authority and responsibility, and professional management

2. (LO 1) Government regulation, double taxation, limited liability, and separation of ownership and control

3. (LO 2) Contributed capital and retained earnings

4. (LO 4) When dividends are declared and when a corporation liquidates

5. (LO 2, LO 6) When it has treasury stock—that is, stock that it has issued but reacquired so that the stock is no longer outstanding

6. (LO 6) Treasury stock is stock that a corporation has issued and bought back. Unissued stock has never been issued.

True-False

1. T (LO 1)
2. F (LO 1, LO 5) It was established to protect the *creditors.*
3. T (LO 1)
4. T (LO 1)
5. T (LO 2)
6. T (LO 1)
7. F (LO 4) It may be both.
8. T (LO 4)
9. F (LO 1) Par value does not necessarily relate to market value (worth).
10. T (LO 6)

11. F (LO 4) No stockholders are ever guaranteed dividends.
12. F (LO 2) Common stock is considered the residual equity of a corporation.
13. F (LO 1) The amount of compensation is measured on the date of grant.
14. F (LO 3) Total assets and total liabilities decrease.
15. F (LO 4) Dividends in arrears are not a liability until a dividend is declared. They are normally disclosed in a note to the financial statements.
16. F (LO 6) Treasury Stock is listed in the stockholders' equity section as a deduction.

17. T (LO 1)

18. F (LO 6) Paid-in Capital, Treasury Stock is credited for the excess of the sales price over the cost.

19. T (LO 1)

20. F (LO 1, LO 6) Return on equity will increase.

21. T (LO 1)

Multiple Choice

1. d (LO 6) When a company reissues its stock, neither losses nor gains are ever recorded. What would otherwise be considered a loss is recorded as a reduction in stockholders' equity.

2. b (LO 6) Treasury stock is issued stock that is no longer outstanding.

3. c (LO 1, LO 2) Authorized stock is the maximum number of shares a corporation is allowed to issue. Authorized shares are therefore the sum of a corporation's issued and unissued shares.

4. d (LO 4) Because the preferred stock is non-cumulative, there are no dividends in arrears. The current dividend of $40,000 will be distributed to preferred stockholders based on 7 percent of the par value of $100; thus, $7,000 will be distributed (.07 × $100 × 1,000 shares). The remaining $33,000 will be distributed, pro rata, to the common stockholders.

5. d (LO 1) Under most circumstances, the liability of a corporation's stockholders is limited to the amount of their investments. They are not responsible for the corporation's debts.

6. d (LO 3) The declaration of a cash dividend requires a journal entry to record the liability and to reduce retained earnings by the amount of the declared dividend. On the date of payment, a journal entry is required to record the elimination of the liability created on the date of declaration and the reduction in cash resulting from the payment. No journal entry is required on the date of record, which is the date on which ownership of the stock is determined.

7. b (LO 3) If stock is purchased after the date of record, the new owner has no rights to the dividend that has been declared but not yet distributed to stockholders.

8. d (LO 4) The call feature on stock specifies an amount for which the corporation can buy back the stock. It is binding on the stockholder and on the issuing corporation in spite of possible differences between the call price and the market value at the time the stock is called.

Exercises

1. (LO 1, LO 3, LO 5)

\multicolumn{5}{c}{**General Journal**}				
\multicolumn{2}{c}{**Date**}	**Description**	**Debit**	**Credit**
Jan.	1	Start-up and Organization Expense	8,000	
		Cash		8,000
		Paid legal and incorporation fees		
Feb.	9	Cash	575,000	
		Common Stock		500,000
		Paid-in Capital in Excess of Par Value, Common		75,000
		Issued 5,000 shares of $100 par value common stock for $115 per share		
Apr.	12	Buildings	240,000	
		Preferred Stock		200,000
		Paid-in Capital in Excess of Stated Value, Preferred		40,000
		Issued 2,000 shares of preferred stock in exchange for a building		
June	23	Cash Dividends Declared	8,000	
		Cash Dividends Payable		8,000
		Declared a cash dividend on preferred stock		
July	8	Cash Dividends Payable	8,000	
		Cash		8,000
		Paid cash dividend declared on June 23		

2. (LO 6)

\multicolumn{5}{c}{**General Journal**}				
\multicolumn{2}{c}{**Date**}	**Description**	**Debit**	**Credit**
Jan.	12	Treasury Stock, Common	300,000	
		Cash		300,000
		Recorded purchase of treasury stock		
	20	Cash	130,000	
		Treasury Stock, Common		120,000
		Paid-in Capital, Treasury Stock		10,000
		Recorded reissue of treasury stock		
	27	Cash	116,000	
		Paid-in Capital, Treasury Stock	4,000	
		Treasury Stock, Common		120,000
		Recorded reissue of treasury stock		
	31	Common Stock	10,000	
		Paid-in Capital in Excess of Par Value, Common	40,000	
		Retained Earnings	10,000	
		Treasury Stock, Common		60,000
		Recorded retirement of treasury stock		

3. (LO 4)
    a. $18,000 (1,000 × $100 × 6% × 3 years)
    b. $33,000 ($51,000 − $18,000)

4. (LO 4)
    a. $6,000 (1,000 × $100 × 6%)
    b. $45,000 ($51,000 − $6,000)

Chapter 13

Self-Test

1. b	(LO 5)	**6.** d	(LO 7)
2. a	(LO 6)	**7.** b	(LO 1)
3. a	(LO 6)	**8.** c	(LO 2)
4. d	(LO 5)	**9.** a	(LO 3)
5. a	(LO 5)	**10.** b	(LO 4)

Matching

1. j	**6.** b	**11.** p	**15.** k
2. c	**7.** n	**12.** d	**16.** h
3. e	**8.** g	**13.** q	**17.** f
4. o	**9.** i	**14.** a	**18.** l
5. m	**10.** r		

Short Answer

1. (LO 5, LO 6) Net loss from operations, cash dividend declaration, and stock dividend declaration are the three instances discussed in this chapter. (Certain treasury stock transactions will also reduce retained earnings.)
2. (LO 6) A stock split changes the par or stated value of the stock; a stock dividend does not. A stock dividend transfers a portion of retained earnings to contributed capital; a stock split does not.
3. (LO 3) It must be unusual in nature, and it must occur infrequently.
4. (LO 1, LO 3) Correct order: 5, 1, 4, 6, 3, 2
5. (LO 1) In the statement of stockholders' equity, in a separate statement of comprehensive income, or in the income statement

True-False

1. F (LO 2, LO 3) The net of taxes amount is less than $20,000.
2. F (LO 5) Restricted retained earnings is not a cash account.
3. T (LO 7)
4. F (LO 6) Each stockholder owns the same percentage as before.
5. F (LO 6) The market value of the stock is needed to calculate the dollar amount for the journal entry.
6. F (LO 6) Its main purpose is to increase marketability by lowering the market price. The decrease in par value is a by-product of a stock split.
7. F (LO 3) This type of gain is not an unusual and infrequently occurring event.
8. F (LO 3) Extraordinary items appear on the income statement.
9. T (LO 3)
10. F (LO 6) It is part of contributed capital.
11. T (LO 4)
12. T (LO 2)
13. T (LO 1)
14. F (LO 4) They are included in the calculation of diluted earnings per share but not of basic earnings per share.
15. T (LO 6)
16. T (LO 1)

1. a (LO 6) A stock split simply increases the number of shares outstanding and reduces the par or stated value of the stock proportionately. It has no effect on retained earnings.

2. c (LO 6) The firm distributed a stock dividend of 1,000 shares (10% of 10,000 shares). The 11,000 shares outstanding after the stock dividend then were split into 4 shares for each 1 share (11,000 × 4), resulting in total shares outstanding of 44,000.

3. d (LO 5) The restriction on retained earnings is simply an indication of the intended use of the restricted amount. It does not change total retained earnings or stockholders' equity. The purpose of the restriction and the amount are usually disclosed in the notes to the financial statements.

4. c (LO 6) On the date that a stock dividend is distributed, Common Stock is credited, and Common Stock Distributable is debited. Retained Earnings will be reduced at the end of the accounting period when Stock Dividends Declared is closed to Retained Earnings.

5. a (LO 3) The cumulative effect of an accounting change should appear on the income statement after extraordinary items and before net income or loss.

6. c (LO 4) The company had 60,000 shares outstanding for 9/12 of the year and 40,000 shares outstanding for 3/12 of the year: 60,000 × 9/12 = 45,000 shares; 40,000 × 3/12 = 10,000 shares; 45,000 + 10,000 shares = 55,000 weighted-average shares outstanding for the year.

7. b (LO 5) There was a $30,000 increase in Retained Earnings during the year, even after a $15,000 cash dividend. Therefore, net income for the year must have been $45,000 ($30,000 + $15,000).

8. c (LO 3, LO 5) Discontinued operations are shown on the income statement.

9. b (LO 7) If a corporation has just one type of stock, it would be common stock. Book value per share would be calculated by dividing total stockholders' equity (retained earnings and contributed capital) by the number of shares issued. The current year's dividends would have already reduced total stockholders' equity. Dividend information would be irrelevant to finding book value per share.

10. c (LO 5) Retained earnings accumulate over time as a result of undistributed income. In each accounting period that earnings are not entirely distributed to stockholders through dividends, retained earnings increase. In periods in which losses occur, retained earnings decrease. Dividends declared and transfers to contributed capital are taken from retained earnings.

11. d (LO 1) The quality of earnings may be affected by the accounting methods and estimates a company uses and by the nature of nonoperating items.

Exercises

1. (LO 6)

		General Journal		
Date		Description	Debit	Credit
Sept.	1	Cash	1,200,000	
		Common Stock		1,000,000
		Paid-in Capital in Excess of Par Value, Common		200,000
		To record issuance of stock		
Mar.	7	Stock Dividends Declared	65,000	
		Common Stock Distributable		50,000
		Paid-in Capital in Excess of Par Value, Common		15,000
		To record declaration of stock dividend		
		(10,000 shares × 5% × $130 = $65,000 debit)		
	30	No entry		
Apr.	13	Common Stock Distributable	50,000	
		Common Stock		50,000
		To record distribution of stock dividend		

2. (LO 2, LO 3)

Operating income before taxes	$100,000
Less income taxes expense	40,000
Income before extraordinary item	$ 60,000
Extraordinary loss (net of taxes, $12,000)	18,000
Net income	$ 42,000

3. (LO 2)

		General Journal		
Date		Description	Debit	Credit
20x3		Income Taxes Expense	24,000	
		Income Taxes Payable		16,000
		Deferred Income Taxes		8,000
		To record income taxes for 20x3		
20x4		Income Taxes Expense	12,000	
		Deferred Income Taxes	4,000	
		Income Taxes Payable		16,000
		To record income taxes for 20x4		
20x5		Income Taxes Expense	28,000	
		Deferred Income Taxes	4,000	
		Income Taxes Payable		32,000
		To record income taxes for 20x5		

4. (LO 7)

Total stockholders' equity		$680,000
Less:		
Par value of outstanding preferred stock	$200,000	
Dividends in arrears	28,000	
Equity allocated to preferred shareholders		228,000
Equity pertaining to common shareholders		$452,000

Book value per share:

Preferred stock = $228,000 ÷ 4,000 shares = $57.00 per share

Common stock = $452,000 ÷ 30,000 shares = $15.07 per share

5. (LO 4) Basic earnings per share $= \dfrac{\$50,000 - \$20,000}{10,000 \text{ share}} = \$3.00$ per share

Chapter 14

Self-Test

1.	a	(LO 1)	**6.**	a	(LO 5)
2.	d	(LO 1)	**7.**	c	(LO 1)
3.	c	(LO 1)	**8.**	b	(LO 2)
4.	c	(LO 3)	**9.**	d	(LO 3)
5.	d	(LO 4)	**10.**	c	(LO 2)

Matching

1. f	**4.** g	**7.** h	**10.** b
2. j	**5.** e	**8.** c	
3. i	**6.** a	**9.** d	

Short Answer

1. (LO 1) Issuing capital stock to retire long-term debt and purchasing a long-term asset by incurring long-term debt

2. (LO 3) They represent noncash expenses that have been legitimately deducted in arriving at net income. Adding them back to net income effectively cancels out the deduction.

3. (LO 1) Money market accounts, commercial paper (short-term notes), and U.S. Treasury bills

True-False

1. T (LO 1)
2. F (LO 3) It is considered an operating activity.
3. T (LO 4)
4. T (LO 3)
5. F (LO 1, LO 3) Depreciation, depletion, and amortization expenses appear in the operating activities section.
6. F (LO 4) An increase in cash flows from investing activities implies the sale of long-term assets; thus, the business would be contracting.
7. T (LO 5)
8. F (LO 3) It is added to net income.
9. T (LO 5)
10. T (LO 1)
11. F (LO 2) Dividends are deducted because in the long run they must be paid to retain stockholders' interest.
12. T (LO 3)
13. F (LO 5) It is disclosed in the financing activities section.

Multiple Choice

1. a (LO 3) Cash receipts from sales, interest, and dividends are used to calculate cash inflows from operating activities. Under the indirect method, they are simply components of the net income figure presented.

2. b (LO 3) Net income in the operating activities section of the statement of cash flows includes a gain on the sale of investments. That amount needs to be backed out of the operating activities section to avoid duplication of cash inflow data.

3. a (LO 3) An increase in accounts payable indicates an increase in cash available to the firm. To reflect the absence of that cash outflow, the amount by which the payables have increased is added to the Cash Flows from Operating Activities section.

4. e (LO 1) The purchase of a building by incurring a mortgage payable does not involve any cash inflow or outflow. The investing and financing activity is disclosed in the schedule of noncash investing and financing transactions.

5. d (LO 5) The payment of dividends is a cash outflow and would be disclosed in the financing activities section of the statement of cash flows.

6. b (LO 3) The increase in inventory represents a cash outflow and would be deducted from net income in the operating activities section of the statement of cash flows. The counter-entry is the adjustment for changing levels of accounts payable.

7. c (LO 3, LO 5) Cash receipts from the issuance of stock are a cash inflow from financing activities. No adjustment to net income is required because the sale of stock is not recorded as a revenue and is not presented on the income statement.

8. c (LO 2) The numerator for all three calculations is net cash flows from operating activities.

Exercises

1. (LO 2)
   a. 2.0 times ($120,000/$60,000)
   b. 13.3% ($120,000/$900,000)
   c. 15% ($120,000/$800,000)
   d. $55,000 ($120,000 – $30,000 – $75,000 + $40,000)

2. (LO 3, LO 4, LO 5)

Harding Corporation
Statement of Cash Flows
For the Year Ended December 31, 20x5

Cash flows from operating activities

Net income		$55,000
Adjustments to reconcile net income to net cash		
flows from operating activities		
Depreciation expense	$14,000	
Loss on sale of equipment	4,000	
Changes in current assets and current liabilities		
Increase in accounts receivable	(24,000)	
Decrease in merchandise inventory	14,000	
Increase in accounts payable	4,000	
Increase in income taxes payable	700	12,700
Net cash flows from operating activities		$67,700

Cash flows from investing activities

Sale of equipment	$11,000	
Purchase of equipment	(27,000)	
Net cash flows from investing activities		(16,000)

Cash flows from financing activities

Repayment of notes payable	($10,000)	
Issue of notes payable	15,000	
Dividends paid	(51,700)	
Net cash flows from financing activities		(46,700)

Net increase in cash		$ 5,000
Cash at beginning of year		103,000
Cash at end of year		$108,000

Schedule of Noncash Investing and Financing Transactions

Conversion of bonds payable into common stock	$15,000

Solution to Crossword Puzzle
(Chapters 12, 13, and 14)

```
                    ¹I        ²S          ³U          ⁴D
         ⁵C  O   M   P   R   E   H   E   N   S   I   V   E
   ⁶N    O           O           A           E               F
   O     M      ⁷A   R   R   E   A   R   S                   I
  ⁸P  A  P  E  R      U           E                           C
   R     L           T      ⁹S ¹⁰P   L   I   T               I
   A     E     ¹¹P   H                R                       T
      ¹²E  X   T   R   A   O   R   D   I   N   A   R   Y
  ¹³R          E           R           C
   E     ¹⁴B   F           I      ¹⁵S   E  ¹⁶G  M   E   N  ¹⁷T
   T     O     E           Z       T       A                 A
   U     T     R           E       A       I      ¹⁸L        X
  ¹⁹R  E  T  I  R  E  D     E       T       N       O         E
   N     O     E                   E       O       S         S
         M  ²⁰D   I   V   I   D   E   N   D   S
```

Chapter 15

Self-Test

1. d	(LO 1)	**5.** d	(LO 3)
2. c	(LO 1)	**6.** a	(LO 4)
3. c	(LO 1)	**7.** a	(LO 6)
4. c	(LO 1		

Matching

1. f	**4.** g	**7.** a	**10.** h
2. b	**5.** e	**8.** j	
3. c	**6.** i	**9.** d	

Short Answer

1. (LO 2) The planning, executing, reviewing, and reporting stages

2. (LO 3) A just-in-time operating philosophy mandates a production environment in which personnel are hired and raw materials and facilities are purchased and used only as needed; emphasis is on the elimination of waste.

3. (LO 7) Competence, confidentiality, integrity, and objectivity

4. (LO 5) Why is the report being prepared? For whom is the report intended? What information should be provided? When is the report due?

True-False

1. F (LO 1) The management accountant provides management with the information needed for decision making.

2. T (LO 1)

3. F (LO 1) The reverse is true.

4. T (LO 1)

5. T (LO 1)

6. F (LO 1) Financial accounting reports must be prepared at regular, equal intervals.

7. F (LO 6) It relates most closely to integrity.

8. F (LO 6) It relates most closely to competence.

9. T (LO 3)

10. T (LO 4)

11. T (LO 3)

12. T (LO 1)

13. F (LO 1) Planning is the first stage; executing is the second stage.

14. T (LO 3)

15. F (LO 3) The *customer*, not the manufacturer, must perceive value in the product.

Multiple Choice

1. d (LO 6) Management accountants are expected to stay abreast of new methods and knowledge in the accounting field so that they can perform their duties as skillfully and competently as possible. Integrity means avoiding conflicts of interest, objectivity refers to fair and complete disclosure of information, and confidentiality forbids the unethical or illegal disclosure of proprietary information.

2. a (LO 6) To maintain their integrity, management accountants may not accept any gift or favor that would prejudice their actions.

3. b (LO 1) The timeliness of the information is important in both financial and management accounting reports because it enhances the usefulness of the schedules, reports, and statements that are prepared from that information. The other choices listed are areas in which the two types of accounting may differ.

4. d (LO 3) JIT, TQM, and ABM all strive for perfection, which is the goal of continuous improvement. Companies that adhere to this concept are never satisfied with what is; they constantly seek a better method, product, service, process, or resource. Although no company ever attains perfection, having it as a goal contributes to a firm's continual improvement.

5. c (LO 1) Management accounting reports are generated to assist managers in the decision-making process. Users' needs are therefore the driving force in their creation.

6. a (LO 1) Much of the work of management accounting is based on allocations, forecasts, and projections, for which there is no exact information; reports and analyses are therefore often based on estimates.

7. c (LO 1) After planning and executing a decision, managers review the expected performance established at the planning stage. Any significant differences are then identified for further analysis.

8. b (LO 4, LO 5) Operating budgets, which are used to plan a company's future, are based on financial data relating to the company's performance in the past. All the other choices listed are based on nonfinancial data.

Exercises

1. (LO 1)

	Financial Accounting	Management Accounting
1.	e	c
2.	g	l
3.	m	b
4.	i	n
5.	a	h
6.	k	f
7.	d	j

2. (LO 5)

Employee	Number of Pizzas Served per Hour	Employee Rating
P. Sanchez	22	Excellent
S. Wang	18	Good
R. Scotti	13	Lazy
E. Butterfield	16	Average
B. Jolita	19	Good
B. Warner	15	Average
G. Cohen	9	The Pits

3. (LO 3)
   1. b
   2. b
   3. a
   4. a
   5. b

Chapter 16

Self-Test

1. a (LO 3)		**6.** d (LO 7)	
2. d (LO 3)		**7.** d (LO 5)	
3. d (LO 5)		**8.** a (LO 5)	
4. b (LO 4)		**9.** b (LO 6)	
5. a (LO 4)		**10.** b (LO 8)	

Matching

1. h	**5.** g	**9.** m	**13.** e
2. c	**6.** d	**10.** f	**14.** n
3. b	**7.** j	**11.** o	**15.** i
4. a	**8.** k	**12.** l	

Short Answer

1. (LO 4) Materials Inventory, Work in Process Inventory, and Finished Goods Inventory
2. (LO 3) Direct materials, direct labor, and manufacturing overhead
3. (LO 3) A materials cost is considered direct when it can be conveniently and economically traced to a specific product or other cost object.
4. (LO 1) For profit or loss determination, product pricing, inventory valuation, and planning and cost control
5. (LO 5)
   Beginning balance, materials inventory
   + Direct materials purchased
   = Cost of direct materials available for use
   − Ending balance, materials inventory
   = Cost of direct materials used
6. (LO 5)
   Cost of direct materials used
   + Direct labor costs
   + Total manufacturing overhead costs
   = Total manufacturing costs

7. (LO 5)
   Total manufacturing costs
   + Beginning balance, work in process inventory
   = Total cost of work in process during the period
   − Ending balance, work in process inventory
   = Cost of goods manufactured
8. (LO 7) Estimated manufacturing overhead is divided by total estimated cost driver activity (e.g., direct labor hours)
9. (LO 6) Overapplied overhead is the amount by which applied manufacturing overhead costs exceeds actual manufacturing overhead costs.
10. (LO 4) Cost of goods manufactured is the total cost of all units completed and moved to finished goods storage during an accounting period.

True-False

1. T (LO 5)
2. T (LO 2, LO 4)
3. T (LO 8)
4. T (LO 3)
5. T (LO 4)

6. F (LO 5, LO 9) A service firm has no direct materials cost.
7. T (LO 8)
8. F (LO 4) The purchase request is prepared first.

9. F (LO 3) They are classified as indirect labor costs (i.e., as manufacturing overhead).

10. F (LO 5) It must be prepared *before* the income statement is prepared.

11. T (LO 5)

12. T (LO 5)

13. F (LO 5) The opposite is true.

14. T (LO 5)

15. T (LO 8)

16. T (LO 6)

17. F (LO 3) The smaller a cost object, the more difficult it is to trace.

18. F (LO 3) It is part of manufacturing overhead and is thus an indirect cost.

Multiple Choice

1. c (LO 3) A direct materials cost can easily be traced to the item manufactured. Other than the legs for the chair, each cost described is not distinctly traceable to the product.

2. c (LO 4) Goods must first be requested, then ordered, then received, then used.

3. a (LO 2) Salespeople are not involved in the manufacture of products. Thus, their salaries are treated as period costs, not product costs.

4. d (LO 4) The proper document to use when buying goods is a purchase order.

5. a (LO 4) A materials request form documents goods released to production.

6. c (LO 8) Activities are what "drive" the costs in an ABC system.

7. b (LO 8) With ABC costing, costs are accumulated for a given activity pool and applied via a cost driver.

8. a (LO 7) One of the criticisms of the traditional method is that it uses a single plantwide cost driver (e.g., direct labor hours) to apply manufacturing overhead to a product cost.

9. d (LO 1) Managers use product cost information in all the stages in the management cycle listed, as well as in the reporting stage.

Exercises

1. (LO 5)

Finished Goods, Jan. 1	$ 75,000
Add Cost of Goods Manufactured	450,000
Cost of Goods Available for Sale	$525,000
Less Finished Goods, Dec. 31	80,000
Cost of Goods Sold	$445,000

2. (LO 8)

Activity Pool	Estimated Activity Pool Amount	Cost Driver	Cost Driver Level	Activity Cost Rate
Setup	$10,000	Number of setups	200 setups	$50
Inspection	6,000	Number of inspections	300 inspections	$20
Building	8,000	Machine hours	4,000 machine hours	$2
Packaging	4,000	Packaging hours	1,000 packaging hours	$4
	$28,000			

Activity Pool	Activity Cost Rate	Product A Cost Driver Level	Product A Cost Applied	Product B Cost Driver Level	Product B Cost Applied
Setup	$50	70	$ 3,500	30	$ 1,500
Inspection	20	250	5,000	150	3,000
Building	2	1,500	3,000	2,000	4,000
Packaging	4	300	1,200	700	2,800
Total			$12,700		$11,300
÷ by Number of Units			1,000		2,000
= Manufacturing Overhead Cost per Unit			$12.70		$5.65

3. (LO 5)

Specialty Company
Statement of Cost of Goods Manufactured
For the Year Ended December 31, 20xx

Direct materials used
   Materials Inventory, Jan. 1 $ 8,700
   Add direct materials purchased (net)   168,300

   Cost of direct materials available for use $177,000
   Less Materials Inventory, Dec. 31   32,600

   Cost of direct materials used $144,400
Direct labor costs   142,900
Manufacturing overhead costs
   Depreciation, factory building and equipment $ 31,800
   Factory insurance   2,300
   Factory utilities expense   26,000
   Indirect labor   42,800
   Other factory costs   12,600

Total manufacturing overhead costs   115,500

Total manufacturing costs $402,800
Add Work in Process Inventory, Jan. 1   34,200

Total cost of work in process during the year $437,000
Less Work in Process Inventory, Dec. 31   28,700

Cost of goods manufactured $408,300

4. (LO 3)

a. OH	**d.** DM	**g.** DM
b. DL	**e.** OH	**h.** OH
c. OH	**f.** DL	**i.** OH

Solution to Crossword Puzzle
(Chapters 15 and 16)

Chapter 17

Self-Test

1. a	(LO 2)	**6.** c	(LO 5)
2. a	(LO 2)	**7.** d	(LO 6)
3. b	(LO 3)	**8.** d	(LO 1)
4. c	(LO 4)	**9.** a	(LO 6)
5. a	(LO 3)	**10.** c	(LO 1)

Matching

1. c	**4.** b	**6.** e
2. g	**5.** d	**7.** a
3. f		

Short Answer

1. (LO 5) Labor, materials and supplies, and service overhead
2. (LO 3) Direct materials, direct labor, and applied manufacturing overhead
3. (LO 4) The costs on the job order cost card are totaled, and the total costs are then divided by the number of goods units produced.
4. (LO 2) Railroad cars, bridges, wedding invitations, or any other unique or special-order products

True-False

1. T (LO 2)
2. T (LO 2, LO 4)
3. F (LO 3) Indirect costs are charged to Work in Process Inventory through applied overhead.
4. T (LO 4)
5. F (LO 4) The job must be completed and all costs recorded on the job order cost card before the product unit cost can be calculated.
6. T (LO 3)
7. F (LO 3) The decrease is to Finished Goods Inventory.
8. T (LO 2)
9. T (LO 4)
10. T (LO 1)
11. F (LO 5) Services are not associated with a physical product that can be inventoried and valued.
12. F (LO 6) Project costing links many different job orders and processes by transferring costs from one job or process to another, collecting and summarizing costs in a variety of ways, and providing appropriate internal controls.
13. T (LO 2)

Multiple Choice

1. c (LO 2) A job order costing system is used if the goods manufactured are unique. A supersonic jet is unique because it is manufactured to the specifications of the buyer.

2. b (LO 3) Manufacturing overhead is applied to specific jobs by increasing the Work in Process Inventory and reducing the Manufacturing Overhead account.

3. a (LO 3) Actual factory overhead costs are entered into the Manufacturing Overhead account; they do not flow through the Work in Process Inventory account.

4. b (LO 3) The Manufacturing Overhead account decreases when the manufacturing overhead costs are assigned to the Work in Process Inventory account.

5. b (LO 2) A process costing system accumulates product costs by process, department, or work cell, not by job or batch of products.

6. d (LO 3) When materials are issued into production, Work in Process Inventory and Manufacturing Overhead are increased, and Materials Inventory is decreased.

7. d (LO 1) During the reviewing stage, managers compare budgeted costs with actual costs to evaluate performance, identify problems and recommend changes.

8. a (LO 3) Costs of a manufactured product include materials, labor, and manufacturing overhead; a factory foreperson's salary would be among the indirect costs included in overhead.

Exercises

1. (LO 5)

Job Order Cost Card Melvin's Septic Service Company	
Customer: Gonzales	
Contract Type: Cost-plus	
Type of Service: Septic Services	
Cost Summary:	
Costs Charged to Job	**Total**
Septic design	
Beginning balance	$ 5,270
Design labor	500
Service overhead (30% of	
design labor)	150
Totals	$ 5,920
Septic tank installation	
Beginning balance	$28,500
Materials and supplies	4,300
Installation labor	12,800
Service overhead (50% of	
installation labor)	6,400
Totals	$52,000
Job site cleanup	
Beginning balance	$ 150
Janitorial service cost	1,050
Totals	$ 1,200
Totals	$59,120
Cost of job	$59,120
Markup (25% of cost)	14,780
Amount billed	$73,900

2. (LO 3)

Materials Inventory			
12/23	2,950	850	12/26
	2,100		

Accounts Payable			
		2,950	12/23

Work In Process Inventory			
12/26	800	3,900	12/29
12/27	1,200		
12/27	3,600		
	1,700		

Manufacturing Overhead			
12/26	50	3,600	12/27
12/26	1,200		
12/27	300		
12/31	2,500		
	450		

Factory Payroll			
		1,500	12/27

Cash			
		1,200	12/26

Finished Goods Inventory			
12/29	3,900	2,000	12/30
	1,900		

Cost of Goods Sold			
12/30	2,000	2,500	12/31
		500	

Sales			
		3,400	12/30

Accounts Receivable			
12/30	3,400		

Chapter 18

Self-Test

1.	b	(LO 1)	**6.** b	(LO 5)
2.	c	(LO 3)	**7.** d	(LO 5)
3.	a	(LO 4)	**8.** a	(LO 5)
4.	c	(LO 4)	**9.** c	(LO 5)
5.	d	(LO 5)	**10.** a	(LO 6)

Matching

1.	d	**3.**	f	**5.**	g	**7.**	e
2.	h	**4.**	c	**6.**	b	**8.**	a

Short Answer

1. (LO 5) Account for physical units, account for equivalent units, account for costs, compute the cost per equivalent unit, assign costs

2. (LO 5)

   Units in beginning inventory × (100% – percentage of completion)
   + Units started and completed × 100%
   + Units in ending inventory × percentage of completion
   = Equivalent units

3. (LO 5) Costs of units completed and transferred out and ending work in process

4. (LO 5)

   Costs attached to units in beginning inventory
   + Costs necessary to complete units in beginning inventory
   + Costs of units started and completed during the period
   = Costs of goods completed and transferred

True-False

1. F (LO 3) A Work in Process Inventory account is maintained for each process, department, or work cell.
2. T (LO 3)
3. T (LO 2)
4. T (LO 3, LO 4)
5. F (LO 4) Units started and completed are only part of the computation.
6. T (LO 4)
7. F (LO 5) A combined unit cost (conversion cost) is computed for direct labor and manufacturing overhead.
8. F (LO 6) Beginning inventory is multiplied by 100 percent.
9. T (LO 5).
10. F (LO 5) Equivalent units for materials and conversion costs must be multiplied by their respective unit costs.
11. T (LO 5)
12. T (LO 1)
13. T (LO 2)

Multiple Choice

1. b (LO 4, LO 5) Equivalent production for conversion costs would be 14,100 units, or the sum of (a) the 10,000 units started and completed during the period, (b) ending equivalent units of 2,100 (7,000 units × 30% complete), and (c) beginning equivalent units of 2,000 (5,000 units × 40% remaining to complete).

2. c (LO 4, LO 6) Average costing treats all units in beginning inventory as if they were started and completed during the period. Thus, equivalent production for conversion costs would be 17,100 units, or the sum of (a) beginning inventory of 5,000 units, (b) the 10,000 units started and completed during the period, and (c) ending equivalent units of 2,100 (7,000 units × 30% complete).

3. d (LO 3, LO 5) The costs necessary to complete ending inventory are costs of a future period.

4. a (LO 5) Equivalent units account for efforts expended; Step 1 accounts for physical units.

5. c (LO 4, LO 6) Using average costing, equivalent production would be 17,600 units, or the sum of (a) beginning inventory of 5,000 units, (b) 12,000 units started and completed, and (c) 600 ending equivalent units (2,000 units × 30% complete).

6. b (LO 4) Conversion costs are the costs incurred to convert raw materials into finished products. They include both direct labor costs and manufacturing overhead.

7. b (LO 5) Step 5 assigns costs to finished goods and ending work in process.

8. b (LO 5) Step 5 assigns costs to finished goods and ending work in process.

9. b (LO 1) Forecasting unit costs and budgeting are two of the uses of process costing information in the planning stage of the management cycle.

10. c (LO 1) A firm that produces custom-made suits would use a job order costing system.

Exercises

1. (LO 5)

Jaquette Manufacturing Company **Process Cost Report: FIFO Costing Method** **For the Month Ended May 31, 20xx**			

	Physical Units		*Equivalent Units*
Beginning inventory	2,000		
Units started this period	24,000		
Units to be accounted for	26,000		

		Direct Materials	*Conversion*
Beginning inventory	2,000	—	1,400 (70%)
Units started and completed	17,000	17,000	17,000
Ending inventory	7,000	7,000 (100%)	2,100 (30%)
Units accounted for	26,000	24,000	20,500

	Total Costs		
Beginning inventory	$ 15,000	$ 12,000	$ 3,000
Current costs	144,750	114,000	30,750
Total costs	$159,750		

Current Costs ÷ Equivalent units		$114,000 ÷ 24,000	$30,750 ÷ 20,500
Cost per equivalent unit		$4.75	$1.50

Cost of goods manufactured and transferred out:

From beginning inventory	$ 15,000 =	$12,000 + 3,000
Current costs to complete	2,100 =	0 + (1,400 x $1.50)
Units started and completed	106,250 =	(17,000 x $4.75) + 17,000 x $1.50)
Cost of goods manufactured	$123,350	
Ending inventory	36,400 =	(7,000 x $4.75) + (2,100 x $1.50)
Total costs	$159,750	

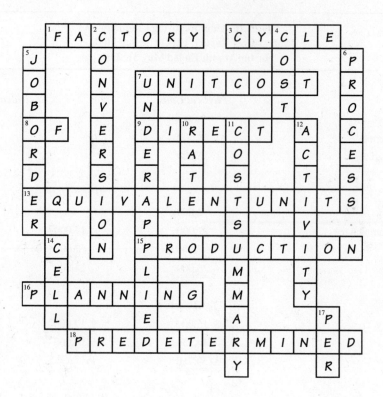

Chapter 19

1. c	(LO 5)	**6.** c	(LO 7)
2. a	(LO 5)	**7.** c	(LO 3)
3. d	(LO 5)	**8.** a	(LO 4)
4. c	(LO 3)	**9.** b	(LO 6)
5. d	(LO 1)	**10.** c	(LO 7)

Matching

1. i	**5.** d	**8.** c	**11.** k
2. a	**6.** f	**9.** h	**12.** m
3. g	**7.** e	**10.** j	**13.** l
4. b			

Short Answer

1. (LO 5) A basic concept of the just-in-time operating philosophy is that all resources—materials, personnel, and facilities—should be acquired and used only as needed.
2. (LO 4)
   Identify and classify each activity.
   Estimate the cost of resources for each activity.
   Identify a cost driver for each activity and estimate the quantity of each cost driver.
   Calculate an activity cost rate for each activity.
   Assign costs to cost objects based on the level of activity required to make the product or provide the service.
3. (LO 3) Process value analysis (PVA) is a method of identifying all activities and relating them to the events that prompt the activities and to the resources that the activities consume. PVA is helpful to managers because it forces them to look critically at all phases of their operations. It improves cost traceability and results in significantly more accurate product costs, which in turn improves management decisions and increases profitability.
4. (LO 5, LO 6) Just-in-time is an operating philosophy, not an inventory system. One of its goals is to minimize inventory. Unlike the traditional manufacturing approach, which requires that inventory be kept on hand to meet customer demands, JIT uses customer orders to trigger production runs. Throughput time is much more important than in traditional manufacturing environments.

True-False

1. F (LO 8) The primary goals of both ABM and JIT are to eliminate waste, reduce costs, improve product or service quality, and enhance an organization's efficiency and productivity.
2. T (LO 5)
3. T (LO 5)
4. T (LO 5)
5. T (LO 5)
6. F (LO 5, LO 6) Machine operators inspect products on a continuous basis.
7. F (LO 6) Queue time is the time a product waits to be worked on after it arrives at the next operation or department.

8. T (LO 6)
9. T (LO 4)
10. F (LO 4) The cost hierarchy of a service organization has four levels: the unit, batch, service, and operations levels.
11. F (LO 4) A bill of activities is used in activity-based costing. It is a list of activities and related costs that is used to compute the costs assigned to activities and the product unit cost.
12. T (LO 7)
13. T (LO 3)
14. T (LO 3)
15. T (LO 1)

Multiple Choice

1. c (LO 4) Batch-level activities are performed each time a batch of goods is produced. Installation of a vehicle's engine is an example of a unit-level activity. Unit-level activities are performed each time a unit is produced.
2. c (LO 5) Variance analysis is a method used to identify causes of differences between expected and actual results of operations. Emphasis on direct labor variance analysis could be found in any production environment.
3. b (LO 5) In pull-through production, the production process begins when a customer places an order.
4. a (LO 5) Because inventory is delivered as needed in a JIT environment and not kept on hand in advance of being needed, the resources traditionally used to store, count, maintain, and move inventories are reduced or eliminated.
5. b (LO 5) Quick and inexpensive machine setups result in cost savings. None of the other choices guarantees that a company will ultimately save money.

6. d (LO 6) Decision time precedes the start of production. Production time begins with the requisition of raw materials and ends with the transfer of the product to finished goods.
7. c (LO 3) A value-adding activity increases the market value of a product or service—for example, using a higher-quality material that increases the value of the product in the eyes of the customer. Recording the daily receipts would not add to the market value of the pizza; thus, it would be a nonvalue-adding activity.
8. a (LO 7) In a JIT environment in which back-flush costing is used, the direct materials costs and the conversion costs (direct labor and manufacturing overhead) are immediately charged to the Cost of Goods Sold account.
9. a (LO 1) In the planning stage, an activity-based system can help managers estimate product costs, as well as identify value-adding activities and determine the resources required for such activities.
10. b (LO 6) Processing time is the actual amount of time spent working on a product.

Exercises

1. a. (LO 4)

Direct materials cost	$28,645
Cost of purchased parts	38,205
Direct labor cost (660 × $7.00)	4,620
Manufacturing overhead (1.6 × $4,620)	7,392
Total cost of the order	**$78,862**
Product unit cost ($78,862/350 units)	**$225.32**

b.

Activity	Activity Cost Rate	Cost Driver Level	Activity Cost
Unit level:			
Parts production	$19 per machine hour	190 machine hours	$ 3,610
Assembly	$9.50 per direct labor hour	42 direct labor hours	399
Packaging/shipping	$13 per unit	350 units	4,550
Batch level:			
Work cell setup	$45 per setup	8 setups	360
Product level:			
Product design	$31 per engineering hour	38 engineering hours	1,178
Product simulation	$45 per testing hour	14 testing hours	630
Facility level:			
Building occupancy	125% of direct labor costs	$4,620 direct labor costs	5,775
Total Activity Costs			$16,502
Cost Summary			
Direct materials		$28,645	
Cost of purchased parts		38,205	
Direct labor cost		4,620	
Activity costs		16,502	
Total cost of order		**$87,972**	
Product unit cost		**$251.35**	

2. (LO 5, LO 6) In both traditional and JIT settings, direct labor and raw materials are classified as direct costs, and a president's salary and plant fire insurance are classified as indirect costs.

Costs that are classified as indirect in a traditional setting and direct in a JIT environment are depreciation, machinery; product design costs; small tools; operating supplies; setup labor; rework costs; supervisory salaries; and utility costs, machinery. All these costs are traceable to a JIT work cell, whereas in a traditional setting, they are included in a plantwide or departmental overhead cost pool.

3. (LO 5, LO 6)

Work in Process Inventory				Finished Goods Inventory				Cost of Goods Sold	
4,890	32,750			32,750	17,880			17,880	
13,300									

Accounts Payable				Accounts Receivable				Sales	
	4,890			28,608					28,608
	13,330								

Chapter 20

Self-Test

1. b	(LO 1)		**6.** a	(LO 4)
2. c	(LO 2)		**7.** c	(LO 5)
3. a	(LO 2)		**8.** b	(LO 5)
4. b	(LO 2)		**9.** b	(LO 4)
5. d	(LO 4)		**10.** c	(LO 2)

Matching

1. d	**4.** k	**7.** i	**10.** c
2. g	**5.** j	**8.** a	**11.** e
3. h	**6.** b	**9.** f	

Short Answer

1. (LO 4) Sales = Variable Costs + Fixed Costs, or Sales – Variable Costs – Fixed Costs = 0

2. (LO 2) A mixed cost is any cost that has both fixed and variable elements. Examples include telephone expense, electricity expense, and water expense.

3. (LO 2) The high-low method breaks down a mixed cost into its fixed and variable components.

4. (LO 4) *Sales* refers to the gross proceeds realized on the sale of a product. *Contribution margin* refers to the portion of sales remaining after all variable costs have been deducted from sales. It is the amount available to cover fixed costs and earn a profit.

5. (LO 4)

Sales	$XX
– Variable Costs	XX
= Contribution Margin	$XX
– Fixed Costs	XX
= Profit	$XX

6. (LO 5)
Estimate service overhead costs.
Determine the breakeven point.
Determine the effect of a change in operating costs.
Compute targeted profit.

True-False

1. T (LO 2)
2. T (LO 4)
3. T (LO 2)
4. F (LO 2) It is a fixed cost because it does not change with volume.
5. F (LO 2) Normal capacity is the most realistic measure.
6. T (LO 4)
7. F (LO 4) A contribution margin is realized on the sale of the very first unit.
8. T (LO 4)
9. T (LO 2)

10. T (LO 3)
11. T (LO 2)
12. F (LO 4) The horizontal (x) axis represents volume, such as units of output.
13. T (LO 4)
14. F (LO 4) Unless the selling price or variable cost per unit changes, the contribution margin per unit will remain the same.
15. T (LO 4)
16. F (LO 5) Service businesses can use C-V-P analysis.

1. c (LO 2) Because part of the fare varies according to activity level and part is fixed, it is a mixed cost.
2. c (LO 4) Breakeven in units is calculated by dividing total fixed costs by the contribution margin per unit; contribution margin per unit is the selling price less variable costs per unit. Thus, $10,000 \div (\$10 - \$8) = 5,000$ units.
3. b (LO 2) Variable costs are directly associated with production levels. If production is zero, variable costs are also zero.
4. a (LO 4) Total contribution margin is the contribution margin per unit multiplied by the number of units sold. When profits (losses) are zero, the total contribution margin equals total fixed costs.
5. d (LO 4) The total-cost line includes all fixed and variable costs. The slope of the total-cost line is determined by the variable costs per unit. Therefore, where the total-cost line intercepts the total-revenue line, revenues equal costs.
6. a (LO 2) When preparing cost analyses and forecasting sales, managers assume normal operating capacity.

7. d (LO 2) When volume decreases, the number of units divided into the (same) fixed cost decreases, increasing the fixed cost per unit.
8. d (LO 4) When the selling price and variable cost per unit both increase by the same amount, the contribution margin per unit remains the same, and thus the breakeven point remains the same.
9. d (LO 5) Solve the following equation to obtain the correct answer: $\$50X - \$35X - \$30,000 = \$45,000$.
10. a (LO 5) Solve the following equation to obtain the correct answer: $10,000(X - \$10) - \$40,000 = \$26,000$.
11. b (LO 4) The weighted-average contribution margin is computed by multiplying the contribution margin for each product by the product's percentage of the sales mix. This, in turn, is used to calculate the weighted-average breakeven point.
12. d (LO 5) Calculating the breakeven point in service businesses requires a thorough analysis of each cost component and a reliable estimate of activity.

Exercises

1. (LO 4, LO 5)
   a. 20,000 units
   b. $260,000
   c. $32,000 loss
   d. 32,500 units

2. (LO 4)

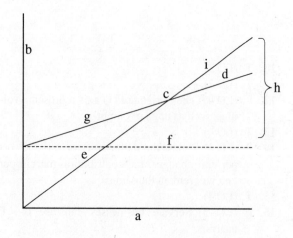

3. (LO 2)
   a. Total cost = $800 + $.25/mile
   b. $4,800

4. (LO 5)
   a. $20,000 loss
   b. $10.00
   c. $50,000

Solution to Crossword Puzzle
(Chapters 19 and 20)

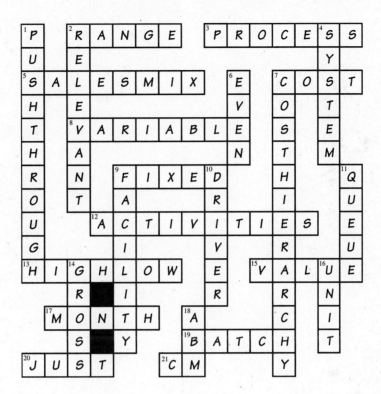

Chapter 21

Self-Test

1. d	(LO 2)		**6.** a	(LO 2)
2. d	(LO 1)		**7.** d	(LO 2, LO 3)
3. a	(LO 3)		**8.** c	(LO 4)
4. c	(LO 4)		**9.** a	(LO 1)
5. d	(LO 4)		**10.** b	(LO 3)

Matching

1. k	**4.** f	**7.** d	**10.** e
2. g	**5.** i	**8.** c	**11.** a
3. j	**6.** h	**9.** b	

Short Answer

1. (LO 1) Budgeting is the process of identifying, gathering, summarizing, and communicating financial and nonfinancial information about an organization's future activities.

2. (LO 2) A master budget consists of a set of operating budgets and a set of financial budgets. The operating budgets are plans used in daily operations. They are the basis for preparing the financial budgets, which are projections of financial results for an accounting period.

3. (LO 4) In addition to providing an estimate of the ending cash balance, the cash budget enables managers to anticipate periods of high or low cash availability and to plan for short-term investments or loans during those periods.

4. (LO 3) The three steps are to (a) calculate the total units of direct materials needed for production, (b) calculate the total units of direct materials to be purchased, and (c) calculate the total cost of direct materials to be purchased.

True-False

1. F (LO 2) A master budget usually covers a one-year period.
2. F (LO 2) A master budget represents an entire organization's budget.
3. T (LO 3)
4. T (LO 2)
5. F (LO 4) Depreciation expense does not represent a cash outflow and is therefore not included in the cash budget.
6. T (LO 1)
7. T (LO 4)
8. F (LO 4) Only cash collected from sales (including prior months' sales) are included as cash receipts.

9. F (LO 3, LO 4) The reverse is true.
10. T (LO 3)
11. F (LO 3) External factors, such as the state of the local and national economies, the state of the industry's economy, and the nature of the competition, are important factors in forecasting sales.
12. T (LO 3)
13. F (LO 4) Preparing the budgeted balance sheet is the final step in the development of the master budget.

Multiple Choice

1. d (LO 2, LO 3) The detailed operating budgets serve as the basis for preparing the financial budgets. Operating budgets are prepared at the departmental level and represent the expectations of the managers responsible for each segment of a firm.

2. c (LO 3) The production budget is the basis for preparing the other three budgets.

3. b (LO 4) The cash budget shows anticipated cash inflows and outflows. Once it has been prepared, certain account balances on the balance sheet can be forecasted (Cash, Accounts Receivable, Notes Payable, etc.). Thus, the cash budget must be prepared before the pro forma balance sheet.

4. d (LO 3) Forecasted sales would appear on the sales budget, not on the direct labor budget.

5. a (LO 4) The sales budget would provide information about the projected *inflows* of cash.

6. d (LO 4) The cash budget consists of the items listed in **a, b,** and **c** plus the beginning cash balance.

7. a (LO 3) Requirements for production in the second quarter are 72,000 pounds (24,000 units × 3 pounds). Add 10 percent of the requirement for the third quarter, or 6,300 pounds (21,000 units × 3 pounds × .10). Subtract materials on hand at the beginning of the second quarter, or 7,200 pounds (24,000 units × 3 pounds × .10). The amount that should be purchased for the second quarter is 71,100 pounds.

8. d (LO 3) A manufacturing organization would prepare a direct materials budget.

9. c (LO 4) (40% × $15,000) + (60% × $10,000) + $20,000 = $32,000

10. d (LO 3) The first step in preparing the direct labor budget is to estimate the total direct labor hours by multiplying the estimated direct labor hours per unit by the anticipated units of production. The second step is to calculate the total budgeted direct labor cost by multiplying the estimated total direct labor hours by the estimated direct labor cost per hour.

Exercises

1. (LO 3)

Donlevy Company
Production Budget
For the Quarter Ended June 30, 20xx

	April	May	June
Expected sales	10,000 units	12,000 units	15,000 units
Add ending inventory	1,200	1,500	900
Units needed	11,200	13,500	15,900
Less beginning inventory	1,000	1,200	1,500
Units to produce ending inventory	10,200 units	12,300 units	14,400 units

2. (LO 4)

Monahan Enterprises
Cash Budget
For the Month Ended June 30, 20xx

Cash receipts		
Sales—May	$52,000	
Sales—June	18,000	
Proceeds from loan*	1,000	
Total receipts		$71,000
Cash disbursements		
General and administrative expenses	$22,000	
Inventory purchases—May	20,000	
Inventory purchases—June	15,000	
Purchase of office furniture	3,000	
Selling expenses	14,000	
Total disbursements		74,000
Cash increase (decrease)		$ (3,000)
Cash balance, June 1		7,000
Cash balance, June 30		$ 4,000

*Amount must be derived.

---

3. (LO 3)

Jeppo Titanium Company
Direct Labor Budget
For the Year Ended December 31, 20xx

	Product	Product	Year
Bending department	X	Y	
Total production units	10,000	20,000	
× Direct labor hours per unit	1	.6	
Total direct labor hours	10,000	12,000	
× Direct labor cost per hour	$10	$10	
Total direct labor cost	$100,000	$120,000	$220,000
	Product	Product	
Welding department	X	Y	
Total production units	10,000	20,000	
× Direct labor hours per unit	2	3	
Total direct labor hours	20,000	60,000	
× Direct labor cost per hour	$15	$15	
Total direct labor cost	$300,000	$900,000	$1,200,000
Total firmwide direct labor cost			
			$1,440,000

4. (LO 1) During the planning stage of the management cycle, budgeting helps managers relate long-term strategic goals to short-term activities, distribute resources and workloads, communicate responsibilities, select performance measures, and set standards for bonuses and rewards.

In the executing stage, managers use budget information to communicate expectations, measure performance and motivate employees, coordinate activities, and allot resources.

In the reviewing stage, budgets help managers evaluate performance, including its timeliness; find variances between planned and actual performance; and create solutions to any significant variances that they detect.

To provide continuous feedback about an organization's operating, investing, and financing activities, managers prepare and distribute reports based on budget information throughout the year.

Chapter 22

1. d	(LO 1)	**6.** a	(LO 2)
2. b	(LO 5)	**7.** d	(LO 2)
3. c	(LO 6)	**8.** c	(LO 4)
4. c	(LO 4)	**9.** a	(LO 5)
5. b	(LO 2)	**10.** b	(LO 3)

Matching

1. j	**5.** i	**8.** d	**11.** h
2. k	**6.** g	**9.** f	**12.** e
3. l	**7.** b	**10.** a	**13.** c
4. m			

Short Answer

1. (LO 1) Managers use standard costs to develop budgets in the planning stage, to control costs as they occur during the executing stage, for comparison with actual costs and the computation of variances in the reviewing stage, and to prepare and distribute reports on operations and managerial performance in the reporting stage.

2. (LO 6) A favorable fixed overhead volume variance exists when the overhead costs budgeted for the level of production achieved is less than the fixed overhead applied to production using the standard variable and fixed overhead rates.

3. (LO 2) The six standards are the direct materials price standard, direct materials quantity standard, direct labor rate standard, direct labor time standard, standard variable overhead rate, and standard fixed overhead rate.

4. (LO 4) A favorable direct materials quantity variable exists when a smaller quantity of direct materials is used than was expected for a particular level of outcome.

5. (LO 5) An unfavorable direct labor rate variance exists when a higher wage is paid than is standard for an employee doing a particular job.

True-False

1. F (LO 2) They are used in establishing direct labor time standards.
2. T (LO 2)
3. F (LO 1, LO 3) It is part of the control function.
4. T (LO 4)
5. T (LO 3)
6. T (LO 5)
7. F (LO 6) The standard overhead rate has two parts: the standard variable rate and the fixed overhead rate.
8. F (LO 5) The total direct labor cost variance is the sum of the direct labor rate and direct labor efficiency variances.

9. T (LO 7)
10. F (LO 3) A flexible budget is also referred to as a *variable* budget.
11. T (LO 6)
12. F (LO 3) Computing a variance is important; however, identifying the *reason* for a variance is critical if corrective actions are to be taken.
13. T (LO 3)

1. a (LO 5) The amount of wages paid is used to calculate the actual direct labor cost.

2. d (LO 4) The direct materials price variance is the difference between the standard price and the actual price multiplied by the actual quantity used. Thus, each of the responses could lead to such a variance.

3. d (LO 6) A static budget forecasts sales and costs for just one level of production.

4. a (LO 6) When the standard overhead applied is less than the actual overhead, a company has an unfavorable overhead variance.

5. b (LO 2) The total budgeted cost would be as follows:

Direct materials:	10,000 units	×	$4.00 =	$ 40,000
Direct labor:	10,000 units	×	1.00 =	10,000
Variable M.O.H.	10,000 units	×	3.00 =	30,000
Fixed M.O.H.				20,000
				$100,000

6. a (LO 2) The total budgeted cost would be as follows:

Direct materials:	20,000 units	×	$4.00 =	$ 80,000
Direct labor:	20,000 units	×	1.00 =	20,000
Variable M.O.H.	20,000 units	×	3.00 =	60,000
Fixed M.O.H.				20,000
				$180,000

7. a (LO 4, LO 7) Because a purchasing manager is responsible for purchasing materials, a favorable or unfavorable direct materials price variance could be used to evaluate his or her performance.

8. d (LO 5) If actual direct labor hours times standard labor rate is greater than standard direct labor hours times standard labor rate, an organization has an unfavorable direct labor efficiency variance.

9. a (LO 3) A flexible budget shows changes in budgeted amounts given different levels of activity. Fixed manufacturing overhead would be constant throughout the relevant range.

10. d (LO 1, LO 7) Standard costing can be used for all these reasons and in every stage of the management cycle.

Exercises

1. (LO 2)

Porcelain	$ .40
Red paint	.05
Blue paint	.02
Molding department wages	.12
Painting department wages	.30
Variable manufacturing overhead	
(.08 hr. x $3/hr.)	.24
Fixed manufacturing overhead	
(.08 hr. x $2/hr.)	.16
Standard cost of one dish	$1.29

2. (LO 3)

Sturchio Company
Flexible Budget
For the Year Ended December 31, 20xx

Cost Item	Unit Levels of Activity			Variable Cost per Unit
	10,000	15,000	20,000	
Direct materials	$ 12,500	$ 18,750	$ 25,000	$1.25
Direct labor	45,000	67,500	90,000	4.50
Variable manufacturing overhead	27,500	41,250	55,000	2.75
Total variable costs	$ 85,000	$127,500	$170,000	$8.50
Fixed manufacturing overhead	50,000	50,000	50,000	
Total costs	$135,000	$177,500	$220,000	

Flexible budget formula: ($8.50 × units produced) + $50,000

3. (LO 4, LO 5)

a. $13,140 F = $\left(\$.60 - \dfrac{\$381,060}{657,000}\right) \times 657,000$

b. $4,200 U = (657,000 - 650,000) \times \$.60$

c. $1,105 U = $\left(\dfrac{\$100,555}{22,100} - \$4.50\right) \times 22,100$

d. $11,700 U = [22,100 - (65,000 \times .3)] \times \$4.50$

Solution to Crossword Puzzle
(Chapters 21 and 22)

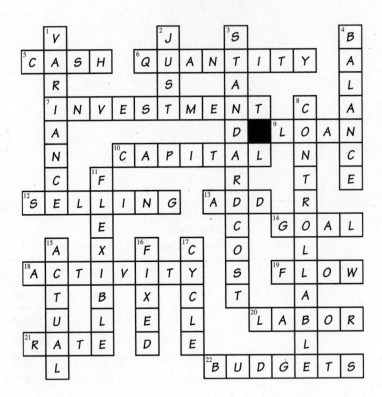

Chapter 23

Self-Test

1. c	(LO 1)	**6.** d	(LO 4)
2. b	(LO 3)	**7.** b	(LO 4)
3. c	(LO 4)	**8.** a	(LO 5)
4. a	(LO 5)	**9.** c	(LO 6)
5. a	(LO 3)		

Matching

1. g	**4.** e	**7.** c	**10.** d
2. h	**5.** b	**8.** i	
3. f	**6.** a	**9.** j	

Short Answer

1. (LO 5) Economic Value Added = After-Tax Operating Income – Cost of Capital in Dollars, or Economic Value Added = After-Tax Operating Income – [Cost of Capital × (Total Assets – Current Liabilities)]

2. (LO 3) Cost center, discretionary cost center, revenue center, profit center, and investment center

3. (LO 4) A traditional income statement assigns all manufacturing costs to cost of goods sold. A variable costing income statement uses only direct materials, direct labor, and variable manufacturing overhead to compute variable cost of goods sold. Fixed manufacturing overhead is considered a period cost.

4. (LO 1) The purpose of a balanced scorecard is to provide a framework that links the perspectives of an organization's four basic stakeholder groups with the organization's mission and vision, performance measures, strategic plan, and resources.

True-False

1. T (LO 3)
2. F (LO 3) In a discretionary cost center, the relationship between the cost of resources and the products or services produced is *not* well defined.
3. F (LO 5) Return on investment is equal to profit margin multiplied by asset turnover.
4. F (LO 3) Performance reports should contain only costs, revenues, and resources that the manager can control.

5. T (LO 4)
6. F (LO 1) The four basic stakeholder groups are investors, employees, internal business processes, and customers.
7. F (LO 5) Asset turnover is the ratio of sales to average assets invested.
8. T (LO 3)
9. F (LO 1) The reports should enable managers to monitor and evaluate performance measures that add value for stakeholders.

Multiple Choice

1. a (LO 4) Fixed manufacturing overhead does not change within a relevant range of volume or activity.

2. c (LO 4) The total variable cost per unit is multiplied by the number of units of output: $8 × 20,000 = $160,000. The fixed overhead costs of $20,000 are added to the $160,000 to equal $180,000.

3. a (LO 1) The four basic stakeholder groups are investors, employees, internal business processes, and customers.

4. a (LO 5) The equation for computing return on investment is operating income divided by assets invested.

5. b (LO 5) Profit margin is the ratio of operating income to sales.

6. c (LO 3) A revenue center is accountable primarily for revenue, and its success is based on its ability to generate revenue.

7. c (LO 4) To evaluate profit, all variable costs are subtracted from sales to arrive at the center's contribution margin. All fixed costs are then subtracted from contribution margin to determine operating income.

8. b (LO 3) The five types of responsibility centers are a cost center, a discretionary cost center, a revenue center, a profit center, and an investment center.

9. a (LO 5) The asset turnover ratio indicates the productivity of assets, or the number of sales dollars generated by each dollar invested in assets.

Exercises

1. (LO 4)

Corwin Company
Flexible Budget
For the Year Ended December 31, 20xx

Variable budget:	
Direct materials (350,000 × $1.80)	$ 630,000
Direct labor (350,000 × $.35)	122,500
Variable manufacturing overhead	
(350,000 × $.60)	210,000
Total variable budget	$ 962,500
Fixed manufacturing overhead	135,000
Total flexible budget	$1,097,500

2. (LO 3)

a. Budgeted sales of $120,000 compared with actual sales of $125,000 results in a favorable variance of $5,000.

b. Budgeted net income of $20,000 compared with actual net income of $18,000 results in an unfavorable variance of ($2,000).

c. The cost of goods sold is budgeted at $62.50 per unit, but the actual production cost was $63.20. Therefore, it cost $.70 more to produce each unit; $.70 multiplied by 1,250 (the number of units sold) results in a variance of ($875).

Chapter 24

Self-Test

1. d	(LO 1)	**6.** a	(LO 7)
2. b	(LO 2)	**7.** d	(LO 1)
3. b	(LO 2)	**8.** c	(LO 1)
4. d	(LO 3)	**9.** c	(LO 3–LO7)
5. b	(LO 4)	**10.** d	(LO 2)

Matching

1. d	**4.** b	**7.** j	**10.** e
2. f	**5.** c	**8.** g	
3. h	**6.** i	**9.** a	

Short Answer

1. (LO 1)
   Discovering a problem or need
   Identifying alternative courses of action to solve the problem or meet the need
   Analyzing the effects of each alternative on business operations
   Selecting the best alternative

2. (LO 2) Relevant decision information is information that differs among the alternatives under consideration. All other information is irrelevant.

3. (LO 3) Outsourcing can (a) reduce a company's investment in physical assets and human resources, (b) improve cash flow, and (c) increase profits.

4. (LO 3–LO 7)
   Outsourcing decisions
   Special order decisions
   Segment profitability decisions
   Product mix decisions
   Sell or process-further decisions

True-False

1. T (LO 2)
2. F (LO 2) Sunk costs are irrelevant in incremental analysis.
3. T (LO 1)
4. T (LO 2) The main concern is with the differences in revenues and costs.
5. T (LO 3)
6. T (LO 4)
7. T (LO 2)
8. F (LO 5) If a segment has a negative segment margin (i.e., if its revenue is less than its direct costs), it should be eliminated.
9. T (LO 2)

10. T (LO 7)
11. F (LO 2, LO 5) Sunk costs are costs that cannot be recovered; avoidable costs are costs that can be eliminated by dropping a segment.
12. F (LO 4, LO 6) A sales mix decision is what is being described.
13. F (LO 4) Special order decisions should also consider qualitative factors, such as the order's impact on sales to regular customers, its potential to lead the company into new sales areas, and the customer's ability to maintain an ongoing relationship with the company that includes good ordering and paying practices.

1. b (LO 6) In making a sales mix decision, a service business must analyze the contribution margin.

2. c (LO 2, LO 3) By focusing on the quantitative differences between outsourcing a product or service and producing or performing it internally, incremental analysis speeds and simplifies the decision making process.

3. d (LO 6) The contribution margins are as follows: Superior, $3 per hour; Deluxe, $4 per hour; and Standard, $5 per hour. To realize the highest operating income, the company should therefore produce all of the required Standard, followed by the Deluxe, and then the Superior, up to the amount possible with the machine hours available.

4. d (LO 3) All choices except **d** are possible benefits of outsourcing; the loss of critical information is one of its potential drawbacks.

5. a (LO 3) Decisions about whether a company should make a product itself or engage another company to make it are outsourcing decisions, as are decisions about whether to use another company to perform an activity that could be performed in-house.

6. a (LO 2) Relevant costs are those that differ among alternatives. When decisions are based solely on cost, relevant costs are the only factors considered.

7. c (LO 7) The incremental revenues resulting from further processing must exceed the processing costs.

8. b (LO 7) The split-off point occurs at the end of joint processing. Until then, joint products are indistinguishable.

9. a (LO 5) An avoidable cost can be eliminated by dropping the segment to which the cost is traced. Relevant variable costs are always avoidable. Some fixed costs may be avoidable.

10. c (LO 7) Joint costs are incurred before the split-off point and are therefore irrelevant to the sell or process-further decision.

Exercises

1. (LO 2)

	Machine A	Machine B	Difference (A – B)
Cost of machine	$10,000	$17,000	($7,000)
Direct labor	16,000	8,000	8,000
Maintenance	300	500	(200)
Electricity savings	(50)	80	(130)
Totals	$26,250	$25,580	$ 67

The company should purchase Machine B because of its lower incremental cost: $25,580.

2. (LO 2, LO 4) $1.75 (All other costs are sunk and are therefore irrelevant.)

3. (LO 4)

Special order price		$600
Incremental costs:		
Design labor	(10 hr × $40)	(400)
Printing labor	(4 hr × $15)	(60)
Incremental gain		$140

Matt should accept the order because it will increase income by $140. Additional considerations include the special order's impact on sales to regular customers, its potential to lead the company into new sales areas, and the customer's ability to maintain an ongoing relationship with the company that includes good ordering and paying practices. The benefit to the community in which the company operates is also a consideration.

¹D	²E	³O		⁴S				⁵O	
	⁶C	E	N	T	E	⁷R	E		⁸T	E	R	M
	S	O				E	G	A
	S	C	R⁹	I¹⁰	S	M¹¹	I	X	O¹²	F
	R	O	N		P	E		R
	E	M	A¹³	C	C	O	U	N	T	I	N	G
	T	I	R		N	T		A
I¹⁴	N	C	O	M	E	S	J¹⁵	O¹⁶	I	N	T
O		M		I		S¹⁷		R	I
N	M¹⁸	A	K	E		B	A¹⁹	N	D	Z
A	A	N		I		L	E	A
R²⁰	E	N	T		L	V	R²¹	A	T	E
Y	A	C²²	A	P	I	T	A	L	I
	G	L		T		G	R²³	O	I
N²⁴	E	E	D		Y	E²⁵	V	A	N

Chapter 25

Self-Test

1. c	(LO 1)	**6.** d	(LO 4)
2. d	(LO 2)	**7.** c	(LO 5)
3. a	(LO 1)	**8.** a	(LO 5)
4. a	(LO 3)	**9.** b	(LO 5)
5. c	(LO 3)		

Matching

1. e	**4.** b	**7.** j	**10.** h
2. d	**5.** f	**8.** i	
3. g	**6.** a	**9.** c	

Short Answer

1. (LO 2) To determine the optimal price for an item, its marginal revenue and marginal cost curves must be computed and plotted. The point at which the two lines intersect is projected onto the demand curve, and a price is determined.

2. (LO 1) Any four of the following would answer the question:
   Demand for the product or service
   Number of competing products or services
   Quality of competing products or services
   Prices of competing products or services
   Customers' preferences
   Seasonal demand or continual demand

3. (LO 1) Any four of the following would answer the question:
   Cost of the product or service
   Desired return on investment

Quality of materials and labor
Labor-intensive or automated process
Usage of scarce resources

4. (LO 3) The sum of the following costs yields the total billing:
   (a) Total cost of materials and parts
   (b) Materials and parts overhead percentage × (a)
   (c) Total labor cost
   (d) Labor cost overhead percentage × (c)

5. (LO 5)
   A cost-plus transfer price is the sum of costs incurred by the producing division plus an agreed-on percentage of profit.
   A market transfer price is the amount that the product would sell for on the open market.
   A negotiated transfer price is a price negotiated by managers that will benefit the entire company.

True-False

1. F (LO 1) Long-run objectives should include a pricing policy.
2. F (LO 1) It is more of an art than a science.
3. F (LO 2) The definition is of marginal revenue, not total revenue.
4. T (LO 1)
5. F (LO 1) It is a possible pricing policy objective.
6. T (LO 4)

7. T (LO 3)
8. F (LO 3) They often use the time and materials approach to pricing.
9. F (LO 5) They bargain for a negotiated transfer price.
10. T (LO 5)
11. F (LO 5) An artificial price cannot increase or decrease total company profits.

Multiple Choice

1. d (LO 1) Charging unrealistically low prices may be a pricing "strategy" to gain market share. It is not a pricing policy "objective."

2. b (LO 1) Effective price setting depends on a manager's ability to analyze the marketplace and anticipate customers' reactions to a product or service and its price. This requires both experience and creativity.

3. c (LO 2) Actual "total cost" behavior and "total revenue" behavior cannot be expected to produce straight lines. Changes in costs are influenced by volume. Changes in price per unit are influenced by competition and other market forces. The lines are therefore curved. These curves produce multiple "breakeven" points at the intersections that occur after the initial "breakeven."

4. a (LO 1) Return on investment is an internal factor that can influence a pricing decision.

5. d (LO 4) The objective of target costing is to avoid this mistake. With target costing, the product is designed so it can be produced in a profitable manner once it is known how much the market will pay for it. Any modifications to the production procedures after the product is marketed are to improve profitability, not to obtain it.

6. b (LO 3) This is the formula used in gross margin pricing.

7. c (LO 3) Service businesses often use "time and materials" to establish prices. The hourly rate, expected time required, a materials list, and an overhead rate should provide a fair estimate of a job's total costs .

8. d (LO 5) The prices that a division charges for goods and services that it provides to another division of the same organization are called *transfer prices*. When the managers of these divisions have discussed and decided on an appropriate transfer price, that price is called a *negotiated transfer price.*

9. a (LO 5) Because they include an estimated amount of profit, transfer prices can be used as a basis for measuring performance. This pricing method enables management to evaluate the contributions that individual production departments make to a company's profitability.

10. b (LO 1, LO 5) Transfer pricing and pricing products for the marketplace have similar objectives and use similar data. The art of price setting is developed through experience in dealing with customers and products. This is as true for setting transfer prices as it is for setting prices for the open market.

Exercises

1. (LO 3)

$$\text{Markup Percentage} = \frac{\text{Desired Profit} + \text{Total Selling, General, and Administrative Expenses}}{\text{Total Production Costs}}$$

$$= \frac{\$382,500 + \$238,000 + \$510,000}{\$680,000 + \$552,500 + \$204,000 + \$263,500}$$

$$= \frac{\$1,130,500}{\$1,170,000}$$

$$= \underline{\underline{66.50\%}}$$

Gross-Margin-Based Price = Total Production Costs per Unit + (Markup Percentage × Total Production Costs per Unit)

$$= (\$1,700,000 \div 850,000) + (\$1,700,000 \div 850,000 \times .665)$$

$$= \underline{\underline{\$3.33}}$$

2. (LO 3)

Zeriscape Landscaping Company

Materials and supplies	$ 46,500
Materials and supplies-related overhead ($46,500 × .4)	18,600
Total materials and supplies charges	$ 65,100
Labor charge	$ 32,800
Overhead charge ($32,800 × .6)	19,680
Total labor charges	$ 52,480
Total billing	$117,580

3. (LO 4)

a. Target cost = $575 ÷ 1.25 = $460

b. Anticipated unit cost of the workbench

Raw materials cost					$120
Purchased parts cost					80
Manufacturing labor	2 hr	×	$14	=	28
Assembly labor	4 hr	×	$15	=	60
Activity-based costs					
Materials and parts handling activity	5%	×	$200	=	10
Engineering activity	$20	×	1	=	20
Production and assembly activity	$15	×	8	=	120
Packaging and delivery activity	$33	×	1	=	33
Sales and marketing activity	$14	×	1	=	14
Total projected unit cost					$485

c. The company should not produce the workbench because its projected cost is $25.00 above the target cost, which means that it would not earn the desired 25 percent profit. The company needs to lower its profit expectations, reduce the product's overall cost, or decide against venturing into this market segment.

4. a. (LO 5)

	Volume = 20,000 units	
	Total Cost	*Unit Cost*
Direct materials	$130,000	$6.50
Direct labor	172,000	8.60
Variable overhead	90,000	4.50
Variable shipping expenses	5,000	.25
Total variable costs	$397,000	$19.85
Avoidable overhead	50,000	2.50
Incremental costs	$447,000	$22.35

b. Unless Ohms Division is willing to pay at least $22.35 per unit, Electra Division should not continue to produce this product. Incremental unit costs exceed the $20 selling price, and Electra is therefore decreasing its profits by continuing to produce the component. The division manager's contention about variable cost recovery is not valid. Revenues must recover all incremental costs, both fixed and variable, to avoid an adverse effect on profits.

Sales (20,000 × $20)	$ 400,000
Less variable costs	(397,000)
Contribution margin	$ 3,000
Avoidable fixed costs	(50,000)
Loss ($2.35 × 20,000 units)	$ 47,000

The division manager should also consider the alternative uses to which plant capacity could be applied. This opportunity cost is not included in measuring the $47,000 loss.

Chapter 26

Self-Test

1. b	(LO 1)		**6.** c	(LO 6)
2. a	(LO 4)		**7.** c	(LO 5)
3. b	(LO 3)		**8.** a	(LO 6)
4. a	(LO 3)		**9.** c	(LO 6)
5. a	(LO 5, LO 6)		**10.** b	(LO 4)

Matching

1. d	**4.** e	**7.** i	**10.** a
2. g	**5.** j	**8.** b	
3. f	**6.** c	**9.** h	

Short Answer

1. (LO 1) Identification of capital investment needs, formal requests for capital investment, preliminary screening, establishment of an acceptance-rejection standard, evaluation of proposals, final decisions on the proposals

2. (LO 2) Cost of debt, cost of preferred stock, cost of common stock, and cost of retained earnings

3. (LO 5, LO 6) Net present value method, payback period method, and accounting rate-of-return method

True-False

1. F (LO 1) Capital investment analysis does not deal with obtaining cash; it involves making decisions about capital investments.
2. F (LO 5, LO 6) The accounting rate-of-return and payback period methods are easier.
3. T (LO 6)
4. F (LO 6) It is the minimum time, not the maximum time.
5. T (LO 6)
6. F (LO 5) The desired rate of return must be known.
7. T (LO 5)
8. F (LO 3) Carrying values are past costs and are therefore irrelevant.
9. F (LO 1) They do this in the planning stage.
10. F (LO 3) They are a source of cash and are therefore relevant.

Multiple Choice

1. b (LO 6) Net income is used to calculate rate of return; net cash inflows do not equate with net income for an accounting period. Some non-cash transactions occur and affect net income, but they have no impact on the Cash account.

2. d (LO 2) The average cost of capital involves all sources of capital used to fund the business. Costs of financing through debt, common and preferred stock, and retained earnings are averaged and weighted by their proportions of the total debt and equity to arrive at the weighted cost of capital.

3. a (LO 4) When used in capital investment analysis, the time value of money restates the estimated cash flows of a capital investment in terms of present value. This analysis restates cash flows using appropriate present value interest factors for timing of the cash flows and the discount rate chosen.

4. b (LO 4) Because of the discount rate used in evaluating the value of money in today's terms, the present value per dollar shrinks as cash flows occur farther in the future. Cash flows that occur sooner are comparatively more valuable per dollar. An investment that has higher cash inflows early in its life would have a greater present value than a similar investment that had the same total cash flows later in its life.

5. a (LO 6) The payback period method shows when an initial investment in a project will be recovered in constant dollars. It is a quick and easy method of ranking investment possibilities.

6. b (LO 1) During the reviewing stage, each project undergoes a postcompletion audit to determine if it is meeting the goals and targets set forth in the planning stage.

7. d (LO 5) The net present value method uses the minimum rate of return as the discount rate.

8. c (LO 3) Estimates of future cash flows should cover the entire life of a project and be as detailed as possible. Cash flows that occur later in the life of a project may be difficult to estimate, but for complete analysis and evaluation, they should not be ignored

9. c (LO 6) The payback period is 4.0 years. It takes four years of net cash inflows to equal the $500,000 initial investment ($160,000 + $140,000 + $120,000 + $80,000 = $500,000).

Exercises

1. (LO 6)

    a. Accounting Rate of Return $= \dfrac{\$8,000}{\$70,000 \div 2} = 22.9\%$

    b. Payback Period $= \dfrac{\$70,000}{\$8,000 + \$14,000} = 3.2$ years

    (The $14,000 in the denominator is depreciation.)

    Because the minimum desired rate of return is 25 percent and the minimum payback period is three years, the company should not invest in the machine.

2. (LO 5)

Year	Net Cash Inflows		Present Value Multiplier		Present Value
1	8,000	×	.862	=	$6,896
2	6,000	×	.743	=	4,458
3	6,000	×	.641	=	3,846
4	6,000	×	.552	=	3,312
5	6,000	×	.476	=	2,856
Total					$21,368

The company should purchase the machine because the present value of future net cash inflows is greater than the cost of the machine.

3. (LO 3, LO 5, LO 6)

    a. Depreciation = ($400,000 – $40,000) ÷ 5 = $72,000

    b. Project's average annual net income = $160,000 – $72,000 = $88,000
       Average investment cost = ([$400,000 – $40,000] ÷ 2) + $40,000 = $220,000
       Accounting rate of return = $88,000 ÷ $220,000 = 40%

    c. Payback period = $400,000 ÷ $160,000 = 2.5 years

    d. Present value factor from Table 3: 5th year at 20% return = .402
       Present value factor from Table 4: 5 years at 20% return = 2.991
       Present value = ($160,000 × 2.991) + ($40,000 × .402) = 494,640

    e. The net present value of all future cash inflows ($494,640) is greater than the $400,000 initial investment. The investment will therefore earn the minimum desired rate of return. Because of this and because the payback period of 2.5 years is less than the 3.0 maximum allowed, the company should purchase the machine.

Solution to Crossword Puzzle
(Chapters 25 and 26)

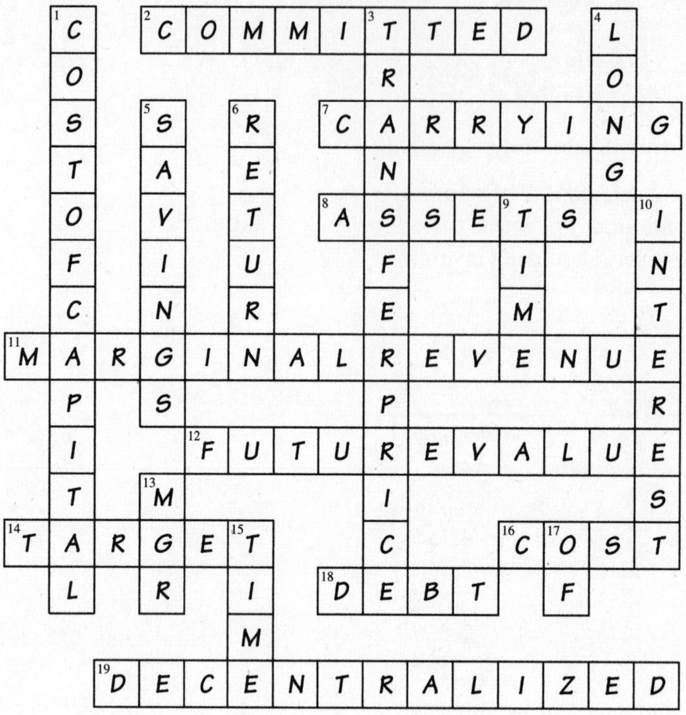

1 COSTOFCAPITAL
2 COMMITTED
3 TRANSFERPRICE
4 LONG
5 SAVINGS
6 RETURN
7 CARRYING
8 ASSETS
9 TIME
10 INTEREST
11 MARGINALREVENUE
12 FUTUREVALUE
13 MGR
14 TARGET
15 TIME
16 COST
17 OF
18 DEBT
19 DECENTRALIZED

Chapter 27

1. d (LO 1)   **6.** c (LO 3)
2. b (LO 1)   **7.** d (LO 3)
3. c (LO 2)   **8.** a (LO 3)
4. a (LO 2)   **9.** d (LO 2)
5. d (LO 3)   **10.** c (LO 5)

Matching

1. b   **4.** a   **7.** i   **10.** f
2. j   **5.** g   **8.** e
3. d   **6.** c   **9.** h

Short Answer

1. (LO 1) An MIS database supplies managers with relevant and reliable information that they can use to formulate strategic plans, make forecasts, and develop budgets in the planning stage of the management cycle; to implement decisions about personnel, resources, and activities in the executing stage; to evaluate all major business functions in the reviewing stage, and to generate customized performance reports in the reporting stage.

2. (LO 2, LO 3) Costs of conformance include prevention costs (e.g., the costs of design review and quality training of employees) and appraisal costs (e.g., the costs of product simulation and development and of vendor audits and sample testing).

Costs of nonconformance include internal failure costs (e.g., the costs of scrap, rework, and downtime) and external failure costs (e.g., the costs of warranty claims and returned goods).

3. (LO 2, LO 3) Nonfinancial measures of quality are measures of product design, vendor performance, production performance, delivery cycle time, and customer satisfaction. These nonfinancial measures supplement the cost-based measures. By focusing on them, managers can detect and correct problems early on, before they have a detrimental effect on the financial statements. Nonfinancial measures of quality thus help managers maximize the net income from operations.

True-False

1. F (LO 2) CAD is the acronym for computer-aided design.
2. F (LO 2, LO 3) Quality can be measured by using both financial measures (costs of quality) and nonfinancial measures (production performance).
3. T (LO 2)
4. F (LO 2) The costs of conformance are incurred to ensure that products do not have defects. As they increase, the costs of nonconformance, which are incurred to correct defects, should decrease.
5. F (LO 4) The description applies to process mapping, not benchmarking.

6. T (LO 2)
7. T (LO 2)
8. F (LO 2, LO 3) Reductions in delivery cycle time have a positive impact on income because they reduce nonvalue-adding activities and shorten the time between a company's payment for manufacturing inputs and its receipt of payment for the products it sells.
9. T (LO 2)
10. F (LO 5) The Malcolm Baldrige Quality Award recognizes U.S. organizations for their achievements in quality and business performance.

Multiple Choice

1. b (LO 1) An MIS not only gives managers access to historical costs; it also provides continuous, detailed records of a company's activities and provides managers with timely measures of operating results.
2. a (LO 2) Costs of conformance are the costs incurred to produce a quality product or service. The inspection of rework needed to correct a defect is a cost of nonconformance.
3. b (LO 2) Costs of nonconformance are costs incurred because of design flaws, poor materials, poor workmanship, poor machinery, or poor management. These avoidable costs increase the cost of a product or service without adding value. The objective of controlling the costs of quality is to eliminate such costs.
4. b (LO 2) $11,200 + $18,900 + $10,100 + $16,400 = $56,600
5. c (LO 2) $13,000 + $10,500 = $23,500
6. d (LO 2, LO 3) Nonfinancial measures of quality are important to TQM for all the reasons stated in **a, b,** and **c.** By focusing on these measures, managers can detect problems at an early stage (before they show up in financial statements) and take steps to correct them.

7. b (LO 2) Production cycle time is the time it takes to make a product and have it available for shipment to a customer.
8. a (LO 2) The costs of conformance are the costs incurred to produce a quality product or service. The costs of nonconformance are the costs incurred to correct defects in a product or service.
9. c. (LO 2) Delivery cycle time consists of purchase order lead time (the time it takes for materials to be ordered and received), production cycle time (the time it takes to make a product), and delivery time (the time between completion of a product and its receipt by the customer).
10. d (LO 2) Company A's conformance costs exceed its costs of nonconformance, but not by much. Company B spends less than Company A on conformance costs, but that is not always the best route to follow. However, because Company B's costs of nonconformance costs are only 20 percent of its costs of conformance it is more likely to have a higher level of product quality than Company A.

Exercises

1. (LO 2)

a.

	20x4	*20x5*
Costs of conformance		
Prevention costs		
Prototype design	$38,000	$42,000
Quality training	20,000	30,000
Total prevention costs	$58,000	$72,000
Appraisal costs		
Product simulation	$ 6,000	$ 9,000
Materials testing	4,000	6,000
Total appraisal costs	$10,000	$15,000
Total costs of conformance	$68,000	$87,000

b.

	20x4	*20x5*
Costs of nonconformance		
Internal failure costs		
Scrap	$ 20,000	$15,000
Rework	50,000	35,000
Total internal failure	$ 70,000	$50,000
External failure costs		
Product warranty	$ 40,000	$25,000
Total external failure	$ 40,000	$25,000
Total costs of nonconformance	$110,000	$75,000

c. The quality improvement program was successful. In 20x4, the costs of nonconformance exceeded those of conformance by $42,000. In 20x5, the costs of conformance exceeded those of nonconformance by $12,000. In addition, the the costs of nonconformance decreased by $35,000, and conformance costs increased by only $19,000. The company is definitely moving in the right direction.

2. (LO 2, LO 3)
- **a.** CC
- **b.** CN
- **c.** CC
- **d.** CN
- **e.** CC
- **f.** CN
- **g.** CC

Chapter 28

Self-Test

1. a	(LO 1)	**6.** d	(LO 4)
2. d	(LO 2)	**7.** c	(LO 4)
3. a	(LO 3)	**8.** c	(LO 5)
4. b	(LO 5)	**9.** a	(LO 5)
5. c	(LO 4)	**10.** c	(LO 5)

Matching

1. g	**4.** e	**7.** h	**10.** d
2. b	**5.** j	**8.** i	**11.** c
3. l	**6.** f	**9.** k	**12.** a

Short Answer

1. (LO 5) Profit margin, asset turnover, return on assets, and return on equity
2. (LO 4) Horizontal analysis presents absolute and percentage changes in specific financial statement items from one year to the next. Vertical analysis, on the other hand, uses percentages to show the relationship of individual items on a financial statement to a total within the statement.
3. (LO 2) Rule-of-thumb measures, analysis of past performance of the company, and comparison with industry norms

4. (LO 1) The risk of total loss is far less with several investments than with one investment because only a rare set of economic circumstances could cause several different investments to suffer large losses all at once.
5. (LO 5) Cash flow yield, cash flows to sales, cash flows to assets, and free cash flow

True-False

1. T (LO 4)
2. F (LO 4) Common-size statements show relationships between items in terms of percentages, not dollars.
3. F (LO 5) The current ratio will increase.
4. T (LO 5)
5. F (LO 5) It equals the cost of goods sold divided by average inventory.
6. F (LO 5) The reverse is true because the price/earnings ratio depends on the earnings per share amount.
7. F (LO 5) Interest is not added back.
8. T (LO 5)
9. F (LO 5) The higher the debt to equity ratio, the greater the risk is.

10. F (LO 5) Receivable turnover measures how many times, on average, the receivables were converted into cash during the period.
11. T (LO 5)
12. T (LO 5)
13. F (LO 5) It is a market strength ratio.
14. F (LO 4) Sales are set at 100 percent.
15. T (LO 3)
16. T (LO 3)
17. T (LO 5)
18. F (LO 5) A higher payables turnover will produce a *shorter* average days' payable.
19. T (LO 1)

Multiple Choice

1. b (LO 5) The interest coverage ratio measures the degree of protection creditors have from a default on interest payments on loans.

2. d (LO 5) The quick ratio measures a company's ability to cover immediate cash requirements for operating expenses and short-term payables.

3. c (LO 5) Asset turnover is calculated using net sales as the numerator and average total assets as the denominator. It is a measure of how efficiently a company uses its assets to produce sales.

4. a (LO 5) A high price/earnings ratio indicates that investors are optimistic about a company's future earnings and growth.

5. a (LO 4) Index numbers are calculated to reflect percentage changes over several consecutive years. The base year is assigned the value of 100 percent; changes from that base are then assigned a percentage so that subsequent amounts can be compared with base amounts. This method, which is used to identify trends, eliminates differences resulting from universal changes, such as inflation.

6. b (LO 1) Of the choices given, only managers are internal users of financial statements. In setting financial performance objectives for a company and in seeing that those objectives are achieved, managers rely on the information presented in the financial statements.

7. d (LO 2) All the factors listed in **a** through **c** contribute to the complexity of comparing a company's performance with the performance of other companies in the same industry.

8. c (LO 5) The turnover of receivables is the number of times receivables are collected in relation to sales in an accounting period. A low number suggests that average accounts receivable balances are high and that credit policy is weak.

9. b (LO 4) Net income is given a percentage in relation to net sales, as are all other components of the common-size income statement. Net sales are set at 100 percent.

10. c (LO 5) Free cash flow is the cash that remains from operating activities after deducting the funds a company must commit to dividends and net capital expenditures.

Exercises

1. (LO 4)

	20x6	20x5	Increase (Decrease) Amount	Increase (Decrease) Percentage
Sales	$200,000	$250,000	$ 50,000	25.0
Cost of goods sold	120,000	144,000	24,000	20.0
Gross margin	$ 80,000	$106,000	26,000	32.5
Operating expenses	50,000	62,000	12,000	24.0
Income before income taxes	$ 30,000	$ 44,000	14,000	46.7
Income taxes	8,000	16,000	8,000	100.0
Net income	$ 22,000	$ 28,000	6,000	27.3

2. (LO 5)

a. 2.0 ($500,000 ÷ $250,000)

b. 1.3 $\left(\dfrac{\$500{,}000 - \$180{,}000}{\$250{,}000}\right)$

c. 1.9 times ($350,000 ÷ $180,000)

d. 192.1 days (365 ÷ 1.9)

e. 12.0% ($106,000 ÷ $880,000)

f. 22.1% ($106,000 ÷ $480,000)

g. 6.0 ($600,000 ÷ $100,000)

h. 60.8 days (365 ÷ 6.0)

i. 17.7% ($106,000 ÷ $600,000)

j. .7 times ($75,000 ÷ $106,000)

k. 12.5% ($75,000 ÷ $600,000)

l. 8.5% ($75,000 ÷ $880,000)

m. .68 times ($600,000 ÷ $880,000)

n. 8 times $\left(\dfrac{\$40}{\$106{,}000 \div \$21{,}200}\right)$

Solution to Crossword Puzzle
(Chapters 27 and 28)

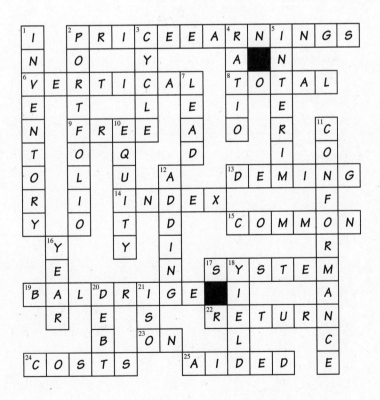

Exercises

1.

Mammoth Mart, Inc.
Work Sheet
For the Month Ended March 31, 20xx

Account Name	Trial Balance Debit	Trial Balance Credit	Adjustments Debit	Adjustments Credit	Adjusted Trial Balance Debit	Adjusted Trial Balance Credit	Income Statement Debit	Income Statement Credit	Balance Sheet Debit	Balance Sheet Credit
Cash	1,000				1,000				1,000	
Accounts Receivable	700				700				700	
Merchandise Inventory	400				400		400	620	620	
Prepaid Rent	750			(a) 250	500				500	
Equipment	4,200				4,200				4,200	
Accounts Payable		900				900				900
Common Stock		3,000				3,000				3,000
Retained Earnings		1,200				1,200				1,200
Sales		9,800				9,800		9,800		
Sales Discounts	300				300		300			
Purchases	3,700				3,700		3,700			
Purchases Returns and Allowances		150				150		150		
Freight In	400				400		400			
Salaries Expense	3,000		(b) 500		3,500		3,500			
Advertising Expense	600				600		600			
	15,050	15,050								
Rent Expense			(a) 250		250		250			
Salaries Payable				(b) 500		500				500
Depreciation Expense			(c) 375		375		375			
Accumulated Depreciation, Equipment				(c) 375		375				375
Income Taxes Expense			(e) 180		180		180			
Income Taxes Payable				(e) 180		180				180
			1,305	1,305	16,105	16,105	9,705	10,570	7,020	6,155
Net Income							865			865
							10,570	10,570	7,020	7,020

2.

		General Journal		
Date		**Description**	**Debit**	**Credit**
		Income Summary	131,900	
		Sales Returns and Allowances		5,300
		Cost of Goods Sold		52,700
		Freight In		3,200
		Selling Expenses		39,400
		General and Administrative Expenses		24,800
		Income Taxes Expense		6,500
		Sales	244,100	
		Income Summary		244,100
		Income Summary	112,200	
		Retained Earning		112,200
		Retained Earnings	50,000	
		Dividends		50,000

Appendix B

Matching

1. a **3.** c **5.** b
2. d **4.** e

Exercises

1. a. J **d.** CP **g.** J **j.** CP
   b. CR **e.** S **h.** J **k.** CR
   c. P **f.** CP **i.** J

2.

				Debits			Credits		
Date		**Account Debited/Credited**	**Post. Ref.**	**Cash**	**Sales Disc.**	**Other Accts.**	**Accts. Receiv.**	**Sales**	**Other Accts.**
Feb.	3	Don Morris	✓	490	10		500		
	9	Land	135	8,000					8,000
	14	Common Stock	311	10,000					10,000
	23	Sue O'Neill	✓	150			150		
	28	Sales		25,000				25,000	
				43,640	10		650	25,000	18,000
				(111)	(412)		(114)	(411)	(✓)

Cash Receipts Journal — Page 1

3. a. Cash payments journal

b. The account number below the Other Accounts total is incorrect; a check mark should be used here to signify that the Other Accounts total is e account number below the Other Accounts total is incorrect; a check mark should be used here to signify that the Other Accounts total is not posted at the end of the month.

c. May 1: Paid DePasquale Supply Co. $800 for supplies previously purchased; paid within the discount period and received a $16 discount.
May 7: Paid Monahan Business Equipment $2,000 cash for purchase of office equipment.
May 13: Paid $350 for ad placed in the Celestial News.
May 19: Paid Deneker Motors $420 for items previously purchased. (No discount granted.)

d. 1. The amounts in the Accounts Payable column were posted to the accounts payable subsidiary accounts (DePasquale Supply Co. and Deneker Motors).

2. The amounts in the Other Accounts column were posted to the general ledger accounts (Office Equipment and Advertising Expense).

3. The 315 is an error, as already explained. The other numbers refer to the numbers of the accounts in the general ledger to which the column totals were posted.

Appendix C

Matching

1. e	**5.** b	**8.** h
2. f	**6.** c	**9.** a
3. j	**7.** g	**10.** d
4. i		

Exercises

1. a. A = \$14,500 (\$10,000 + \$3,000 + \$1,500)
B = \$13,000 (\$10,000 + \$2,000 + \$1,000)
C = \$13,000 (\$10,000 + \$2,500 + \$500)

b. A = \$7,000 (\$10,000 + \$3,000 − \$6,000)
B = \$8,000 (\$10,000 + \$2,000 − \$4,000)
C = \$10,500 (\$10,000 + \$2,500 − \$2,000)

c. A = (\$8,000) (\$10,000 + \$3,000 − \$21,000)
B = (\$2,000) (\$10,000 + \$2,000 − \$14,000)
C = \$5,500 (\$10,000 + \$2,500 − \$7,000)

2.

<table>
<tr><th colspan="5">General Journal</th></tr>
<tr><th colspan="2">Date</th><th>Description</th><th>Debit</th><th>Credit</th></tr>
<tr><td>a.</td><td></td><td>Cash
G, Capital
H, Capital
I, Capital
   J, Capital
      Recorded purchase of one-third interest by J</td><td>12,000
800
800
400</td><td>

14,000</td></tr>
<tr><td>b.</td><td></td><td>Cash
   J, Capital
      Recorded purchase of one-third interest by J</td><td>15,000</td><td>
15,000</td></tr>
<tr><td>c.</td><td></td><td>Cash
   G, Capital
   H, Capital
   I, Capital
   J, Capital
      Recorded purchase of one-third interest by J</td><td>21,000</td><td>
1,600
1,600
800
17,000</td></tr>
</table>

Appendix D

Matching

1. c	**3.** b	**5.** a
2. e	**4.** d	

Exercise

1.

General Journal				
Date		**Description**	**Debit**	**Credit**
		Accounts Receivable, Mexican company	5,000	
		Sales		5,000
		Recorded sale of merchandise		
		($100,000 × $.05)		
		Cash	4,500	
		Exchange Gain or Loss	500	
		Accounts Receivable, Mexican company		5,000
		Recorded receipt of payment		
		($100,000 × $.045)		

Appendix E

Matching

1. c	**4.** d	**7.** g
2. h	**5.** f	**8.** i
3. b	**6.** e	**9.** a

Exercise

1.

General Journal				
Date		**Description**	**Debit**	**Credit**
		Cash	12,000	
		Dividend Income		12,000
		Recorded cash dividend from Tewa*		
		($80,000 × 15%)		
		Investment in Rorris Company	19,500	
		Income, Rorris Company Investment		19,500
		Recognized 30 percent of income reported by Rorris Company		
		($65,000 × 30%)		
		Cash	15,000	
		Investment in Rorris Company		15,000
		Recorded cash dividend from Rorris		
		($50,000 × 30%)		

*Tewa's earnings of $110,000 are irrelevant because Jamal is using the cost adjusted to market method to account for the investment.

Appendix F

Matching

1. d   **3.** f   **5.** a
2. b   **4.** e   **6.** c

Exercises

1. a. $747 ($1,000 \times .747$)
  b. $4,122 ($1,000 \times 4.122$)
  c. $1,126 ($1,000 \times 1.126$)
  d. $1,745.81 ($100,000 \div 57.28$)
2. Present value = $2,000 \times 4.494 = $8,988
  The purchase should not be made because the present value of the future cash savings is less than the initial cost of the equipment.
3.

		General Journal		
Date		**Description**	**Debit**	**Credit**
(a) Jan.	1	Equipment ($10,000 × .826)	8,260	
		Discount on Notes Payable	1,740	
		Notes Payable		10,000
(b)	1	Interest Expense ($8,260 × .1)	826	
		Discount on Notes Payable		826
(c)	1	Interest Expense ($1,740 − $826)	914	
		Notes Payable	10,000	
		Discount on Notes Payable		914
		Cash		10,000